ABORIGINAL AUSTRALIANS

A history since 1788

FULLY REVISED FOURTH EDITION

RICHARD BROOME

ALLEN&UNWIN

The photographs on the chapter headers are of the rock face of Ngamadjidj Shelter in the Grampians–Gariwerd National Park, taken by the author and reproduced courtesy of the Budja Budja Cooperative, Halls Gap.

First published in 2010

First published in 1982
Reprinted ten times.
Second edition published in 1994
Reprinted four times.
Third edition published in 2002
Reprinted seven times.
Fully revised fourth edition published in 2010.

Allen & Unwin
83 Alexander Street
Crows Nest NSW 2065
Australia
Phone: (61 2) 8425 0100
Fax: (61 2) 9906 2218
Email: info@allenandunwin.com
Web: www.allenandunwin.com

Cataloguing-in-Publication details are available
from the National Library of Australia
www.librariesaustralia.nla.gov.au

ISBN 978 1 74237 051 4

Internal design by Lisa White
Maps by Mapgraphics
Index by Trevor Matthews
Set in 11/15 pt Minion by Bookhouse, Sydney
Printed in Australia by Griffin Press

15 14 13 12 11 10 9 8 7

CONTENTS

PREFACE

The first version of this book appeared in 1982. It has been in print ever since, with two new editions in 1994 and 2002, which each contained an added chapter. The original thirteen chapters had never been revised until now. This current fourth edition is a completely rewritten, revised, updated and changed book. It might warrant a new title, but it does owe much to the first three editions and the 50,000 copies in circulation, so only the subtitle has been changed.

Books, even those with single authors, are joint enterprises. Like icebergs, they are supported by a greater mass than is seen. Much has changed in the terrain of Aboriginal history since 1982 and this new edition, its footnotes and its bibliography reflect that. As with earlier editions, it owes enormous debts to all those historians who toil in the field of Aboriginal history. Dr Heather Radi and Dr John Hirst, who inspired and assisted the first edition, should not be forgotten. Those who originally reviewed the book provided ways of enriching this edition. La Trobe University has provided me with leave to write all the editions of this book. We are in great measure shaped by those with whom we converse. My colleagues at La Trobe University and other universities have given me great support over the years—more than they can ever realise. Many generations of students at La Trobe University have helped to shape this book as well. Aboriginal friends and acquaintances have provided inspiration and assistance. Professor Lynette Russell, Director of the Indigenous Research Centre at Monash University, kindly read this fourth edition. Elizabeth Weiss at Allen & Unwin encouraged me to bring the book to a fourth edition for which I thank her. Aziza Kuypers steered it deftly through publication. David Harris acted as an assiduous proofreader in the final days and expunged many errant commas.

The images in this edition, many of them new, were generously provided by those acknowledged in each caption. Special thanks must be extended to Brendan Edwards and the Budja Budja Cooperative of Halls Gap for permission to use the rock art images from the Ngamadjidj shelter in the Grampians–Gariwerd National Park, Victoria, at the header of each chapter. I must also thank Leah King-Smith for permission to use her wonderfully rich and deep image from the 'Patterns of Connection', (1991) Untitled No. 7—'Aunt Sally'—to grace the cover of the book.

My family and friends have given me great succour during the long hours of writing. Our Burmese furry friends—Sandy and Cocoa—have slumbered alongside my keyboard, brightening my labours. My adult children, Katherine and Matthew, were not born when the first edition was begun, but have emerged into fine adulthood as this book appeared in its various editions. They take an interest in its progress through various forms, sometimes bemused by such an obsession with the past, as my newspaper scrapbooks mount steadily to 75 volumes. My wife and great friend Margaret Donnan provides unyielding support and constant interest in what I do, despite her own demanding career. The first edition was dedicated to her. This is the one part of the book that will never change. So to Margaret I again dedicate this book, with heartfelt love and affection—always.

Richard Broome

April 2009

NOTE OF WARNING

This book, which is a history, contains many references to deceased Aboriginal people, their words, names and sometimes their photographs. Their words used here are already in the public domain and permission has been sought to use photographs. Many Aboriginal people follow the custom of not using the names of those deceased. Individuals and communities should be warned that they may read or see things in this book that could cause distress. They should therefore exercise caution when using this book.

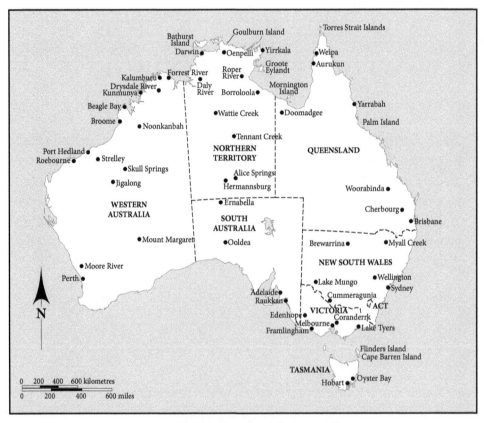

Location of places in Aboriginal Australia.

Prologue

ENDINGS AND BEGINNINGS

In Dareton, New South Wales, in 1965, eleven-year-old Malcolm Smith and his brother Robert 'borrowed' pushbikes leaning against a bus shelter and went joy-riding. This small act led to the involvement of the police, welfare officers and the court. Malcolm's widowed father, who was in seasonal work and thus not always present, was judged as an unfit parent. The boys were taken and placed in a series of homes and foster care placements, where their Aboriginality was undermined, even denigrated. As a confused youth, Malcolm found himself behind bars, where his Aboriginal identity was somewhat affirmed by other young Koori men. The gaol door revolved and he was finally reconnected with family, as best any fostered youth could. In 1980, in the hope of pleasing and defending his sister, he outraged her by killing her boyfriend, who had been bashing her. He was sentenced to four years for manslaughter. In Long Bay gaol he expressed interest in the Bible and was given a tape of the Book of Matthew. He began to paint religious images but became delusional, said he was Jesus Christ, then claimed he was evil. Mental turmoil mounted, reflecting his alienation from family and his Aboriginal cultural roots. Self-hate engulfed him and, driven by the passage in Matthew: 'And if thine eye offend thee, pluck it out' (Matthew 18:9, King James Bible), he drove the handle of an artist's brush into his eye and brain while in a toilet cubicle, collapsed and died. He became one of 99 cases investigated in 1990 by the Royal Commission into Aboriginal Deaths in Custody.[1]

How did a joy-ride unleash such a terrible chain of events? The short answer is that Malcolm was a colonial subject—although it is a little more complex, as his brother Robert did not suicide. However, both took a joy-ride that led to their being taken out of their family and placed into a system that managed young Aboriginal people, because it viewed their culture and Aboriginality as inferior, and requiring of alteration—even eradication. His father's love and desire to have him back was of no account. Malcolm was a victim of the practices of colonialism and the ideas of superiority and racism embedded within. The psychological pressures of this set of colonial practices led to defiance through repeated crime, to be sent back to his Koori mates in gaol; and then to self-hate: the twin responses to colonial pressures first identified by Frantz Fanon and Albert Memmi in their 1960s classics about the colonial condition.[2]

This book will trace Australia's history of its colonial relationship with Aboriginal people, for as an earlier version of this book stated in 1982: 'until recently the Aborigines rarely appeared in our history, so that we have been presented with half a history'. This retelling of our history, begun by many historians in the 1970s and synthesised here, will reveal how colonialism created practices that refashioned Aboriginal people into the colonised and oppressed, and other Australians into coloniser oppressors—but not entirely so. Aboriginal people also resisted these practices, physically, mentally and culturally, while some white Australians resisted assuming the role of colonisers. This book will tell this 200-year story, which ranges over diverse cultural groups, living under seven colonial/state and one federal regime, in as much complexity as is possible in one volume.

This is a story of how settlers in overwhelming numbers, bearing new diseases, plants, animals and new technologies, and with the blessing of the British Imperial Government, supplanted the original owners of a continent. Ecological change, disease, violence and force of numbers swept away Indigenous economies and supplanted them with new forms shaped by global capital. Patrick Wolfe and others have identified three strategies of settler colonialism: confrontation, incarceration and assimilation, which he has termed 'the logic of elimination'.[3] To justify these acts, settlers created images and knowledge that eulogised themselves as pioneers and wealth creators, and denigrated Indigenous people as non-producers and not worthy of owning land. This discourse justified dispossession, and was followed by a Civilising Mission to change those seen not as different, but inferior. Albert Memmi termed this creation of false images and discourses the 'usurper complex', by which those who take power unlawfully have to justify such acts—to themselves and others. All these pathways of dispossession and denigration led to the social, economic, cultural and bodily impoverishment of Aboriginal people—and outcomes such as those following Malcolm's joy-ride. It was perhaps not inevitable—but the practices of colonialism narrowed and shaped the options of both Indigenous and settler Australians, which this book will explicate.

ON WORDS

This book will use multiple words to describe the historical actors. The original owners will be referred to where possible by their own local names that stem from traditional times, such as Eora and Woiwurrung. Also, local names will be used that have been acquired, employed and accepted by Aboriginal people since colonial contact—for instance, Lake Condah or Cherbourg people.

When the need arises to describe those in wider regions, Aboriginal names that are widely, but not universally, accepted by original owners may sometimes be used. These include names such as Koori, Murri, Yolgnu, Nyoongar and Nyungah, for those of the south-east, north-east, north, west and southern parts of the continent respectively. Those in Tasmania now refer to themselves as Pallawah. Aboriginal names exist for non-Indigenous Australians, notably Gubba in the south and east and Balanda in the north.[4]

When all original owners are referred to, which is necessary in a continent-wide study, it is necessary to use European words, as no Indigenous word exists. This book will use interchangeably: Aboriginal people, blacks, Aboriginal and Torres Strait Islander people, Indigenous people, original owners, Aboriginal Australians and Indigenous Australians to describe all those whom Canadians succinctly refer to as 'First Nation' peoples. Those who came to settle after 1788 will be called settlers, whites, non-Indigenous people, Europeans, British, and other Australians, where appropriate.

This book was originally entitled *Aboriginal Australians* and this name has been retained for this fourth edition. The word 'aboriginal', which comes from the Latin *ab origine* (meaning 'from the beginning'), emerged in seventeenth-century English to mean 'the original inhabitants of a land'. As an English word of that era, it also became a colonial word to mean Indigenous people, as opposed to the colonists.

The word 'aboriginal' was not at first used in Australia. The English discoverer of the east Australian coast, James Cook, who claimed the continent for Britain in 1770, called the original owners 'natives' and occasionally 'Indians'. Early colonists mostly used 'natives', although 'the blacks' also came into use on the frontier, as the language of race intruded. Both these terms remained in common usage until the twentieth century. On 4 May 1816, a government proclamation used 'natives', 'black natives' and 'Ab-origines', probably the first use of this last term.

The words 'aboriginal', 'aborigine' and their plurals did not become common until the 1840s and existed along with 'blacks' and 'natives', which had a long life. Indeed, 'native', which often became derogatory, was used until the middle of the twentieth century, even in legislation. The word 'aboriginal' and its other forms did not overtake 'native' in common usage until the late nineteenth century. For much of its life, 'aboriginal' was used without a capital 'A', which gave it a derogatory edge. However, it has been capitalised conventionally since the 1960s, revealing new respect. It is now embraced by most Indigenous people, especially its derivative form 'Aboriginality', which relates to the politics of identity. 'Aboriginal people', which is used in this book, is now becoming the term preferred to 'Aborigines' or 'Aboriginals'.

Words used in quotation marks, such as 'half-caste', are those of historical speakers. Some of these are now offensive, but are used to explain the discourses of settler colonialism. They should never be taken at face value, but seen in their context as settler ammunition, used to construct the mythologies of the 'usurper complex'.

1

REFLECTIONS ON
A GREAT TRADITION

Indigenous groups across Australia have many oral stories about their past, which form part of a Great Tradition of knowledge. These stories explain the Aboriginal genesis in different parts of the country and reveal the shaping of a formless land by great ancestors. In some traditions, these ancestral beings broke through the crust of the earth to begin the processes of life as the sun burst forth and the wind and rains came. Other great ancestors formed the landscape by rushing or writhing through it, by shaping beings from bark and breathing life into them, as did Bunjil, or bearing a sacred dillybag from which life was brought forth, as did the Djanggawul sisters. The stories are as numerous as the 500 or more Aboriginal languages and groups across ancient Australia, but the significance is the same. Great ancestors shaped and breathed life into the land and made it rich for the people. The stories stretch way back, for the people believe they have always been in this land.

Those from another great tradition—that of Science—listen not to the ancient stories of the great ancestors, but to what the human remains and rocks say. The remains have been telling a shifting story for the past hundred years, as more and more discoveries are made, and new techniques of interpretation are invented. They are fitted into a worldwide story by scientists who estimated from the evidence that early forms of hominids evolved in Africa about four million years ago. Modern humans, *Homo sapiens*, emerged some 150,000 years ago, and with great ingenuity and fortitude migrated across the face of the earth in the last 100,000 years or so. Those who reached Australia between 40,000 and 60,000 years ago did so before humans colonised much of the European landmass. To reach Australia, they traversed islands and straits when sea levels were low. Even at the lowest levels, they voyaged courageously at times in raft, canoe or on flotsam, beyond the sight of land. It is likely that a number of migrations occurred as people sought new lands, for the remains reveal that humans of both a robust and a gracile frame lived here. At some stage in the last 10,000 years the dingo reached Australia as well, as a semi-domesticated companion animal.

The remains and techniques of dating rock, soil strata and campfire charcoal tell us there were people living on the shores of an ancient and rich Lake Mungo almost 40,000 years ago. They lived a prosperous but simple life in the dunes by this inland beach. Skeletal remains mark their presence. Recently, footprints have been discovered in petrified mud, which reveal a wondrous glimpse of an extended family's leisurely stroll by this fertile shore. The Mungo people lived off marine life and foraged for fauna and flora in the dunes. At night by the campfire, under a glorious star-filled canopy, they were inspired to create and embroider their own Great Tradition. Skeletal remains reveal this, indicating cremations of their dead, and burial practices enriched by ochre and ritual positioning, to signify the importance, love and respect they attached to their kinsfolk.

After a generation of tussle, the keepers of the stories and the keepers of the human remains are reconciled to the value of each others' knowledge. Archaeologists in the 1990s agreed to return the remains for reburial in keeping places, and Aboriginal elders in the region have used scientific study to prove in a different way what they knew: that their ancestors possessed among the earliest of human cultures.

Aboriginal and Torres Strait Islander people managed massive environmental changes over at least 40 millennia in this land, greater than those facing Australians today. Sea levels oscillated by scores of metres, and the continent experienced periods which were significantly colder and wetter than today, culminating 20,000 ago. A period of warming and rising sea levels followed, and ancient coastlines shrank. The giant megafauna which roamed the land when they arrived became extinct; debate still rages about the human involvement in that demise. While parts of the ancient rainforests of the continent survived, and coastal and riverine environments such as the Murray Valley remained hospitable in the face of global warming, other groups were forced to adapt to drier and arid conditions in the vast central regions of Australia. Mungo, among many other fertile lake regions, dried, and desert areas expanded. Drought became a feature of much of the landscape under the influence of the El Niño Southern Oscillation, which affected surface temperatures in the Pacific Ocean,

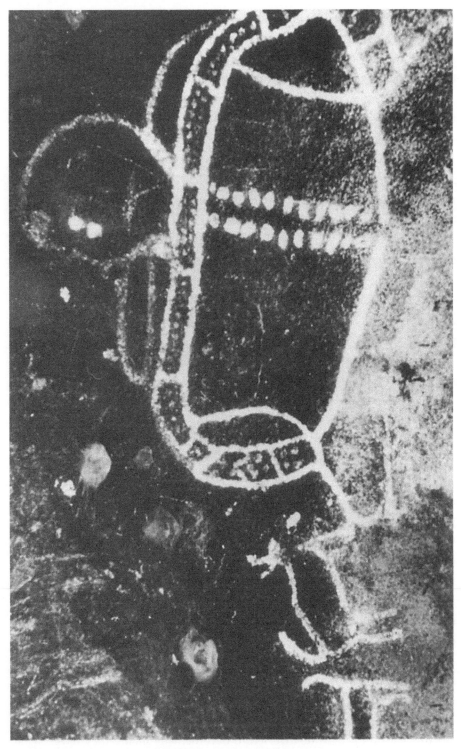

Bunjil, the Great Ancestor, and his dogs; Grampians, Victoria. PHOTOGRAPH BY THE AUTHOR.

bringing periodic droughts to vast regions of central and southern Australia. Australia, baked by the sun, and less frequently drenched by rains, developed the lowest water run-off rate of any continent. Only the tropical north was well watered, and periodically relieved by flooding rains.

The Australian continent, which separated from the great super-continent Gondwana over twenty million years ago, slowly drifted north since that time and became an arid, fire-prone and low-energy ecology. This reflected the longstanding absence of tectonic and glacial activity on this ancient flat continent, activity that usually refurbishes soils. The ancient land was leached by wind and rain over millions of years to the point of low fertility, with poor soil quality and subsequent modest fishing grounds due to poor rainfall and a low nutritional run-off. This ecological poverty led to greater biodiversity of plant and insect life, but poorer resources of larger faunal mammals, compared to, say, North America, which is a more fertile, higher-energy continent. (However, some species were in greater abundance, such as small reptiles.) Thus the drying, arid and fiery continent presented significant challenges for human survival—and yet Aboriginal people survived.

Aboriginal people managed this difficult environment, which still confounds most current-day Australians, through adapting their economies and technology. They learned to live with fire and to use it to shape the land to their needs. Indeed, scientists, some of whom have called this 'fire-stick farming', have argued Aboriginal people shaped the land by fire to aid the production of grasslands for kangaroo grazing and to more easily trek through their country. By doing so they expanded the natural fire processes of this parched continent, which favoured a biota ruled by eucalypts, wattles and banksias and other sclerophyll species. They learned to consume a large variety of bush foods, and so rarely went without. They emerged from the so-called 'stone age' long ago, as their tool kits became smaller, more refined and specialised, and were increasingly made of bone and wood. Weaving string and ropes for bags and netting was developed. Food-gathering strategies evolved using new technology such as netting to trap birds, baskets to catch fish or eels, and bark or wooden canoes and bone hooks for fishing. Those groups who needed covering to ward off the cold sewed cloaks of animal skins. They experienced few diseases which racked their bodies, except for an annoying and at times debilitating skin disease, yaws. Life was not always easy when drought arrived, but they adapted.

It is often wondered why Aboriginal people did not develop agriculture. But the question should be inverted to become: why *should* they have? What makes agriculture particularly a superior economy? It might feed many, but only if many need feeding. Agriculture, which developed in the Fertile Crescent of modern-day Iran and Iraq, has lasted so far less than 10,000 years, whereas the Aboriginal foraging economy was at least four times as old. Indeed, hunting and gathering is in world terms several million years old. Aboriginal people survived for over 40 millennia with a non-agricultural economy, which suited the land, and was sustainable with the land. Farming in Australia after just 200 years is in significant trouble, causing such degradation as to demand a massive rethink of agricultural and pastoral techniques.

Nor were conditions in Australia generally conducive to the development of farming. Research has revealed that, while parts of Australia, North America and South Africa have a temperate climate like that of the Fertile Crescent, these ecologies lacked the building blocks of agriculture, which the Fertile Crescent had in abundance. In Australia (and North America and other temperate zones, for that matter), there were few of the favoured seeds for plant domestication, and none of the animals that have been domesticated by humans to eat and to help power farms: pigs, sheep, goats, cattle, horses. The largest animals in Australia were the megafauna—large versions of kangaroos, wombats and the like, which proved resistant to domestication. Thus Aboriginal people in general continued to forage for food when they needed it and from where it grew—and successfully so. They developed an economy that provided all they desired, and which some economists and anthropologists have since termed 'affluence'.

However, about 5000 years ago, some Aboriginal groups experimented successfully with creating food surpluses. On the fire-cleared western plains of New South Wales, the colony's Surveyor-General, Thomas Mitchell, in the mid 1830s saw vast fields of 'hay ricks', formed of millet grass, cut and drying so that the grain fell into the middle of the stack. It would be collected, ground and baked into bread by the ancestors of the Wiradjuri. This was clearly a clever agriculture, a seed economy for part of the year at least, which was done with minimal effort, without fertiliser, cultivation, threshing and with little further impact on the land. At Brewarrina, extensive fish traps were formed in the Barwon River by channels made of rocks carried and placed by the ancestors of the Wiradjuri. Fish aplenty were farmed by the people. Similarly, Gunditjmara in the Western District of Victoria made eel farms through extensive labour with digging sticks, their shallow wooden dishes, muscle and sinew. They shaped extensive channels and waterways over some hectares, even linking river systems. These channels directed migrating eels into fenced barriers complete with woven baskets to trap more eels than could be eaten. So plentiful was this food that the people formed stoned-walled houses with wicker and tuft roofs, held big gatherings and ceremonies, and lived off eels for months. Further north, some of the Torres Strait Islanders became gardeners under the influence of Melanesians, but remained fishers and foragers as well.

Scientists have called these new food strategies of rudimentary and intelligent farming 'intensification'. Such changes must have accompanied changes in leadership to mobilise this activity for future gain. The farming was rudimentary, in that its technology was simple, but it was efficient. It was intelligent, as it emerged out of the local ecology and remained only a part of the food supply, never exposing the people to famine. They escaped the experience of the Irish when their agri-monoculture potato-cropping failed repeatedly and disastrously before and during the Great Famine of the 1840s.

The general economic affluence that allowed most Aboriginal people to gather food in three to five hours per day thus left time for rest, sociality and to develop their Great Tradition. It was natural that this tradition revolved around the land. Local country provided food and water, formed the wondrous space through which they moved each day, and the place they slept at night under a starlit canopy. They invested the land with stories and formed a holistic relationship with it. The great ancestors who shaped the land were also embedded in it, and were still powerful. The people shared some of that power too. They were connected to the land through totemic animals determined by their birthplace and clan, and for which they were responsible. Through ritual and ceremony the people played a role in revitalising the land and its abundance. The great ancestors gave meaning to life and the rules by which life should be lived. These rules were learned by each young male and female in initiations that grew them into knowledge of the Great Tradition. This tradition—this Dreaming or Tjurrkupa as it is called in Central Australia—was all-encompassing and never doubted. It was also a sustainable tradition, for people were in a custodial, not exploitative, relationship to land.

Each family was attached to a landowning clan, which owned an 'estate' of land that was theirs to manage and nurture. It had recognised boundaries, denoted by hills, a river or some other recognisable landform. Through kinship relations, marriage and other agreements, people moved beyond their owned estates to forage across a wider range of land according to the season. Groups used each other's estates through reciprocal rights or ceremonies of permission to form these foraging ranges. Thus land was owned and mutually recognised as owned, the title deeds being the stories told and the paintings emanating from those stories. The land of others was not coveted, for without ownership of the story, ownership of land was meaningless.

Women, the great food providers of the Aboriginal economy, digging rakai, a rush at Matarauwaitji, Blue Mud Bay, Arnhem Land, in 1936. COURTESY OF THE DONALD THOMSON COLLECTION, MUSEUM OF VICTORIA.

The important rules of this Great Tradition revolved around land and people, enmeshed into one. Thus all people were interrelated. The great Aboriginal questions upon meeting were: what is your country and who are your kinfolk? Kinship was the social cement of Aboriginal society. People lived in small groups foraging across the land. They were part of a clan held together by either patrilineal or matrilineal descent. These clans or landowning groups were also part of larger cultural–linguistic groups we have called 'tribes'. Marriage rules sensibly required out-marriage into another clan, and sometimes even another language group; for language groups were sometimes part of a larger cultural confederation. Thus individuals had multiple identities, names and social connections. This social system held people together through codes of kin relations, which were invisible to the eye, but if mapped would form complex grids on a page, far denser than maps of great city underground rail systems. Aboriginal people knew these complex networks from a lifetime of practice.

These grids of relationship came with rights and obligations which kept the people secure and insured against scarcity. Internal conflicts were managed by these kinship systems, and while kin violence was part of their world, as with any society, kinship acted to contain it. Kinship also protected the people from outside dangers. Aboriginal society was one of friends and enemies. Kinsfolk were friends, and all others beyond a language group or confederation of language groups were enemies. Loyalties to one's kin group meant enemies had to be killed if they ventured close, as they might wield sorcery, the cause of all mature deaths. Enemies might steal hair or faeces and work malevolent magic through these things or 'sing' someone to death in other ways. Vigilance was necessary. Clever men in each group were revered as they knew cures against sorcery. For minor illnesses other elders knew countless bush medicine prescriptions.

For millennia the Great Tradition was renewed, refined and reinvented. Ritual paintings on bodies, on rock shelters and bark were continually refreshed and retouched. But then change—the possibility of which always existed with the Great Tradition—quickened. Outsiders arrived on the shores of the great southern continent. At first there were brief, almost dreamlike, contacts with European navigators. The Dutch came, and then some English and French visited, who were all borne like large ungainly birds across the water, only to vanish the same way after brief landings.

On the northern coast from about 1720 men also came from the island of Macassar in the Celebes to gather marine life: trepang or sea slug from the shallow coastal waters. They came annually for a short season and stayed for only a few weeks in any one place. The Macassans formed camps on the land, cured the trepang in kilns, and interacted with the people. They exchanged items such as food, pipes and tobacco, glass and pottery for labour and sex. Then they disappeared until the following year. The people interacted with the Macassans and some journeyed to Macassar with them as wives or workers. A genetic link exists today between these two peoples, which has been recognised in visits and festivals. The touch of these contacts was light, however, for the Macassans offered few threats to Aboriginal culture and none to their land. Some things were learned—how to make dugout canoes—but the Great Tradition was unaltered by almost 200 years of this contact.

Yet microbes also made the journey with these Macassans. It is without doubt that the deadly smallpox virus, *Variola major*, made the trip on the Macassans' praus, to wreak havoc on Aboriginal groups as far down as the continent's southern coast. Possibly 50 per cent of those first making contact with the disease perished, and Aboriginal society began to experience unprecedented shocks.

One of the world's greatest navigators, Lieutenant James Cook, searched the Pacific in 1770 for the Great South Land of the European imagination. Cook was also sent to the newly discovered Tahiti to record the transit of Venus across the Sun. English astronomers sought to measure no less than the known universe by readings in Tahiti and London. These two great European quests brought Cook to the east coast of what was then known as New Holland, the north and west coasts having been found by the Dutch over a century earlier. Cook sighted first Point Hicks on the south-east coast, named after his midshipman, then coasted north observing people or their fires through his telescope. He stopped at Botany Bay and tried to engage with the Eora. Cook and his men watched from their small landing cutter as two brave Aboriginal men with raised spears defied their landing. This was a pivotal moment in Australia's history as two groups encountered each other for the first time across a cultural and ecological divide, ushering irreversible change to the great southern continent and its original owners. A shot was fired, wounding one warrior in the leg. He ran off—to survive or not, we will never know. Cook visited some huts and left gifts, but to his amazement, the gifts were untouched the next day—unlike in Tahiti, where the people had traded voraciously. He thought less of the first Australians for it, as all 'civilised' people traded. He also saw no buildings or gardens, and remarked they roamed the land in search of their subsistence 'like wild Beasts'. Later, when the *Endeavour* was holed on the Great Barrier Reef, Cook and his crew managed to beach the ship at Cook Town, where it was repaired. Again, brief contacts were made with the local people. Cook then sailed north and took possession of the east coast at what became known as Possession Island.

As Cook voyaged north from the continent he wrote with humane insight about his encounters with Indigenous people, critiquing with subtlety his own society: 'They live in a Tranquillity which is not disturbed by the inequality of Condition. The Earth and Sea of their own accord furnishes them with all things necessary for Life. They covet not Magnificent Houses, Household stuff, etc; they live in a Warm and fine Climate; and enjoy every Wholesome Air . . .'

It was a rare moment of openness to the 'otherness' of Aboriginal society. But Europeans wouldn't read Cook's insight for a hundred years. The editor of his journal, John Hawkesworth, thought the description nonsense, applied as it was to the Indigenous people of New Holland. How could a backward people live in 'tranquillity'? But not wanting to waste fine words, Hawkesworth attached them instead to Cook's description of those he encountered at Tierra del Fuego. A new editor a century later corrected the error, and restored Cook's observation of non-material oneness with the land to Aboriginal people and their Great Tradition.[1]

2

THE EORA CONFRONT
THE BRITISH

FIRST ENCOUNTERS

The Eora, the original owners of the foreshore that became Sydney, were named from their words for 'yes' (*e*) and country (*ora*): their very name affirming their ownership. From time immemorial they were a fishing people who used the bush seasonally to hunt and gather other foods. They and adjoining groups, the Dharug (of which the Eora were an eastern part), Kuringgai and the Dharawal, formed the 3000 interlinked Aboriginal people of the Cumberland Plain, which stretched to the Blue Mountains. Their descendants now use Eora as a collective regional name. On 26 January 1788 unprecedented cultural encounters burst forth at Port Jackson, part of a terrible drama that slowly unfolded across the continent, as two very different peoples came face to face within the framework of colonialism.

Unbeknown to the Eora, other peoples over the previous 350 years had been drawing nearer. In a great imperial expansion, the seafaring Portuguese reached India in 1498 and Malacca in 1511; and Ferdinand Magellan, with Spanish patronage, first circumnavigated the globe in 1519–22. The Spanish, who penetrated Pacific islands in 1606, were followed by the British and French a century later. These adventurers 'discovered' and claimed lands already occupied. Australia was first penetrated, but not claimed, by the Dutch in 1605, when Janz in the ironically named *Duyfken* (Little Dove) clashed with people on the northern Gulf coast. Lieutenant James Cook then claimed eastern Australia at Possession Island in 1770. Searching for a Pacific sea base and a convict settlement, the British government despatched a fleet in 1786 containing a thousand people, nearly three-quarters of them convicts, to found a colony.[1]

At their first sight of British sails entering Port Jackson on 26 January 1788, the Eora were stunned, then anger arose as some raced shorewards shaking their spears. With growing anxiety they observed a people almost as numerous as themselves unloading strange stores, equipment and animals. The invaders behaved like savages, landing without permission, and then felled trees, and cleared the ground of undergrowth and pitched shelters. Their cove was rapidly transformed by straight lines of tents, by fences for stock, the air punctuated by shouts and curses, orders and parades. When the female convicts were finally landed, disorder arose as rum-primed, amorous men rushed upon them until all were cooled by a sudden downpour. Aboriginal bewilderment arose in succeeding weeks and months as they observed the new inhabitants and their unfamiliar social structure. Overseers commanded convicts, flogged them and to their horror, even hanged some. Officers in different dress poked at Aboriginal graves, which was even more shocking. To the Eora these newcomers were barbaric, for they asked no permission and offered no respect, which explains their general avoidance of the British for two years.

However, contacts did occur, both with the Dharawal in mid-January 1788 at Botany Bay, and with the Eora soon after. Governor Arthur Phillip and his fellow officers left descriptions of these encounters. Both sides showed bravery as goods were cautiously offered, examined and exchanges made of food, implements and ornaments. The Eora wondered if the British were spirits and not human, being white, and pondered their gender as they were clothed and clean-shaven. One of the sailors was ordered to drop his pants, to which the Eora responded with a knowing cry of recognition. There were other common human understandings as the men on both sides of the cultural frontier eyed off the other women. British officers, amazed and titillated by Aboriginal semi-nakedness, wrote approvingly of the charms of Aboriginal women, while Aboriginal men were caught gazing at convict women and talking and laughing among themselves. The thoughts of women about men across the sexual frontier were not recorded. Such moments of common humanity, however, were lost as tensions arose. The Eora objected to land clearing and sought to wrest some fish out of the British nets, asserting ownership of resources. Phillip mistook this for hunger and ordered the fish be shared. The Eora sampled British metal tools and the British souvenired Aboriginal weapons—both deemed it a theft. At least seventeen encounters occurred in the first month. During most, the

Aboriginal fishers were an important part of the coastal Eora's economy, depicted here by Joseph Lycett, c. 1817. COURTESY OF THE NATIONAL LIBRARY OF AUSTRALIA (NLA.PIC-AN2962715-S17).

Eora showed boldness, even aggression, in defence of their ownership of land. They entered the British settlement only twice in this time.[2]

These encounters at Port Jackson mirrored those of the French Baudin expedition with the Nuenonne at Adventure Bay, Tasmania, in 1802. The French acted in a more sensitive manner, by first embracing the Tasmanians before pressing them with gifts. The French wrestled, danced and exchanged goods with the adults and frolicked with the children. The Nuenonne inspected their clothing and blackened the faces of the French with charcoal. Despite sharing food and laughter, there were moments of tension, but overall the encounter was marked by cautious curiosity, and some joy—far different to the more wary Eora–British encounters. These also differed from meetings with Sydney sealers, who by 1800 were gathering seal skins on Bass Strait islands with the help of captured or bartered Aboriginal women, whom they generally mistreated. The French were perceived as temporary sojourners, whereas the Eora soon realised the British intended to stay.[3]

Cultural encounters are by nature marked by misunderstandings. Language barriers obscure meaning. Even gestures can be misinterpreted, as winks and handshakes in one group are mere twitches or touches to the other. Governor Phillip observed cuts on Eora women's temples—marks of mourning—but to him they were signs of Aboriginal men's brutality to their women. The Eora noted Phillip's missing front tooth and mistook it for a sign of men's initiation, which to them it was. Natural misunderstandings arising from cultural difference were exaggerated as these two peoples held radically different orientations. The Eora lived a life largely without possessions, looked to the past, the community and a religiously based Great Tradition for inspiration, while the British valued material items, eyed the future and lauded the individual, science and the Enlightenment.

SEVEN DETERMINANTS OF CONTACT

Seven other factors shaped these colonial encounters and those elsewhere across the continent, which will be elaborated in turn: first, the British brought no treaty with them; second, they came with a particular exclusivist view of land and society; third, the British held preconceptions of Indigenous people as savage; fourth, the colony they formed was a penal colony; fifth, the encounters were shaped by Aboriginal people themselves through their own agency; sixth, particular individuals on both sides helped shape the action; and seventh, the logics of colonialism began to take hold.

The British government offered treaties to Indigenous peoples before and after taking Australia. It offered treaties to Indian tribes in North America during wars there in the 1750s with the French, and offered a treaty at Waitangi, New Zealand, to the Maori in 1840. However, it offered no treaty to Aboriginal landowners in Australia. Lieutenant James Cook's voyage was formative in this decision. Cook was ordered to search for 'a Continent or Land of great extent' in the south-west of the Pacific and 'with the Consent of the Natives to take possession of Convenient situations in the Country in the name of the King'. Cook took but a cursory look at the east coast of Australia, mostly from the deck of the *Endeavour*. He admired Aboriginal people, but perceived them as being without structures of religion and government; without agriculture or interest in trade; and indeed without clothing and permanent shelters. To Cook, they roamed in search of food daily, 'like wild Beasts'.[4] Cook decided their consent for the British taking possession was not necessary, as the land seemed 'waste' and unowned. The British buccaneer William Dampier had similarly described Aboriginal people he met on the western Australian coast in 1688 as 'the miserablest People in the world', constantly facing starvation, and without agriculture or forms he recognised as those of a society.[5]

These two Eurocentric English misrepresentations, the only ones known to the British government when the First Fleet was being assembled, implied that Aboriginal people, not being farmers, were not sovereign owners to be offered treaties. Two prevailing views of the international law of possession had existed in the late eighteenth century. One held that a people's presence on land gave them ownership, so that all occupiers—even hunters and gatherers—were owners. Another subset of this view was that both Indigenous owners and those who settled had shared rights to a land. However, the other view argued that land was 'waste' until people acquired property rights through mixing their labour with the soil. The British government, influenced by Cook and Dampier, viewed non-farming Aboriginal people as not owning land, and therefore did not offer them a treaty.[6] This infringed the rights of Aboriginal people and lowered respect for them from that moment on.

Second, the British brought radical ideas of land ownership to Australia. These had been developed over the previous 200 years in Britain, where communal title to lands deemed 'commons' had been eradicated by a farming revolution. In this movement, large landowners who wielded power in both houses of parliament expropriated the common lands through hundreds of parliamentary Enclosure Acts from the 1770s. They added these enclosed commons to their enlarged and improved farms. Private property and all on it, both animals and resources, came to have a higher value in the late eighteenth century than human life. And this was an *exclusive* right, for poaching and game laws in England forbade trespass and put the property rights of an owner above that of the liberty, even the life, of another person. This extreme emphasis on exclusive property rights also produced a land revolution in Australia as Aboriginal communal property rights were challenged by a more exclusive regime. This view began to bite once Governor Phillip issued grants of land to officers and freed convicts, who, in turn, warned Aboriginal people off 'their' newly acquired property.[7]

The third determinant of contact were the discourses of savagery that the British carried in their heads—a way of thinking that was very old and bound to the word 'civilised'. 'Savage' came from the Latin *salvaticus*, meaning 'wood'; that is, being wild and untamed, and opposite to the Latin *civicus*, meaning 'citizen' and pertaining to city; that is, cultured and ordered. From Greek times there was a belief that wild men who were large, hairy and uncontrolled in their passions lived beyond civilised society without family, society or religion. In essence, those who thought themselves civilised needed a wild man ('Other') to be their opposite, to help define what it was to be 'civilised'. As Europe's colonial expansion unfolded, the idea of the wild man—'the savage'—was transferred onto Indigenous people; they appeared as a new Other to Europeans.

Africans were not only seen as savage and heathen but different in skin colour—not that blackness was given the significance it later assumed. In the English language the word 'black' from the fifteenth century assumed new and loaded meanings of 'dirty' and 'evil', as opposed to 'white' being defined as 'clean' and 'pure'—ideas played out in Shakespeare's *Othello* (1603). African slavery, which had to be rationalised as people were bought and sold and suffered appalling conditions, further linked savagery and blackness into a body of ideas that argued that the savage was wild, violent, treacherous and animalistic.[8]

A variant of the savage was the 'noble' savage. This emerged from the ideas of Jean Jacques Rousseau, a Genevan-born philosopher who, in his *Discourse on Arts and Sciences* (1750), argued that as arts and civilisation developed, moral virtue declined. True virtue and even physical strength was deemed greater in natural man, who lived in perfect harmony with his fellows and environment. This idea was soon exemplified by a Tahitian noble named Omai, who returned to England with Cook in 1774 and was dined, painted, presented to the King and feted in British society as a man of natural manners and true virtue.[9] A line of exotic Indigenous visitors followed him to Europe. The Romantic idea of the noble savage found favour with the educated of Europe and also influenced Pacific explorers who went in search of them. The French artists on D'Entrecasteaux's 1793 voyage to Tasmania painted the Tasmanians with heroic Greek-like bodies and poses—clearly revealing how the mind can shape the eye. On Baudin's succeeding voyage in 1802, scientists tested Tasmanians with a dynameter to compare their strength with French sailors. Some officers of the British First Fleet, notably Captain-Lieutenant Watkin Tench, also arrived with the idea of noble savagery firmly in their heads.

While basic savagery was the dominant view of Aboriginal people among the first settlers, especially convicts, and noble savagery was very much a minority view, mostly among Phillip and his officers, both were unreal. The idea of savagery was the more resilient as it suited the context of conflict that soon developed, and the idea of nobility soon faded with the reality of contact. Neither idea was a sound basis for practical relations with the Eora, who were neither noble nor savage, but human and different. Conversely the Eora in their own way were civilised, for they were guided by a moral code and law. Conversely the newcomers, many of them untutored convicts from the streets of urban Britain, were by definition law-breakers—and some were indeed savage.

The fourth factor was the penal nature of early colonial society. Its immediate origins lay in the American Revolution. The assertion of independence by

Noble savagery as depicted in 'Natives of Botany Bay', by R. Cleveley. FROM *THE VOYAGE OF GOVERNOR PHILLIP TO BOTANY BAY* BY JOHN STOCKDALE, LONDON, 1789.

American colonists in 1776 soon denied Britain its dumping ground for convicts, who had been cast off to New England colonies as indentured labour since 1717. Its deeper origins lay in a harsh criminal code which emerged from a social crisis in Georgian England. Agricultural reconstruction pushed rural labourers into poverty and to London and regional cities in search of work. Population increased and unemployment rates climbed to one in three as the labouring classes scrambled for work. Conditions in new factories, and living conditions in slums, were primitive. The death rates of children under five were one in two among the urban poor. Alcohol abuse, violence and social disruption marked the lives of those termed the 'casual poor', whose ranks filled the gaols. Historians argue the 'casual poor' exhibited traits of brutality, mistrust, misogyny and social alienation, born of broken families and dismal social and economic conditions.[10] Many transported to Australia were further degraded by an authoritarian convict system in which about 40 per cent of males were flogged for new misdemeanours. While debate rages about the qualities of convicts, many of whom were reclaimed by a new colonial start, most were poor ambassadors for the sensitive task of cultural interaction. Some convicts, damaged by social conditions at home and the convict system in the colony, vented their frustrations and aggressions on

Aboriginal people. Indeed, Governor Phillip attributed much early interracial violence to the convicts.

Convict society was infused by convict attitudes and shaped by its penal and remote status. God-fearing people shunned it and free settlers were at first denied entry, leaving New South Wales to hardened men and their gaolers. When free immigrants arrived after 1813 they were generally not first-rate respectable types, but adventurers looking for the main chance in a remote outpost of empire. Few were open to intercultural dialogue with Indigenous people so different from themselves. A great contradiction lay at the heart of New South Wales. Governor Phillip was ordered 'by every possible means to open an intercourse with the natives, and to conciliate their affections, enjoining all our subjects to live in amity and kindness with them', and to punish those who 'wantonly destroy them'. He was also to report 'in what manner our intercourse with the people may be turned to the advantage of this colony'.[11] Good intentions clashed with the order to possess, to dominate and to colonise. This contradiction between humanitarian conscience and belief in British supremacy continually infected the history of Australian colonisation.

The fifth factor shaping colonial encounters was Aboriginal action, based on motives of survival and ideas of kinship, reciprocity and land, and the sixth was individual motivations, both of which will be elaborated together. The Eora initially shunned white settlement. Perhaps they thought the British were spirits of the dead or strange beings from the periphery—but either way, they were to be avoided. Once they detected their humanity, the settlers were perceived as dangerous strangers who might invoke sorcery, as the power of outsiders to work dreadful magic was a great fear in Aboriginal society. However, Aboriginal avoidance also stemmed from a sense of offence. These strangers had not requested permission to enter Eora land, which is what respectful visitors did in the Aboriginal world. They chopped and burned the land, shot kangaroos and took fish—all without permission. The newcomers were wild men, barbarians ignorant of right behaviour, who were to be shunned.

As the months passed, Phillip's anxiety to engage the Eora turned to urgency as crops wilted in the alien soils. Food shortages made it imperative that he learn more of the country's resources. However, Eora avoidance made this impossible. After a year, Phillip determined to kidnap several Eora, teach them English, and make them intermediaries between the two races. This change from apparent friendship to coercion made him appear treacherous to the Eora. Arabanoo, captured at Manly, quickly learned the language and was much admired by the British officers. However, he perished in the disastrous smallpox epidemic that destroyed half the Eora in mid-1789. (None of the British, who were immune, died.) The following November, Bennelong was also kidnapped, but this clever fellow escaped six months later with a smattering of English, a love of wine and a fund of stories. Phillip's hopes for a dialogue were again dashed. Phillip encountered Bennelong at Manly months later and, while attempting to approach him in friendship, the Governor was speared—almost fatally—by another Eora man. Why this occurred is unknown, but was probably reflective of Aboriginal ideas of kinship and reciprocity: payback for the kidnappings.[12]

Governor Phillip survived his spearing and bore no grudge. However, after another year punctuated by scattered violence and growing frustration, Phillip overreacted to the fatal spearing of his huntsman, John McEntire, in December 1790, allegedly by Pemulwoy. (McEntire was said to be notorious for cruelty to 'blacks'.) Phillip gave orders that ten men in the Botany Bay area were to be captured, slain and their heads severed and brought back in bags as an example, but that women and children and property were to be untouched. However, Captain-Lieutenant Tench's detachment heading south towards the Dharug became lost in marshes and none were captured.[13] Clearly, Phillip's unrealistic romantic view of the Eora had soured. Others, like Tench, were simply bewildered by the Eora's failure to respond to British overtures. But Phillip did not lose faith entirely, and while he remained in the colony extended friendship to certain Eora individuals.

This friendship was as much due to the Eora as to Phillip. The Eora initially controlled the British by avoidance, but when that proved impossible due to the latter's refusal to leave, the Eora used kinship to manage the strangers. Bennelong befriended the opposing headman Phillip, camped at the bottom of the Government House garden, ate at Phillip's table, and called him 'Beenena', which meant father. Barangaroo, Bennelong's wife, asked Phillip if she could have her child born at Government House. Phillip refused, thinking the hospital a safer place. Barangaroo's request was no idle one, but a significant attempt to gain a number of advantages. First, it would cement kinship relations with Phillip, who would be cast in the role of another provider for her family; second, her child would be associated with the headman of the new power in the region; and third, her child would fill a vacuum in land custodianship, as the Cadigal clan who owned the land on which Government House stood had been decimated by smallpox, and Aboriginal law denoted that land must not be left without custodians.[14] Other Eora fraternised with the British, exchanged sexual favours in return for flour, tea and tobacco, and sold them fish and artefacts. This

Both in early Sydney and Van Diemen's Land, British officials offered, but could not achieve, equality for Aboriginal people before the law. Governor Davey's proclamation to the Aborigines in Van Diemen's Land, 1816, explains this offer. COURTESY OF THE NATIONAL LIBRARY OF AUSTRALIA (NLA.PIC-AN7878675).

prolonged encounter, made inevitable once both groups occupied the same space, was accelerated when smallpox fractured Eora society.

These close encounters became deeper entanglements, as both groups influenced each other. The Eora learned English, used European steel implements, consumed new foods such as flour, tea and sugar, and camped around the settlement. Few British imagined they might learn from the Eora, but some gathered smatterings of other ways of living and a few even pondered the difference. Phillip and Captain David Collins described their culture and ceremonies as best they could. Lieutenant William Dawes collected vocabulary. Phillip at times even let his observation overrule his preconceptions. In March 1788 he observed Aboriginal drawings of humans and animals on shields, implements and rocks—some in 'superior style'—which he thought odd for a people who had not created clothing. Yet pondering it, he concluded that perhaps the climate was not as cool as he supposed, otherwise 'they would doubtless have had clothes and houses, before they attempted to become sculptors'.[15]

Captain-Lieutenant Tench, a man of the Enlightenment, observed the Eora and other groups closely, formed friendships, and wrote sensitively about their religious and cultural life, albeit all through a Eurocentric veil. Tench detected belief in a 'superior power', although Collins did not, and witnessed Eora at church services, where they 'always preserved profound silence and decency, as if conscious that some religious ceremony on our side was performing'.[16] Watkin Tench soon rejected the 'noble savage' ideal, preferring to see the Eora in a more complex way. He wrote that as a nation they 'rank very low, even in the scale of savages', but he added that they 'possess a considerable portion of that acumen, or sharpness of intellect, which bespeaks genius'.[17] He admired the beauty of a young Eora woman, Gooreedeeana, but was all the same shocked when she appeared like a 'savage' in body paint. The sympathetic Tench departed the colony within four years, along with Phillip and several other open-minded officers such as William Dawes.

As settlement spread from Sydney Cove, violence escalated. By the late 1790s the Hawkesbury River area, 60 kilometres north-west of Sydney, supported more than 400 European farmers who claimed exclusive rights to the rich river flats. The Dharug complained that farms were barriers to the river and their food supply. The dispute soon became deadly. When the Dharug crossed the farms or took corn in retaliation, settlers fired on them. The Dharug hit back, forming raiding parties and setting fire to crops. 'Mosquito' led one group until he was captured and transported for murder to Van Diemen's Land, where two decades later he led the Oyster Bay tribe in raids on settlers. He was caught and hanged in 1823.[18] Open warfare soon erupted on the Hawkesbury and the government reluctantly provided troops in 1795 to protect the settlers and their crops. Captain Paterson wrote that 'it gives me concern to have been forced to destroy any of these people, particularly as I have no doubt of their having been cruelly treated by some of the first settlers who went out there'. However, the crops were vital and had to be defended.[19] The bodies of any Dharug killed were to be placed in iron gibbets and hung from trees as a warning. The fiction of their equal status before the law was exposed.

The Dharug, led by Pemulwoy, made a daring raid on Parramatta. They were beaten off and Pemulwoy severely wounded, but he escaped to fight on. By 1801 Governor King ordered soldiers to patrol the farms on the Georges River and shoot any Dharug on sight. After four more settler deaths and some convict women being 'cruelly used', allegedly by Pemulwoy's band, orders were given for his capture—dead or alive. Two settlers killed him in June 1802. King despatched Pemulwoy's severed and pickled head to Sir Joseph Banks, commenting: 'altho' a terrible pest to the colony, he was a brave and independent character'. Pemulwoy's son, Tedbury, raided farms until 1810. The tribal guerrilla warfare on the outskirts of the Cumberland Plain was so effective that, as late as 1816, Governor Macquarie forbade Aboriginal people from carrying weapons within two kilometres of a house or town, or from congregating in groups of more than six, even when unarmed. He authorised settlers to establish vigilante groups and formed three new military outposts. The ten most wanted Aboriginal 'murderers' were outlawed and thus liable to be shot on sight.[20]

The seventh factor in shaping early colonial encounters was the logic of colonial possession. The land was taken from the Eora, the Dharug and the Kuringgai rhetorically, as well as by force. David Day argues, in his book *Conquest*, that dispossessing another people of their land has three stages: a legal claim, a practical assertion of ownership, and a moral assertion of ownership.[21] We have already seen how the British justified not offering a treaty to reinforce the legal claim by Cook at Possession Island in 1770. The practical assertion of ownership took many non-violent forms and was practised over decades after 1788.

Names and cropping were practical ways of denoting ownership. From the first moment of sighting Sydney Cove, the British renamed the land in their own image and after their own places, officials and politicians back home. Even the continent was named by 1813 after a suggestion by Matthew Flinders that it be called Australia after the Latin *terra australis*—south land. Once named, the land was laid out in straight lines, surveyed and mapped, again to denote ownership. Towns and villages were then gradually built and land was granted to officers, ex-convicts and free settlers who after 1813 peopled the land in increasing numbers. The British First Fleet's 1000 people equalled the Eora's population in 1788. After the smallpox epidemic in 1789, they equalled all Indigenous people on the Cumberland Plain. By 1820 there were 30,000 British in the colony, by then the equal of all Indigenous people in New South Wales. Many settlers fenced, built and tilled the soil to confirm their claim. To the British, planting a crop or erecting a hut had always been an effective assertion of ownership. Army officers and officials soon aped the gentry back home, building fine villas and estates across the Cumberland Plain, and laying it out to agriculture. In doing so, they totally transformed the Aboriginal landscape into an English one—or as near as they could; fomenting a revolution of ecology and power in this space more complete than any European political revolution. This was the Australian Revolution, the outcomes of which are still reverberating.

The moral claims took numerous forms as the British tried to justify their possession by boosting themselves. Albert Memmi called this the 'usurper complex', by which taking another's possessions have to be rationalised.[22] The British claimed to be a civilised people bringing the arts and sciences to a backward land. They had no doubt that they were superior to the Indigenous people they called 'savages'. The British claimed all the trappings of a fine civilisation: Christianity, law, forms of government, technology, refined morals and manners. They viewed the world as progressing through various stages of development from hunters and gatherers and pastoralists to farmers and townspeople who created Art and Science. They were advanced; Aboriginal people were not—of this they had no doubt. It was ironic then that this supposed advanced civilised society also produced poverty, crime and inequality in England, and a penal system in Australia.

The 'usurper complex' also justified possession by denigrating Indigenous people. Europeans—even sensitive ones like Watkin Tench—authored books claiming to know what Aboriginal people were like. They even invented general labels for them, like 'natives', and shunned the names the people used for themselves—although Aboriginal people did not have a general term for indigenes, only local ones. This newly invented knowledge about Aboriginal people was a form of power: even Tench's affectionate account still asserted that they 'rank very low, even in the scale of savages'. As the struggle for the land unfolded, the abuse of those who were now considered enemies deepened. Many British—notably most convicts—regarded the Eora as inferior and dangerous savages. The convict artist Thomas Watling was resentful that they

Ignoble savagery. 'Scene in Sydney Street', by J. Austin. COURTESY OF THE NATIONAL LIBRARY OF AUSTRALIA (NLA.PIC-AN8953984).

were treated, he believed, better by Phillip than convicts. He wrote to his aunt in England of Aboriginal people that 'irascibility, ferocity, cunning, treachery, filth and immodesty, are strikingly their dark characteristics'.[23] Artists began to lampoon the Eora in caricatures, making them even more alien; others gave them liquor and goaded them to fight. The long denigration of Aboriginal people had begun.

However, around 1800 most European explanations of human difference were not based on racial arguments of inherent inferiority or superiority, but rather cultural and environmental assumptions. The British 'knew' they were superior out of a staunch ethnocentrism—the belief their own group was the best—and on their observations of material development and ideas of progress. They had metal, structures of government and empires based on fine ships; Aboriginal people did not. Watkin Tench argued in 1792 that the British were superior, but only as they 'have been born in more favoured lands, and who have profited by more enlightened systems . . . by the fortuitous advantage of birth alone, they possess superiority; that untaught, unaccommodated man, is the same in Pall Mall [London], as in the wilderness of New South Wales'. To

Tench, human difference was a product of environment. Education and enlightened thinking in Britain underpinned British superiority—not anything to do with race. The Christian view that all men were brothers from the one creation also strengthened the environmental view, as people had diverged only since the Creation 7000 years before. These views underpinned the idea that Aboriginal people could and must be changed.[24]

THE CIVILISING MISSION

The desire to 'improve' Aboriginal people, combined with the need to bolster British moral claims to possess Australia, created the Civilising Mission. Tench identified this quest as introducing to the Eora education, work and Christianity, which would bring them 'knowledge, virtue and happiness'.[25] Governor Arthur Phillip articulated this idea too, but with some doubts of a practical man as to 'whether many of the accommodations of civilised life be not more than counterbalanced by the artificial wants to which they give birth'. However, he concluded that 'to teach the shivering savage how to clothe his body', how to shelter himself, and to teach those 'ready to perish for one half of the year with hunger, the means of procuring constant and abundant provision, must be to confer upon them benefits of the highest value and importance'.[26]

This Civilising Mission was pursued seriously by Lachlan Macquarie, a stern but humane Governor from 1809 to 1822. The darker side of Macquarie's paternalism caused him to send a military expedition against the Eora on the periphery of settlement in 1814, whom he termed 'outlaws'. But the kinder facets of his paternalism—of guiding and helping—prompted his ameliorative effort to incorporate Aboriginal people into colonial society. In December 1814, on the advice of a missionary named William Shelley, he established a Native Institution to educate children vocationally and 'to effect the Civilization of the Aborigines of New South Wales, and to render their Habits more domesticated and industrious'.[27] It was Australia's first assimilation policy. It also became a vehicle for the first removal of children via the dormitory system. Although entry was voluntary, once there, children were supposed to remain until around fifteen years of age.

Six children began this great experiment under Shelley's tutelage. By 1817 seventeen were enrolled. They displayed their 'progress' at the annual Parramatta Feast sponsored by Macquarie as a reconciling effort. In 1817 the *Sydney Gazette* reported the children entered 'appearing very clean, well clothed and happy', read aloud from books, and allegedly engendered pride in the adults. One supposedly exclaimed: 'Governor that will make a good settler,—that's my Pickaninny! [child]'.[28] In 1819 Maria, an Aboriginal girl of fourteen years, won first prize in the school examination, ahead of twenty Aboriginal and 100 European children. Macquarie was delighted, declaring Aboriginal pupils reveal 'good Natural Understandings, and an Aptitude for learning whatever is proposed to be taught them'. The *Sydney Gazette* hailed the Institution as the instrument of 'civilization and salvation of thousands of fellow creatures, at present involved in gross darkness'.[29] However, Commissioner Bigge, investigating Macquarie's administration in 1820, was less sanguine and anxious at the annual cost of £15 13s per child. By 1823, with Macquarie recalled home for overspending, and his successor indifferent, the institution was closed and its few remaining pupils returned to the Blacks Town settlement.

Despite the loss of the Governor's patronage, the Native Institution failed because its aims did not match the Eora's aspirations. The parents used it as a crèche while they travelled, but removed their children when they chose for Macquarie did not enforce their stay. The teaching of the three Rs seemed irrelevant to parents who valued traditional education more. The school was supposed to produce a group of young adults who could fit into the new society and be marriage partners for each other, as few colonists showed any inclination to intermarry with Aboriginal people. However, the school never had more than twenty children and most retained little of their learning once out of school, as it was not deeply embedded or frequently used like their traditional learning. Only Maria—the examination winner—fulfilled the experiment in assimilation. She married a convict named Robert Lock in 1824. Maria was promised a marriage dowry of a cow and some land. She received the cow finally in 1827 after repeated written requests. By using her education she wrote several petitions and gained 40 acres in 1832. They raised ten children before Robert died in 1854 and Maria in 1878. Their descendants still live in the area today.[30]

To 'civilise' Aboriginal adults, Macquarie granted land for farming to engender 'the productive Effects of their own Labour and Industry to the Wild and precarious Pursuits of the Woods.'[31] Macquarie typically believed hunting and gathering was marked by scarcity and want, and did not see it as an appropriate and intelligent use of land. He could not know the Aboriginal economic mode was twenty times older than that of agriculture. In 1815 Macquarie settled sixteen Kuringgai families from Broken Bay on land at George's Head in prefabricated huts with provisions, seed, clothes and a boat. The enterprise failed, but not because the Eora were incapable of farming, as some had already grown crops successfully. Rather, it was more the case that their

Great Ancestors were successful hunters and gatherers, not farmers, and there being no sound reason to change, they sold their farms and spent the money. It was too hopeful to expect the Kuringgai to change in one generation, and arrogant to expect that they should.

The Christian aspect of the Civilising Mission began formally in the 1820s, although several clergy housed Aboriginal individuals earlier. Two men, Bennelong's son and a man called Jemmy, were baptised around 1821. Reverend Lancelot Threlkeld began a mission at Lake Macquarie in 1827 among the Awabakal, Rev. William Watson and Johann Handt worked among the Wiradjuri at Wellington Valley in 1832 and several small missions operated in Port Phillip and Moreton Bay around 1840. These were important efforts, since missions provided sanctuary for Aboriginal people amid wild times on the frontier. The missionaries had no doubt Aboriginal people were fully human, as Acts 17:26 pronounced 'God hath made of one blood all nations of men for to dwell on all the face of the earth'. They observed Aboriginal culture and learned an Aboriginal language, although usually with the intention of subverting the culture. Missionaries considered Aboriginal people heathens who were to be taught Christian truth, civilised and remade into black brothers. Reverend Threlkeld advised: 'first obtain the language, then preach the Gospel, then urge them from Gospel motives to be industrious'.[32]

Missionaries were at first optimistic. When food was available at the missions Aboriginal people gathered, no doubt out of curiosity as well. Services were held and mission buildings and gardens erected. Intense work focused on the children, who were often placed in dormitories where they were regimented and taught reading, singing and domestic arts. The missionaries initially filed favourable reports. Threlkeld, aided by an Awabakal man named Biraban, translated Luke's Gospel by 1831—the first part of the Bible available in an Aboriginal language. At Wellington Valley, Rev. James Gunther wrote: 'Their intellectual faculties are by no means so inferior as is generally supposed; their mind is quite capable of culture; of this I have many decisive proofs . . . at least the young men and boys very soon acquire and speak the English language correctly and fluently. You can draw out their minds so as to reflect and reason.'[33] A superintendent of agriculture in the valley taught 'habits of industry, order and subordination', and a number of young Wiradjuri men were employed there as agricultural labourers.

However, when supplies ran short, as they invariably did, the people drifted off to local pastoral stations to seek work and rations. Conversions proved elusive. A Wiradjuri man at the Wellington mission named Fred did seem genuinely interested. He recited the Lord's Prayer in his hut, led his kinfolk in prayer and requested baptism. However, Rev. Watson refused the sacrament as he was not convinced of Fred's complete faith.[34] Unlike the Pacific islands, where missionaries might convert the chief and then the whole community followed, each Aboriginal person was a new battle. Reverend Gunther at Wellington wrote despondently: 'we are very apt to think our giving instruction to them is like writing on the sand, the impression of which may be effaced by the first breeze or wave that passes over it'.[35] Threlkeld had other problems. By the time he finished his translation into Awabakal, all the people had perished.

The missions themselves were like marks in the sand that left little trace once they failed from myriad problems. They were underfunded, despite some government help, and their food cropping struggled like that of other pioneers. Once supplies failed, their effort faltered. The Wellington Valley missionaries were also deeply divided by personality clashes and differences in method. Reverend Watson's virtual kidnapping of children to fill the dormitory with potential converts not only alienated the other missionaries but infuriated the Wiradjuri. Even if the missions had run smoothly, they would have failed to make conversions because the missionaries held deeply Eurocentric ideas of Aboriginal people. They misread their nakedness, their refusal to do constant work, their polygamous family structure and much else about the lives of hunter-gatherers. The Wiradjuri and others found the rigid evangelical thinking of the missionaries perplexing and their lectures against sin tiresome, preferring the more robust behaviour of stockmen and shepherds. As one Wiradjuri man asked Watson: 'What for you speak much about God, and devil, and dying? No other white fellow, no other master, talk that way'.[36] Above all, the missions failed because Aboriginal people resisted their overtures. Reverend Handt wrote in November 1832 that the Wiradjuri 'seemed to be very indifferent' to his preaching—and while his despair was natural, so too was the disinterest of the Wiradjuri, who had their own sustaining religious ideas and good reason to reject the alien beliefs of their overlords. Missionaries, being part of the colony, were conquerors too, whether they liked it or not.

THE ABORIGINAL DOMAIN

Observers claimed that there was no sense of inferiority whatsoever in the remaining Aboriginal people of Sydney, later to be termed 'fringe dwellers'. A colonial doctor named Peter Cunningham found his 'donation' of money in a Sydney street repulsed by an Aboriginal man as he had not given enough.[37]

These were not Aboriginal beggars, for their view of sharing did not allow such an interpretation. Besides, some no doubt saw a street donation as paying rent to the original owners. Each in his or her way found a means of surviving. Bennelong attached himself to Phillip, and travelled to England with him in 1793, accompanied by his friend Yemmerrawannie. The two intelligent and gregarious men visited high society, the theatre and learned to write while there. Yemmerrawannie rests in the village of Eltham, Kent, having died there of pneumonia.[38] Back in Sydney, Bennelong remained a traditional man, despite this British veneer, until his death from spearing in 1813.

Bungaree, a Kuringgai man, made several sea voyages with Europeans, acting as an emissary when other Aboriginal peoples were encountered. He journeyed with Flinders to circumnavigate Australia in 1813. Bungaree, who mimicked Sydney identities for coins, died a traditional man in 1830, survived by his wife Cora Gooseberry and two sons. Cora camped about Sydney living on rations, handouts and showing rock art to those interested, till her death in 1852. One son, Young Bungaree, gave boomerang exhibitions in the Sydney Domain in the 1840s. The other son, John Bungaree, was a boarder at the Sydney Normal School in the 1830s—paid for by some philanthropist—and became a pastoral worker and native policeman. John Bungaree was less assured than his parents, once remarking: 'I wish I had never been taken out of the bush, and educated as I have been, for I cannot be a white man, and they will never look

Bennelong, by James Neagle. COURTESY OF THE NATIONAL LIBRARY OF AUSTRALIA (NLA.PIC-AN7566576-V).

on me as one of themselves; and I cannot be a blackfellow, I am disgusted with their way of living.'[39]

A generation after settlement the Eora, Dharug and Kuringgai remnant camped mostly around Sydney Harbour and survived by catching and selling fish along the foreshore, seeking rations or earning money doing odd jobs. Mahroot, alias 'the Boatswain', a 50-year-old Dharug man from the Cooks River area, who grew up with Commissioner Allen before becoming a whaler, told a select committee in 1845 that of the 400 in his group when he was a boy, there were now four. There were 50 Aboriginal people still living in the Botany Bay area, but from mixed groups, and seven of them were of mixed descent. They lived off fish and possums, although supplies were less than formerly—'you look all day to get one or two'. Mahroot also sold fish and earned a little rent from a piece of land given to him at Botany. Mahroot gave an account of a people still living a traditional life as best they could at Botany—largely separate from white society, although two women lived with white men there. They did not use hospital services out of fear, but Mahroot thought a few might let their children be schooled. Asked if it would be good if children went to school to become like white fellows, he replied in quiet defiance: 'it would not do them any good at all'.[40]

Other Aboriginal people further inland also became semi-dependent on the European invaders, as access to their land and resources was restricted, although bush tucker was still gathered along with European food. By the 1820s, they had come from 150 kilometres away to receive handouts and a blanket at the Parramatta Feast, which they perceived as easy takings. No article of trade in return was demanded and the blanket could quickly be traded for alcohol, food or tobacco. Wishing to stop this annual migration into Sydney's outskirts, the government transferred the blanket distribution to the interior in the 1830s. By then, Aboriginal people saw it in moral terms as compensation from Queen Victoria for their loss of land. When the government ended the distribution in 1844 to cut costs, and because it allegedly encouraged idleness, Aboriginal people cried out in anger: 'What for!'[41]

By the 1820s, few Aboriginal people accepted Governor Macquarie's invitation to join colonial society, as the remnants of the Sydney people thought it a bad deal. They had their own cultural ideas that had held them in good stead, and besides it was *their way*. When asked if the people at Botany would farm if they had land, Mahroot replied 'they would not stop by it'.[42] Aboriginal people also saw, as John Bungaree found, that the offer to join white society was a poor one. Europeans would only accept them as the lowest class at the bottom of the new colonial society, confined there by their Aboriginality. They, like anyone else, wanted to be able to reach the top, to be gentlemen as Bennelong had experienced in London, but that was not possible within the inequalities of colonialism. So they considered the colonial offer—and rejected it. It was not their world, and nor was it an equal and just world for them, for their original ownership and respect for their culture was denied.

3

RESISTING THE INVADERS

Unlike the Eora, who were surprised by sails from nowhere, Aboriginal groups inland were forewarned of invasion as the British drove their flocks from the Cumberland Plain after 1815. Detailed information about European explorers preceded them by hundreds of kilometres along Aboriginal tracks. Distant groups learned of pale, ghost-like strangers, weird animals and baggage, which proved to be loaded drays, horses and stock. Before seeing the strangers, Aboriginal people also possessed their technology. John Batman peered into a Kulin woman's bag near the future site of Melbourne in 1835 and saw pieces of metal hoop traded from the north. Other items—nails, glass from bottles and metal pieces—preceded the frontier. European diseases were also vanguards of their European hosts.[1]

Aboriginal people could not imagine what might be the outcomes of later contact. If they could have foreseen events, they might have been less willing to guide explorers and show settlers the country. They might have met the intruders more frequently with violence and less often with cautious welcome. Settlers were more prescient, knowing of global colonial adventures—for instance, in the Americas where Spanish conquistadors had levelled the great Aztec and Inca empires in the south, and the French and English had dispossessed half the indigenous people of the north. In 1835 the explorer Major Thomas Mitchell wrote when south of the Murray: 'As I stood, the first European intruder on the sublime solitude of these verdant plains . . . I felt conscious of being the harbinger of mighty changes; and that our steps would soon be followed by the men and the animals for which it seemed to have been prepared.'[2]

BATTLES FOR THE LAND

Aboriginal groups soon realised Europeans intended to stay—and without permission. Timberoon confronted the Aboriginal Protector George Robinson at Burrumbeep in 1841, by stamping and yelling: 'Country belonging to me; country belonging to me. My Country!' An elder warned Edward Curr across a watercourse near the Murray in 1840, spitting and yelling that the water, the fish and the ducks all belonged to his people.[3] Each encounter was a dramatic clash between Indigenous people who believed land was a spiritual essence under their custodianship and was not transferable, and intruders who treated it as a valuable commodity to be exploited, bought and sold. This moral clash between original owners and harbingers of progress was re-enacted across the continent as settlers spread from Sydney and beachheads at Hobart (1804), Brisbane (1824) and Perth (1829), then later from Melbourne (1835) and Adelaide (1836). The north and north-west were settled after the 1870s (see map, overleaf).

In retrospect, the fact that settlers won the struggle for the land suggests the frontier was a place of white power. But victory for either side was less easy to predict at the time. In many places, but not all, violence became a distinctive marker of settlement. This has been challenged recently by conservative thinkers who argue that much of what has been said about such violence is exaggerated, unproven and even historical fabrication. The British Empire was a 'good' empire ruled by law, they contend. Where violence existed, Aboriginal people were not patriots fighting for land, but outlaws after European goods. While the British did intend to uphold the rule of law, this proved impossible on the far-flung frontier. Also, police and magistrates were not always even-handed, favouring settlers against 'savages'. The weight of evidence clearly shows violence and a culture of violence initially permeated most frontiers. Settlers did not doubt they were fighting a war and called it such. Aboriginal people who carried buckshot in their bodies and mourned their many dead had no doubt either.

History was running against Indigenous people as global capital connected Europe's productive capacity to the resources of new lands. In 1822 the British government reduced import duties on Australian wool to one-sixth that on German wool, to favour its own colonies. A rapid expansion of sheep numbers followed and a quarter of a million immigrants, mostly British and Irish, flowed to the Australian colonies by 1850. The frontier expanded rapidly, spurred on by a fantastic land grab that was unique in world history. About 4000 Europeans called 'squatters', along with their twenty million sheep, occupied over 400

million hectares of Aboriginal land, stretching from southern Queensland to
South Australia by 1860.[4] Aboriginal people were soon outnumbered in their
own land. The British government, which initially tried to confine settlement
to resemble a settled and elite property-holding state like England, from 1836
sanctioned this illegal occupation with an annual licence system.

If god-fearing farming families had occupied the land, settlement would
have been far slower and fear and violence might have been far less. But arid
lands did not favour farming and pastoralism took hold. Sheep flourished on
the dry western plains and their wool was light and of high value for transportation.
Pastoralism created a gendered society, demanding itinerant seasonal male
workers for shearing, and few permanent workers, mostly single men to reduce
costs. In the outback around 1840 there were 38 white men to every white
woman, which boded ill for local Aboriginal women who were subsequent
targets for men's libidos. Half the workforce were or had been convicts, whose
ways were mostly less than genteel.[5] Sheep country was of low human density,

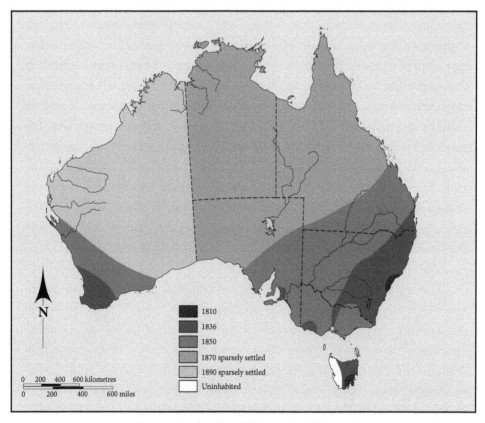

The moving frontier of European settlement.

a male domain, with few towns and fewer clergy, police, judges or families to civilise the frontier.

Young adventurers eager for profit but fearful of failure pushed into Aboriginal lands. The bush was immense, alien and melancholy, to European minds. Life savings were sunk in risky ventures: scab or foot rot in their sheep or Aboriginal resistance could wreck their hopes. Pastoral runs were large and isolated with few workers, mostly lone shepherds, who might not see each other for a week. Aboriginal people were imagined as fierce and treacherous; so the discourse of savagery played with settlers' minds—fear eating away at some. Tom Browne, who occupied 20,000 hectares of Gunditjmara land near Port Fairy, journeyed along a ti-tree-lined track. 'I began to think about the blacks, and whether or not they might attack us in force. At that moment I heard a wild shrill cry, which considerably accelerated the circulatory system. I sprang to my gun.' To Browne's relief, the noise proved to be a wild swan.[6]

Aboriginal people came to dread the bleating of sheep on their kangaroo grasses and the sound of settlers' axes cleaving their trees. But Aboriginal people were facing more than just settlers and their sheep: they were facing ecological revolution. In his classic account of Europe's biological expansion, *Ecological Imperialism* (1985), Alfred Crosby identified and explained how settlers came as part of an ecological package. Their cattle ate out the native grasses and their cloven hooves trampled the waterholes. The sheep demolished the precious staple foods like the *murnong* or yam daisy in a few seasons. The disturbance of the soils gave way to opportunistic weeds, which hitched a ride to the new world in the settlers' baggage or were purposely transplanted by homesick settlers. Weeds, as Crosby argued, 'sprout early and seize bare ground. Direct sun, wind and rain do not discourage them.'[7] Game such as kangaroo and bush turkey were scared off and replaced on their grasslands by introduced stock. Within a few seasons settlers noticed the difference in the country. But how much more did the keenly observant original owners see?

Aboriginal anger mounted as their world began to alter. They found pastoralists claimed exclusive possession and barred their entry to sacred places. As their food supplies were disrupted, Aboriginal people sought European foods as supplements. They requested food at the hut door, but when the largesse of stock owners dried up they took food off the hoof by stealth, and roasted their mutton chops over a secret fire. They soon learned that what to them was proper use of resources on their land was to most squatters stealing—and English poaching laws held property above life until 1832. Squatters were in turn angered when Aboriginal people ransacked unattended shepherds' huts for flour, tea and sugar, knives and even guns—appearing to settlers to be common thieves. But as Yagan, a Nyoongar man from Swan River, explained in 1843:

> The wild black fellows do not understand your laws, every living animal that roams the country, and every edible root that grows in the ground are common property. A black man claims nothing as his own but his cloak, his weapons, and his name . . . He does not understand that animals or plants can belong to one person more than to another.[8]

Once Aboriginal people learned the art of stock management, the taking of a few sheep escalated into the removal of whole flocks. There are numerous instances of Aboriginal sheep yards being found in remote areas. In the 1840s, Billy Billy of the Pyrenees area 'borrowed' some of William Clarke's sheep to stock his own station, 'made a bush yard and shepherded the sheep during the day and yarded them in the usual way at night'. He did this for several years until he was discovered.[9] Aboriginal men sometimes rode stolen horses with bark saddles to manage stock. More crudely, other groups broke the legs of stolen sheep to immobilise them until they returned to dine on lamb roast. Such maiming of sheep infuriated squatters—the same emotion felt by Indigenous owners when pushed off their land. After finding 100 of his sheep with their legs broken, an enraged John Cox pursued the offenders: 'It was the first time I had ever levelled a gun on my fellow man. I did so without regret or hesitation in this instance . . . I distinctly remember knocking over three blacks, two men and a boy, with one discharge of my double barrel'.[10]

Weapons became paramount. Not every settler carried them, but most were armed. Shepherds who were free men carried rifles instead of crooks, often with pistols in their belts. Huts were built with slit windows to repulse Aboriginal attacks. George Carrington, a shepherd in southern Queensland, wrote of his first night alone: 'I lay now broad awake, and the perspiration streamed from every pore. My hearing seemed unnaturally sharpened . . . all around the hut I fancied I heard the cracking of dry sticks and of rustling grass.'[11] His fear was driven by images of 'the savage', but also was not misplaced, for Europeans were initially outnumbered and even 'outgunned'.

Until the 1850s, most guns had unreliable flintlock firing systems. A primary charge ignited by a moving flint exploded a secondary charge, which propelled the bullet. The 'hang-fire', or time delay, between the first charge which gave off a flash, and the second which propelled the bullet, not only gave the enemy time to duck, but also made it very difficult to hit moving targets. Wet weather affected the powder, causing misfires, but even in dry weather misfires averaged one in every six shots. Flintlocks were reloaded with two sets of powder, wadding that had to be rammed, and a ball. An experienced shooter took over twenty seconds to reload and fire, and even when fired by experts, these smooth-bore firearms were wildly inaccurate beyond 50 metres. However, at close quarters the flintlock's nineteen-millimetre lead ball travelled at high speed, making evasion unlikely. If the wound was not fatal, the ball still shattered flesh and bones on impact, making recovery difficult.[12]

The skills of Aboriginal warriors were honed by a lifetime of hunting. Their spear-throwing almost equalled the speed and accuracy of the legendary English bowmen. Aboriginal spears flew 50 metres a second, but could be evaded. However, Gideon Lang wrote in 1865: 'A blackfellow, with some eight or ten spears in his hand and some paddy-melon sticks, will throw them all while a white man is reloading after firing two shots; and I have known one man to be pierced in the thigh by two spears successively, thrown at seventy yards off.'[13] These skilled Indigenous warriors initially outnumbered early settlers in any one area. Also, being practised in inter-tribal skirmishes, their tactics and military skills were superior to those of settlers, given that most settlers had no weapons or military experience. Aboriginal warriors also used traditional methods of fire to destroy property and drive shepherds out like game. Settlers clearly did not outmatch Aboriginal warriors until the 1860s, when the advent of breech-loading, repeating rifles and more widespread use of horses made them invincible, vanquishing the Aboriginal resisters.

Fear on the frontier bred violence as some Europeans shot first and asked questions later. Those with convict backgrounds toughened by abject poverty and the lash were probably more inclined to use violence to solve problems. When Edward Curr remonstrated with an ex-convict shepherd, who had just shot down an unarmed Aboriginal man, the shepherd replied: 'as many of them as comes here when I am alone I'll shoot'.[14] Gross abuses occurred in Tasmania, where the historian Clive Turnbull reported some Aboriginal people were flogged, branded, castrated and mutilated by hardened convicts.[15] However, ordinary men who were fearful and protecting property also opened fire on Aboriginal people.

Violence took other forms as well, being expressed for example through language. Aboriginal people were denigrated as 'savages' and likened to orang-outang or wild animals by the most embittered settlers. White brutality was played out also through sexual relations; some station workers even held Aboriginal women captive. Reverend Threlkeld wrote from Lake Macquarie mission in 1825 of his torment 'at night [by] the shrieks of girls, about 8 or 9 years of age, taken by force by the vile men of Newcastle [convicts]. One man came to see me with his head broken by the butt-end of a musket because he would not give up his wife.'[16] When a law of 1837 prohibited the keeping of Aboriginal women, some stockmen dressed their women as boys and continued to cohabit with them. A minority of Aboriginal women, assessing their options in a changing world, provided sexual and domestic services more willingly.

Aboriginal people met violence with violence. At first, revenge was taken in accordance with Aboriginal law, specifically on those Europeans thought responsible for transgressions; this paralleled traditional Aboriginal feuding. However, as violence escalated, and as large-scale killings occurred from the actions of settler punitive parties, Aboriginal revenge became more generalised. Aboriginal bands declared they would attack, kill and drive out all Europeans in their area. The shock of violence had shifted the responses of many Aboriginal groups from traditional feuding to a new way of viewing events—a war against all intruders. The government soon found itself deeply involved in these clashes, shattering any efforts at even-handedness.

Escalating violence beyond the Cumberland Plain first erupted at Bathurst, where relations with the Wiradjuri had been calm. A small military outpost was created in 1815 and initially settlement was forbidden. By 1821, however, tensions rose as settlers brought 30,000 head of stock to Bathurst, scouring the native grasses. The Wiradjuri, seeing their resources diminish, and led by Windradyne, attacked stock and stole crops. A guerrilla war ensued, with deaths on both sides in fierce clashes. After about twenty shepherds were killed in various incidents, martial law was declared for five months in August 1822, and 75 troops of the 40th Regiment were despatched. Local tradition claims that several massacres of Wiradjuri occurred before the declaration of martial law, and at least one after. Governor Brisbane was informed of about fifteen deaths, but if local knowledge is correct, the Wiradjuri death toll was closer to a hundred. Reverend Threlkeld was told of 45 Wiradjuri being shot in a swamp, whose heads were severed, boiled down and shipped to England. The sheer ferocity of the fighting lends credence to this story.[17]

Fierce fighting also erupted in Van Diemen's Land in 1824 after two decades of low-level violence punctuated by periods of calm. The escalation followed the island's pastoral expansion in the 1820s, as emigration boosted the settler population tenfold and a million sheep spread through the midlands. Ecological change followed as sheep and weeds disturbed the ancient grasslands. Aboriginal warriors hit back as their lands were eaten out and denied them. Twenty-four

Europeans were killed during the years 1824–26, forcing Governor Arthur to switch from a policy of 'amity and kindness' to treating Aboriginal people as 'open enemies'. In 1827, another 30 Europeans were killed and pastoral development halted. The Executive Council advised Arthur to 'inspire them with terror' as Aboriginal outrage was said to 'amount to a complete declaration of hostilities against the settlers generally'.[18] Arthur declared martial law in November 1828 and settler bounty parties took revenge. However, Aboriginal Tasmanians or Pallawah continued the most successful frontier defence in Australia, killing over 50 settlers from 1828 to 1830. Tongerlongerter led the Oyster Bay tribe in war, stating: 'they and their forefathers had been cruelly abused, that their country had been taken away from them, their wives and daughters have been violated and taken away'.[19]

Governor Arthur pursued two policies in 1830: seeking peace through the Protector George Augustus Robinson and also declaring a complete mobilisation of the army and citizenry, convict and free alike. He tried to round up Aboriginal people by means of a 50-kilometre line of 2200 men beating through the country, to herd them onto the Tasman Peninsula and end the war. The strategy failed

NATIVES ATTACKING SHEPHERDS' HUT.

'Natives attacking shepherds' hut', by Samuel Calvert. COURTESY OF THE NATIONAL LIBRARY OF AUSTRALIA (NLA-PIC-AN8957159).

to capture any blacks, but heavily pressured the Aboriginal people, who then numbered less than 200.[20] George Robinson, together with his those he called his 'ambassadors', Trugernanna, Woorrady, Pagerly and Dray, spoke to the Aboriginal remnant over the following year and brokered a peace.[21] Henry Reynolds argued convincingly that the Pallawah only agreed on condition they could periodically return to their lands—a promise that was never kept.[22] Some have argued that the Tasmanian frontier was one of genocide; however, a war for the land was in progress in which the Aboriginal owners were considered 'open enemies'. Henry Reynolds concluded: 'there is little evidence to suggest that he [Arthur] wanted to reach beyond that object and destroy the Tasmanian race in whole or part'. This is true of other colonial administrations, but authorities still favoured settlers in most cases when trouble erupted.[23]

The local Swan River administration also became drawn into warfare after settler incursions onto Aboriginal lands led to the loss of European lives and property near Perth. Governor James Stirling abandoned 'amity and kindness' and authorised settler 'acts of hostility' against Aboriginal people. In 1833 the Government Resident in Perth offered settlers use of the government armoury, 'for those who may require it, ready to inflict a prompt and heavy punishment on the natives'.[24] Matters were further complicated and tensions increased when some Aboriginal groups aligned themselves with the whites against their traditional enemies.[25] When his brother was killed in a robbery, Yagan, a Whadjuk man, led raids on settlers. He was outlawed and a reward equalling a shepherd's annual wage was posted for his capture. In 1833 he was shot dead by two young settlers feigning friendship, his head severed and his skin bearing his tribal markings stripped from his back. The *Perth Gazette* was incensed at such barbarity by whites. Yagan's head was sent to England where it was displayed at the Liverpool Royal Institute. After further 'outrages', Governor Stirling led a punitive party in October 1834 against the Pindjarup, who had threatened incendiary attacks and to 'destroy all the whites in the district'.[26] The Governor's force ambushed an Aboriginal group that included families. Stirling admitted to fifteen deaths, but other witnesses claimed 30 people trapped in a waterhole were massacred. In 1994, Yagan's Nyoongar descendants tracked down his head, which had been taken from the Liverpool Royal Institute and buried in 1964 due to its deterioration. His skull was returned to Perth and awaits reburial by the community after a search is conducted for the rest of his remains.[27]

European property losses were enormous in the frontier war, although some pastoral runs were left untouched due to good local relations. Many head of stock were killed for food and thousands of others as a military strategy: some properties lost hundreds of sheep annually in swift and effective guerrilla raids. Huts were looted and burned, vegetable plots raided and set fire to, and some stations were completely abandoned. The experience of George Mackay, who was driven from his run at the Ovens River near Beechworth in 1838, was not unique. He returned, only to have a servant killed and his huts and stores destroyed. Four horses (each worth a shepherd's yearly wage) were killed, and all but seven of his 3000 cattle driven off and lost.[28] Many properties were similarly affected. At the Darling River in 1845, Major Thomas Mitchell wrote that the 'humiliating proof that the white man had given way, were visible in the remains of dairies burnt down, stockyards in ruins, untrodden roads.'[29] Even when not driven off, pastoralists found workers hard to come by and wages were forced up by the dangers. Even in towns, people grew fearful. Later in the century, Gilberton in Queensland was abandoned for a time due to terror of Aboriginal attacks.[30]

Aboriginal military tactics were rooted in their long mastery of the environment. They used the element of surprise, emerging from the bush and striking fast and hard, then withdrawing to eat mutton and celebrate their victory with a corroboree. Only rarely did they adopt European guns for killing, although they were practised in their use: guns did not fit their warrior code. William Thomas, who knew Aboriginal people around Melbourne better than anyone, stated 'they never use them in battle: they consider guns a cowardly means of defence.'[31] However, some fought pitched battles with settlers, such as the six-hour fight between George Faithful and Duangwurrung people in 1838. This fight followed a conflict at the Broken River near Benalla in north-east Victoria in which eight of Faithful's men were overwhelmed and killed in revenge for the killing of some Daungwurrung at the Ovens.[32] In the last six-hour battle, Faithful witnessed Aboriginal women and children running boldly forward, even between his horse's legs, collecting spears for their warriors to reuse.[33] Aboriginal treatment of white victims could be cruel. One man found dead in 1841 in the Western District of Victoria was staked to the ground with his limbs ritually defleshed.[34]

Europeans hit back with equal barbarity, perpetrating massacres. The word 'massacre' should not be used too freely, for its overuse labels Aboriginal people as passive victims awaiting slaughter. However, in the Liverpool Plains area of northern New South Wales a series of killings in 1838 *were* massacres of defenceless people. In response to frontier conflict, which left many cattle and half a dozen shepherds dead, Captain Nunn and 23 troopers were sent to the Namoi River area to create calm. Against orders, Nunn pursued and cut down as many as 100 Aboriginal people, many dying while trapped. Six months later, at Myall Creek Station, a posse of twelve armed stockmen, eleven of them convicts or ex-convicts, roped about 30 old men, women and children together. They led them away before putting them to the sword and hacking off their heads and burning their bodies. Only naturalised blacks—those who agreed to act like Europeans and join the local economy as workers—were spared. After two trials prosecuted tenaciously by Attorney-General John Plunkett, and a vigorous and popular defence of the accused, seven of the stockmen were hanged for murder. This outraged many settlers, since capital punishment for killing Aboriginal people was unprecedented. However, half of Sydney's population supported the government's prosecution of these men.

More killings, often in secret, followed as vigilante groups rode hard, bent on subduing all Aboriginal resistance.[35] Tradition says a few malevolent settlers in various districts gave out poisoned flour. In November 1847, at Kangaroo Creek south of Grafton, a settler offered work to 23 Gumbaynggirr people and paid them with flour and tobacco. The people consumed the flour and died agonising deaths. The station owner, Thomas Coutts, was tried after four of his men reported the incident. The prosecution was reluctantly dropped by Attorney-General John Plunkett as there was 'not sufficient legal evidence' to convict Coutts, because the white workers were not present and Aboriginal evidence was inadmissible. Plunkett, who was certain of Coutts's moral guilt, tried to get an Act passed in 1849 to admit Aboriginal evidence but it failed by one vote.[36]

Frontier violence was normalised by killings and stories of them. Henry Meyrick, a Gippsland squatter, wrote in the 1840s that he became 'familiarized with scenes of horror—from having murder made a topic of everyday conversation'.[37] In *Scars on the Landscape*, Ian Clark listed 107 violent incidents in Western Victoria, most well substantiated. Of the estimated 400 Aboriginal deaths, about three-quarters occurred in incidents involving the deaths of five or more people—some of which were clearly massacres.[38] The listing of particular slaughters from sites across southern and eastern Australia could go on—if one could stomach it. People of both races were being brutalised by a ruthless battle for the land, begun by European encroachment, but settlers were more efficient at massacring, simply because of the combined power of guns, horses and government troopers.

In many parts of Australia, from the Coorong to the Darling Downs and inland to the Darling, many Aboriginal communities fought guerrilla campaigns against the invaders before the 1850s. So intense was the resistance and destruction in some areas that alarmed Europeans referred to the 'black war' on the frontier. Aboriginal people living in regions of dense bush or mountains were the most successful. The Pallawah fought and evaded capture for almost a decade, defending their land and peppering the intruders. Most groups, however, were defeated in a matter of months or a year or two. In the early 1840s, Gunditjmara people of the Port Fairy region used the impenetrable volcanic scoria country as a strategic base for their guerrilla raids. They were routed only when caught in open country after a resistance of several years. The Milmenrura people of the Coorong region also carried out an effective resistance in the early 1840s, sometimes in very large groups (said to number up to 300), raiding stations, burning pastures, and dispersing and destroying stock. Several military detachments were needed to quell them. Aboriginal 'clever men' also used sorcery—the traditional means of dealing with enemies. Edward Parker, Aboriginal Protector in the Loddon area, was told in 1840 that a great plague, the Mindi, would descend on the whites and destroy them. Others threatened lightning, droughts and winds.[39]

However, Aboriginal fighting skills were not matched by organisational capacity. Their traditional economy did not create surpluses to feed a warrior class, complete with military leaders and support systems. Also, their traditional emphasis on the local group as sovereign, and the lack of strong traditional inter-tribal military links, meant that settlers mostly fought individual tribes. Thus each battle was really the Milmenrura versus the British, or the Gunditjmara versus the British, and not Aboriginal peoples versus the British.

Scattered evidence suggests that some Aboriginal people made tentative steps towards adapting their traditions to the new military needs. A few used guns in the fighting. Others learned how to evade the fire of a flintlock by drawing fire and then attacking during the reloading phase, or recognising when a gun misfired after the initial flash. A few military leaders have been identified that do not appear in the traditional mode. In Tasmania, a Sydney Aboriginal man, Mosquito, transported there as previously mentioned, led the Oyster Bay tribe in its resistance against settlers before being hanged in 1823. A woman named Walyer, who had earlier lived with white sealers, taught some Pallawah to use guns and led them against settlers. In other places, it was reported that large groups of several hundred warriors sometimes attacked, but whether they had gathered for a ceremony or war is unknown.[40]

Colonial governments across the British Empire created Indigenous military units to quell Indigenous resistance. In Australia these paramilitary forces were euphemistically called the 'Native Police', suggesting Aboriginal people were lawbreakers. A more military label would admit that a war was being waged against sovereign Aboriginal tribes, rather than an action against 'criminal' black citizens. Forces were established in Port Phillip in 1842, in New South Wales in 1848 (officially in 1855), and in Queensland in 1859. They differed considerably in their purpose. The Port Phillip Native Police aimed to civilise the men into being role models for other Aboriginal people—disciplined workers with a settled family life. The Queensland force, on the other hand, marked the absolute 'rock bottom' of Aboriginal policy for it had no humanitarian or educative intent. Several hundred Aboriginal men from Queensland and as far south as the Murray River region were enlisted to destroy troublesome blacks to consolidate colonial expansion.

Aboriginal men enlisted for various reasons. Many were attracted by the military-style uniforms, which in Port Phillip were handsome and complete with leather belts and gold braid. Troopers were equipped with rifles, sabres and other supplies—and horses, which were rare and valuable items in colonial society. The men were also given good rations and a small wage. These things promised to attract young women, usually the preserve of older men. The life promised to be exciting, with military-style drilling with guns and horses, and journeys into foreign country. Being a trooper induced some respect—especially from relieved settlers who valued their presence.

Native police by William Strutt in 'Victorian the Golden, Scenes, Sketches and Jottings From Nature 1850–1862', plate 55. REPRODUCED WITH THE PERMISSION OF THE VICTORIAN PARLIAMENTARY LIBRARY.

The Port Phillip Native Police, which lasted for a decade, was unique in a number of ways. It was formed in a more hopeful atmosphere and with a civilising intent. Superintendent Charles La Trobe included the troopers in his parades on civic occasions in Melbourne. Troopers in Port Phillip also had general policing powers, including the power to arrest whites. The Port Phillip force was unique in another sense, being formed with strong Aboriginal consensus. Billibellary, headman of the Woiwurrung or Yarra people, was open to dialogue with settler society. He enrolled his son in the first mission school and also persuaded 22 young men to join the Native Police. He enlisted too. What is surprising is that the other 22 were all men of power and status in Aboriginal society—either elders or sons of elders. Marie Fels has argued that they joined for their own reasons—to secure their power within Aboriginal society and also to enlarge it into the new sphere of settler society. They became troopers as one way of remaining Aboriginal.[41]

It must also be remembered that the Aboriginal world was one of friends and enemies, which meant that troopers were willing to take action against distant peoples they considered enemies. In Port Phillip, Buckup, a Kulin man of the Melbourne region, was in charge of a small detachment of Aboriginal troopers from his country. On arrival at Tom Browne's station at distant Port Fairy, Buckup dismounted, saluted and said to Browne in settler language: 'Believe the blacks been very bad about here.'[42] He and the other troopers dealt a decisive blow to the Gunditjmara resistance there, for these were in no way his people.

In Port Phillip such military excursions were less frequent than in Queensland where the force had no humanitarian gloss, was poorly led and lasted three times as long, until the 1890s. Although the Native Police in Victoria killed over 100 Aboriginal people, the Queensland troopers killed perhaps a thousand,[43] and became an important factor in the final defeat of the Aboriginal resistance in that colony. Unlike settlers, who lacked military and bush skills, troopers could pursue Aboriginal quarry deep into the bush. There, beyond the control of European officers, and armed with the new and deadly breech-loading Snyder and Martini-Henry rifles, they killed with little compunction. Few prisoners were taken in the bloody encounters that were euphemistically reported as the 'dispersal of blacks'. Their activities are detailed in Jonathan Richard's *The Secret War: A True History of Queensland's Native Police* (2008).

Becoming an Aboriginal trooper in Queensland was a means of surviving in a colonial world rapidly disintegrating into chaos. Some re-enlisted time after time, others deserted despite the unofficial penalty of execution, and some eventually used their military skills fighting alongside other Aboriginal people.

Those who remained were often brutalised by life in the force and trapped in a war of nightmare killings of those considered enemies. Some adopted the language of colonisers, speaking gleefully at the end of an action about how many 'niggers' they had shot. Some may have internalised European values and weakened their Aboriginal identity, as new identities form when old ones are not sustained. They were young men who were away from their own communities and traditions and they were being moulded into European-like troops by drill and regimentation, the bearing of new names and the wearing of new clothes. As sociologist Peter Berger has said of social roles: 'It is very difficult to pretend in this world. Normally, one becomes what we play at.'[44] This had been the case of boy soldiers in the late twentieth century in Africa, pressed into service and shaped into killers. Young Aboriginal troopers, confused and bewildered by the destruction of their traditional society, and adrift from the rules of traditional behaviour and morality, took a path that meant survival, even if this included the job of killing other people who were just as displaced as themselves. Ironically, life in the force was so hard, and disease and alcohol had such a debilitating effect on them, that few of these troopers had long lives.[45]

In the battle for the land, the language of war prevailed, exaggerating differences between Aboriginal owners and settlers. During martial law at Bathurst in 1824, William Cox, a pastoralist and magistrate who lost stock in Wiradjuri raids, reportedly told a public meeting that the 'best thing that could be done, would be to shoot all the Blacks and manure the ground with their carcases, which was all the good they were fit for'.[46] In 1835 Rev. W. Yate told a government inquiry: 'I have heard again and again people say that they were nothing better than dogs, and that it was no more harm to shoot them than it would be to shoot a dog'.[47] Peter Cunningham, a colonial doctor, reported that a settler told him blacks were the 'connecting link between man and the monkey tribe'.[48] In the 1840s phrenologists made claims about head shape and brain size to 'prove' European superiority and thereby to justify dispossession. But Aboriginal difference was still not explained universally by racial ideas of biological inferiority. Within the savagery of the Myall Creek massacre, those deemed 'naturalised'—that is, the Aboriginal stockmen who worked and dressed like Europeans and knew English—were spared, as were a few 'useful' women. The settlers' thoughts of war and lust, as much as those of race, determined their ideas and actions.

In the story of frontier violence, only a minority of settlers actually practised violence against Aboriginal people, although the majority thought it inevitable in the clash over land. Neil Black, in the Western District, felt relieved he leased land that was already opened up. He found a grave of twenty Aboriginal bodies killed by his predecessor, and commented: 'a settler taking up a new country is obliged to act towards them in this manner or abandon it'.[49] Many were indifferent to those they displaced as long as they kept clear of 'their' runs. John Hepburn, a Port Phillip squatter for twenty years, admitted: 'after all my residence amongst them I never learnt a word of their lingo'.[50] He and others imbibed the colonial discourse that maintained Aboriginal people were inferior and that they would inevitably fade away.

A few people were interested in Aboriginal people or concerned for their welfare, however. Edward Curr, a young well-educated squatter on the Murray around 1840, formed close friendships with the Bangerang people. He admired their physical and intellectual abilities, learned their bush craft, and often hunted with them. Thomas Chirnside, who settled near the Grampians in 1839, was distant, but allowed Aboriginal people to use their now shared land, and provided flour and mutton in return for the safety of his sheep. In the early 1840s, pastoralists Dr Richard Penny and David Wark badgered the government for medical supplies to help the Ngarrindjeri and others of the Coorong in South Australia. Numbers of Queensland pastoralists refused the services of the deadly Native Police, even warning local Aboriginal people of their impending arrival.[51]

PROTECTIVE EFFORTS

Government policy was contradictory in the frontier period—attempting an impossible balance between claiming Aboriginal people were British citizens, and then labelling them as 'enemies' once they resisted the invasion of their lands. Martial law, punitive expeditions and the Native Police utilised by local colonial administrations at flashpoints in the colonial wars were complemented by more protective measures to save Aboriginal people devised by the distant British government.

With the battle to end slavery in the British Empire won by 1833, humanitarians in the British Parliament looked to new causes. Led by Thomas Fowell Buxton, a deeply evangelical man, they gained a select committee in the House of Commons to examine the condition of Indigenous people in the Empire. Governor Arthur gave evidence and regretted events in Van Diemen's Land, calling for a treaty to stop such loss of life in other colonies. The Committee's report condemned the destruction of Indigenous people in many colonies and called for better protection and a civilising mission to compensate those it deemed as 'original owners'. In 1838 the British government, influenced by these Exeter Hall humanitarians, bypassed the squatter-dominated New South Wales Legislative Council to establish an Aboriginal Protectorate in the Port Phillip District. George Robinson (fresh from his Tasmanian 'triumphs') and four others were appointed as protectors. The project began with great hopes and the considerable outlay of £20,000 in the first four years—paid for out of the colonial land fund; that is, money raised from leasing and selling Aboriginal land. The Aboriginal people were paying for their own protection, but settlers similarly claimed *they* were paying for it—which they resented. Protectors were to move with Aboriginal people, learn their language, and protect them from cruelty and injustice and guard their property. This last provision was absurd in light of the European land-grabbing.[52]

This high-minded attempt was doomed. The Protectors, being family men, soon settled and formed home stations, where they tried to farm. Being inexperienced farmers working on alien soil, they generally failed. They were also providing rations for Aboriginal people, but when government funding dwindled in the recession of 1842 and rations dried up, the people drifted away. Other settlers were hostile as the money came from the land fund; besides, they viewed these protective efforts poorly in the midst of what they termed a 'black war'. Nor did the Aboriginal people necessarily appreciate the Civilising Mission of instilling Christianity, Western education and farming on the protectorate stations. An old Djadjawurrung man complained angrily to Protector Parker at the Loddon Protectorate station that the Europeans had firstly stolen their country and now they were 'stealing their children by taking them away to live in huts and work, and "read in book" like white fellows.'[53] He need not have feared, because Aboriginal people on southern frontiers before the 1850s resisted attempts to change them. They remained at the stations only while rations were available, then travelled to live off bush tucker, returning when more rations arrived.

The Port Phillip Protectorate and the less elaborate ones in South Australia and Western Australia were sincere but ineffective attempts to save Aboriginal people through rationing, education and providing a refuge for them. They achieved some good amid the 'black war', as most protectors quelled some violence by their presence. But the effort ended in Port Phillip in 1849 and in other colonies by 1857. Thereafter, occasional rations and a blanket a year each were all the help many Aboriginal people received from colonial governments. Furthermore, the protective effort was increasingly a controlling one. In 1842 William Thomas was told to keep Aboriginal people out of Melbourne as part of his duties. In Western Australia, Protectors soon became little better than policemen, keeping Aboriginal people from town lest they cause trouble or offence by their nakedness. They induced Aboriginal people to work, and stymied Aboriginal resistance with the aid of the two policemen who accompanied them. Protector Symmons reported happily in 1855 of a 'general abstinence from aggression, friendly subservience to the wants and wishes of the settlers and submission to the constituted authorities on the part of the Aborigines'.[54]

There was one important legacy of the humanitarian sentiment in Britain that produced the Protectorate. Earl Grey, Secretary of State for the Colonies, passed the Waste Land Act 1848, which set policy over the alienation of (Aboriginal) lands by lease on the eve of settler attainment of responsible government. It had two important humanitarian benefits about land for Aboriginal people—access rights and reserves—which Earl Grey explained to the Governor of New South Wales, Charles Fitzroy. Grey wrote:

I think it is essential that it should be generally understood that Leases granted for this purpose give the grantees only an exclusive right of pasturage for their cattle, and of cultivating such Land as they may require within the large limits thus assigned for them, but that these leases are not intended to deprive the Natives of their former right to hunt over these Districts, or to wander over them in search of subsistence in the manner to which they have been heretofore accustomed, from the spontaneous produce of the soil: except over land actually cultivated or fenced in for that purpose . . . a distinct understanding of the extent of their mutual rights is one step at last towards the maintenance of order and mutual forbearance between the parties [settlers and Aboriginal people]. If therefore, the limitation which I have mentioned above on the right of exclusive occupation granted by Crown Leases is not, in your opinion, fully recognized in the Colony, I think it is advisable that you should enforce it by some public declaration, or if necessary by passing a declaratory enactment . . . Reserves should be established where they do not exist; particularly in Districts recently brought within the range of occupation and those already set apart for this purpose should be turned to account with all speed . . .[55]

Over succeeding years settler governments often ignored these 'mutual rights'. However, they became a crucial consideration 150 years later in the High Court Wik case (see Chapter 13).

THE COST OF WAR

After fierce resistance Aboriginal groups were defeated by deaths from disease
carried by European hosts, from poor nutrition in conditions of war (see Chapter
4) and from violence by settlers, who were not better fighters, but arrived in
overwhelming numbers. The Europeans were also assisted unwittingly in the
war by other troops of conquest: sheep, cattle and the relentless weeds that
followed settlement. Aboriginal lands were altered ecologically and the Aboriginal
economy undercut by violent dispossession and change. What then was the cost
of this dispossession and war?

Australia's frontier history was a bloody one. Just how bloody is difficult to
determine, as many Aboriginal killings went unrecorded or were covered up, and
not all European deaths were tallied. About 1700 violent European deaths occurred
by Aboriginal hands across Australia: 176 in Tasmania, 80 in Victoria, over 100
in Western Australia, 50 in parts of northern New South Wales, and 800 in
Queensland. Untallied deaths in the rest of New South Wales, South Australia, the
north-west and Northern Territory might add 400 more. (Henry Reynolds claims
the Australia-wide total may well exceed 3000.) The number of Aboriginal casualties
is less certain, but some historians estimate that more than ten Aboriginal people
fell for every European, giving a death toll of 17,000. Aboriginal casualties from
white violence might even be as high as 20,000 across the entire continent.[56]

'The Avengers', by Samuel Thomas Gill. COURTESY OF THE NATIONAL LIBRARY OF AUSTRALIA (NLA-
PIC-AN2377344).

During the so-called 'History Wars' in the years around 2000, frontier deaths again became controversial. In a series of articles in 2000, Keith Windschuttle claimed the frontier was not lawless, and that the violence and death tolls were wildly exaggerated. He has since written a book about Tasmania in which he denies a war of resistance existed, claiming Aboriginal people were outlaws after goods, rather than patriots defending land.[57] However, at a national conference in 2002, fifteen leading historians gave papers documenting the avalanche of evidence from the time that proves Windschuttle wrong.[58] Aboriginal people also refuted his view. The late Eddie Kneebone, a Bangerang man, painted a multi-panelled work to show the impact of settlement on the north-east of Victoria, beginning with the so-called Faithful Massacre at Broken River in 1838. Kneebone wrote in his attached notes that in the aftermath 'the troops came on horses with guns and swords, hunted and killed the Aboriginal people as they found them . . . some of the settlers . . . joined in the carnage and poisoned the waterholes frequented by Aboriginal groups'. He added the 'land truly did bleed and their bones fell like rain'.[59] Kneebone represented this visually with a curtain of blood across half of his painted panels.

As the frontier receded, settlers were less keen to refer to a frontier war, instead casting a veil over this aspect of their history. Aboriginal resistance was relegated to a casual remark about 'treacherous' blacks being simply one more obstacle over which gallant pioneers triumphed. The whitewashing of frontier history began within a generation of its closure. In Australia, two frontier histories emerged which were still evident in the recent 'History Wars'. The settlers' or winners' view was represented in the Melbourne *Age* in 1896:

> The favourite theory at Exeter Hall is that the disappearance of the native races is due to the cruelty and malignity of the white settlers. Those who are acquainted with the history of this colony from its first settlement are aware that no such charge can be alleged against the Victorian people, and that the black race has decayed, and is rapidly dying out from causes quite outside the power of the white man to control.[60]

Aboriginal people were being blamed for their own demise. The Aboriginal or losers' view was represented by Dalaipi, a Queensland Aboriginal man, who at about the same time stated:

> We were hunted from our ground, shot, poisoned, and had our daughters, sisters and wives taken from us . . . What a number were poisoned at

Kilcoy . . . They stole our ground where we used to get food, and when we got hungry and took a bit of flour or killed a bullock to eat, they shot us or poisoned us. All they give us now for our land is a blanket once a year.[61]

The second version is nearer the historic truth.

4

CULTURAL RESISTANCE
AMID DESTRUCTION

Within weeks of the European invasion of each Aboriginal country, Indigenous groups witnessed a novelty: interlopers without knowledge of or custodianship over Aboriginal land, who refused to leave that land. Following disputes and violent confrontations, Aboriginal control of the land was eventually lost and Indigenous people 'came in' to pastoral stations, towns and missions. This 'coming-in' was sometimes forced by loss of food supplies, the impact of diseases, and frontier violence. The Pallawah in Tasmania came in during 1830–31, after 30 years of European occupation and a decade of war. In open country covered rapidly by sheep and attendant European weeds, and with few places of retreat or sustenance, groups were forced in more quickly. Some clans had sufficient bush foods to remain apart, but chose to engage with Europeans. The government's offer was one of change as Governor Gawler explained. Ignorant of the Great Tradition that dwelt in Aboriginal minds, Gawler told Aboriginal people in Adelaide in 1838: 'Black men. We wish to make you happy. But you cannot be happy unless you imitate white men. Build huts, wear clothes and be useful . . . you cannot be happy unless you love God . . . Love white men . . . learn to speak English. If any white man injure you tell the Protector and he will do you justice.'[1] Precisely why did Aboriginal people come in and on what terms?

NEW FOODS, WORK AND DISEASES

Curiosity drove much initial interaction. Aboriginal people examined explorers' equipment and fingered their cloth jackets and metal buttons. Those entering stations or settlements were amazed at huts, which harboured metal mugs and pans, books, pocket watches and glass items. Above all, they were attracted by food. Annette Hamilton has argued: 'when the news came that the whites had abundant, if strange, food, more than they could possibly eat, this was like news of Eden—or the super water-hole, in Aboriginal terms'. They moved to food as they always had, but as Hamilton added; 'not in order to take part in white society, not in order to experience social change, but in order to beg the food'.[2] Their hunter-gatherer lifestyle stressed the daily gathering of food for the least output of energy. If Europeans staying on Aboriginal land without permission had abundant food, why not claim a share, and save gathering bush foods? Pastoral stations with food on shelves and meat on the hoof, and butchers and bakers shops in settlements, attracted much Aboriginal interest. The Parramatta Feast had attracted Aboriginal people from as far away as the Bathurst Plains, who trekked across the Blue Mountains to attend the official feast in Sydney in the 1820s. Great inter-tribal gatherings were held in Melbourne around 1840, to the annoyance of Melbourne residents, partly stimulated by official feasts to welcome the Governor and also the Protectors. The largest comprised 800 people. European food supplies probably allowed groups to hold larger and longer gatherings than ever before.[3]

The lure of basic food in the context of the collapse of the Aboriginal economy was only outmatched by a desire for exotic stimulants, namely tobacco, tea and sugar, which were requested universally from settlers across the country. Although Aboriginal people rarely left their traditional lands, some groups voluntarily travelled long distances from their country in search of tobacco. In the 1920s, the Warmala people of the Northern Territory developed an appetite for tobacco through contact with prospectors and travelled to distant pastoral stations to ensure a steady supply. Engineer Jack Japaljarri recalled that his father said before their arduous journey: 'we want to gettem longa tobacco, go longa tobacco, get it tobacco'.[4] His group did not intend to stay permanently, but once there, camped to maintain their tobacco supply through work. The eminent anthropologist William Stanner, who witnessed this search for tobacco, remarked: 'the search for stimulants . . . must have been to them something like the spice-trade to medieval Europeans. The new things gave a tang and zest to life which their own dietary lacked. In becoming their own voyagers, the Aborigines claimed, coaxed and fought an opening into an incomprehensible new world'.[5] Stanner's marvellous image of voyaging stressed the active agency of Aboriginal people who, with a 'zest for life', were determined to fight for a place in the new colonial world—and remain Aboriginal.

Once engaged with European society, the problem for Aboriginal people was how to manage relations with whites and maintain the flow of food, tobacco and useful goods. They employed traditional strategies of building reciprocal obligations through the kinship system. Naming was vital in this, for names had ritual and kinship significance. Bennelong had named Governor Phillip 'father' and took the Eora name of 'son' in 1789. Derrimut exchanged names with John Pascoe Fawkner, the first European settler on the site of Melbourne in 1835. Most settlers experienced the same strategy, which Aboriginal people used naturally, as all people in their world were connected and controlled through kinship. Edward Curr remarked that the Bangerang people were 'aware that their Ngooraialum neighbours had all got white names, so they took the matter up, and several came to me daily to be named. The result of it was that in the course of a week or two, I christened the whole tribe, men, women and children'. They repeated their names—Plato, Jolly Chops, Tallyho—until memorised.[6] While Curr thought himself in charge, Aboriginal people were attempting to assimilate him and other Europeans into their code of moral behaviour—the mirror image of the European Civilising Mission.

Aboriginal groups exchanged items—lyrebird feathers, weapons and information—for food and tobacco, as reciprocity was intimately connected to kinship. They offered their women, which was a traditional way of creating friendliness, obligations and repayments between groups in potential conflict. This was welcomed by sex-starved European men unaccompanied by their own women. However, misunderstandings were frequent and led to trouble. While a sexual joining was the creation of ongoing kinship ties and obligations to an Aboriginal group, to the minds of Europeans it was short-term prostitution, an exchange solely between a man and a woman. However, there were also consensual relations. Some Aboriginal women offered themselves and formed permanent liaisons with shepherds or stockmen to gain access to European food, goods and shelter for their children in difficult times—and to share in the power of settlers. A few European men formed satisfactory and lasting relationships with Aboriginal women and cared for the offspring of their union. There were even several interracial marriages in each colony, although most consensual liaisons were de facto ones.

Aboriginal strategies to access goods did not always succeed without cost. After the first handouts, settlers demanded work in return for rations. Aboriginal workers—and not exclusively men—ferried sheep across creeks, cut timber for huts and sheep folds, and in time engaged in shepherding, sheep washing and shearing. More than 500 Aboriginal men and women worked seasonally in south-eastern Australia during the 1840s. Many workers supported family, who also resided seasonally on the stations, catching bush tucker to supplement the rations earned by their working members. Aboriginal workers enjoyed stock work because of its excitement and closeness to their traditional lands, and many employers praised their work skills. William Taylor, who settled the Wimmera, commented of his Aboriginal workers: 'several of them have shepherded for eight to ten months at a time, and were the best shepherds in the district. Not being afraid of losing their flock, they allowed them to spread over a large tract of country. They were also useful in pointing out the permanent waterholes'.[7] Edward Curr also noted that 'as scrub-riders and rough-riders the average Bangerang excelled the average stockman. He had better nerve, quicker sight, and stuck closer to his saddle'.[8] During labour shortages in the gold rushes, their work was particularly valued. In 1852, at Mt Cole in Victoria, 40,000 sheep were washed by Aboriginal labourers for twelve shillings a week, and two or three received £1 a week as bullock drivers.

In the towns they earned money as fishermen, water carriers, messengers, domestic servants and boatmen. In the 1840s, scores were involved in whaling at Encounter Bay and Albany on the southern coasts. At Twofold Bay, Rev. Threlkeld

'*Going to Work*', *by Samuel Thomas Gill.* COURTESY OF THE NATIONAL LIBRARY OF AUSTRALIA (AN2381127).

reported Aboriginal men crewed two whaleboats, and 'lived in huts with their families . . . some of their women are good washerwomen'.[9] Many were good workers, some whalers rising to the position of 'boat steerer', which meant they were in charge of black and white crewmen. Such jobs provided food in the form of whale meat and a fund of stories about their exploits. Nebinyan, a Nyoongar man from the Albany region, sang of his whaling adventures for decades after.[10] Robert Dawson, manager of the Australian Agricultural Company's estate at Port Stephens in New South Wales from 1826 to 1830, remarked of a boat's crew comprised of Gampignal people, who 'handle the oar with the expertness of experienced seamen'. He gained pleasure from their company and employed others as guides, messengers, labourers and domestics. They offered their labour willingly. But while he employed 'a considerable number', they were not always the same people as some 'tired of labour'.[11]

Aboriginal workers 'tired' of work for a variety of reasons. First, they shunned the European work ethic that demanded labour beyond which was needed to put food on the table. Traditionally, Aboriginal people worked in short efficient bursts to allay hunger. Many likened Europeans to bullocks, for they worked constantly, seemingly without reason. Aboriginal people were unimpressed with accumulation for future wealth and status. Second, they soon realised their pay was not equal, as they received just rations, or rations and wages at less than half the rates of whites. Some workers in the Plenty Ranges near Melbourne even struck briefly for fairer wages in the mid-1850s.[12]

Aboriginal people also believed they were not obliged to work for white settlers in return for goods. They sought to impose their own moral code onto Europeans—what we might call 'right behaviour'. Europeans had usurped their land and resources and in return Aboriginal people demanded support. Many Victorian pastoralists sensed this over time and reported as much to an 1877 royal commission in Victoria. Joseph Watson of West Charlton said most of the twelve Aboriginal people around his station worked part of the year, but 'expect to be fed and clothed the remainder of the year'.[13] Hugh McLeod of Benyeo Station, Apsley, declared: 'the Aborigines consider they have a right to be kept by the squatters'.[14] James Dawson, a Camperdown pastoralist who knew the people extremely well, revealed that this view carried over from the frontier to reserves and missions. He stated that the Framlingham reserve people near Warrnambool were, by the 1860s, 'fully aware of the position the occupation of their country by the white man has placed them in, and of their strong claims on him for proper maintenance and protection. They are very sensitive on that point, and assert that they are entitled to be well housed, well clothed, and well fed, in consideration for the loss of their "hunting ground".[15]

The act of 'coming-in' placed Aboriginal people in the unequal power relationship of colonialism. Their efforts to impose Aboriginal kinship and Aboriginal morality on settlers often did not get the desired response. Settlers did not comprehend the significance of exchanging names; they did not understand or did not want to meet the wider obligations of joining with an Aboriginal woman; and many settlers did not agree to make payments for the 'proper maintenance and protection' of original owners for the settlers' use of Aboriginal land. On the contrary, settlers believed it was Crown land that had been leased to them and made productive. Yet the act of 'coming-in' also demanded much from Aboriginal people physically and culturally. They were exposed to poor food, tobacco and alcohol, were subject to diseases, and were more prone to inter-tribal fighting and to cultural denigration and rupture.

Traditionally, Aboriginal people ate balanced vegetable and meat diets, gathered by short but sometimes hard bursts of work. Running down an animal, digging with a stick and yandy for yams, and burrowing in pursuit of a ground animal was energetic activity. After settlement they accessed European foods— flour, tea and sugar, with occasional meat or offal—which were nutritionally poorer and gained with less physical effort than their former diet. Some bush vegetables, eels and fish, and some small game were still consumed. But as bush foods diminished on traditional lands, or work slowed their gathering of it, dependence on a narrow range of white foods increased. Flour and sugar eroded good health, and malnutrition was evident, which made people less vital— prompting settler claims of inherent laziness. Aboriginal people who were dependent on handouts of rations ceased to be self-supporting individuals, which affected their self-esteem. Their attachment to settlers and their work lessened ritual life and induced boredom. They filled the void with craving for tobacco and alcohol.

Such craving for tobacco was widespread and, as with convict workers, it was used as an incentive to extract work. Aboriginal people in many regions traditionally enjoyed a narcotic made from the *pitcheri* bush (*Duboisia hopwoodii*), which, when mixed with ash and chewed, gave a pleasing narcotic feeling of an altered reality. Its use was firmly controlled by complex kinship and trading networks, a limited supply, and elders who knew the secrets of its intricate preparation.[16] However, Aboriginal use of European tobacco was not controlled by tradition and not counterbalanced by traditional daily activities. Pastoralists gave it out as rations with flour, tea and sugar, often in exchange for work.

Edward Curr remarked that Aboriginal leisure hours at his run were 'divided between putting the pipe to its legitimate purpose and begging my tobacco . . . the words, terrible from their repetition, i inyanook bakka, mitta cowel, ingarnica! (give little tobacco, Mr. Curr, smallest!) rang forever in my ear.'[17] It clearly was a colonial-derived habit and in time became a health hazard.

Settlers also introduced alcohol to those with no known tradition of drinking fermented vegetable matter. At the first meeting at Botany Bay in early January 1788, two Aboriginal men were offered wine as a gesture of genteel English sociality, but refused. Other early offers were repulsed until Governor Phillip offered it to Bennelong in late 1789, who accepted it as a marker of gentility. He developed a fondness for wine, but not low-caste spirits. Over the years he drank to excess. Others around early Sydney were offered wine and sometimes made to fight.[18] Problem drinking soon emerged to have a disastrous impact on tribal and family life, and led to terrible ill health. European observers rated it high on the list of destructive forces for Aboriginal people. Too many drank themselves to death, with one-third of the Port Phillip Native Police reportedly dying from the effects of drunkenness. The government finally acted: what was first offered to Aboriginal people by whites was denied them by special legislation in most colonies from 1838. Some continued to drink illegally and binged secretly around town on cheap wine or 'all-sorts'—cheap mixtures of rum, tobacco and leftovers concocted by publicans. Others found it in surprising places: Tommy Walker took Holy Communion at the Port McLeay mission in South Australia, drained the cup eagerly and cried out boldly, 'Fill 'im up again!'

Aboriginal people initially accepted alcohol to engage with settlers. Some drank to emulate whitefellas who were notorious for their own drinking and drunkenness. One intoxicated man overheard by Rev. Threlkeld claimed he drank to feel 'merry good, merry good, make me merry drunk, me drunk like a gemmen (gentlemen)'.[19] However, as colonialism dispossessed Aboriginal people of land and turned them into 'have-nots' in the new colonial world, some turned to alcohol to escape their predicament. Others drank out of boredom, to make time pass, as the rhythms of their traditional life were disrupted. Some sought to shock their colonial masters with a counter-culture of violence and drinking. One Aboriginal drinking song exclaimed: 'Give me some drink! Give us drink for us to swallow! Why do you crawl about down there on the ground? I'm rolling about, lying as if I'm asleep.' Another contained the refrain: 'I'm silly from drink, I am lost'.[20]

While the loss of land was the greatest legacy of colonialism on Aboriginal people, disease proved to be their greatest killer. Even before they laid eyes on

'Bushman's Hut', by Samuel Thomas Gill. COURTESY OF THE NATIONAL LIBRARY OF AUSTRALIA (AN7150080).

Europeans and other strangers, Aboriginal people felt the sting of diseases previously unknown to them. With no immunity, they died in great numbers. Smallpox killed half the Eora of Sydney in 1789 and thousands in other regions. It probably originated from Macassan fishers on the far north coast, but it is theoretically possible that it escaped from the First Fleet medical kit, although there is no evidence it did.[21] It swept south and west, killing people on the far southern coast. Telltale pockmarks on Aboriginal faces were still visible when Europeans arrived in Port Phillip Bay in 1804 and in other parts of Victoria in the 1830s. Survivors gave gruesome accounts of how their communities were decimated by unknown ailments, presumably magic sent by sorcerers from hostile tribes. In what was a common story, Dungog people told J. Fraser in 1840 of one such epidemic: 'the disease was of a very virulent type, and after a week or so, they were unable to bury the dead, and day by day kept moving onwards, leaving their dead on the ground'.[22] Face-to-face contact with settlers created another smallpox epidemic around 1829.

Diseases formed part of the European ecological package, along with new plants, animals and ways of using land. And these did not have to be as spectacular as smallpox to be destructive among a people who had no experience of such diseases. Indeed, there were few great epidemics like that of smallpox, but rather a gradual but constant loss of life. Less exotic diseases such as dysentery, scarlet fever, typhus, measles, whooping cough, respiratory diseases including influenza and even the common cold killed many, whose lack of immunity encouraged exaggerated symptoms. Tuberculosis, which thrived in poor living conditions among a health-deprived people, later became prevalent. Newly impoverished diets induced malnutrition, and no doubt over time raised blood pressure and cholesterol levels and heralded diabetes.

Venereal disease was another unintended gift of colonialism as Old World diseases were brought to the New. Those willing to discuss genital diseases claimed many were affected. Captain Fyans alleged that venereal diseases infected two-thirds of the Port Phillip Aboriginal people in the 1840s, and some estimates for colonial Queensland ranged higher than this.[23] Venereal disease was certainly common, but its incidence was probably exaggerated due to confusion with yaws, an indigenous skin complaint that produced similar surface eruptions. It was called *bubburum* by the Kulin of central Victoria and was one of the few indigenous diseases prevalent in Australia before white settlement. It was not a killer, but drove people to despair with itching. However, many Aboriginal people of all ages also did suffer from venereal diseases. They used traditional explanations and healing for illnesses, but made an exception with venereal disease, which they realised was from sexual contact. The Kulin asked the Aboriginal Protector William Thomas to treat their venereal skin eruptions with copper sulphate solution. Dr Cussen treated more radically by amputation of arms, legs—even penises. Colonial medical officers gave assistance, but always too little, too late. Several doctors around Adelaide in the 1840s gained funds for Aboriginal health but these were quickly withdrawn.[24]

Venereal diseases were made more rampant by European pastoral workers being without their own women. Aboriginal people stereotyped settlers as lustful, the lower Murray people calling them 'kringal kop', meaning 'white people whose noses come first'; that is, who nose about the camps for women.[25] Many took Aboriginal women in relations not of agreement or care, but of force, violence and rape. Some Aboriginal women were detained in huts in chains; others were bought and sold like property, abused and beaten, and discarded once infected by venereal disease. It was alleged that in this era before the discovery of the existence of germs, some knowingly tainted Aboriginal women with venereal disease in the desperate and ignorant belief that they would thus lose the infection themselves. Aboriginal women suffered discomfort, sometimes death and often infertility as a result of such diseases. Governor Bourke was so alarmed by the frequent reports of these acts of barbarism against black British subjects that in 1837 he outlawed the forced detention of Aboriginal women by whites.

The power of tradition shaped Aboriginal understandings of diseases and fatalities. People believed that deaths occurred because of the malevolent acts of distant sorcerers. William Thomas debated with a Kulin man in early Melbourne, expressing disbelief that an Aboriginal sorcerer could visit a sleeping victim, open the victim's side, extract their kidney fat which was their life force, seal up the wound perfectly, and then wait for the victim to fade away slowly to death. The man took Thomas's knife, cut a sapling and then pressed the bark together. When Thomas could not see where the cut lay on the branch, the man declared: 'like it that the spirit of a black on another'.[26] Post-settlement deaths from disease received the same explanation of sorcery. The Woiwurrung and Boonwurrung people around Melbourne claimed smallpox was a visitation by Mindi the Great Snake, sent against them by enemy sorcerers. The Wiradjuri linked disease to the actions of a dangerous Being to the south-west, while the Euahlayi of northern New South Wales believed their enemies sent disease on the wind and it dropped down on its victims.[27] Sorcery demanded counter-sorcery to neutralise it. Perhaps Aboriginal faith in their own sorcery was eventually shaken when the many sick could not be restored to health, especially once sorcerers themselves were struck down. If faith in healing and the power of sorcery was questioned, then life itself was uncertain. But on early frontiers, Aboriginal belief in tradition mostly held firm.

APPROPRIATING AND ACCOMMODATION

Aboriginal people adopted European items they valued. They earned, bartered or 'borrowed' bottles and scrap metal to make blades, which they fashioned by grinding in traditional ways. They shaped weapons, carved wood and scraped possum skins with these new blades. Daniel Bunce saw possum-skin cloaks being embossed with traditional designs, not by mussel shells or stone blades, but slivers of glass and sharpened metal spoons.[28] They bought or traded guns, which they dismantled, cleaned or had serviced in Melbourne's gun shops. There were 26 firearms in Aboriginal camps on the Yarra River in 1840, and men fired these into the air each night in delight at their noise and destructive power. While they were rarely used against settlers, the New South Wales Legislative Council banned Aboriginal gun ownership in 1840, despite William Thomas's view that 'I have known one gun to be almost the support of an encampment in the Bush'.[29] This was overturned in 1841 by the British government, which ruled that the Act failed to treat Aboriginal people as lawful British citizens.[30]

The item most widely appropriated by Aboriginal people was in fact the European dog, which became ubiquitous in Aboriginal camps throughout the south-east, and eventually across the continent. The dingo, which had been brought from South-east Asia about 10,000 years ago, was used for hunting, but was only semi-domesticated, unlike the European dog, which was a companionate animal. And unlike the European dog, the dingo could not bark as a watchdog. Their interest in dogs was initially most evident in Tasmania among the Pallawah people. Convict sealers, who gathered seal pelts on Bass Strait islands from 1800, visited the Tasmanian coast for water and supplies. They exchanged tobacco, tea and sugar for skins with Aboriginal groups and soon sought the seasonal use of women for comfort, and as co-workers, offering dogs in exchange. The Pallawah were delighted by the deal and by 1810 gathered each November to await the sealers' return. The Pallawah of north-east Tasmania, led by Mannalargenna, chose some of their own women to go annually with the sealers. They also raided other Aboriginal groups to steal more women to barter for dogs. Mannalargenna and his group used these dogs for hunting and to enlarge their power by gift exchange. By the 1820s, George Robinson noticed the Pallawah secured their dog with leather collars and leashes. On the mainland, Aboriginal groups also embraced the dog, each camp having packs used as watchdogs and as hot-water bottles on cold nights.[31]

New items could potentially disturb traditional patterns. The stone axe was produced by an intricate cultural exchange in which axe blanks travelled over long distances, were exchanged perhaps several times, and then hafted onto a handle in a painstaking way. Axes were owned by older people, often men, and their borrowing acknowledged the owner's authority and power. Stone axes were controlled by the stories of particular clans explaining how the axe was first created and from where it came. However, the settlers' steel axe was soon valued greatly as being more efficient than the stone axe. Peter Beveridge, a settler, saw Aboriginal people on the Murray 'clucking with the[ir] tongue' in admiration over the first steel axe they had sighted.[32] Settlers and missionaries sometimes rewarded Aboriginal effort with steel axes, subverting traditional axe-head exchange cycles. Younger people who engaged with or worked for whites received them, endangering the usual power relations within their own society. The vast trading systems that distributed stone-axe heads over great distances, and the Dreamtime stories that explained these axes, were diminished as the demand for them dwindled. However, traditional ideas were not so entirely subverted.

While an initial assessment in the 1930s of the impact of steel axes on the Yir Yiront of Cape York by anthropologist Lauriston Sharp was pessimistic, later research revealed the resilience of traditional systems in controlling and explaining the presence of these new steel axes. But social disruption could occur if sufficient new items flowed across the cultural divide.[33]

Aboriginal young people were quick to experiment with new things, being less steeped in their own culture, and with less to lose and more to gain from the European presence. There is some evidence that young men used the disruptions created by white contact to avoid traditional obligations and have greater access to young women, who were usually monopolised by older men. Some women also willingly took up with white men to access the resources of settlers. Yet, if elders suspected young people of turning from traditional ways, they tried to discipline them by physical violence or threats of sorcery. Some even threatened to withhold traditional knowledge from them, and youths returned to traditional ways after such pressure. Moorehouse, the Aboriginal Protector in South Australia, related in 1843 how two Aboriginal girls, who were his domestic servants and pupils, left his service after being commanded by their parents and older women to live with their promised husbands, being threatened with sorcery if they did not obey. Years later, and far to the north, an Aboriginal man from Charlotte Waters suddenly declared to his employer that he was going to get circumcised by his people. When called a fool, he replied: 'Well, I can't put up with the cheek of the women and children. They will not let me have a lubra, and the old men will not let me know anything about my countrymen.'[34]

A few—usually those isolated from their kinfolk in European-style schools—experienced greater change, and some chose to become like settlers. Maria, who as we saw in Chapter 2 came through Macquarie's Native Institution and married Robert Lock the convict in 1824, made such a choice, although Maria was exceptional. Most Aboriginal people either found the gap between individualistic European culture and communally based Aboriginal culture too wide to bridge, or their efforts were shunned by whites and opposed by blacks. In the late 1840s, two Gunai brothers from Gippsland, Tommy and Wurrabool (Harry) Bungeelenee, were brought in with their mother to Melbourne, who then left them at the Merri Creek Aboriginal School. They received tuition with several other Aboriginal children, becoming showpieces each Sunday at the Collins Street Baptist Church by singing and reading, dressed in white trousers and jackets. Hoping to go to Hobart in 1851 with their school teacher Edgar and his family, they were instead adopted out to a Melbourne schoolteacher named Hinkins and his wife. They were baptised, Harry being renamed John, after Hinkins. In 1854 they were presented to the Governor wearing white suits and blue scarves and sashes in their straw hats. When John died from respiratory disease Thomas became morose and rebellious and was sent to a training vessel for wayward boys. He then entered the Victorian public service. He aspired to whiteness, three times denying his Aboriginality, the third time scoffing at the idea he might marry an Aboriginal girl. Thomas Bungeelenee successfully applied to become a member of the Oddfellows' Lodge, the social destination of respectable young colonial men. Shortly after his initiation into this white man's lodge, he died of gastric fever, requesting on his deathbed the 23rd Psalm—the comfort of Christians—be read. Each colony had a few such stories, with most individuals losing their earlier identity, without successfully assuming another.[35]

Most Aboriginal people rejected such cultural crossovers as they felt superior to the early settlers—and indeed, most explorers relied on the assistance of Aboriginal guides during their journeys.[36] One guide told George Haydon in Gippsland in 1844: 'now white man berry clever, no mistake, make him house, and flour, and tea, and sugar, and tobacco, and clothes, but white fellow no find out when another white man walk along a road—I believe sometimes white man berry stupid'.[37] Indigenous people quickly identified European inadequacies. Reverend Threlkeld's bumbling efforts to learn Awabakal were corrected endlessly

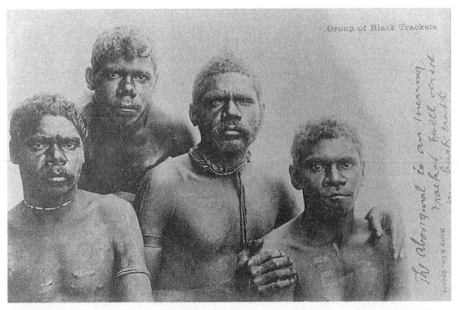

Aboriginal trackers were unrivalled bushmen. COURTESY OF THE MITCHELL COLLECTION, STATE LIBRARY OF NEW SOUTH WALES.

by his Aboriginal teachers who rebuked him, saying: 'What for you so stupid, you very stupid fellow.'[38] Bangerang people teased Edward Curr because he could not make a gun, a tomahawk, or sugar, tea and flour, whereas they could make all they used. This belief in their superiority underpinned their continuing confidence in their own culture. Most Aboriginal people saw little value in European ideas and sometimes ridiculed them, even Christian ideas. When Peter Beveridge told the Murray people about God creating the world, they replied logically that the world was not made, it was always here. If God did make it, they asked—with the eternal question—where then did the Earth come from out of which it was made?[39] Similarly, Eora people in Sydney confounded a missionary by replying to his explanation of life after death: 'if black man jump up again what for bury him?'. Others who tired of these 'silly' European views simply laughed or replied: 'We don't want talk: we want tobacco, pipes, bread.'[40] When settlers expressed scepticism in turn about Aboriginal sorcery or religious ideas, Aboriginal people replied that whites were ignorant about such matters.

Most Aboriginal people conformed to their Great Tradition that had shaped their culture for countless generations. The adoption of steel blades, clothes or guns were insignificant things in their overall cultural pattern. Bennelong dined with Governor Phillip and travelled to England, but he did it for amusement and adventure rather than any great fascination or respect for European civilisation. On his return he went back to his own people and culture. Aboriginal ways persisted all through the upheavals of the invasion and what we do know of Aboriginal culture, which was observed by settlers, missionaries and officials, is testimony to Aboriginal determination to maintain faith with tradition, maintain ceremonies and remain Aboriginal, despite the disruptions and deaths.

This adherence to Aboriginal cultural pathways can be seen in their attitude to work. In short, they refused to internalise the European individualist ethic of hard work and thrift. The Aboriginal stockmen did sufficient work to obtain the food needed for themselves and their kin, but their real life laid waiting back at the camp, where European work-clothes would be discarded and corroborees held far into the night. Edward Curr commented that, although he was intensely interested in corroborees, the Bangerang people held so many in the 1840s that he became bored with them. When ceremonial obligations called, or seasonal pursuits beckoned, workers simply left the stations. Hugh Jamieson, a Mildura pastoralist, wrote of Aboriginal people in the summer months in the 1840s: 'the various tribes, have the greatest desire to abandon every employment, and indulge in the roving life . . . alternatively hunting, fishing, and levying contributions on both sheep and cattle, as they slowly and indolently saunter along the banks of the Murray and Darling. Nothing could induce them to return from 'these wild and roving excursions of the tribes' until they were ready.[41]

Aboriginal people developed strategies of non-cooperation to deal with settlers. In 1843 Father Raymond Vaccari, a Passionist missionary at Moreton Bay, claimed Gabi Gabi people exhibited 'an extreme sloth and laziness in everything, a habit of fickleness and double-dealing, and uncontrollable vindictiveness, so much so that they will stop at nothing in the pursuit of revenge. They are deceitful and cunning and prone to lying. They are given to extreme gluttony and if possible will sleep both day and night.'[42] Similar comments were made about Indigenous people and slaves in other places who proved uncooperative and resistant to the European work ethic. Aboriginal people felt no shame in asking for food without working for it, which to them was not begging, but a sharing of what was due to original landowners.

DESTRUCTION

Invasion for some groups meant near or total extinction. However, the Pallawah people of Tasmania were wrongly numbered among these extinctions through the myth of 'The Last Tasmanian'. Complex circumstances on the Tasmanian frontier meant that Pallawah women were split into different groups by 1810—a dispersal that actually ensured the survival of the Pallawah. Some were taken or went with convict sealers to the Bass Strait islands and Kangaroo Island, some to the southern coast of the mainland, while others remained in Tasmania. Those living with sealers experienced a hard life among rough conditions and even rougher men. Some died, some escaped, and some were rescued: around 1830, humanitarians including George Robinson urged that these women be taken from the immoral and brutish sealers because they believed the women were being ill-used. The humanitarian middle-class view emerged that they were slaves of these men, a claim adopted by some historians.[43]

However, it was never that simple. Some women forged a life with the men to whom they bore children and they refused to be rescued. Some also refused to join mainland Pallawah on the great experiment of moving to Flinders Island. Instead, they continued as skilful partners in the sealing industry on islands in the Furneaux group. When sealing became unsustainable due to the mass slaughter of seals, they showed their white sealer men how to live off the land, and to fashion a new industry by catching mutton birds for their down, their meat and their boiled-down fat. This had been a traditional trade for Pallawah, so they knew the techniques to enable the sealer community to transform into mutton-birders. The people applied for a teacher catechist in 1851. In 1872 seven islander families settled on Cape Barren Island south of Flinders Island. They were ministered to by an Anglican missionary teacher and struggled to gain the right to land and mutton-bird leases. By 1900 the community numbered over 100 and fiercely rejected becoming 'like white people'.[44] Those few who were taken to Kangaroo Island were less able to sustain their Aboriginality amid a white majority. Their story is told by Rebe Taylor in *Unearthed* (2002).

In 1831, about 300 surviving Pallawah in Tasmania who agreed to be moved from their lands were taken to Gun Carriage Island, then Swan Island and finally Flinders Island. George Robinson had promised them a refuge free from harassment where their culture would be respected. They moaned when they first arrived on what was a windy sterile Bass Strait island far different to their homelands, but while at first conditions were materially harsh, they were left alone. Early visitors to Flinders Island witnessed corroborees, which suggested some contentment. But deaths, mostly from diseases, were constant. In 1835 the missionaries George Robinson and Robert Clark arrived at the settlement called Wybaleena, the name for 'black man's houses'. The 123 remaining Pallawah experienced new difficulties as the Civilising Mission began in earnest: the people were bombarded with Christianity and the work ethic. The children were schooled and catechised; women were taught domestic skills of cleaning, sewing and cooking; they and the men, who worked in the garden, were read the Bible at night and endured questions about God, the Devil, Heaven and Hell. Robinson rehoused the people, renamed them, insisted on cleanliness and clothing, and issued the weekly *Flinders Island Chronicle* which the young people wrote, testifying to a new-found faith. He also introduced a weekly market to teach them about work and trade. Some children were removed to the Orphans School at Hobart, and the death toll mounted. Wybaleena was becoming a hell for most Pallawah. Robinson preached eulogies, buried the people in neat rows, mourned them, and marked their names on his graveyard blueprint. When he left in early 1838 to become the Chief Protector of Aborigines at Port Phillip, taking fifteen Pallawah with him, only 65 remained at Wybaleena.[45]

A succession of new commandants were less interested in the Civilising Mission, so the people had more freedom to roam the island, conduct ceremonies and engage in old feuds over dogs and women. When the Port Phillip group returned in 1842, minus two of their number who had been hanged in Melbourne for robbery and murder, a more rebellious attitude developed. They refused to work without pay, and lived communally again with their many dogs. They wrote letters of protest and in 1846 eight men—Walter Arthur, Chief of the Ben

Lomond Tribe, John Allen, Davey Bruny, Neptune, King Alexander, Augustus, King Tippo, and Washington—petitioned the Governor. They complained of tyrannical treatment by one commandant, their poor conditions and how they had been betrayed. Their petition asserted 'that we are your free children that we were not taken prisoners but freely gave up our country to Colonel Arthur then the Governor after defending ourselves . . . Mr Robinson made for us and with Colonel Arthur an agreement which we have not lost from our minds since and we have made our part of it good'.[46] This remarkable statement of dignified independence reached the desk of Queen Victoria, who received it 'graciously'.

The petition prompted an inquiry and a Colonial Office demand that the people be moved back to Tasmania. Settlers unsuccessfully opposed the idea, fearing either the 37 middle-aged Pallawah and their ten children, or the claims on land they might make. In 1847 the Pallawah were overjoyed to be back on the mainland at a former convict depot at Oyster Cove—the ten children going straight to the Hobart Orphan School. They moved into freshly painted houses and received good rations. Walter Arthur and his wife Mary Anne built a house and farmed. But soon despair returned. Some drank in taverns, women prostituted themselves and the Arthurs gave up farming. The settlement fell into an unkempt

Pallawah survivors at Oyster Cove, 1859. COURTESY OF THE F. ENDACOTT COLLECTION, MUSEUM OF VICTORIA.

state and the population declined from 30 in 1851 to 14 in 1859. Walter Arthur died in a boating accident while drunk in 1861.[47] By 1868 only three Pallawah survived, along with the Pallawah women and their children living with former sealers on Bass Strait and Kangaroo islands. These sealing women and their European husbands forged to this day a viable community, who have now reclaimed Wybaleena and their Pallawah identity. Their story is told in Lyndall Ryan's *The Aboriginal Tasmanians* (1996).

Many mainland groups in south-eastern Australia did pass into oblivion, and within the second generation after contact. George Robinson noted the absence of clans in the Western District of Victoria as early as the 1840s; Awabakal and other peoples in New South Wales were completely gone by 1850. Mahroot, one of four Dharug survivors out of 400 of his people at first contact in Sydney, lamented in 1845:

> All black-fellow gone! All this my country! Pretty place Botany! Little Pickaninny, I run about here. Plenty black-fellow then; corrobbory; great fight; all canoe about. Only me left now, Mitter—Poor gin mine tumble down (die). All gone! Bury her like a lady, Mitter—; all put in coffin, English fashion. I feel lump in throat when I talk about her but—I buried her all very genteel, Mitter.[48]

Other groups were similarly depleted and teetered on the point of extinction by the 1850s. Around Adelaide, the Aboriginal population declined from 650 to 180 in the fifteen years after 1841; around Geelong, the decline was from 279 to 36 in eighteen years; while Edward Curr stated that on the Murray the Bangerang dropped from 200 to 80 in the first decade of settlement.[49] The 'last of his tribe' became a great colonial cliché. However, it was usually based on the racialised view that those of mixed descent who survived were not 'true Aborigines'.

How did this destruction occur on southern frontiers? Disease was by far the greatest killer, as we have seen in the previous chapter, and white violence also played a part, including the activity of the Native Police. *Inter se* killings also occurred; that is, Aboriginal deaths at the hands of other Aboriginal people. Why was this so?

The Aboriginal world was one of friends and strangers, the latter being considered dangerous and to be feared. The Aboriginal Protector on the Loddon River, Edward Parker, was told by a Worngarragerra man in the 1840s that the Lake Boloke people 'are foreign in speech, they are foreign in countenance, they are foreign altogether—they are no good'.[50] These traditional feelings of enmity were fed by the belief that deaths were caused by the sorcery of others, usually outsiders, and that revenge must be taken—a life for a life. The European terms 'wild myalls' and 'wild blackfellows' were used frequently by Aboriginal people to denote outsiders who must be killed if they intruded without permission into local territory. Indeed, the power of tradition meant that people feared strangers from distant tribes as much or more than they did Europeans. This was one reason why Native Policemen could be used successfully to disperse or kill other Aboriginal people.

The settlers' penetration of Aboriginal lands accelerated the level of inter-tribal fighting because of Aboriginal beliefs about death, sorcery and strangers. First, the settlers' presence encouraged Aboriginal people to travel beyond their traditional boundaries to get access to European foods and goods. Aboriginal groups which did not have traditionally friendly relations interacted violently in the scramble for white resources, and friction and deaths ensued. Young men travelled as guides or accompanied stock into strange new lands, and it was the highest act of loyalty to one's group to kill such an Aboriginal stranger, who might work sorcery against them. The Aboriginal belief that all unnatural death was caused by sorcery also lay behind the increase in inter-tribal fighting after settlers arrived. Deaths caused by European diseases—the actions of unseen microbes and viruses—were blamed on sorcery, and revenge killings followed. Billibellary, a Melbourne tribal elder who succumbed to respiratory disease in 1846, believed when near death that he was the victim of sorcery. An inquest held by his people led to a revenge party heading north.[51] When deaths occurred due to visible white violence, Aboriginal people who believed that the Europeans were ignorant of sorcery may have thought settlers were merely puppets of Aboriginal sorcerers. Thus more inter-tribal killings might have followed.[52]

Inter-tribal violence witnessed by settlers was often not war but law: judicial proceedings between groups carried out in a traditionally controlled fashion. Protector William Thomas witnessed such a dispute between the Barrabool and Buninyong peoples at North Melbourne in 1844. An hour of heated arguing was followed by a ritualised fight controlled by elders, in which many spears were thrown, but always with restraint. The fight resulted in only a few wounds, and harmony was finally restored by a concluding reconciling ceremony.[53]

However, inter-tribal or *inter se* fighting of a more deadly kind was also traditional. The escaped convict William Buckley, who lived with the Wathaurung people for 33 years around Geelong, gave descriptions of vicious fighting between groups before settlers arrived. Many people—not just male warriors, but women and children—died in these deadly encounters.[54] Evidence exists that such traditional fighting continued after the Europeans' arrival, although it was possibly exacerbated by the settlers' presence. In Tasmania, even when the Pallawah were reduced to several hundred survivors, inter-tribal fighting still occurred. In 1830 Mannalargenna led Oyster Bay and allied people against the Big River tribe in a dispute over women. Similar fighting occurred among them on Flinders Island. In 1835, the year of Melbourne's settlement, Gunai people from Gippsland raided the Boonwurrung at Western Port, killing 25, who were revenged in 1838 when seven Gunai were killed by Boonwurrung. Twenty-five Djadjawurrung were killed by Duangwurrung (Goulburn River people) in the late 1830s. A fight between the Avoca and Murray peoples in 1848 resulted in sixteen deaths. Edward Curr reported of the 1840s that the Wongatpan at times slept in great discomfort in canoes amid mosquito-filled reed beds, fearing an attack. About 250 Aboriginal people were killed by other Aborigines in inter-tribal fights in the Port Phillip District between 1835 and 1850. If the number of Aboriginal people killed by the Native Police is added to this death tally, possibly 400 Indigenous people were killed by other Aboriginal people in Victoria alone—a significant death toll.[55]

Of course other forces, notably disease, played a far greater role in the Aboriginal population decline, as we have seen. What, then, was the relative weight of these various factors: disease, white and black violence, malnutrition caused by ecological change, and a loss of purpose—all of them legacies of colonialism? Quite accurate figures of Aboriginal depopulation exist for the Port Phillip District because of the presence of Aboriginal Protectors who kept detailed records; whether Port Phillip was representative of other colonies is unclear. Despite the presence of the Port Phillip Protectorate, the violence on the Victorian frontier created a ratio of Aboriginal to European deaths of twelve to one, similar to Australia-wide estimates of ten to one. Overall, a pre-contact Indigenous Victorian population of about 10,000 in 1834–35, conservatively speaking, declined to 1907 by 1853—a decline of 80 per cent in eighteen years.[56] Indeed, if smallpox is included, a huge population loss had already occurred before 1835. Using demographic modelling, Noel Butlin estimated that the Aboriginal population in Victoria might have numbered 50,000 in 1788, but was more than halved in 1790 by smallpox, and halved again by smallpox around 1830, just before European settlement.[57] Settlers faced a much depleted people.

What caused this dreadful depopulation after 1835 of another 80 per cent? It has been estimated that in Port Phillip, of the 8000 Aboriginal deaths in the first two decades of settlement: 4000–5000 were from disease (up to 60 per cent); 1500–2000 were from violence (up to 25 per cent), including 1000–1500 from white violence; 150 by Native Police; 250 from *inter se* fighting; and 1000–2000 dying from natural causes (up to 25 per cent), no doubt hastened by malnutrition and ecological stress. Each region within Port Phillip was unique, however. Edward Curr claimed, perhaps optimistically, that only two of the 120 Bangerang deaths on the Murray over a decade were due to violence and that most died from disease- and alcohol-related causes. He did not consider how loss of resources and ecological change might have been part of the equation. The same lack of violence was true in the case of the depopulation around Melbourne. In Gippsland and the Western District, white violence played a more significant part in the Aboriginal death toll. Overall in Port Phillip, about six out of every ten Aboriginal deaths was due to introduced diseases, two from white and black violence and two from natural causes in a context of rapid ecological change. Eight of every ten deaths in the frontier period were a legacy of colonialism, or as Alfred Crosby might call it 'ecological imperialism'. This ratio most likely operated on all Australian frontiers.[58]

This horrific 80 per cent decline in one generation was exacerbated by an extremely low Aboriginal birth rate. The Aboriginal Protector William Thomas recorded 135 deaths among the Woiwurrung and Boonwurrung around Melbourne from 1839 to 1859 and only 28 births. Other observers noted the lack of children. Gonorrhoea reduced fertility and syphilis reduced the livebirth rate, while poor diets and living conditions reduced infant survival. William Thomas lamented that most of the 28 children born did not survive the first month.[59] He hinted at infanticide, which Billibellary, a Woiwurrung elder, agreed sometimes occurred. But settlers gave too much weight to infanticide as a factor in population decline. The evidence for it remains slim and the settlers' claims were value-laden, shaped by the discourse of savagery.[60]

It is true that a certain fatalism crept in as Aboriginal people witnessed death and destruction around them. Derrimut, a Boonwurrung man, exclaimed to William Hull, a settler, in the 1840s: 'You see . . . all this mine, all along here Derrimut's once; no matter now, me soon tumble down . . . Why me have lubra? Why me have piccaninny? You have all this place, no good have children, no good have lubra, me tumble down and die very soon now.' Billibellary also reported: 'the Black lubras say now no good children, Blackfellow say no country now for them, very good we kill and no more come up Pickaninny.'[61] Without their land, their places to hunt and their sacred sites to give meaning to their lives, some felt life was simply not worth living.

'Billibellary, chief of the Yarra Tribe on Settlement being Formed', by William Thomas.
COURTESY OF LA TROBE AUSTRALIAN MANUSCRIPTS COLLECTION, STATE LIBRARY OF VICTORIA.

There are clues to the outcomes of demographic disaster. The death of 80 per cent of the population created huge gaps in the kinship system, left children without close guardians, made correct marriage partners scarce and ceremonial obligations difficult to perform. Much ceremonial life was lost as ceremonies formerly held over days became impossible to sustain without access to sites and without sufficient elders with deep knowledge of the law. Adults who were once providers and conveyors of knowledge were reduced to beggars and scroungers on the fringes of white society. Stress, and perhaps even mental illness, pushed people to alcohol abuse and violence. The bodies of Aboriginal people were emaciated by colonisation—some even scarred from the violence. The disruptions were obviously countless and complex, and now largely unknowable.

The fabric of Aboriginal society and the Aboriginal family was torn. Rifts were created between those who spoke English and associated with settlers and those who did not; between the young who experimented with new things and the old who stressed tradition; between men and women who had different opportunities and pressures within colonialism. Aboriginal women, formerly independent providers, perhaps suffered most. Not only were they sexual targets of white settlers, but their role as the family's main provider was undermined. Women became dependent on rations to sustain family where bush tucker declined or became unavailable. Of Aboriginal women's yam and tuber food gathering at the Swan River, archeologist and historian Sylvia Hallam concluded that rations of bread were needed because European ideas of exclusive possession symbolised by fences, and enforced by guns and the law, 'deprived Aboriginal women of access to the land to which they held rights and the carbohydrate staples they used to harvest there'. Rations of food and clothing were often not directed to women, being paid to Aboriginal men by European men. Aboriginal men were the main cash wage earners in the growing cash economy, which further skewed men's power over women on the frontier. Work for women was confined by European gender roles to domestic work—although some became shepherds—and prostitution. Some also lived with European men, which gave them access to resources that Aboriginal men did not have. Aboriginal women experienced violence from men on both sides of the frontier. Violence from Aboriginal men to their women was frequently reported by colonial observers, and while it is impossible to determine whether this was new or traditional behaviour, there is no doubt frontier conditions gave rise to fraught gender relations.[62]

The survivors eked out an existence as dwellers on the fringes of white society. They were considered hopeless remnants, but in reality were courageous battlers, fighting tenaciously for existence in their camps on riverbanks or near pastoral runs throughout the colonies. They followed traditional Aboriginal rhythms: roved across country, worked and cadged a bit, and gathered possum, small game, eels, fish and bush vegetables to supplement government rations and food purchased from seasonal wages. The campers, called 'fringe dwellers', were often in poor health and some drank and smoked to excess when able.

They were outcasts living in tents and shacks around towns and riverbanks who shared a folklore of injustice and bewilderment. Some lived as lone individuals. The Piltindjeri people from the Lower Murray region sang this lament around their camps: 'Where are my friends, my clanspeople? . . . They are all gone . . . I am lonely . . . They are all dead, my clanspeople. I am sorrowful and lonely.'[63]

Yet, not all was lost. Some Aboriginal people were sustained by what has been called by Harvard philosopher Jonathan Lear 'radical hope'; that is, a hope based on tradition for a future in a new world.[64] Billibellary, the tall, athletic *ngurungaeta* or elder of the Woiwurrung people of Melbourne, had one such 'radical hope'. He engaged with European society, being a signatory of the conciliatory Batman's treaty in 1835. After seven days of negotiations in 1842, he joined the Native Police because of its potential and to enlarge his power. He enrolled his eldest son in the first mission school and sent his youngest two children to the Merri Creek School to given them skills in the new colonial world. He became close friends after 1839 with William Thomas, the Aboriginal Protector. They often discussed the Aboriginal future around a campfire. Billibellary admitted women practised infanticide, but did not give way to fatalism, promising to stop it. He cracked the heads of young men who were drunkards. He respected Thomas but did not become Christian—even on his death from influenza in 1846. His radical hope involved agriculture, through which his people had a future in the colonial world on portions of their traditional lands. In 1843 Billibellary called for land to be handed back, telling Thomas: 'If Yarra blacks had a country on the Yarra . . . they would stop on it and cultivate the ground'.[65]

In Tasmania Walter Arthur embraced farming, and also Christianity, as a way forward. He too remained Aboriginal and determined to be part of a 'free people', as the 1846 Pallawah petition asserted. This was their radical hope. Indeed, it is almost certain that Billibellary and Walter Arthur met in Melbourne and discussed the state of their world and its future, as Walter Arthur was in Port Phillip with George Robinson from 1838 to 1842.

Such radical Aboriginal hopes did not end when these two men died, for Billibellary had two sons, Simon Wonga and Tommy Munneringa, who kept his radical hope alive—as we shall see.

5

RADICAL HOPE QUASHED

Some Aboriginal people who lived through the first generation of contact on southern and eastern frontiers revealed a tenacity for survival. However, this was not by a rejection of the new world in which they now lived, but by what Jonathan Lear calls 'radical hope'; that is, by embracing it realistically in an Aboriginal way.[1] Aboriginal people, having adapted to great environmental changes during the previous 50,000 years, were very practised at intelligent approaches to change. This chapter will examine three instances of 'radical hope', two of them linked back to Billibellary, a Woiwurrung elder of Melbourne: the hopes of the Kulin of Central Victoria, the Ngarrindjeri of the Coorong, and the Yorta Yorta–Bangerang of the Murray, all of whom embraced farming and a settled existence to remain Aboriginal.

THE MAKING OF CORANDERRK, RAUKKAN AND CUMMERAGUNJA

After the Aboriginal Protectorate stations were abandoned in 1849, about 2000 Aboriginal people in Victoria were left to their own devices. The Kulin did have access to rations from government depots at Warrandyte and Mordialloc when needed, and the Wotjobaluk could access the Moravian and Anglican missions at Lake Boga and Yelta on the Murray River. Aboriginal people in New South Wales were also unsupervised and uncared for by government. Most lived and worked as station hands in the 1850s and were highly valued by the settlers as rural labour became scarce during the gold rushes. They supplemented rations or low wages with bush tucker, and a few even farmed at Mount Franklin, near the old Protectorate station.

Billibellary first articulated the Kulin's call for land in 1843, a claim restated
by the Kulin a number of times. In 1859 a deputation of seven Kulin led by
Simon Wonga, Billibellary's son, visited William Thomas, the Aboriginal
Guardian, again requesting 'a block of land in their own country where they
may sit down, plant corn, potatoes, etc—and work like white men'.[2] In March
1859, these tall 'robust, well-made men, apparently equal in power to the average
European', as the *Argus* described them, met with Gavin Duffy, Minister for
Lands, who granted them 1820 hectares on the Acheron River.[3] The timing was
propitious as the Victorian Parliament had the previous month received a select
committee report recommending 'reserves for the various tribes on their own
hunting grounds'.[4] Eighty Kulin pioneered the Acheron, clearing, fencing,
building, and planting six hectares of wheat and vegetables. However, with no
government stake of supplies and equipment, the able-bodied men soon dispersed
to earn needed cash as rural labourers. The pioneering venture was threatened
by local settlers, including the most powerful pastoralist in Victoria, Hugh Glass,
who coveted their land for grazing purposes. The Kulin were shifted to Mohican
Station eight kilometres away in November 1860, a colder, less favourable area,
with no traditional meaning to the Kulin. The victorious white settlers moved
in with their stock and burnt the Kulin's fences, huts and crops. The Kulin were
so disillusioned by the government's broken promises over land that at first only
four women went to the new Mohican site.

In June 1860, the Victorian government established a Central Board for
the Aborigines to establish reserves and appoint managers to control them, to
create local guardians in most areas, and to administer the affairs of Aboriginal
people. Six reserves were created, namely: Coranderrk near Healesville;
Framlingham and Lake Condah in the Western District; Ebenezer to the north;
and Ramahyuck and Lake Tyers in the Gippsland area. Protector William Thomas
wrote vehemently to the new Board about the Kulin's removal from the Acheron
site: 'this, the fate of Aboriginal industry, is enough to deter Aborigines from
ever after having confidence in promises held out to them'.[5]

Eventually, 35 Kulin led by Simon Wonga pioneered at Mohican Station,
where only about sixteen hectares were suitable for farming, compared to 400
hectares at Acheron. John Green, a Presbyterian lay preacher and friend of the
Kulin for several years, was appointed 'General Inspector of Aborigines' by the
new Board. Green criticised the Kulin's removal to Mohican Station and conveyed
their dissatisfaction with the place, which one declared was 'no good'; whereas
the 'old station very good, plenty hot, plenty work, plenty wheat, potatoes and
cabbages, plenty of everything'. If the government gave back their old station,

'by and by black fellow need no more things from him; Black fellow buy them himself'.[6] This was a clear statement of radical hope: of Aboriginal initiative and self-reliance. As Mohican Station proved unsuitable, the Kulin were moved to a third site, and for a third time they commenced pioneering.

In March 1863, the Kulin defiantly moved and squatted at a fourth place, a traditional camping site on the Yarra flats at Healesville, named 'Coranderrk' after the native Christmas bush. Simon Wonga, his cousin William Barak, seventeen other Kulin and one Bangerang man attended Governor Sir Henry Barkly's levy for the Queen's Birthday in May 1863 to petition for land. The government graciously gazetted 930 hectares there in June (extended to 1960 hectares in 1866) as an Aboriginal reserve. A message from Queen Victoria shortly after offered her protection, which led to a view among the Kulin that Coranderrk was a direct gift from her.[7] For the fourth time, the Kulin cleared land like white people—but this was their land of choice. The men quickly constructed nine bark huts and the women made and sold enough rugs to buy boots, coats and hats for all, and a few horses. Within two years 105 resided there—almost all the remaining Kulin. Simon Wonga told the Duangwurrung, with biblical allusions, when they arrived in 1865: 'Mr Green and all the Yarra blacks and me went through the mountains. We had no bread for five days. We did this to let you know about the good word. Now you have come to the Yarra. I am glad.'[8] Before long a score of Bangerang, mostly children, also arrived from the Murray River.

Coranderrk prospered despite the challenges of pioneering facing all farmers, and some unique difficulties. Since 44 of the 105 residents in 1865 were children, there were only twenty able-bodied men to clear the heavily timbered reserve. Also, as the Central Board provided little money and few rations, the men had to hunt for several days a week and periodically work on adjoining properties to get money for seed, stock and equipment. The women and old men made baskets, rugs and artefacts for sale. Their efforts were vital to the settlement's survival. So too were Green's contributions from his own salary, for he was made Coranderrk's manager. Despite the little time that could be devoted to development, by 1874 the Coranderrk men had cut materials for, and erected, 32 cottages, various outbuildings, yards and seven kilometres of boundary fencing. The community had 65 hectares under crop and managed 450 head of stock. In twenty years 1215 hectares had been converted from dense bush to improved pasture. The Board insisted on a shift to hop cultivation in 1872, claiming it was a better cash crop. The people proved to be not only the colony's fastest hop pickers, but their hops won first prize at the Melbourne International

Exhibition, and demanded the highest prices on the Melbourne market. By 1875 Coranderrk was virtually self-supporting.[9]

Significant changes were taking place elsewhere on Victorian reserves where half the remaining Aboriginal people chose to live. These changes were partly forced. The loss of land and people had pushed them onto reserves and the settled life of agriculture, where managers, who usually were missionaries, actively pursued the Civilising Mission by means of work, schooling and even teaching them cricket. But Aboriginal people also explored new ways when the old no longer seemed possible. An old Lake Tyers man said to the manager as he thrust his daughter forward: 'Marry her in your way to a young man here, like the white people.'[10] He seemed pressured by circumstances to relinquish tradition, but for others there seemed a radical hope that the old might be reborn in the new. Secretary to the Board, Robert Brough Smyth, wrote in 1864: 'Wonga and Barak . . . are very intelligent men, and in their behaviour would compare favourably with the better class of other races'.[11] Soon Aboriginal houses on the reserves were furnished in settler mode, complete with rugs, sofas, rocking chairs, clocks, pictures and wallpaper; some even possessed harmoniums. Many dwellings had flower gardens, fruit trees and picket fences around them. One visitor remarked in the 1870s that reserve homes were 'equal to those of English workingmen and superior to those of many selectors in the district', while their young people had 'a better education than most of the farmers' children'.[12]

Aboriginal women who lived permanently on the reserves, as opposed to their men who did part-time labouring around the district, experienced the greatest changes. This is evident in the numerous surviving photographs, which reveal women dressed in Victorian finery and coiffure. This was partly due to the close contact between the women and the missionaries' wives. Mary Green, like her husband John, was close to the Coranderrk people. Anthropologist Diane Barwick noted that 'a genuine camaraderie developed as they shared the same classes, met to sew, crochet and embroider, sang in the choir and practised on the harmonium, worked in the dairy and bakery, prepared festive suppers for church events and social evenings, sat up with the sick and wept together over children's coffins'.[13] Sorrow increased as tuberculosis and other respiratory diseases raged at Coranderrk to blot these happy early years. Of children born before 1900 on the Victorian Aboriginal reserves, half died in infancy.[14]

Despite new modes of dress, housing, economic patterns and numerous conversions to Christianity, the Aboriginal people, who practised these things on all reserves, did not abandon their traditional values. This was their radical hope: to change materially, but culturally to remain in essence the same. They

Tending the hop gardens at Coranderrk, 1882, taken by Fred Kruger. COURTESY OF THE NATIONAL LIBRARY OF AUSTRALIA (NLA.PIC-VN3082703).

still practised kinship ties and obligations, feared the effects of sorcery, practised certain rituals, especially relating to personal hygiene and funerals, hunted and collected bush foods in their leisure time, and maintained a deep attachment to the land and its governing stories. The evidence suggests that by a radical hope, many were trying to survive and retain the best of both worlds—to forge an Aboriginal existence within a European economic mode: farming with an Aboriginal idiom. Even Christianity was embraced and blended with Aboriginal spirituality.

Such transformations occurred on all six Victorian Aboriginal reserves, but Coranderrk was a model of this—and not just because it was the largest and most fertile, and thus conducive to successful farming. Coranderrk's leaders—Simon Wonga, then his cousin William Barak, after Wonga's death from tuberculosis in 1874—followed the legacy of Billibellary, who had first attempted this cultural balancing act. Barak in particular developed a very close friendship with, and a trust of, John Green. Green was a Christian and, although displaying a touch of paternalism, displayed little ruling and much caring compared to the typical paternalist. Whereas other reserve managers lacked faith in the people and tried to dominate them, Green trusted them and their abilities. He treated them as adults and allowed them 'to rule themselves as much as possible'. He created a court, which the residents ran, and which decided the rules and punishments.

The people decided drinking alcohol should be prohibited. Punishment for a second offence was loss of the right to marry. Green let the men organise the farm work, which was done in teams of four, possibly traditional groupings. Green worked beside the Kulin, not over them. He visited them in their homes, unlike most of the other reserve managers. He continually stressed that Coranderrk would become their permanent home—Queen Victoria had promised that—if they could make it productive. He empowered Billibellary's radical hope with this promise.

However, their efforts existed in an age when governments gave little state help to individuals, black or white. The Victorian government refused to give the Kulin individual blocks or title to their reserves, which created insecurity and dampened their radical hope. Their anxiety about land title increased in the face of covetous European neighbours, especially at Coranderrk, which had proved so productive. The Board refused to pay Aboriginal workers any wages during the 1860s, despite improvements being made to the land (owned by the Board and not by them). At Coranderrk the workers also supported the large number of orphans who were resident there, as well as their own families. After numerous protests by Green and the Kulin, the Board finally paid a small male wage to supplement rations, at a third of the European rate, but at Coranderrk the men had to buy their own meat out of their wage to encourage a market mentality. The Kulin clearly understood the market, which should have pleased the Board. They protested to a royal commission into the reserve in 1881 that their wage was not enough to buy sufficient meat to feed their families. They showed their enthusiasm for individual enterprise by persuading Green to distribute the food surplus according to the capitalist principle of the largest share to the best workers, and not according to need.

Not all Aboriginal people in Victoria made such agricultural and market adaptations or held such radical hopes about change. The land on other reserves was less fertile and the supervision less sympathetic. Also, by 1869 when the Central Board became the Board for the Protection of Aborigines and acquired the power to compel people to move to the reserves, only a quarter of all Aboriginal people in Victoria lived on reserves. Even by 1877, less than half did so. In 1877 those off the Aboriginal reserves were more likely to be adult males and of full descent, who were doing labouring work on pastoral properties, whereas most women and children were on reserves. These rural labourers moved on and off the reserves as the work dictated. Others were country campers, who lived permanently off the reserves. They made moral claims on local landowners for rations and generally adhered to the old ways.

Ngarrindjeri people of the Coorong region, to the south-east of Adelaide, also embraced new enterprises. In 1859 George Taplin established Raukkan (Point McLeay) mission for the Aborigines' Friends' Association. Many Ngarrindjeri settled there to stabilise their community after the frontier decimation. They quickly revealed a willingness to work and to be educated, but finding employment was a problem. There was little work at Raukkan as the reserve was initially only 180 hectares, which was too small to support a community of 200 people. Even when the reserve was enlarged to 688 hectares in 1872, it was barely bigger than a family farm. Also, the mission had few funds with which to stock the land. The Ngarrindjeri mastered the trades of saddlery, blacksmithing, carpentry, stonemasonry and baking, but there was no paid work for them at Raukkan. They established a fishing enterprise, yet distance from markets in a pre-refrigeration era rendered this futile. Eventually, they set up a wool-washing plant on the shore of Lake Alexandrina and made a good income from it.

Life favoured the Ngarrindjeri for a generation. They prospered almost as well as Aboriginal people at Poonindie mission near Port Lincoln in South Australia, who, with sufficient land, farmed successfully and were by 1850 self-sufficient after fifteen years of pioneering. Some Ngarrindjeri gained leases to small blocks of land near Raukkan. John Sumner took up the first in 1868, but was forced to relinquish it after three years of effort with little success. However, Napoleon Bonney, William MacHughes and Henry Lambert leased farms in the early 1870s and made profits, and their descendants still farm in the area today. By 1901 there were a dozen Ngarrindjeri families on individual farms in the district. A number converted to Christianity and a few acted as missionaries to the local Europeans. Indeed, after George Taplin died in 1879, the Ngarrindjeri Christians kept the church going in the face of the religious indifference of the succeeding manager.[15]

Success at Raukkan, Poonindie and Coranderrk influenced events in southern New South Wales. Daniel Matthews, a Cornish migrant and Echuca storekeeper, visited Coranderrk in 1866 and was deeply impressed with the reserve. Being a deeply Christian man and already concerned about the plight of the Yorta Yorta and Bangerang camping around the Murray towns, Matthews in 1874 created an Aboriginal refuge, Maloga, on his own selection on the Murray's banks near Echuca. Matthews scoured the country for destitute Aboriginal people to bring to Maloga. Matthews and his equally zealous wife Janet believed Aboriginal people could live dignified and worthwhile Christian lives, if given the chance. Like John Green, for the first five years Daniel and Janet Matthews poured their own savings into the mission, which struggled without significant outside support.

Mindful of antagonists who accused Matthews of making slaves of the residents, Matthews was careful never to use Aboriginal labour unless he could pay his workers. Therefore, development was painfully slow and he did much of the building himself, a story told in Nancy Cato's *Mr Maloga* (1976).

Maloga progressed steadily once funds flowed from the Aborigines Protection Association, a private body that was partly government funded. G.E. Morrison, who visited Maloga in 1881, remarked that the 80 Aboriginal residents 'are healthy and clean looking, dress neatly, and keep their cottages tidy and trim . . . [they] sang some sacred songs, and sang them well too, and in good time. Their repertoire is extensive; they can sing from memory 74 hymns.'[16] These Christian converts still held traditional ideas about family, community and land, and practised rituals such as cutting their heads and wailing in grief at Christian funerals. Maloga developed as a village like Raukkan and Coranderrk, and by 1886 there were fourteen neat dwellings complete with furniture and vegetable gardens, and eleven other buildings. Just as John Green inspired Matthews, so too did Daniel Matthews inspire Rev. J.B. Gribble to establish Warangesda mission near Brewarrina in 1880, and others later in Queensland and Western Australia. A fuller account of these missions and others is found in John Harris's *One Blood: 200 Years of Aboriginal Encounter with Christianity; A Story of Hope* (1990).

Aboriginal people inspired each other into radical hope as well. Bangerang and Kulin, who were not traditionally friends, came together at Coranderrk after some Bangerang, mostly children, were brought there by Daniel Matthews in the late 1860s. Some Coranderrk exiles sought refuge at Maloga around 1880, and William Barak took his son David there in 1881 to try unsuccessfully to restore his health from tuberculosis. While there, Barak imparted news of Coranderrk's promise and his hopes for it. Inspired by Coranderrk people and under encouragement from Matthews, 41 Maloga men (and David Barak, who was convalescing there), petitioned the New South Wales government for land in July 1881.[17] They rehearsed the history of their dispossession, outlined their training and their desire to adopt 'more orderly habits of industry', and declared: 'we believe we could, in a few years support ourselves by our own industry, *were a sufficient area of land granted* to us to cultivate and raise stock . . . we more confidently ask this favour of a grant of land as our fellow natives in other colonies have proved capable of supporting themselves.'[18] The government replied after two years of rumination over its non-existent Aboriginal policy. In 1883 it created its own colony's Aborigines Protection Board, following Victoria's example, and reserved 730 hectares for Aboriginal use adjoining Maloga, and some land at Brungle as well.

Winter quarters, Maloga station, taken by Nicholas John Caire, 1883. COURTESY OF THE STATE LIBRARY OF VICTORIA (H38469).

Despite his compassionate rescue of the people from destitution, Matthews ruled Maloga by rigid Christian and puritanical standards. He opposed traditional marriage rules and withdrew rations until Christian marriage was accepted. He banned corroborees and other traditional practices, including the language. Daniel and Janet Matthews were authoritarian, unlike John and Mary Green, and failed to treat Aboriginal people as adults and equals—so much so that Janet Matthews later sent her son John to England to prevent his possible marriage to a Maloga girl.[19] These attitudes prevented any syncretism of two cultures emerging. By the mid-1880s, Maloga residents, especially younger ones with an independent spirit, resented the Matthews's paternalistic control, which they had outgrown. Some shunned the endless 6.30 a.m. prayer services and were threatened with expulsion. Tensions grew with the younger generation of men, who owned horses and were self-assured from their ability as stockmen. John Atkinson left with his family and farmed some land nearby; others, chastised by Matthews for drinking and attending footraces without permission, soon enough joined him.

Most people left Maloga in 1888 for the new government reserve nearby, which they named Cummeragunja (affectionately 'Cummera'), meaning 'my country'. The living conditions were poor and the residents worked for rations only, but gradually the settlement took shape. Within five years, 570 hectares had been cleared and 40 cottages erected together with the necessary outbuildings, fences and tanks. It was a thriving village by 1908, containing over 300 Yorta Yorta and Bangerang, and 46 cottages, a school, meeting hall, church and many other buildings. Most houses were neatly furnished, complete with gardens and fruit trees. Doug (after 1972 Sir Doug) Nicholls's family had a pedal organ and his father later owned a car of sorts. William Cooper and John Atkinson asked unsuccessfully for individual blocks as early as 1887, Cooper wanting land for economic independence: 'this small portion of a vast territory which is ours by Divine Right'.[20] Individual farming commenced after 1895, following the repeated requests of the people for blocks of their own. By 1898, twenty individual blocks as well as the communal farm operated. The desire for individual blocks outran the available land. In 1899 twenty men sowed 140 hectares on their blocks with good yields and personal profits. Until about 1910, the Cummeragunja farmers in most years exceeded the average wheat yield in the district.[21]

Thomas Shadrach James, a Mauritian schoolteacher who married William Cooper's sister Ada, also boosted the radical hope of the Cummeragunja people. 'Granpa James' gave a generation of children a good rudimentary primary education. He also reinforced the pride and self-assurance the children gained from their parents and elders who were independent farmers. He instilled them with Christian, self-improving values, and helped forge what became one of Australia's first and most important Aboriginal political elites in the generation after the 1930s. Aboriginal memories of these years recall 'Cummera' as a tightly knit, secure environment for growing up. Doug Nicholls remembers it as a carefree, wonderful place by the river, an endless source of diversion. Margaret Tucker (later MBE) recalled her childhood as the happiest years of her life. Food was plentiful, supplemented by bush tucker of possum, fish, crayfish, ducks and scrub turkey. Christmas holidays brought treks into the bush to refresh traditional skills and replenish bonds with their land. The men proudly gained premiership flags in district cricket and football competitions spanning decades from 1898, and 'Cummera' men won fourteen professional running titles over a generation. Bobby MacDonald introduced the crouch sprint start in the 1880s before it was officially sanctioned, and William Cooper's son Lynch won the World Sprint championship in 1926 and the Stawell Gift in 1928.[22] By 1900, Cummeragunja people had reached the stage of prosperity and stability that Coranderrk, Raukkan and Poonindie had attained by 1880. These were model settlements of radical hope. They attracted distinguished visitors, who were generally impressed by the people's initiative and determination to succeed on the land, but who did not always detect the tenacity of their Aboriginality. However, their prosperity was soon undermined by government apathy and white opposition.

THE EROSION OF AUTONOMY

The initiatives of those at Raukkan were stifled by ill luck and the discrimination of settlers and governments, as explained in Graham Jenkins's *Conquest of the Ngarrindjeri* (1979). The community survived by seasonal work on pastoral properties, the wool-washing enterprise and financial donations, but other employment remained a problem. Subdivision of pastoral properties for farms reduced the amount of seasonal work in the district, and the South Australian government consistently refused them more land, which meant that the farming they desired to follow was not viable. The government also denied them ownership of Raukkan, or even freehold title to building land, to enable them to build their own homes securely. In the 1890s, their successful wool-washing venture ended when new irrigation schemes on the upper Murray reduced the river's downstream flow. In 1891 five Ngarrindjeri learned bootmaking and within a year their instructor reported that their workmanship was 'equal to any other work in the same class'; however, no boot manufacturer was found who would employ these or other Aboriginal bootmakers. The only alternative was to establish a factory at Raukkan itself, but the Aborigines' Friends' Association could not provide sufficient capital. The government refused help, in keeping with prevailing ideas of making citizens self-reliant. Besides, it was unlikely that a Raukkan factory could compete with the prices of the larger-scale factories in Adelaide. Ngarrindjeri initiative and willingness to become self-supporting was continually thwarted, and Raukkan became a community without a secure future.[23]

Poonindie had no future at all. This reserve, which had been self-supporting since the 1860s, was dismantled by the South Australian government in 1894 to open the land for European settlers.[24] In Victoria and New South Wales the attack on Coranderrk and the Cummeragunja took two forms: bureaucratic and legislative.

Bureaucratic control increased with an 1869 Act that gave the Victorian Aborigines Protection Board greater power over reserves, and control over work and wages, the movement of adults and the removal of children. Once Coranderrk's economy was switched to hop production, the Board assumed tighter control and skimmed any profits for general revenue. This intervention led to bitter quarrels between John Green and the Board, finally resulting in his resignation. The Board sought to close Coranderrk in 1875 and move the people to the Murray, hoping to save the steep running costs and the high incidence of respiratory disease. The move would also please covetous settlers who might pay handsomely for Coranderrk's fertile land.

These events led to a state of rebellion at Coranderrk for the next decade. The people pushed for the retention of their reserve, which, declared Barak, was 'my father's country'. The people also pushed for the reinstatement of their friend John Green. A resident remarked of Rev. Strickland, the fifth new manager after Green: 'He does not sympathise with us. He does not go amongst us. When he does, he just passes through, makes himself quite a stranger . . . My wife heard him say that he would not like to live here at all, because it was just like living in hell.'[25] Trouble was also present on other Victorian stations, especially at Ramahyuck and Lake Condah, where the managers insisted on ruling the residents like schoolchildren. The punishments they inflicted, including thrashing, withdrawal of rations and expulsions from the station, were met with further recalcitrance from Aboriginal residents. Rebellion broke out several times around 1880 at Lake Condah as Rev. John Stahle and his wife Mary battled with Ernest and Maggie Mobourne in particular over discipline problems.[26] However, resistance was strongest at Coranderrk causing Rev. Hagenauer, the Ramahyuck manager, to complain: 'if the angel Gabriel came to manage Coranderrk he would not be able to do it satisfactorily'.[27]

The Coranderrk residents, led by William Barak and his 'speakers' Robert Wandin and Tom Dunnolly, instigated protests through petitions, strikes, interviews with the press, letters to the editor, discussions with sympathetic residents in Healesville, and two 70-kilometre walks to Melbourne to meet with government ministers. One Melbourne paper, the *Leader*, wrote of a deputation in 1882: 'From each face there comes a calm, steadfast, civilised look; each of these manly figures is costumed in civilised and decent fashion; the attitude of each individual is not slouching but erect, as that of a self-respecting man, conscious of his manhood.'[28] These men were driven by the hope that the land was theirs and they were going to make the farming community work in an Aboriginal and permanent way. Their steadfast Aboriginality is symbolised by the wonderful traditional artworks that William Barak began to paint around this time, which now reside in Federation Square in Melbourne.[29] The results of these protests were a royal commission in 1877 and a parliamentary inquiry in 1881. The Kulin's petition to the commission called for Green's reinstatement and 'then we will show the country that the station could self-support itself'.[30]

Coranderrk families at their Christmas holiday camp, Yarra River. From left to right: Jim Young, Elsie White, Julia Russell (seated), Bill Russell, Dan Russell, Michael Davis, Joe McDougall. COURTESY OF THE F. ENDACOTT COLLECTION, MUSEUM OF VICTORIA (XP2214).

The inquiries opposed the Board's sale of Coranderrk and recommended funding for maintenance to ensure it remained self-supporting. (It stayed silent, however, on Green's reinstatement.) The Victorian Chief Secretary, Graham Berry, was so impressed with the Coranderrk people's stand that he made the reserve a 'permanent reservation', which could only be revoked by Act of Parliament and not simply at the Board's whim. However, the Board's coercive and petty control of Coranderrk remained to undermine the independence of the people.[31]

In 1907, Cummeragunja's promising development was ended by the New South Wales Aborigines Protection Board when it revoked the twenty individual smallholdings. It argued the men misused their blocks and had sown fewer crops by leasing the blocks to outsiders for grazing purposes during 1903–07. However, this was an intelligent business decision during the Federation drought that killed two-thirds of the state's livestock and forced hundreds off the land, before being ended by flooding rains. The 'Cummera' farmers, by good farm management, gained some return by leasing the remaining grass, but the Board did not agree. The Board's motives for ending the people's individual success were a desire to make the able-bodied and successful support the whole community.

Ironically, those Aboriginal families who adopted the European ethic of individual enterprise were rewarded by being forced into a co-operative effort. Not only were the individual blocks revoked, but a European overseer was appointed to manage farming at Cummeragunja.[32]

The second attack on these two communities was legislative. It stemmed from European concern about Aboriginal reserves as welfare places in an age of minimal government support, and anxiety about the number of light-skinned Aboriginal residents of part-European descent. This concern for 'whites' being reared among 'blacks' was compounded as Coranderrk was an asylum for orphans, most of whom were of mixed descent. Those of mixed descent formed 62 per cent of Coranderrk's residents in 1877, as opposed to 7–42 per cent at other Victorian reserves. These fears led to the expulsion of so-called 'half-castes' from reserves under the Victorian Aborigines Act of 1886. The Act stated that only 'full bloods' and 'half-castes' under eight or over 34 years of age were entitled to aid and to reside on reserves. The Board argued it was 'unreasonable that the State should continue to support able-bodied men who were well able to earn their own living'. It stated the Act would 'merge the half-caste population into the general community'.[33] In one move, the Board's costs would be reduced and the Aboriginal race would vanish as the 'full bloods' aged and died, and the 'half-castes' were blended to whiteness. This was a deliberate policy of absorption, and the New South Wales government adopted the Victorian Act almost verbatim in 1909.

The impact of this dispersal policy on Aboriginal people was disastrous. Those removed to fend for themselves faced a tough time. Besides the difficulties of supporting large families on seasonal and low rural wages, they faced job discrimination and felt the chill of white prejudice. Most were ejected on the eve of the 1890s Depression, although the government offered rations to those in 'necessitous circumstances' for three years and clothing for up to five years. Some remained in miserable circumstances, causing the Victorian government in 1910 to reverse its policy and allow those in need to return to reserves. However, Coranderrk and other reserves were by then in decline, as the 1886 Act ruined the viability of these once-thriving settlements by removing their younger and able-bodied workers. At Coranderrk there were only fifteen able-bodied men left after the dispersals. Hop production declined, and little cash flowed into the reserve from outside seasonal labour. Coranderrk became rundown and its residents dispirited. This situation was paralleled in other Victorian reserves and later at Cummeragunja, where the population was halved within ten years as 150 left and farming dwindled. The reserves' very success led to their demise. Diane Barwick noted ironically: 'because they had proved competent farmers and achieved a working-class standard of living the Board believed that the dispersal policy would benefit the half-castes, giving them complete independence and new opportunities for 'absorption' into the general population. Because they had made the land profitable, there was intense political pressure for its resumption and sale.'[34]

A third attack of closures followed these bureaucratic and legislative controls. Neighbours, who had always clamoured for Aboriginal reserve lands, quickly applied pressure once the settlements declined after the dispersal policy. In 1893 Coranderrk lost 970 of its 1960 hectares. There was no public outcry since this was done stealthily as part of a multi-item land bill. Framlingham and Ramahyuck were also radically reduced in size. All reserves were closed and most leased and finally sold over the next two decades, except Lake Tyers in Gippsland, where the reserve remnants were sent in 1925–26. Its population, which was still regulated by an Aboriginal Act, swelled to about 250 people. Coranderrk, which the people's protest had secured as a 'permanent reserve', was harder to sell, but parliament succeeded in doing so in 1948 after refusing to hand it to Aboriginal returned servicemen.[35] Cummeragunja also came under attack as sections were leased to neighbours in the 1920s, and all but 80 hectares revoked in 1959, allegedly because it was 'no longer needed by the Aborigines'. Other New South Wales reserves were sold up. Indeed, Heather Goodall has revealed that half of the 27,000 acres of Aboriginal reserve land in 1911 were revoked by 1927, and another quarter leased out to white farmers.[36] This second act of dispossession of Aboriginal land—a repeat of frontier times—also took place in other colonies. In South Australia by 1913, of the 97 Aboriginal reserves gazetted after the 1830s, 64 had been sold or leased to Europeans.[37]

The reserves, in spite of being places of control, had succeeded in the goal for which they had been established: to protect the Aboriginal remnant. This has been demonstrated by researchers Janet McCalman and Len Smith, who painstakingly reconstructed the Victorian Aboriginal population backwards from genealogies. They found that almost all Aboriginal people today are descended from families who lived on Victorian reserves.[38] William Barak and those many other Aboriginal people who fought to retain their reserves sensed their importance. It was Billibellary's radical hope to get land to farm like white people, in order to survive as an Aboriginal community. Even that hope seemed lost with the closure of many reserves by 1910. Coranderrk, which had been started by Billibellary's son, Simon Wonga, was a mere shell by this time. However, by then Billibellary's policy had done its work for Aboriginal survival.

Campers at Aggie's Swamp, Swan Hill, c. 1910. From left to right: Kathryn Farrell, Jacky Logan and Agnes Edwards. COURTESY OF JAN PENNEY.

REMOVING CHILDREN

Those on reserves, especially menfolk, had often worked off the reserves in the rural economy for part of each year to earn cash wages. The 1886 and 1909 Acts increased the number of Aboriginal people living off reserves. Under these Acts, it was young people of mixed descent who felt the sting of Aborigines Protection Board controls and their absorptionist policies. Indeed, the people called them 'Destruction Boards' for they broke up families in a racist policy which operated dependant on the colour of one's skin. The fragmentation of families increased in New South Wales after the passage of amending legislation in 1915, which increased the powers of the Aborigines Protection Board. The Board could now, without parental consent or court approval, take Aboriginal children of mixed descent as young as a few weeks old, and place them in foster or training homes and then into apprenticeships or work. Of course, children were also taken from white families for neglect in this era, and even at the parents' request, due to unruliness or poverty. However, research has shown that authorities tried to reunite white families, whereas there was no attempt to bring together Aboriginal parents and their removed children, pointing to a racist motivation in these removals.[39] Peter Read, who researched child removal in New South Wales between 1909 and 1940, believes between 5000 and 6000 children were separated from family during that time—the case books showing it was not only for alleged neglect, but sometimes just for 'being Aboriginal'.[40] This was the logic of the 1886 Victorian Aborigines Act which encoded the Protection Board's aim of the 'absorption of the whole race into the general community'.[41] But what did the removal policy mean for individuals?

Doug Nicholls never forgot the day his sixteen-year-old sister Hilda was officially kidnapped: 'the police came without warning except for the precaution of ensuring that the men had been sent over the sandhills to cut timber. Some of the girls eluded the police by swimming the Murray. Other Yorta Yorta children were forced into the cars, with mothers wailing and threatening the officers with any weapons at hand'.[42] These children were not neglected youths who needed protection, but healthy, happy adolescents with loving families. A Yorta Yorta woman, Margaret Tucker, was rounded up at Moonahculla at the age of thirteen and packed off with her sister to the Cootamundra Domestic Training Home for Aboriginal Girls. Tucker was bundled into a police car while her mother wrestled with the police and 'my last memory of her for many years was her waving pathetically, as we waved back and called out goodbye to her, but we were too far away for her to hear us'.[43] Many years later, she learned her mother was found wailing and dishevelled in the bush outside Deniliquin, which Tucker recalled in the film *Lousy Little Sixpence*.

Margaret Tucker was taught to cook, sew and clean. At fifteen she was placed in an apprenticeship in Sydney, to provide cheap domestic labour for a European family. Her first mistress was extremely vindictive. Although trained for housework, Tucker had to also undertake child-minding, gardening and lawnmowing. She was never given sufficient to eat for such heavy work, nor adequate clothing, and stole food from the pantry to quell her rumbling stomach. She was beaten when caught. Margaret Tucker became a lonely, frightened teenager who was never allowed out or to see her family hundreds of kilometres away. She was driven to attempt suicide with rat bait. This attracted the attention of the Protection Board and she was shifted to a succession of far kinder mistresses in Sydney and Walgett. Yet she remained cheap domestic labour. After nine years of domestic service under the Board's guardianship, she had earned the meagre sum of £80, whereas European women then earned £50 a year.[44]

Jimmie Barker, a Murawi man of mixed descent who served his apprenticeship on a pastoral property for four years from 1915, was paid the paltry sum of £32 over that period. On his first day, his boss told him that he must not run away and if he did he would be captured and gaoled: 'I must not address anyone by their Christian name, and must do everything I was asked to do. Any refusal or rudeness would be dealt with by him. He stressed that I must not raise my hands to anyone, even in self-defence. If any black touched a white man he would be shot down.'[45] This was the black experience in the wider white world into which these young people were dispersed. From their apprenticeships, both Tucker and Barker went back in the 1920s to the settlements of Cummeragunja and Brewarrina respectively. However, the missions were increasingly becoming places of control, rather than the islands of Aboriginal protection, independence and radical hope they initially had been.

Increasingly, Aboriginal settlements in south-eastern Australia came under government instead of mission control, which decreased their humanitarian tone. With the stifling of Aboriginal agricultural initiative, the settlements became ration depots, not farms. Once a week, the now dependent residents lined up for their rations and, at some missions, management extended to morning musters where the orders for the day were given. When young Jimmie Barker and his brother first moved to Brewarrina reserve from a fringe camp in 1912, he experienced the daily muster of the 50 Aboriginal boys who were lorded over by the manager, who carried a stockwhip and barked orders. Jimmie recalled: 'It was during this first morning with the manager and the boys that I realised that something different and unpleasant had come into our lives. We had no freedom, things were not right.'[46]

Physical violence was part of life on the mission. Aboriginal schoolchildren were cuffed on the ear, or punched or kicked—sometimes to the point of severe injury—by their European teachers. They were also subjected to daily denigration, which humiliated Jimmie:

> During my first lessons from these men I learnt that as I was black, or partly coloured, there was no place in Australia for me. I learnt that anyone of my colour would always be an outcast and different from a white person. It gave me the firm idea that an Aboriginal, even if he was only slightly coloured, was mentally and physically inferior to all others. He was the lowest class known in the world, he was little better than an animal; in fact, dogs were sometimes to be preferred. As I was less than twelve years old it was impossible to disbelieve men of authority who were much older. I tried to stop their remarks from bothering me too much, but it was hard to adjust to being treated with such cruelty and contempt.[47]

Aboriginal people on reserves withdrew into their own domain to maintain a private life and regain some self-esteem. This protected their Aboriginal identity beyond the scrutiny of reserve managers and police, who acted as guardians where there were no managers. With initiative thwarted, some channelled their energies into less positive directions—cards, alcohol and a craze for sport—by which they overcame the boredom of reserve life and maintained pride and identity. The more the managers opposed these activities, the more some people pursued them. There were a thousand and one ways to resist the manager's control and retain some autonomy. The Coranderrk people even established their own alternative church services in 1916 and refused to attend those conducted by the manager.[48]

Above all, the maintenance of a private life and identity by Aboriginal people depended upon continuing many traditional ideas. The kinship system and its basic values of rights and obligations towards others remained. Missionaries lamented that religious ideas, mourning rites and belief in sorcery survived. Aboriginal reminiscences of the early twentieth century are full of accounts of how the old people still taught the young traditional stories, hunting skills and fear of malevolent spirits. The people battled on, surviving the increased controls placed on them by petty managers and burgeoning government departments, supposedly in the name of protection. Jimmie Barker remarked of the years around 1910: 'Despite our miserable condition at the Mission many of the old people clung to their beliefs. These had to be kept secret when white people were around, but talking among ourselves gave us some comfort'.[49] Pride, identity and a radical hope for the future were needed, as the world outside the reserves was increasingly being shaped by hardening racial ideas.

6

THE AGE OF RACE AND NORTHERN FRONTIERS

The rise of science and the rage for classifying the world from the seventeenth century onwards inevitably led to considerations of human difference. The conjunction of this discussion in European scientific circles with European imperialism, colonial exploitation and growing secularism created a shift from an environmental to a racial explanation of human difference in the decades after the 1850s. This was the very moment that settlers were pushing into frontiers across the northern half of Australia from Queensland, across the top to Western Australia. They carried with them increasingly fixed ideas about Aboriginal people and their alleged inferiority, more so than settlers on southern frontiers.

THE INVENTION OF RACE

As eighteenth-century scientists contemplated the world around them, they pondered human difference and its causes and consequences. Johann Blumenbach, one of the first to turn to this topic in *The Natural Varieties of Mankind* (1775), pioneered the study of skulls and comparative physiology. He believed humans were one species, but formed five races distinguished by physical and cultural features: the Caucasian, Mongolian, Ethiopian, American and Malay. Georges Cuvier, who wrote half a century later, listed three races instead, and claimed ethnocentrically that the Caucasian was the dominant and most beautiful. Robert Chambers, who like Cuvier thought in terms of hierarchies of races, argued in his *Vestiges of Creation* (1844) that, while humans were a single species, some races were more developed than others, and some more degenerate: mere vestiges of past forms. The biblical view of creation—that all humans were from one creation—formed a barrier against the development of racial views of innate difference. However, Charles Lyell, in his *Principles of Geology* (1830–31), demonstrated that the world had to be far older than the Bible claimed, for the physical processes at work on the earth's rocks had taken far longer than the biblical dating of a creation 7000 years before. Lyell also showed that the fossil record revealed multiple extinctions of species through earth's history. Such thinking challenged human equality based on the view that all were descended from the founding parents, Adam and Eve. Charles Darwin carried Lyell's book with him on the *Beagle* as he voyaged in the mid-1830s contemplating the natural world.[1]

Whereas the Bible stressed unity, science and pseudoscientific ideas such as phrenology now emphasised disunity. Samuel Morton, in his *Crania Americana* (1839), argued—from measuring skulls—that Native Americans and African peoples had no ability for civilisation and were better in slavery: freeing them would lead to their extinction. As polygenic ideas and the assessment of skulls to 'measure' ability grew, the improving and assimilative hope of the Civilising Mission faded.[2] Others argued in similar vein. Charles Smith discussed the idea of competition between races and extinctions in his *Natural History of the Human Species* (1848), but this only formalised what many people had thought for some time. The young Charles Darwin had written while visiting New South Wales in 1836: 'wherever the European has trod, death seems to pursue the Aboriginal . . . The varieties of man act on each other; in the same way as different species of animals—the stronger always extirpate the weaker.'[3] Darwin observed what colonialism caused, but claimed it was a natural phenomenon. Robert Knox, in his *Races of Man* (1850), emphasised racial difference and competition, believing that fair, stronger races always exterminated the black ones, which were weaker. He took no pleasure in this, but stated it as fact.

Few colonists read these books, but the main idea of immutable racial inferiority filtered down into popular thinking, to take its place alongside the discourse of Aboriginal 'savagery'. It rested alongside another and older idea of the Great Chain of Being, which ranked all living creatures in a hierarchy. Europeans ranked highest of the human races and Aboriginal people lowest, nearest the animals. The pseudoscience of phrenology was influential in such claims of inherent difference, phrenologists claiming the head's shape and its bumps indicated the brain within, and different personality traits and abilities. By reading these signs, an individual's characteristics and abilities—or that of a race—could be revealed. Practitioners of this 'science' told colonial audiences that Aboriginal skulls revealed deficiencies in the so-called moral and intellectual organs of the brain, and excesses in those areas allegedly controlling the passions, aggression and the observational instinct.[4] It 'confirmed' the older claims of savagery. Once again, Aboriginal people were treated as being all the same on the basis of assumptions now seen as ludicrous, but which were believed by many at the time to be scientific 'truths'.

Since the abominations of Nazism in the Second World War, the idea of race has been rejected as wrong, but also unscientific. So-called racial characteristics—hair, eye and skin colour, and shape of facial features—form an inconsequential amount of the total human genetic make-up, and have no explanatory power biologically. The UNESCO Declaration on Race and Racial Prejudice of 27 November 1978 stated categorically:

> All human beings belong to a single species and are descended from a common stock . . . Any theory which involves the claim that racial or ethnic groups are inherently superior or inferior, thus implying that some would be entitled to dominate or eliminate others, presumed to be inferior, or which bases value judgments on racial differentiation, has no scientific foundation . . .[5]

Human genome research in recent years has confirmed the similarity of all peoples. Robert Knox's reading of history as driven by racial causation can just as easily be explained by the environmental and other advantages enjoyed by European colonisers, as Jared Diamond has argued in his influential book *Guns, Germs and Steel* (1998).

However, Knox and others who claimed race was the key to understanding history became widely influential in the late nineteenth century. The idea of race assumed massive social power and importance in human behaviour, becoming the dominant explanation of human difference in Western thinking, and the key justification for discrimination against others in custom and law. Human difference was allegedly fixed and explained by skin colour and other racial characteristics. Humans were categorised into races that were claimed to be immutable, each group having innate racial characteristics shared by all, which explained ability and behaviour. 'Inferior' Indigenous races could never be part of colonial societies and thus education was pointless as their 'inferiority' was unchangeable.

Not all accepted this view. Most Christians still believed Aboriginal people were fellow children of God who had unfortunately degenerated into paganism and immorality. Mr French told the Victorian Select Committee on Aborigines in 1858 that 'the general intelligence of the adults seems little if at all inferior to that of the average of white men'; Mr Strutt said that they were 'in many ways as intelligent as the white race'; while Mr Aitken thought them 'intelligent and quick'. Their degeneracy was deep, but with assistance and time, they could become the equal of Europeans. However, others agreed with Mr Gottreux, who claimed their intelligence to be 'very low, incapable of mental instruction'.[6] Pessimism, as well as views driven by racial thinking that we may call racist, became predominant. By the 1850s, the 'last of his tribe', immortalised in Henry Kendall's poem of the same name, became a governing colonial idea as colonists prophesied, and some even hoped for, the Aboriginal demise.

The reservoir of racial ideas held by a growing majority of settlers was boosted when Charles Darwin's ideas about evolution in the natural world were applied by social theorists to human development (but not immediately or fully by Darwin himself). Darwin proposed in *On the Origin of Species* (1859) that new species evolved through a mechanism of 'natural selection', by which favourable variations developed to form new species, and previous forms died out. Many who believed in the superiority of the white race argued that Darwinian thought, when applied to human societies, explained why the black races vanished in the face of European colonisation.

DISPLAYING SAVAGERY

Evolutionary theory led to a worldwide scientific interest in Australia's Aboriginal peoples, deemed the most 'primitive' of all. Investigations of human and cultural remains 'proved' various race-based notions, which further downgraded Aboriginal status in circular arguments. Scientific interest in Aboriginal remains led to abhorrent grave robbery by collectors to service a global trade in Aboriginal relics and remains. The intersection of violence and disease-induced deaths on Australian frontiers with the rise of anatomical science enabled European and Australian museums to collect shelves of Aboriginal skulls and other remains to indulge the fancies of anatomical theorists. Edward Ramsay, curator of the National Museum in Sydney, was in contact with collectors and exchanged remains with overseas museums for other valued items. Ramsay published various editions of his *Hints for the Preservation of Specimens of Natural History* between 1876 and 1900, which included the advice that: 'SKELETONS of

Aborigines are much wanted . . . Skulls of Aborigines found suspended around native dwellings are of little value, but authentic skulls may be obtained from the graves of the natives of each tribe.'[7]

The most intense interest focused on the Aboriginal Tasmanians, who became the subject of no fewer than 120 scientific and pseudoscientific books and articles by scholars worldwide in the late nineteenth century.[8] When William Lanne, a whaler and the last 'full blood' Aboriginal Tasmanian male, died in 1869, there was an unholy scramble for his body. Despite the best efforts of the government, two doctors, William Crowther and George Stokell, competed for the remains—the former to send them to London's Royal College of Surgeons for study, the latter to obtain them on behalf of the Royal Society of Tasmania. It is believed Crowther severed the head and Stokell then cut off the hands and feet to prevent Crowther getting more. The body was buried with due deference by Hobart's citizens and Lanne's fellow sailors—for he was a whaler—but then it was exhumed for an inquiry and later lost. The government, genuinely appalled by the desecration and its failure to prevent it, passed an Act regulating the use of human remains.[9]

Trugernanna, at the time reputedly the 'last' Pallawah woman, died in 1876 in fear of a similar fate. Her body was exhumed after two years for scientific study on condition of not being displayed. However, this condition was broken in 1904, when her remains were displayed in the Hobart Museum until 1947. After vigorous protests, Trugernanna's ashes were scattered in 1976 on the waters of D'Entrecasteaux Channel, as was her wish. However, she was not the last 'full blood' or the 'last Tasmanian' as popularly thought. Suke, another woman of full descent, lived at Kangaroo Island until 1888, and other Pallawah descendants of sealers and their Aboriginal women survived on Bass Strait islands.[10]

Members of the public also evinced a desire to view the 'savage'. Phineas Barnum, the American showman, made exotic displays respectable with his American Museum in New York after 1841. A global trade emerged to exhibit 'freaks' and 'savages' and some Aboriginal people were soon enmeshed in it. In 1883, nine people were taken from Palm Island by American entrepreneur Robert Cunningham, who toured the group overseas. If they went willingly in the face of inducements, it is likely they had little idea of what they were about to embark upon. They were billed as 'cannibals' and 'savages' and performed for audiences across America and Europe. Ethnographers in several European capitals examined and measured them. After three years the group had dwindled to three, tuberculosis claiming most of the others. Billy, Jenny and her son Toby chose to take another tour through Russia and England before Cunningham ended the tour in 1888. Nothing else is known of them. Cunningham took another group of eight in 1892 and two, another Billy and Jenny, returned to Australia in 1896. The remains of another member, Tambo, were repatriated in 1994, after being found in a funeral director's premises in Cleveland, Ohio, the year before. After his death in Cleveland in early 1884, Tambo's body had

Cape Barren Islanders, surviving Pallawah people, March 1893. COURTESY OF THE JOHN WATT BEATTIE COLLECTION, NATIONAL LIBRARY OF AUSTRALIA (NLA.PIC-VN3410795).

been exhibited in a dime museum for some years. The experiences of these, at first unwilling, performers are narrated in Roslyn Poignant's *Professional Savages* (2004).

Governments also colluded in this display of Aboriginal people. In 1886 a Colonial and Indian Exhibition was held in London to display the British Empire to the world. Most colonial governments supplied exhibitions. The Victorian government sent a diorama depicting native life, as well as two boys, William Clark and Willie King from Ramahyuck mission in Gippsland. The diorama showed a bush setting with a native encampment and plaster models of an Aboriginal family—the father skinning an animal, the mother preparing some food and a child watching on. Others were in the background—all were naked. Lynette Russell observed that the exhibition was 'shameless voyeurism, the sanctioned display of nudity given scientific and imperial approval'. She added: 'the objectified and essentially naked bodies represent civilisation's antithesis. The people are objects on display like silent specimens in a frozen zoo'.[11] However, the two boys' civilised demeanour subverted this display of savagery. Certainly, while en route to England they charmed their fellow ship's passengers with their intelligent conversation, William Clark's accordion play, and their participation in playing drafts and attending church services. They survived and were returned home—no doubt with a wealth of tales.[12]

NATIONAL DREAMING

Social Darwinism, or the 'doomed race' theory, gathered wide acceptance in 'white man's countries' by the 1880s. Of Australia, Henry Reynolds remarked: 'local knowledge and evolutionary theory conspired to place the idea of the dying race beyond the reach of debate'.[13] The notion explained what most believed: that some races were better than others, and the weaker ones faded away. In January 1888 the *Age* stated: 'where two races whose stages of progression differ greatly are brought into contact, the inferior race is doomed to wither and disappear . . . The process seems to be in accordance with a natural law which, however it may clash with human benevolence, is clearly beneficial to mankind at large by providing for the survival of the fittest'.[14] Vincent Lesina told the Queensland Parliament in 1901: 'the law of evolution says that the nigger shall disappear in the onward progress of the white man. There is really no hope at all'.[15]

There was to be no lament. Like the law of Providence, the law of Social Darwinism absolved settlers for the disappearance of Aboriginal people—it was the working of this law, not white colonialism, that was at fault. Indeed, history

THE AGE OF RACE AND NORTHERN FRONTIERS 107

was rewritten during the Australian nationalist dreaming period from the 1880s, to claim settlers treated Aboriginal people kindly and did everything to ensure their survival.

The notion of the 'survival of the fittest' assumed differing levels of racial worthiness. It induced anxiety in white settler societies—Australia, the United States and South Africa—about race competition and the mixing of races. This has been recently outlined in Marilyn Lake and Henry Reynolds's *Drawing the Global Colour Line* (2008). Settler Australians believed that their coming national greatness rested on their being part of the British Empire, and above all, part of the white race. Australians, Britishers and whiteness were differing parts of the one seamless identity.[16] Popular thinking argued that the Anglo-Saxon race must be kept pure, since intermixing would create racial contamination and decline. The *Bulletin* stated in 1901: 'If Australia is to be a country fit for our children and their children to live in, we must KEEP THE BREED PURE. The half-caste usually inherits the vices of both races and the virtues of neither. Do you want Australia to be a community of mongrels?'[17] The Labour movement's journalist William Lane, with powerful crudeness, wrote in 1888 that he would rather his daughter was 'dead in her coffin than kissing a black man on the mouth or nursing a little coffee-coloured brat that she was mother to'.[18] Newspapers routinely published such racial obscenities, fed by nationalist dreams of being exceptional and ambiguous fears of invasion from 'the coloured races' to the north.[19] These ideas were played out in the Jack Johnson–Tommy Burns world heavyweight title fight in Sydney in 1908. This first official match between a black and a white, won by the African-American Johnson, was billed as a 'race war' and caused a frenzy of anxiety.[20] Needless to say, despite the frequent use of Aboriginal women by European men, there were only a handful of interracial marriages in colonial society.

Social Darwinism defined Aboriginal policy. The *Age* in 1869 urged more funding for Aboriginal people, but by 1888 argued assistance was useless, since Darwinian law meant 'the spread of the progressive races and the squeezing out of the inferior ones'. In 1896 it claimed 'the black race has decayed, and is rapidly dying out from causes quite outside the power of the white man to control'.[21] While many shrugged helplessly in the face of this 'inevitable' outcome, a veil of silence was often drawn over the details of colonial history. Unproven and strange eugenic claims to justify Aboriginal 'inability to progress' were made in allegedly reputable places, like Alan Carroll's pseudoscientific *Science of Man and Australasian Anthropological Journal*. An article in 1898 alleged that once Aboriginal children passed puberty 'the sutures of the cranium begin to consolidate, and the forepart of the brain ceases to develop as it does in other races'.[22] By 1900 most settler Australians held derogatory views towards Aboriginal Australians, which were a mixture of ignorance, indifference, fanciful racial theories, a belief in white superiority, and the need to rationalise the continued dispossession of Aboriginal land. In this vein, settler Australians shaped their Constitution, which failed to count Aboriginal people with other Australians, and passed immigration laws that excluded people of colour and expelled Pacific Islanders from Queensland in 1906. The settlers' national dreaming was of a white Australia.

NORTHERN FRONTIERS

By 1850 southern Australia was in the possession of European invaders, except for vast unwanted and virtually unknown tracts of arid country from the Great Victoria Desert and the Nullarbor Plain in the west to the Simpson Desert and the Channel Country in the centre. Between 1840 and 1860, the interior was penetrated by men like Charles Sturt, who dreamed to 'be the first to place my foot in the centre'.[23] By 1848 arduous and daring expeditions by Eyre, Sturt, Leichhardt and Kennedy had crossed the Nullarbor, ventured into the Simpson Desert and the Channel Country, crossed the eastern half of the Top End and traversed Cape York. By 1858 A.C. Gregory had crossed the east Kimberley and Top End in reverse and travelled into the Channel Country. By 1862 Burke and Wills and also McDouall Stuart had crossed the continent and F.T. Gregory pushed into the Pilbara. Between 1869 and 1879, John Forrest, Ernest Giles, Alexander Forrest and Peter Warburton criss-crossed Western Australia via the Victoria, Gibson and Great Sandy deserts and across the west Kimberley, consolidating colonial claims on the continent through the making of maps and the planting of flags.[24]

European explorers received a mixed reception from Indigenous landowners. Most owed much of their success, even their lives in some cases, to Aboriginal guides. Wylie, a Nyoongar man from Albany, saved Edward Eyre with bush tucker on the Nullarbor in 1840, being later rewarded with weekly rations, £2 and a medal.[25] Some Aboriginal people assisted explorers on their lands, notably those at Coopers Creek who saved John King of the Burke and Wills expedition from starvation in 1861.[26] Others displayed hostility and set fire to the land to drive them off. Stuart was ambushed twice, and Giles and his men were fortunate to escape an attack at their camp. He wrote: 'I ordered these intruders out. Thereupon they became very saucy and disagreeable and gave me to understand that this was their country and their water.'[27] Any Aboriginal lands and resources that looked promising were claimed, mapped and opened to pastoral settlement by colonial governments, without negotiating with the original owners. Northern Queensland was settled in the 1860s, Central Australia and the Northern Territory in the 1870s, and the Kimberley in the 1880s.

As in the south, a violent struggle for the land was acted out on northern frontiers, ameliorated by some humane encounters. But in many ways the two frontiers were very different, due to their varied terrains and being 40–80 years apart in their making, which created differences in technologies and ideas. First, the huge northern frontier was mostly arid and extremely inaccessible, which made settlement slower and development of an economic base more difficult than in the south. Second, the European population remained small because of this aridity and very fearful: the distance and the lack of police meant there were few restraints on settler violence. Besides, in the remote north the police were both Protectors of Aboriginal people and agents of their conquerors. Third, the immensity of the northern frontier meant many areas were not fully conquered and the land open to ecological transformation for a generation. Fourth, the northern frontiers were settled in an era of new gun technology in which accurate, multi-shot, rapid-fire rifles existed. Marksmen bearing these new arms could hit targets over 500 metres away. Very effective close-quarter handguns were also in use, as were horses, which could help run down warriors. Fifth, following the granting of responsible government to most Australian colonies in the 1850s, colonial authorities were in charge, not the British government. Colonial administrators took a more hard-headed approach to relations with Aboriginal people. Finally, Western racism after the 1850s, as we have seen, claimed Aboriginal people were 'primitive' and inherently of a lower type and so morally did not have a right to stop settlement by more 'progressive' races.

Pastoral expansion spilled into the Darling Downs after 1840 and steadily spread into southern Queensland. Trouble erupted into the usual pattern of invasion and resistance, as on southern frontiers. But some spectacular events, together with new racial attitudes and gun technology, compounded frontier violence. Eleven people, including eight members of the Fraser family—Martha, three of her sons and four daughters—were massacred by Jiman warriors as they slept at their Hornet Bank property, west of Taroom, in 1857. This was an act of premeditated revenge by the Jiman for the rape of their women, shootings and the invasion of their land. The Native Police and armed settlers took revenge, in which Gordon Reid has estimated 150–300 Jiman were killed. Then, in 1861, nineteen of the Gregson family at Cullin-la-Ringo were killed by Kairi in revenge for two deaths and invasion. Noel Loos argues 'these two events left indelible scars on Queensland's race relations'.[28]

By the end of the 1860s, the relentless surge of pastoral adventurers saw much of Far North Queensland intensively grazed by sheep and cattle. The battle for the land continued as settlers sought to 'keep out' the original owners who tried to defend their heritage. In reply, cattle and sheep were stolen by Aboriginal warriors, then yarded and eaten at leisure. The land was burned to drive settlers away. Gold discoveries on the Gilbert, Mitchell and Palmer rivers brought over 20,000 diggers to the region, many of them Chinese, increasing the violence to both land and people. The Strau family were killed on the Palmer Road west of Cooktown in 1874, causing outrage. W.H. Corfield, a bullock owner, wrote: 'If at any time I felt a compunction in using my rifle, I lost it when I thought of the murders of Strau, his wife and daughter, and the outrages committed on them.'[29] Placenames in the region—'Battle Camp' and 'Butchers Hill'—attest to the subsequent retribution. Author Mary Durack wrote of her grandfather Patrick Durack's pioneering at Coopers Creek: 'settlers now openly declared that Western Queensland could only be habitable for whites when the last of the blacks had been killed out—by bullet or by bait'.[30]

The Queensland frontier became an armed camp and its Native Police were the shock troops. This force was introduced from New South Wales to prevent Aboriginal attacks by constant patrolling, to act as a punitive force after incidents and to capture Aboriginal 'criminals'. Equipped with horses, Snyder rifles and Aboriginal bush craft, the small force of 120 troopers in 1860 made a large impact. The white officers believed in the rule of force, Commandant Morriset stating in 1861 that 'blacks only understand brute force . . . the more lenient you are the worse they become'.[31] The black troopers far from home, who were not acting against their own people, and who were encouraged by a culture of brutality in the force, took swift retribution. A Burketown journalist in July 1868 reported Sub-Inspector Uhr and his Native Police's revenge for the killing of a settler named Cameron: 'everybody in the district is delighted with the wholesale slaughter dealt out by the native police, and thank Mr Uhr for his energy in ridding the district of fifty-nine myalls'.[32] Later reports were more circumspect about the number and labelled the killings as 'dispersals'. The force was disbanded in 1896 after scandal over its violence to Aboriginal people.

The Aboriginal defence of country was vigorous. Warriors resisted incursions ferociously by killing vulnerable settlers. They also destroyed about 5 per cent of settlers' cattle per annum, took valuable horses and stole supplies from bullock teams en route to stations or the diggings. Geoffrey Bolton estimated that 15 per cent of the first pastoralists in North Queensland were killed in Aboriginal attacks, so deadly was their defence of country.[33] Noel Loos's exhaustive research on the Aboriginal resistance in North Queensland revealed there were 470 reported 'allied' deaths at the hands of Aboriginal resisters: 304 Europeans, 102 Chinese, 43 Aboriginal people, fourteen Pacific Islanders and seven others.[34] Other unreported deaths no doubt occurred. But the cost was high for Aboriginal people. Some estimates—and that is all we can say—suggest a death rate of one white to every ten Aboriginal people. After researching *Invasion and Resistance* (1982), which covers the violent North Queensland frontier over four decades to 1896, Loos stated: 'to suggest at least 4000 Aborigines died as a result of frontier resistance in North Queensland between 1861 and 1896 is probably so conservative as to be misleading'.[35]

The pastoral adventurers broke out of North Queensland in the 1870s and followed the Coast Track pioneered by Leichhardt in 1845, from Burketown to the Roper River via Borroloola. Dillon Cox overlanded stock to the Top End in 1872, creating a rush once stock regulations were watered down to make development easier. Stations were established to the south on the Barkly Tablelands as a quarter of a million head of stock arrived by the early 1880s. Gold discoveries at Halls Creek in the eastern Kimberley in 1885 brought over a thousand diggers across this track from Queensland. The area, the most remote in Australia, attracted a surfeit of ruthless and criminal types; racial attitudes carried by most people added to the explosive mix. The Inspector of Police, Paul Foelsche, when writing to friends, called a punitive party a 'nigger hunt'. The editor of the *Northern Territory Times*, during one cycle of killing and revenge, described Aboriginal people as 'a race of creatures resembling men in form, but with no more trace of human feeling in their natures than the Siberian wolves'.[36]

These incursions placed enormous pressure on the Garrwa, Marra and other peoples of the region and their resources. They retaliated against this invasion of their lands by destroying stock and horses, stealing supplies and killing overlanders, miners and others. Punitive expeditions by white vigilante parties followed, bolstered by horses and efficient weapons. Aboriginal men—and sometimes women and children—were killed; women were taken as workers and companions, and children as rouseabouts. There is sufficient documentation in diaries, government reports and newspapers to indicate violence and terror were the dominant frontier pattern. The *Northern Territory Times* exhibited frontier philosophy:

> We are invading their country . . . They look upon us as enemies and we
> must do the same by them when they molest us . . . Shoot those you

cannot get at and hang those that you do catch on the nearest tree as an example to the rest; and let not the authorities be too curious and ask too many questions of those who may be sent to perform the service.[37]

Judge Charles Dashwood was one who did ask questions, remarking in 1899: 'organised parties went out—they were not authorised to do it—to shoot the natives right and left, whether they committed any offence or not'.[38]

Other officials were complicit. After the killing of three miners at Daly River, local officials equipped vigilante parties, which scoured the country for eight weeks. A police expedition took action as well, Corporal George Montagu reporting that about 30 Aboriginal people who were trapped in a waterhole were taught 'a lesson'. He added coldly and infamously: 'one result of this expedition had been to convince me of the superiority of the Martini-Henry rifle, both for accuracy of aim and quickness of action'.[39] This remark caused his transfer south. The Aboriginal Protector, Dr Robert Morice, believed 150 Aboriginal people were probably killed in the two months of 'dispersals'.[40] An inquiry was held after uproar in Adelaide, which at the time administered the Territory, but it was a whitewash, claiming Montagu had exaggerated and that perhaps two Aboriginal people were shot in self-defence.[41] Tony Roberts lists 52 recorded incidents (from 1872 to 1903) in the Gulf region, in which there were multiple killings of Aboriginal people, compared to nineteen European deaths. He estimates that these killings, together with single deaths and unrecorded deaths, amounted to over 400 violent Aboriginal deaths at white hands in the Gulf region—a ratio of white to black deaths of 1 to 20.[42]

The Western Australian government, formed of pastoralists, opened up the Kimberley region following John Forrest's favourable report in 1880. By 1882, 77 people held leases to eighteen million hectares of Aboriginal lands. By 1885 Nat Buchanan, Patrick Durack and sons overlanded cattle from northern Queensland via the Coast Track. The Kimberley languished from poor markets until boosted temporarily by the Halls Creek gold rush of 1885–86. Land adjoining the King Leopold and Durack Ranges was quickly stocked with cattle. A weak and underfunded Aborigines Protection Board existed under a Western Australian Act of 1886, which also created powers to control Aboriginal people. In 1892 an amending Act made cattle spearing a criminal offence, permitted Indigenous people to be whipped for certain offences, increased gaol terms for cattle theft, and gave power in 1893 to magistrate pastoralists to adjudicate on cases involving their own stock.[43] There were now no obstacles to clearing the land. The inaugural member for Kimberley, Francis Connor, himself a pastoralist,

Prisoners in neck chains at Roebourne Gaol, Western Australia. COURTESY OF JOHN OXLEY LIBRARY, QUEENSLAND.

told parliament in 1893: 'no doubt there will be a lot of sentiment spoken about putting these blacks off their own country, and no doubt exception will be taken to the idea of dispersing them. But I hold that it is simply a question of whether the natives are to have this country or the whites.'[44]

Open struggle for the land soon ignited. Cattle spoiled waterholes and ate out country, causing hungry and angry warriors to kill stock in retaliation. Several stockmen, including 'Big John' Durack, were also killed in 1886 by Aboriginal defenders. It was a savage war. Durack's mates who gathered for revenge found his body dug up, 'pounded with heavy stones and the crushed remains pinned down with spears'. The punitive party failed to find the culprits after following false trails for four days.[45] Pastoralists demanded action and police patrols scoured the stations looking for cattle killers. Such patrols continued for over a decade. In 1895 a series of police raids out of Wyndham surprised Aboriginal camps mostly at dawn, and shots were fired at fleeing people. Police records listed 50 or 60 rounds often being fired. Deaths resulted.

In the most deadly encounter, on 11 November 1895, Sergeant Thomas Wheatley wrote: 'left camp at 6.30 am and followed the tracks and came upon the natives in a large lagoon, the assistants told them to come out of the water and reeds, two of them came which we arrested, the rest of them tried to escape but in doing so we fired on them killing twenty men the women and children making good their escape'.[46] The 'assistants' were Aboriginal trackers who were equally severe on Aboriginal strangers fleeing arrest. After a six-week patrol, fourteen prisoners and two witnesses, all in neck chains, were brought to face trial. At least one officer tried to arrest a pastoralist for a double Aboriginal murder, but he was threatened with a gun and the culprit escaped. The officer was blackballed by pastoralists and was not supported by the Police Commissioner.[47] Mary Durack commented 'no native brought to justice in Kimberley was acquitted nor was any white found guilty on a charge involving the treatment of an aboriginal'.[48]

The police in this pastoralist-run colony were used for conquest as well as policing. When the King Leopold Ranges were settled after 1900, the same cycle of cattle spearing, resistance, pacification, clearance and arrests occurred. Scores of Ngarinyin men were rounded up and transported to court in neck chains along with Aboriginal witnesses. The police received a ration payment per head per day, so they profited from the clearances. From 1904 to 1908, 283 men and 50 witnesses were rounded up, tried, invariably found guilty, and imprisoned for two or three years. After that, they were naturalised—speaking pigeon— disconnected from land, and ready to work. Communities without men struggled to survive and eventually moved in, or were lured by rations, onto the stations. The Ngarinyin came to be with cattle; the land was secured by whites, and cheap labour was assured.[49]

Some Aboriginal cattle spearers who were gaoled escaped, including 34 from the Roebourne gaol, and seventeen from the Derby lock-up in 1901.[50] Others were never caught. Aboriginal 'offenders' could not be tracked through stony country or during the wet season, even by Aboriginal trackers. Bands of young Aboriginal 'outlaws' roamed the stony rises, beyond the station sphere of influence, attacking property and taking cattle. Jandamarra, a Bunuba youth, worked as a police tracker before freeing some relatives from custody in 1894 and shooting a police officer in the process. He escaped capture, although wounded, and was at large for three years raiding stations before retreating to the Oscar and Napier ranges. He was killed in a shoot-out with police in Windjina Gorge in 1897.[51] Others evaded police: Nemarluk raided cattle in the Daly River region in the 1930s, being supported and admired by the 'tame station blacks' in the way of some Australian bushrangers.[52]

Most Aboriginal people whose land was usurped by pastoralists were forced in by defeat, exhaustion or starvation, or lured by food and tobacco. Some groups in Queensland were described in the 1880s as having a hunted and anxious look as they begged food and medicine from settlers. One elderly man complained in Cooktown in 1895 that he could not hunt in his own country because 'whitefellow along a yarraman [horse] too much break him spear, burn yamboo [humpies] cut him old man with whip; white man too much kill him kangaroo . . . we like our own country; only white man no good.' A young woman with him added: 'I think altogether we die soon'.[53] Some living on the outskirts of settlements were wracked by alcohol or opium addiction and disease, while women survived by prostitution. In 1900, Ardock Station in Queensland continued the not uncommon frontier practice of confining women for sexual purposes. Nine Aboriginal women were constrained by rabbit-proof fencing for the use of white station hands.[54]

One salvation for some Aboriginal people was their use as labour in the north—where cheap convict labour was not available, unlike southern frontiers. A number of European bosses valued their Aboriginal labourers and treated them well, sometimes paying them an incentive if not wages. However, many did not care well enough for their labourers, thinking the Aboriginal labour supply plentiful. Food supplies and housing were generally at or below the bare minimum, and working conditions were arduous. European workers experienced hard living as well, which is why so few worked in remote areas, but unlike Aboriginal workers they were paid wages. In addition, Aboriginal workers suffered physical and verbal abuse. Some legislation was passed to protect them, but it generally lacked sufficient powers to make a difference. For instance, in Western Australia the 1873 Pearl Fishery Regulation Act and the 1886 Aborigines Protection Act set some minimal regulations on use of Aboriginal labour, but these were rarely policed.

Aboriginal labour, not land, was the desire of pearlers who sought shell off the coastlines of northern Australia. The trade began in Western Australia in 1866 on pearling grounds off Roebourne and then Broome, in Queensland in the 1870s, and the Northern Territory in the 1880s. About a thousand people were employed in the industry in each colony. In the early swimming phase, when shell was collected in shallow waters, the labour used was mostly Aboriginal, but Torres Strait or Pacific Islanders were also employed in Queensland. The work was strenuous, with long hours and little pay. Many in fact were forced to work: in the west, Aboriginal men were often brought forcibly from the inland— termed 'blackbirding'—and placed on the Lacepede Islands north of Broome, before being sold to pearlers and forced to dive. Some became accustomed to the life and stayed willingly. Women proved to be the best divers, but the 1871

Groote Eylandt pearl divers. COURTESY OF JOHN FAIRFAX AND SONS LTD, AND THE MITCHELL COLLECTION, STATE LIBRARY OF NEW SOUTH WALES.

Pearl Fisheries Act forbade their use because of the moral dangers of having women on luggers.

By the 1880s, new techniques for suited divers ushered in skilled Asian divers and Aboriginal men were relegated to work as deckhands. From providing 500 workers to each colonial branch of the industry in the swimmer phase, Aboriginal involvement declined. In Broome there were fewer than 50 Aboriginal men in pearling by 1900. Aboriginal deckhands had more work in Queensland, where they gathered trepang as well. Aboriginal communities also provided goods and sexual services to the fleets, much to the disapproval of the authorities, who tried to stop this race mixing, fearing it would undermine white Australia. Many permanent liaisons and marriages developed. Aboriginal people mostly valued the connections with Asian crew, which Regina Ganter has traced in *Mixed Relations* (2006) and Peta Stephenson in *The Outsiders Within* (2007).[55]

HUMANITARIAN REACTION

The violence and exploitation across northern frontiers created great angst among humanitarians inside and outside the country, and eventually some among colonial authorities themselves. One such Protector was Rev. John Gribble, a bold cleric who had once successfully challenged Ned Kelly to return his watch at the Jerilderie hold-up. Gribble founded Warangesda mission in New South Wales in 1880. Invited to begin a Church of England mission in Carnarvon, Western Australia, in 1885, Gribble soon confronted racial attitudes and the harsh treatment of Aboriginal people. At Albany, while en route, a conversation almost led to blows when Gribble told a man who claimed blacks were little better than monkeys that he was little better than one himself.[56]

Gribble toured the back country along the Gascoyne River and discovered Aboriginal labour for the most part was forced, not free, their treatment was inhumane and the use of neck chains barbaric. He made his views known and quickly faced a hostile local community, which petitioned the bishop for his recall. Shopkeepers even refused to sell him supplies. Gribble addressed hostile meetings at Carnarvon, and later, Perth. His journal and opinions, which outlined his condemnations of the labour system, were published in the Perth press in 1885; Gribble was subsequently bashed on a coastal steamer. His bishop, siding with the pastoralists, quickly revoked his licence to preach. Gribble published a book, *Dark Deeds in a Sunny Land* (1886), which exposed the kidnapping, forced labour, brutality and rape of Aboriginal people in the west. The press slandered him as a 'lying, canting humbug' and the Church's mission committee closed the Carnarvon mission. Gribble became a labourer to survive and sued the *West Australian* newspaper. However, in a hostile town, he lost the spectacular case. Gribble left Perth in 1886, beaten but not bowed: he established the Yarrabah mission in Queensland in 1892 just before his death.[57]

Several administrators in the Territory tried to ameliorate the ill-treatment of Aboriginal labour. J.L. Parsons worked from 1885 to institute an Act similar to Queensland's Native Labourers Protection Act (1884) and also urged the creation of some reserves to protect Aboriginal people. He was unable to convince the politicians in Adelaide who managed the Territory; however, a dozen reserves were created in 1892 to both protect and remove Aboriginal people. These totalled 4775 square kilometres, a mere 0.4 per cent of the Territory's land. Charles Dashwood, who in 1892 became both Judge of the Northern Territory and the Government Resident, made new investigations into the condition of Aboriginal people. He pushed hard for protective legislation but his draft bill of 1899 was defeated by pastoralist self-interest and a government concerned at the costs of the Territory's administration.[58]

The contradictory aims of protection, removal and exploitation found common expression in the Queensland Aborigines Protection and Restriction of the Sale of Opium Act of 1897. This Act grew out of an alarming report by Archibald Meston in 1896. He pointed to the pitiful condition of the Cape York people, who were suffering death and destruction at the hands of unscrupulous pearlers and pastoralists, and emaciation through disease, malnutrition, and use of alcohol and opium. Protection was needed, but the means enacted were heavy-handed, and applied to all Queensland Aboriginal people no matter what their condition. This Act, which emerged from the specific conditions of Cape York, became the model for Aboriginal legislation in Western Australia (1905), South Australia (1911) and the Northern Territory (1911). Indeed, these restrictive Acts and their refinements maintained rigid controls over Aboriginal people in northern Australia until the 1960s.

The Queensland Act of 1897 expressed not only humanitarian concern but racist assumptions. These twin forces—white racism and humanitarian paternalism—converged to control Aboriginal lives for the next three generations. All people who were deemed 'Aboriginal', no matter their degree of descent or self-definition, or whether they needed protection or not, were placed under the Act. They or their children could be moved to a reserve and kept there against their will with no right of appeal. They were denied other rights, such as the vote or the freedom to drink alcohol. A 1902 amendment, which reflected European obsessions about purity of race and fears of contagious diseases,

Street scene in Broome, c. 1900. COURTESY OF THE NATIONAL LIBRARY OF AUSTRALIA (NLA-PIC-AN24393928).

prohibited sexual fraternisation with Europeans and Asians, and prevented Chinese from employing Aboriginal workers. The minister's approval was needed for interracial marriages, and was rarely given. Exemptions existed, but after 1902 could be revoked by the Chief Protector of Aborigines. The able-bodied were encouraged to work, but were regulated in yearly contracts like serfs, not free workers, whether they needed these or not. Compulsory labour contracts stipulated Aboriginal wages and minimum standards of food and accommodation, which were not always fulfilled, due to inadequate inspection.

The Queensland Act was in many ways a well-meaning effort to save Aboriginal people, and over the years, more money per head was spent in Queensland than by any other administration. Yet it also cleared Aboriginal people from their land, provided a labour pool for employers and created a restrictive regime over people's freedoms. It was paternalistic to think that people needed to exist under such controls to be saved. If Aboriginal people needed to be segregated on reserves to be protected from unscrupulous whites, why did they also require management there? Racial ideas had embedded in white Australians the view that Aboriginal people were childlike, incapable and had to be taught to work and to be civilised. Some doubted this was possible and imagined reserves would simply be a hospice for a 'dying race'. A never-ending flow of regulations under the Queensland Act of 1897, and its nine amending Acts to 1979, rigorously controlled Aboriginal people. European reserve superintendents had to be obeyed at all times by the Aboriginal inmates. They had the right to search Aboriginal people, their dwellings and their belongings, to confiscate Aboriginal property, read Aboriginal mail, confine Aboriginal children to dormitories, expel people to other reserves far from family, and order compulsory medical inspections. Aboriginal inmates laboured up to 32 hours a week on the reserve without remuneration. Threatening or abusive language, card games, intoxication, traditional dancing and ritual were prohibited, as was 'any act subversive of good order and discipline'.[59]

Wherever they lived across most of Australia by 1900, Aboriginal people, besides those few who were exempt or who had 'passed' into white society, came under special Acts. They were denied civil rights, and generally felt the chill of white prejudice. Racism not only permeated the community, but was enshrined in Acts that treated Aboriginal people as different and inferior. As outlined in Erving Goffman's classic study *Asylums* (1975), Aboriginal lives on managed reserves established by these Acts resembled those of prisoners or institutional inmates.[60] Aboriginal traditions were attacked by regimented efforts to remake people. Their identities were threatened by European names and clothes, by removal from their traditional lands, and by their incarceration among Aboriginal people from many different groups. Inmates lost much of their free will and were subject to orders, discipline, a loss of privacy and removal if they tried to resist. Was it any wonder that these controlled environments over generations produced dependent people without a sense of initiative and responsibility? But few cared. Aboriginal Australians were out of sight and other Australians were soon unaware of much that Aboriginal people suffered on isolated reserves.

It should not be glibly thought that all Aboriginal people were controlled in this way. Aboriginal administrations across the country did not have the resources and sometimes the will to manage everyone. In Queensland there were three main reserves—Cherbourg, Woorabinda and Palm Island—and three missions: Hopevale, Mapoon and Yarrabah. However, half the people lived on country reserves under minimal police surveillance. The same occurred for most of the time in Western Australia, the Northern Territory and South Australia, which adopted and refined the 1897 Queensland Act. Victoria and New South Wales followed different policies. Indeed, Victoria from 1886 and New South Wales after 1909 pushed Aboriginal people into the wider society to be 'absorbed'; the only Victorian reserve by the 1920s was at Lake Tyers. More reserves survived in New South Wales, but only a minority were closely supervised by managers whose powers were not as extensive as Queensland managers in any case. The Tasmanian government controlled its Aboriginal remnant—who called themselves Cape Barren Islanders—but through missionaries.

In the first half of the twentieth century, Aboriginal inmates on reserves and missions always found ways to resist controls placed upon them. Goffman detected the 'underlife' and 'free places' that existed even in the most rigorously controlled institutions. Aboriginal people also developed attachments to these places and 'colonised' them, which made reserves less alien and more like home. This accelerated once a generation was born there. Many other Aboriginal people lived in fringe camps or on cattle stations, where they experienced the more indifferent surveillance of local police or bosses. Freedoms were never completely extinguished.

7

WORKING WITH CATTLE

Colonialism involves the exploitation by invaders of Indigenous peoples—their land, resources and labour. In the Australian case, Aboriginal people were cleared from their land by superior European numbers and firepower. Their economy was also displaced by pastoralism geared to global capital, and their land and waters altered by the impact of introduced stock. They became cheap labour in this new world. In the south, they survived as seasonal labourers and some even embraced farming on missions as a radical hope to regain land, as we have seen. In the north, the process of clearance was slower and the traditional Aboriginal economy survived longer and was never completely overlaid. Also, as there were fewer settlers and no convicts, Aboriginal people provided a larger proportion of the labour than in the south. They collected animal skins and worked in mining and pearling as we have seen. About 10,000 Aboriginal men and women also worked in the pastoral industry until the 1960s.

WHITEFELLA WORK

The shift from reliance on their traditional economy was often gradual. Some bartered their labour willingly for tobacco, flour, tea and sugar, similar to the largely peaceful exchanges with Macassan trepangers in the Top End since about 1720. Aboriginal people slotted itinerant European doggers (dingo hunters), crocodile and buffalo shooters and miners into the same pattern, exchanging work or goods intermittently for food and tobacco. These strangers, like Macassans, did not stay or demand land. Aboriginal people in a sense controlled these small-scale economic systems, producing sufficient skins, tails, wolfram or tin to sustain the trade and keep themselves in a steady supply of desired trade goods. A few resourceful Aboriginal people sold tin to the miners, stole it and resold it, while others bargained gold nuggets with the various prospectors to get the best return of flour, sugar and tobacco.[1] Most lost out in these exchanges as doggers exchanged insufficient flour for dingo scalps, which earned a government bounty of 7/6d each. Once Aboriginal traders realised this, they sold direct to mission or government agents where possible for a higher price. Some profited through mining. About 150 winnowed tin in a yandy on the Shaw tin fields in Western Australia in 1906, making £6 a month. In such exchanges, Aboriginal people controlled the working situation and blended it with their traditional life and food gathering.

Those seeking stimulants and food, or to slake their curiosity, were attracted to settlements such as Broome and Darwin (formerly Palmerston), the grubby capital of the Northern Territory. Once near towns they were less in control, subsumed into the bottom of the colonial class and racial structure. They provided casual labour and the women sexual services to the pearling ports once Asian suited divers took over gathering shell. Those servicing the Broome luggers camped in the sand dunes along Broome's Roebuck Bay. In the 1920s, about 20 per cent or over 500 of the Territory's Aboriginal workers found work in Darwin.

Darwin was a typical colonial town, highly stratified socially and residentially along racial lines. The white colonial masters, bureaucrats and employers lived in fine houses at leafy Myilly Point, the Chinese in a shanty town, and Aboriginal people in humpies in the Kahlin Compound or among the mangroves at nearby Frances Bay. Xavier Herbert, who was an Aboriginal Protector for a time, caught the racist mood of Darwin in his robust novel *Capricornia* (1937). His central characters, the Shillingsworth brothers of Melbourne, arrive in serge suits and bowler hats looking for fortune and adventure. Within hours, they are fitted with white suits and pith helmets by Chinese tailors—symbols of authority and white prestige. Their egalitarian innocence vanishes as they join a world of rigid class divisions and racial cliques. Oscar Shillingsworth hires a 'smelly native and his lubra' as domestic labourers for a pittance, and rises through the ranks of a society based on the exploitation of cheap black labour.

It was widely believed around 1900 that white people could not thrive or work in the north and were dependent on black labour. J.W. Bleakley, Queensland's head of Native Affairs who reported into the Territory in 1929, claimed 'life in Darwin for many of the white families would be almost impossible without some cheap domestic labour, and the aboriginal is the only suitable labour of the kind procurable'.[2] Territory Aboriginal workers were controlled by the 1911 Aboriginals

Ordinance, which approved who could be employers. At one stage, Asians were not permitted to employ Aboriginal labour due to deep fears of miscegenation.[3] Aboriginal labourers and domestics received a wage one-eighth that of European workers. Aboriginal workers (unless exempt) were also locked up at night: the local Larrakia in a compound at Kahlin Beach, and the out-of-town blacks at one further from town. The administration claimed to be protecting Aboriginal women from moral danger but anxiety about racial intermixing with Europeans, and especially Asians, underpinned their incarceration. The compound, situated three kilometres from town, was a wretched collection of galvanised huts with earth or concrete floors and no beds. Most inmates preferred to sleep in their own wurlies or on the adjoining beach.[4]

In Darwin, the Larrakia and others were vulnerable to disease and demoralisation as well as exploitation. Many contracted respiratory and venereal diseases. In 1929 Bleakley expressed concern at the cohabitation between the healthy and those with contagious diseases. Fortunately, those suffering from leprosy were isolated but on a barren island as outcasts to fend for themselves. Some Larrakia were ravaged by drug addiction as Chinese employers often paid wages in opium ash, while others drank 'metho', home-made grog, wine and beer, all purchased through illicit networks. Aboriginal people also consumed Darwin's Western goods and amusements. Reverend Lazarus Lamilami from Bathurst Island recalled his youthful addiction to gambling when visiting Darwin in the 1930s. Another Territory man, Marmel of the Uwadga, related how he was estranged from his wife who worked for a European and became enthralled by Western music and films.[5] These were mainly American 'westerns' in which whites defeated Native Americans: Aboriginal Territorians were generally prevented from attending films which might lower white prestige or give them rebellious ideas. They enjoyed westerns and affected cowboy dress when able. Did they see parallels with their own colonial history as they watched cowboys gun down Native Americans, especially when viewed from segregated seating?

Most Aboriginal workers in North Queensland, the Territory and the Kimberley were employed in the cattle industry. It was a colonial frontier world that remained largely unchanged until the 1960s. In this world, pastoralists were top dog. Some of them were owners, while others were managers for big southern-owned or overseas companies like the English firm Vesteys. Legislation shaped this colonial economy. Aboriginal Acts in Queensland (1897), Western Australia (1905) and the Northern Territory (1911), and their amendments and regulations, had similar employment provisions, allegedly to protect Aboriginal people. European employers needed a permit, which broadly set out the term of

Aboriginal employment and the rations, clothing, medical care and wages owed. However, the regulations were often vague, with no minimum standards, and as time passed a lack of inspectors meant these were often flouted, perhaps with the exception of Queensland. Besides, the wise colonial official knew when to turn a blind eye to abuses as employers could make trouble.

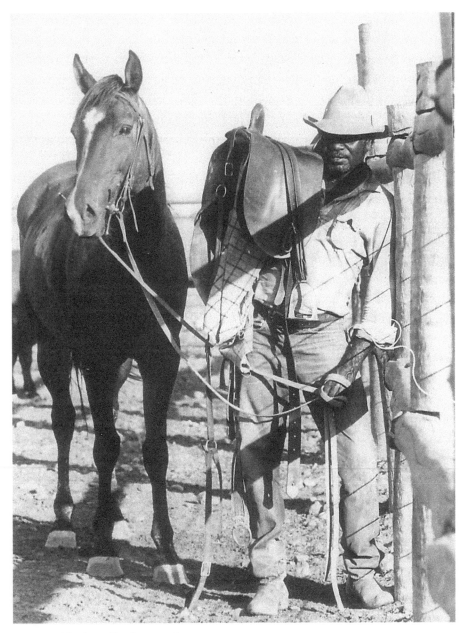

Northern Territory stockman. COURTESY OF THE *HERALD* AND THE *WEEKLY TIMES*.

The cattle industry grew on the basis of cheap labour, which was justified in several ways. First, pastoralists argued, and governments accepted, that Aboriginal labour was 'inferior' and not worthy of wages anywhere near equal to those of European workers. Second, the pastoralists argued, and governments accepted, that they supported the Aboriginal family with rations and a living area, and thus did not have to pay a wage to sustain a family. Third, pastoralists argued, and governments accepted, that without a viable cattle industry, the north would be empty and open to foreign intervention. The first two arguments were specious, as Aboriginal people were not inferior workers and the sustenance given families was little better than flour and offal. The third may have been true, but was no reason for exploiting Aboriginal labour. What, then, was life like for Aboriginal people who lived and worked on cattle stations?

Those lured to stock work by flour or tobacco, or those 'tamed' into working with cattle by coercion or loss of food resources, faced a tough world. Except during the wet season, Aboriginal workers laboured from sunrise to sunset, admittedly as did white workers, but this differed from their traditional world in which work was for sustenance and ceased when sufficient food was gained. Marmel recalled the rhythms of the stockmen's day: 'The sun, peeping over the rim of the land, found us with breakfast finished and ready with the saddle and horses to go on the muster. Sun overhead was dinner time; darkness found us eating our damper and beef around the campfire.'[6] Working with cattle was dangerous. To run down a wild bullock on horseback in the scrub, leap from a moving horse and throw the beast, was a tough and skilful exercise. If the bullock failed to go down, the stockman faced a snorting fury and might need to dash for cover or a tree.

At first, Aboriginal workers were inexperienced, inefficient and often unwilling workers, but they soon developed great skills at station work. As one European ringer, who did not mouth the usual northern platitudes about Aboriginal incompetence, said: 'A white man rides around all day looking for cattle; an Aborigine rides around all day looking for cattle tracks. When he finds the tracks he will find the beast; a white man might wander for days and not see a beast.'[7] Aboriginal men and women developed a liking for station work. It was new and challenging, and close to nature and often their land. Even when they worked away from home country, the unfamiliar environment evoked pleasant memories. As Marmel tended a restless herd at night, he 'would think of my homeland with its lily lagoons covered with ducks and geese. I would chant the songs that reminded me of those places I knew so well as a boy.'[8] Other workers chanted songs reflecting their colonial condition:

Ay-yay, ay-yay
Billy gibbit blanket,
Billy gibbit tea,
Ay-yay, ay-yay,
Poor Fellow me.[9]

When they earned a little cash, many adopted a cowboy-rodeo style of dress. George Dutton, who drove cattle in the border country, and earned good wages because he was on the New South Wales side of the border, always looked flash in made-to-measure clothes and long-necked spurs. At the Top End, others might only afford a hat and shirt. But all took great pride in their ability to handle cattle as well as or better than European stockmen. In a sense, horsemanship, like initiation, became a test of their manhood and an additional basis of their Aboriginal identity.

Aboriginal women were just as indispensable as Aboriginal men, perhaps more so. They were domestics and cooked around the homesteads, and sometimes cooked in the stock camps. Women and children accompanied the quieter cow and calf musters. Women also did gardening, road repair work, fence building, transport work and general maintenance on the stations. Women were also employed as stock workers, equipped with trousers and boots, and with calico tied around their breasts and hair. They matched men in most stock work except the throwing of beasts. Women also provided sexual services, for, as one racist northern quip went: 'the women drovers work all day in the saddle and all night in the swag'. Indeed, their sexual and companionate services were as vital to the maintenance of the industry as any stock work they performed. They laboured as hard as their men, and possibly harder, since men often passed over disagreeable jobs to the women and sat back to watch them work.[10]

Whites shared a frontier mythology based on racist assumptions that claimed all Aboriginal workers were lazy and incapable. The reality was that Aboriginal workers were more than competent and vital to the pastoral economy because few white workers cared for life in the isolated north with its difficult climate. Moreover, the cattle industry was undercapitalised, faced large market challenges due to remoteness and cattle diseases, and by world standards was inefficient. It was profitable only because Aboriginal workers were forced to accept below subsistence wages. Bill Harney, an author and adventurer who knocked about the north all his life in numerous occupations, maintained in 1957 that 'the very economy of the industry depends on aboriginal labour. Many cattlemen try to brush over this lightly during a conversation, but inwardly they are aware of it.'[11] Their denial was based on their begrudging dependence on those whose land they had usurped and whose labour they exploited.

The white mythology was also adamant that Aboriginal people, being inferior and poor workers, needed to be controlled with a firm hand, for any kindness would be construed as weakness. Fear, the mythology warned, must never be shown, and white supremacy must always be upheld. European women must never allow Aboriginal men to be familiar and European men had to assert their superiority in the saddle and in the stockyards. Maintaining public social distance was vital, except for the unstated exception of private sexual relations between white men and black women.[12]

However, a complex interrelationship of paternalism enmeshed black and white on the cattle stations. European men worked alongside Aboriginal workers, needed their labour, and in paternal fashion called them 'our Aborigines', and the men 'boys'. At times, managers cared for sick workers or their children with fatherly tenderness. Indeed, most European children in the north were reared by Aboriginal house servants and some were even suckled at the breasts of black wet-nurses. Aboriginal people resented the controls and poor conditions they suffered, but most accepted it was the way their world worked. Many developed respect and even affection for their own European bosses. They called them names like 'Maluka', which meant 'boss', as Aeneas Gunn was called on Elsey Station. His new southern wife was called 'Missey' by the Aboriginal staff that had to show her the ropes. These relationships were transpositions from Aboriginal society where ritual bosses grew the younger men and women into the law.

Affections of a sort could flow both ways. Patsy Durack of Argyle Station in the east Kimberley was angry when one of his workers, Billy Joe, was arrested by the police for absconding. Billy Joe had not told Durack he was in trouble or sought Durack's protection. Powerless to prevent his gaoling, furious at the police who took him and no doubt concerned at the loss of Billy Joe's labour, Patsy Durack muttered: 'they oughtn't to take Billy Joe. I reared that boy, just like my own son.'[13] There was no suggestion Billy Joe was his natural son, but simply that he felt that all Aboriginal people on the station were under the control and care of the master. Black and white on stations were enmeshed in an ambivalent relationship of attraction and repulsion—of mutual dependence.[14] However, power was tilted wildly in the whites' favour, as revealed by their comparative material conditions—their food, clothing, shelter and wages.

CONDITIONS OF STATION LIFE

While European workers enjoyed butter, jam, fruit, vegetables and sometimes beer with their beef, Aboriginal workers received beef with the occasional potato, bread, tea and sugar, and a weekly tobacco ration. Their families and kin back at the camp, who provided a reserve pool of labour, received less. Although Aboriginal workers' diets improved marginally over the years, a 1946 survey found they consumed more meat, bread and sugar than other Australians, but far less fruit, vegetables, milk and eggs. They received sufficient bulk, but it was 80 per cent higher in starches than the diet of other Australians and very low in calcium and vitamins A and C. A Western Australian Aboriginal Protector noted in 1953 that where station 'diet is poor there is a lack of vitality amongst Aborigines and a lethargy which is not apparent to any marked extent where Aborigines receive varied and sufficient rations which contain elements of a balanced diet'.[15] Studies in undernourishment have confirmed this view. Bush tucker supplemented and balanced their diet somewhat, but the cattle-trampled bush made it harder to gather foods, which also were diminished by the continual demands of permanent camps on cattle stations.

Clothing was basic and only work equipment—boots, trousers, shirts, hats, blankets, camp sheets, towels and soap—were issued, mostly one item at a time. The clothing given out was of a basic quality and design, especially manufactured in Darwin 'for use of natives'. Women who worked in the house or who gained favours from men often dressed a little better or at least had a change of clothes. The men, having only one set of clothes, were caught in a vicious circle. Marmel explained: 'Having no extra clothes to change into, we were always dirty; and because we were dirty we were not thought fit to be given things to eat out of. Our hands were our plate, our pannikin was a used tin from a rubbish heap.'[16] Even in the 1960s, observers pointed out that most Aboriginal workers were not supplied with cutlery, tables or chairs by their employers. Most sat about the kitchen grounds—or on the proverbial woodheap—to eat their tucker.

Housing revealed the starkest differences along race lines. This was less evident in the initial years, when many undercapitalised stations teetered on the brink of ruin and all lived in primitive huts. But with success, and the arrival of European women, most stations assumed an air of comfort, if not affluence. Homesteads were built on a rise where possible to receive the breeze and were cooled by verandahs and shady trees. Most had tennis courts and some boasted lawns with peacocks. Aboriginal servants often pulled manual fans to cool the boss at his dinner. The men's quarters were segregated: one for whites and the other for Aboriginal stockmen. At a distance, the Aboriginal camp was situated in a treeless wasteland of dust and heat. A path wound its way there, used at night by those on both sides of the racial divide seeking sexual adventures. The camp dwellers lived in traditional shelters. The camp had no running water, power or sanitary arrangements, although the homestead had all of these. Permanent camps became unsavoury and unhealthy places, resulting in appalling infant mortality rates. Some stations provided galvanised iron sheds for their workers, which were like ovens in the northern summer—although they did cool quickly at night. These material conditions were damned by Ronald and Catherine Berndt, anthropologists who investigated conditions for the English company Vesteys in the 1940s. They soon became aware that Vesteys was not interested in Aboriginal welfare, only whether its reserve of cheap labour might be sustainable. The Berndts' report, embargoed by Vesteys which did not like its frank exposé, was finally published as *End of an Era* (1987). Similar conditions persisted on many northern cattle stations until the 1960s, as Frank Stevens and other investigators found.[17]

Cash wages for Aboriginal workers varied in each state or territory. They were highest in Queensland, where Aboriginal administration was the most efficient. Wages were paid in Queensland from 1901, although employers often tried to evade payment. In 1911 they were set at a third of the white wage, and by 1918 at two-thirds the rate of white station hands. In 1930, in the face of the Depression, this differential was suspended for twelve months, but was still not restored by the 1960s. Trust accounts were created in 1909, managed by Protectors (often police) to ensure that employers paid wages. In 1915 two-thirds of the wage was to be banked if clothing was provided, and one-third if not; those with families were to bank one-fifth. The administration of so many accounts was difficult, but poor administration gave way to misuse as workers' moneys were directed into general Aboriginal welfare funds and some were misappropriated by police. This has given rise to the recent claims for compensation of 'stolen wages'.[18]

In the Territory, wages were not paid officially, but some stations chose to pay a small wage. Those on the Barkly Tablelands near the Queensland border were forced to make some payments by market forces.[19] However, the wage was always in the form of a credit at the station's store, where prices were high and managers operated the books. Trust accounts existed for some workers but the same abuses existed, historian Ann McGrath remarking: 'Aborigines lost their earnings while the government pocketed their salaries plus interest.'[20]

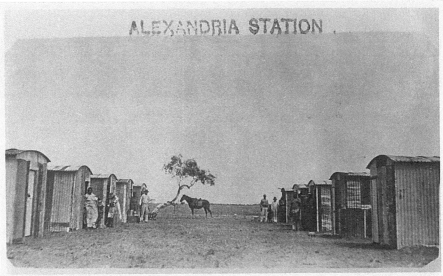

Manager's house (top) and Aboriginal workers' quarters (bottom) at Alexandria Station in the Northern Territory, c. 1920. COURTESY OF THE MITCHELL COLLECTION, STATE LIBRARY OF NEW SOUTH WALES.

In 1916, A.O. Neville, the new Western Australian Chief Protector of Aborigines, tried to reform labour conditions for Aboriginal workers. He also aimed to introduce Queensland's scale of payments and the trust account system, but the pastoral lobby resisted the move. By 1930, despite a lack of reform legislation, half the 5000 Aboriginal stockmen in Western Australia received a wage of generally ten to twenty shillings a week—less than a quarter of white wages. Their wages remained at that level until about 1950. Those still unpaid were usually found in the far northern regions or the interior of the state.[21]

Therefore, until the Second World War, only about half the Aboriginal stockmen in the north received wages, and those who did were paid well below the European rate. Trust funds hived off some of that—often never to be seen again. Whenever the various governments tried to persuade pastoralists to increase the payments—and A.O. Neville was one who lobbied for this— cattlemen claimed the industry could not afford it. They argued they supported the whole Aboriginal camp, not just the workers, although intermittent handouts of offal and bread was hardly support. Government pressure for change was countered by pastoralists' claims that they would be ruined and development in the vital defence region of the north halted. They also threatened to end rationing of non-workers in the camp. Through such blackmail the cattlemen held the upper hand until the 1960s.

To maintain dominance over an exploited labour force, European bosses used various forms of control. Spatial segregation was one technique, making the homestead and its grounds strictly out of bounds to Aboriginal people, except for domestic staff. Even in bush stock camps, white workers camped and ate apart from the black stockmen, occasionally joining them in after-dinner yarning. To be more familiar or to lose at joint card games would, Europeans believed, lower white prestige and endanger their control over labour. Aboriginal people also valued their own domain and most of the time probably welcomed the separation. The two separate worlds of black and white were only bridged by the 'rock and rolling' in the white stockmen's beds.

Language was another means of maintaining dominance and separation. Pidgin English was the lingua franca on most stations. This simple, bastardised form of English (a European, not an Aboriginal invention) was imposed on station blacks and confined them to menial labour because they could not speak 'proper' English. Also, most could not read, which limited their knowledge of the few rights they had, and insight into their trust accounts. Pastoralists also refused to educate Aboriginal station children, as this might make them 'cheeky'. Besides, schooling was considered superfluous for pastoral labour. Then a generation later, pastoralists argued against equal wages on the grounds that Aboriginal workers were illiterate.

Pastoralists created disunity by placing Aboriginal workers from more than one tribe in the camp where possible, and promoting the outspoken leaders to positions of leading hands to isolate them from their followers. Jack Sullivan, or Banggaiyerri, was a mixed-descent man of the Djamindjong people, who was brought up by his Aboriginal mother. When aged twenty, he 'went to the white side', working for the Duracks at Argyle Station in the east Kimberley. As a leading hand, he said: 'there was some reasons to hate the blackfellers in my days. I had to work them same as the white men, I had to liven them up. When they did not do what you told them, bang you went, knocked them over and all that . . . In those days we, white men and half-castes, treated the blackfeller like a dog. We could go in and belt him or take his stud [woman] away for a night.'[22]

Punishments included cutting rations or privileges such as tobacco, killing all or culling some of their beloved camp dogs, dismissing workers back to the camp and hiring others, and threatening to expel people from the station camp altogether. Men were punished by having to do women's work dressed in female clothes. Outstripping all other forms of control was violence: Aboriginal workers were punched, kicked, beaten with belts, whips and stirrup-irons. Matt Savage, a long-time Territory resident, claimed that European stockmen with a reputation for being hard on Aborigines were prized and paid extra.[23] Aboriginal people who existed on the fringe of the stations, and survived partly by cattle spearing, experienced the worst violence, as Aboriginal oral history reveals.[24]

Police, who were also Aboriginal Protectors, were not loath to use force to support employers of Aboriginal workers. The regulations forbade absconding from work contracts, so police tracked down runaway workers and brought them back to face a thrashing or prison. The police, who shared the prejudices of most Top End whites, sometimes exceeded the violence of European stockmen. As Marmel recalled of one police response while merely enquiring about a job:

> As I looked around, the policeman pointed at me and barked, 'Hey you, what's your name?'. Startled by the harsh voice, I could only stare and stutter, but a crack over the ear made my tongue loosen and I almost shouted the word, 'Marmel'. 'Not cheeky, Marmel—or is it Marmalade? Ha, ha, ha!' he laughed at some joke that I could not see, but a cackle from Jimmy, and a loud laugh from Ned [both Aboriginal trackers in the policeman's employ] gave me my cue, and I, too, laughed at something I could not understand, while my ear was buzzing with the pain of the blow. Then the policeman stopped laughing, and Ned stopped, and so did I.[25]

Aboriginal oral history contains many such vivid memories of violence, and even killings.

Violence on the stations was often lessened by the presence of white women, even though they often firmly believed that the exploitation of black labour was natural. Jack Dale, who worked at Mount House Station in the King Leopold Ranges, Kimberley, recalled that in the old days 'we never know white ladies and kids. All we know these old hard bloke, that's all.' But then some white women came. 'They were really good too. Everything was settling down then. All this wild business they settled down.'[26] There is evidence of a massacre near Elsey Station. However, knowledge of this was kept from Mrs Aeneas Gunn, the author of *We of the Never Never*. While women perhaps did have an impact on mitigating violence,[27] outback author Ion Idriess believed white women also learned not to ask too many questions about 'irregularities'.

Gender clearly shaped frontier relations. Aboriginal women probably suffered the worst abuse, as sexual oppression has always followed conquest and exploitation. It was doubly inevitable on the north Australian frontier where the rough-and-tumble European adventurers came without their own women. Male chauvinism and racism combined to permeate the attitudes of most European men in the north. Bill Harney, who knew the Top End as well as anyone, said that there were two kinds of single men in the Territory: 'those who have lived with native women and admit it and those who will not admit it.'[28] Many whites claimed that they were lured to the north by adventure, money and Aboriginal women. The old Territory joke was that Europeans were 'sexplorers' who sought the joys of 'black velvet'. This was the slang term for Aboriginal women, which reflected a whole set of attitudes to race and sex that determined the sexual exploitation of black women by white men. Women were vulnerable and their men quite powerless to protect them. Venereal disease was one of the side effects of sexual encounters, forced or not. Legislation in each state and the Territory tried to prevent abuses, by forbidding the keeping of Aboriginal mistresses or consorting with Aboriginal women, but the law was unpopular and impossible to enforce.[29]

This sexual exploitation pervades Herbert's powerful novel *Capricornia*, together with some interracial love matches, which were few and far between in the real life of the Territory. Exploitation in the form of chauvinism existed even in so-called 'love matches'. Matt Savage, married for 40 years to an Aboriginal woman and proud of their children, could still remark of his wife, Mudburra: 'I got her young and treated her rough and she thrived on it.'[30] Aboriginal women gained in some ways from their sexual association with European men, although the perks they received only lasted as long as did their health, youth and beauty.

Young stockwomen at Alexandria Station in the Northern Territory, c. 1916. COURTESY OF THE
MITCHELL COLLECTION, STATE LIBRARY OF NEW SOUTH WALES.

Perhaps their access to the homestead, the men's quarters and European food and goods added to their power for a time.

Overall, white contact caused a decline in the status of Aboriginal women. In the eyes of the Europeans, they were just 'lubras' who could be used for work and sexual purposes, while in the eyes of Aboriginal men, their women also lost respect. Previously their food-gathering activities had made them a vital part of the family's economic life, but this function was now reduced, and it was largely the man who provided much of the family's sustenance by stock work. While women previously had provided the more consistent and larger food supply, the sustenance they earned by any concubinage and some station work was more erratic and less under their control. Aboriginal women were therefore more dependent on their husbands than they had been in the traditional world.[31]

Yet the relations of men and women are complicated, especially over time. When Ann McGrath interviewed Aboriginal men and women about their memories of the sexual frontier, the men mostly recalled the force and violence, while the women, not dismissing this, tended to romanticise and see the positives of the encounters. Both acknowledged they organised prostitution for profit. But the men, who lost their women's companionship and perhaps some self-esteem, viewed it more severely than the women, who gained more from the transaction in economic terms, and perhaps had a sense of being valued.[32]

Offspring from these black–white sexual encounters often suffered difficulties. Usually they remained in the camp with their Aboriginal mothers, as few European fathers cared to look after them. However, when they grew to working age, the station owners were pleased to include them in their labour force. Some cattle owners boasted that they could breed all their future labour from Aboriginal women. Many children of mixed descent—'yella fellas' in the Territory's parlance—were destined to experience an identity crisis.

Aboriginal children of mixed descent were always in danger of being taken from their mothers as governments sought to 'protect' them from tribal influences. The Aboriginal Acts made the Chief Protector of Aborigines the legal guardian of all Aboriginal and 'half-caste' children. He had the right to remove 'half-castes' from their parents to an institution. In the Territory, authorities built a 'Half Caste Home' to separate those of mixed race from other groups; one at Alice Springs in 1914, dubbed the 'Bungalow', and one in Darwin in 1923. Little funding made for poor conditions and Bleakley in 1929 recommended the homes be disbanded and the children sent to missions or places in the south (if they were 'white enough').[33] European residents, who saw the homes as a future source of cheap labour, quashed his proposal. Charles

Perkins, who later became Under-Secretary of the Department of Aboriginal Affairs and Chairperson of the Aboriginal Development Commission, was one of the children who were taken from their mothers and placed in the Bungalow; he was later sent for an education to an Anglican hostel in Adelaide.

Schooling at the homes was poor, Differ in *Capricornia* claiming the teacher 'barely taught 'em more than A.B.C. and the fact that they're base inferiors . . . they were only Niggers'. Both homes were overcrowded and poorly equipped, leading to much criticism from visitors. M.H. Ellis publicly deplored conditions at the Bungalow around 1930, as it housed 50 children in two galvanised-iron buildings with no running water, giving each less than a metre wide and two metres long of floor space for their bedding. Ellis quoted official reports from 1921 that some girls visited men in the adjoining hotel for dalliances. Maise Chettle, who taught there in 1935–36, had more positive memories. She was greeted by the manager and his wife, who was the matron, and 82 children who 'all looked squeaky clean with hair combed and plastered down; the boys in freshly laundered khaki shirts and shorts, the girls in blue striped cotton frocks'. Their destiny, at least for the girls, was to work for whites in the wider world and perhaps marry a white worker and whitewash their Aboriginality.[34]

Despite white coercion and control, Aboriginal people were able to resist these pressures through various strategies. They forged and told their own campfire stories of injustice—of dispossession, of massacre, of rape—which gave them comfort. They also felt superior in the new world of cattle. One Aboriginal stockman remarked: 'We teachem the cattle business. How to gettem horse. Teachem the bridle. How to get on. How to hold bridle. You teachem but they don't want to live with you. It's common practice for the white stockmen to sit on their arse while the Aborigines do all the work.'[35] Others played the role expected of them. If white bosses believed them to be poor and lazy workers, they were willing to play up to this image. Mrs Gunn's labour troubles with her domestic staff in *We of the Never Never* are a perfect example of this. Her domestic staff declared themselves 'knocked up' and unable to work after just a few tasks. One manager claimed that his 'dumb' and 'lazy' Aboriginal workers could not be trusted to apply even a few drops of oil periodically to the bore-water rigs and that 25 had blown up in two years at a cost of $5000 each. Strangely, the bore at the Aboriginal camp never broke down.[36] Other strategies reaped rewards. Aboriginal stockmen on a muster could kill a prime cow, enjoy the good beef and then turn it over to disguise the carcass to look like a natural death or a dingo killing. Aboriginal boys were expert at spearing vegetables through the cat door of the station store, or at tunnelling under the floor to drain out the flour and sugar from the bags on the bottom row. Mrs Gunn reported stockmen withheld information about the location of waterholes on the vast properties so that they could hide there when they absconded. In the early years, the workers would also often warn the 'wild myalls' on the station's fringe of an impending assault on them by the white stockmen.

While endless racist jokes about blacks circulated around the Top End, Aboriginal people also told their own with comforting effect. Within the colonial world, power is gained by 'joking down', but also by 'joking up' the racial hierarchy.[37] European stockmen were given derisive nicknames to be used among the black stockmen, often disguised in their own language. Aboriginal workers knew much about the private details of the white stockmen from their women and used this back in the camp to ridicule their white bosses. Mrs Gunn observed Aboriginal workers mimicking the futile mustering efforts of Chinese stockmen and was herself the object of mimicry and camp jokes.

Daring Aboriginal men used open defiance, even violence. After beating up an Aboriginal worker, King Billy, Matt Savage was attacked and almost killed in an ensuing brawl until saved by other white stockmen. Another Aboriginal stockman, Banjo, rebelled and killed a white stockman, and then proceeded to hand out boots, clothing and food from the station store to his fellow Aboriginal workers. He fled but was tracked down and shot dead. This was the problem for Aboriginal resisters; they had little real power and so their resistance was often futile. Without horses, runaways in the early part of the century were generally tracked down by mounted Aboriginal stockmen and their white bosses. Marmel was one of a minority who successfully escaped and lived in an isolated sandstone basin for six years with other runaways and resisters, until he grew tired of being confined to a piece of country which was not his own.[38]

Those of mixed descent were given a little more latitude by European stockmen. For instance, Sandy McDonald of the Northern Territory claimed he always carried a gun and was prepared to stand up for his rights, and so did George Dutton in the far west of New South Wales.[39] Jack Sullivan in 1933 challenged Patsy Durack to pay him more or he would leave. 'I want to be up with the white man. I want it [his pay] brought up to the white line.' And Durack agreed. Sullivan recalled 'a lot of working men were there behind me and they pulled out and made him pay that. The whole mob. I had a lot of good mates.' He failed to say who those mates were: black, white or brindle.[40]

The colonial world of cattle inevitably changed Aboriginal working life, and to some degree challenged Aboriginal culture. Gender roles were altered as traditional food gathering was usurped by rations and bush skills became rusty. The role of women as providers diminished, making polygamy less attractive for Aboriginal men, which further altered power relations between men and women. Tradition was weakened for groups decimated by frontier violence or for those amalgamated on properties with locals whose ritual authority prevailed. The initiation of Clancy McKenna, a mixed-descent Nyamil man from the Pilbara, was interrupted by station work around 1940 and never completed.[41] Elders accused young people of being too absorbed by gramophones, illustrated magazines and comics that drifted into the camps.[42] The colonial world denigrated Aboriginal people through racial stereotypes and wracked their bodies with ill health. The Berndts surveyed eleven stations in 1944–45 leased by Vesteys, and found falling birth rates, due to infertility induced by venereal disease and poor nutrition; infant mortality rates were one-third.[43] All these elements had a corrosive effect on Aboriginal culture.

The world of cattle also created resistance, because people made cattle work their own. While their real life was ceremony and the Great Tradition, their day job enthralled them too. They liked cattle work, for it was tough and challenging. It gave them esteem as men and women. Ruby de Satge, who was a female drover in Western Queensland and the Territory, loved the work and saw 'Australia from horseback, enjoying the droving trips'.[44] As Ann McGrath wrote: 'the mobility and status provided by horse riding, stock work and mustering allowed stockmen and women as individuals, and the station community as a whole, a certain feeling of pride'.[45] They told stories at the camp and ever after about their working lives, which they considered a 'no shame job'.

Aboriginal culture thus proved resilient as people incorporated cattle work into their life and probably their spirituality. They certainly fitted their ceremonial life around the work. Both Ann McGrath and Dawn May have detected a *modus operandi* on cattle stations as the people shifted their ceremonial life to the wet season when there was little cattle work. Similarly, bosses sanctioned wet season holidays, gave people tucker for the road and often a lift down the track in trucks to set them on their way, knowing they would return in a month or more. McGrath concluded of this mutual agreement: 'Generations of Aboriginal station dwellers co-operated with white people, but they were never really colonised . . . They incorporated different animals, technologies, skills and kin into their cultural landscape, but it remained *their* country, their world. In their lives, they knew, and continue to know, great pride and strength.'[46] How, then, do we characterise their cattle work?

Reverend John Gribble used the words 'bond service bordering on slavery' and 'species of slavery' when castigating Western Australian pastoralists in his book *Dark Deeds in a Sunny Land* (1886). He wrote of Aboriginal people being run down, captured, tamed and taken into service by signing agreements they did not understand. If they ran away because of bad treatment, they were caught and returned to labour. Young women and girls were under the control of white pastoral workers. He concluded that assigning 'native women against their will for purposes of immorality is a sign of slavery'.[47] In 1890 a British journalist, Arthur Vogan, published *The Black Police* in which he exposed violence, child abuse and exploitation of labour on the frontier. He printed a 'Slave Map of Modern Australia' showing mild and severe forms of 'slavery' in various colours, the north being the 'worst'. It was reprinted by the *Anti-Slavery Reporter* in London. Women and feminist reformers used the word 'slave' in the 1920s when campaigning for a better deal for Aboriginal people. Mary Bennett, in her now famous pamphlet *The Australian Aborigine as a Human Being* (1930), used the words 'akin to slavery' to describe cattle workers. She also referred to the International Labour Conventions and the League of Nations Slavery Convention (1926) in condemning labour practices in Australia and sought to improve human rights for Aboriginal people. Unionists also used the word 'slave', but in self-interested ways, to reduce Aboriginal employment and preserve jobs for white workers in the cattle industry.[48]

Were Aboriginal workers 'slaves' or, as Gribble and Bennett said, 'bordering' on and 'akin to slaves', and what does that mean? The African-American sociologist H. Orlando Patterson developed a model of slavery in which he listed six elements. To Patterson, slavery was: a product of direct force; a substitute for death; a powerless condition; a state of natal alienation—that is, separation from home and kin; a property-less state; and a life without honour.[49] While there was force or coercion involved in much Aboriginal labour, it was not a substitute for death, at least under the law in Australia. Aboriginal people were under an oppressive regime but not powerless, as we have seen. Most were not separated from kith and their home country, although some clearly were. They had only a little personal property, but were not property-less, and in theory most earned wages. Finally, their love of cattle work and being close to country and their ability to continue ceremony, language and culture meant they had honour in their lives; and the work itself was 'no shame job'. Aboriginal workers were on balance not strictly slaves, despite the emotive beauty of this word for many people.

If slavery does not apply, what other alternatives do we have for a worker who is not a slave but not free? Some have argued that Aboriginal labour was a 'reserve labour' force, which remained untrained and largely unprotected (unlike slaves, who were worth money). Some thought there would be an endless supply of wild myalls to 'tame'.[50] But this reserve of labour faded before the evidence of dwindling numbers and does not say enough about the condition of the relations between worker and boss. Claire Williams and Bill Thorpe use the term 'colonised labour', a 'variant or derivation of slavery', to described low-paid workers in a colonial context, loss of Indigenous land and the creation of a racialist society marked by special and discriminatory legislation to control Indigenous people. 'Colonised' labour is like slavery in being 'suffused with force and the repressive elements of power', but unlike slavery in that it was not valued and led to chronic under- or unemployment.[51] Aboriginal workers were low-paid and coerced, yet 'colonised labour' is also an inadequate term as it fails to explain the way Aboriginal people embraced cattle work and now bemoan its passing. So we are without a suitable term for Aboriginal pastoral labour, which was coerced, low-paid, unfree, yet often embraced by the labourer as a source of pride and agency.

TWILIGHT OF THE PASTORAL WORLD

The Japanese military incursions into Australia's northern border zones in the early 1940s fractured the colonial world of the north. The Australian army brought new men and new ideas to the north and they formed different relations with the thousand or so Aboriginal labourers and domestic workers in army camps and defence construction projects. The workers received a cash wage of ten pence per day and they and their dependants received full army rations. Their work was praised and they mixed well with the regular troops, although some gambled their newfound cash.[52] These army wages profoundly affected the pastoral industry. Encouraged by the army's positive reports about Aboriginal workers, the Northern Territory administration investigated and held a conference on wages with pastoral representatives in January 1947. This meeting recommended a wage scale of between 12/6 and 20 shillings a week. The amount was still not equal to white wages, and was never enforced, but a change had been set in motion, finally rendered inevitable by the war.

Aboriginal people in the Pilbara region of Western Australia appropriated the strike weapon to fight for equal wages. They planned a pastoral strike at a secret meeting at Skulls Springs in 1942, of groups from all over the Pilbara concerned at threats to traditional life. The elders invited Don McLeod to the meeting. He was a 40-year-old white Australian, a builder born at Meekathara, who had defended Aboriginal rights in Port Hedland. During the discussions,

Two drovers at Tennant Creek in the Northern Territory, c. 1950.
COURTESY OF THE ARGUS COLLECTION, STATE LIBRARY OF VICTORIA (H2002.199/59).

McLeod, who was by then a communist, urged strike action. Six weeks of protracted translations and discussion followed before agreement was reached. Elders concurred, as 30 De Grey River Station men had successfully struck in 1941 over poor food. Messengers with sacred boards were sent to communities in the region. Dooley-Bin-Bin, a 44-year-old Nyanamada tribesman, and 36-year-old Clancy McKenna, of mixed descent, were selected as McLeod's co-organisers. These three also met secretly with Pilbara Aboriginal communities, planning how the strikers could live off the land by running cattle and prospecting for minerals; reclaiming land and making culture strong would follow. However, the strike was to be delayed until the war's end so as not to appear unpatriotic.

Rumours of a strike leaked, but whites dismissed the idea as impossible. However, on 5 May 1946, strikes broke out on twenty of the 22 Pilbara stations.

The strikers demanded 30 shillings a week plus keep and better conditions. The pastoralists and the Perth press flew into a rage of wild statements about Aboriginal workers being under the control of communists and outsiders, not crediting that they could plan such a thing themselves. Dooley was arrested while the strikers were mining tin with yandies (wooden dishes) at Marble Bar and charged with enticing Aboriginal people from their work. As he was led away in neck chains to Port Hedland, he called: 'It was in the yandy that our mothers carried us. Now the yandy carries us again—keep working!' McKenna and McLeod were also arrested on charges of being within proximity of Aboriginal camps. McLeod's bail was set at £300—the equivalent of a year's wage—and he was find £100. Dooley and Clancy were each sentenced to three months gaol. A campaign in Perth in support of the black strikers was waged by an unlikely coalition of churchmen, women's groups, trade unions and communists. Despite pastoralist and police harassment and many arrests, the Aboriginal strikers held out. Soon the gaols were full and, as the strike entered its second year, the police began to resent being used as a political force.

After three years of industrial action, the pastoralists surrendered. In the Mt Edgar agreement of 1949, they offered £3 a week plus keep—twice the strikers' original demands, but not equal wages. However, despite their victory, few of the strikers returned to the stations. It became clear as the strike developed that they desired freedom from colonial wage labour. Six hundred of the strikers formed a mining company instead, which grossed £50,000 in 1951. Subsequently, they paid a deposit on three pastoral properties. Unfortunately, a fall in metal prices, a lawsuit by another mining company, ill luck and bad management all forced the community into bankruptcy. The Western Australian government, which sought to quash the experiment and return them to the understaffed cattle stations, intervened. The strikers responded by forming the Pindan Mining Company.[53]

The Pindan Mob aimed to be an independent co-operative community, connected to the wider Australian economy, but not controlled by it. Despite initial difficulties, a lack of cash and equipment, some food shortages and internal dissensions, the Pindan Mob managed adequately on their own property purchased from mining profits. If they were no great economic success, due partly to falling metal prices and other economic factors, they were certainly a cultural success. Led by their elders, the mob maintained traditional law for internal affairs, but used Australian law to regulate relations with outsiders. They also voluntarily changed aspects of traditional law. Incorrect marriages and divorce were tolerated, although persons seeking positions of influence were chosen largely from those who had married traditionally. Fighting and traditional revenge were banned, which was important in a community drawn from a number of different cultural groups. Mother-in-law avoidance was modified, so mixed work parties could travel to mining areas together, these relatives having to face away from each other in the back of the truck. While initiations flourished, the elders agreed to allow European doctors to do the actual circumcisions in hospital to prevent possible infection.[54]

The Pindan Mob practised radical hope, like Billibellary and William Barack in the century before them. They strengthened culture and adapted successfully to the market economy on their own cattle station at Strelley, where they still live comfortably today. They insist that their government-funded school teach traditional culture in their own language, through texts prepared by the elders in collaboration with non-Indigenous teachers—an independent stance that developed from their prolonged strike action. A film, *How the West was Lost*, and a book of the same title by Don McLeod, record their pride in their achievement and their willingness to modify tradition to make it strong. Pindan elders in the film, for instance, deliberately speak the names of dead leaders— normally taboo—in order to honour their great leadership and pass this to the young. Their strike inspired many. Allan Muriwulla Barker declared in 1976: 'Now to me a revolution is when I picked up a pick and shovel and starved in the strike of '46 . . . Aboriginals are standing up. Look at that strike.'[55]

The effects of the war and the three-year Pilbara strike reverberated across pastoral properties, ending the worst abuses of Aboriginal labour, but they did not bring equal pay. In the 1950s, Aboriginal workers on Territory cattle stations earned less than half the European wage.[56] In 1962 the Federal Council for the Advancement of Aborigines and Torres Strait Islanders (FCAATSI), a coalition of back and white advocates for Aboriginal equality, took up the cause. The Equal Wages Committee of FCAATSI was led by Barry Christophers, a Melbourne general practitioner and communist. This committee pressured trade unions, until then largely indifferent to the rights of Aboriginal workers, to join a campaign for equal wages. The Australian Council of Trade Unions adopted a policy of eradicating discrimination against Aboriginal labour. This cleared the way for the North Australian Workers' Union to sponsor an equal wage case for Territory pastoral workers in the Federal Arbitration Commission in 1965.

The Commission, in a historic judgment in 1965, decided that 'there must be one industrial law, similarly applied to all Australians, Aboriginal or not'. But there was one catch. The union had presented little evidence, thinking their case that Aboriginal people should be treated equally was self-evident. But John

Kerr (later the Sir John Kerr who dismissed a prime minister in 1975), presented a voluminous case for the pastoralists, quoting Territory opinion and anthropological writing which alleged that Aboriginal workers were less efficient than other workers. The commissioners rejected the racist claim that all Aboriginal workers were 'slow', but ruled that 'a slow worker' clause be inserted into the award, whereby individual workers judged inefficient by a committee were to be paid less than the award wage. The Commission did not canvass much alternative opinion of Aboriginal ability or talk to Aboriginal people themselves. Despite the lack of any strong evidence (except the usual general claims that the industry would be ruined by equal wage payments to Aboriginal workers), the Commission also accepted the pastoralists' application to delay implementation of equal wages until 1968. This decision saved pastoralists $4 million in wages and deprived Aboriginal workers of the same amount. John Kerr received $80,000 for his efforts.[57]

Aboriginal anger was instantaneous. One man declared: 'I am not going to work till 1968. I bin wait long enough. We bin starvin' since we first learnt to ride a horse. We bin wait too long. I bin want them legal wages now—this year.'[58] Aboriginal stockmen at Newcastle Waters walked off the job in June 1966 and, soon after, 200 Gurindji people left Vesteys' Wave Hill Station and squatted on traditional land at Wattie Creek. The Wave Hill walk-off was not just about wages. Research has revealed that Aboriginal stockmen were also angry about the continued use of their women by white workers, who manipulated stock-camp work rosters to leave Aboriginal workers in the bush on weekends, enabling white workers to access Aboriginal women back at the station. Elder Vincent Lingiari told the writer Frank Hardy, 'some them white fellas play bloody hell with black gin women, leave Aborigine natives out in the bush for that. When Aborigine stockmen come back they have to pack up and go away again. That not right.'[59] The walk-off over pay and women escalated into a land claim. Lingiari declared: 'the issue on which we are protesting is neither purely economic nor political but moral . . . on August 22, 1966, the Gurindji tribe decided to cease to live like dogs . . .'[60]

The Gurindji and others maintained their dignity but they lost their jobs. After 1965, pastoralists mechanised with fences and helicopters to minimise their workforce, and employed European stockmen in preference to Aboriginal labour. The Gibb Committee in 1971 revealed that Aboriginal labour had declined by 30 per cent in some areas, with an almost corresponding increase in European labour. Some pastoralists illegally evicted Aboriginal people from their stations, despite traditional access being part of the leases. Aboriginal people in the cattle industry have a unique work history, unmatched by other Australians: they moved from no wages, to small wages, to 'equal' wages, to unemployment.

The generations of little or no formal training left Aboriginal workers ill-equipped for new types of employment. The mining industry, that other great industry of the north, did little at first to soak up Aboriginal unemployment. It was slow to provide jobs and training, and Aboriginal workers were offered only the lowest-paid unskilled work and still used as a reserve labour force. Nabalco's manganese mine at Gove employed 2700 people in 1971, but only 30 Aboriginal people. At Comalco's bauxite mine at Weipa, Aboriginal workers formed 10–20 per cent of the unskilled workforce in the 1970s, without standard benefits. In 1969, following public criticism, Aboriginal workers finally gained the bonuses, paid holidays, and board and lodging that other workers received. Mining companies made initial promises of job training for Aboriginal people, but few efforts were made until the 1990s. Instead, they fell back on old stereotypes that Aboriginal workers lacked initiative, and had high rates of absenteeism. The companies initially also made little effort to consult with the people, and to

Indigenous workers upgrading the rail track at Comalco's bauxite mine in 1971. COURTESY OF THE WOLFGANG SIEVERS COLLECTION, NATIONAL LIBRARY OF AUSTRALIA (NLA.PIC-AN13116334-2-V).

understand the cultural and other issues from generations of living dependent and managed lives on cattle stations and missions.[61]

The one early exception was GEMCO (then of BHP), which mined manganese at Groote Eylandt. Significant consultation was carried out between the company and the landowners over the location and protection of sacred sites. Aboriginal workers formed 18 per cent of the workforce by 1970. They received training, were paid equally, and were employed in all of the company's operations, not just on the end of a shovel. Several rose to management level and others operated bulldozers then valued in excess of $80,000. The company took great pains to communicate job instructions to Aboriginal workers and low absenteeism resulted. The rigid racial segregation that existed at Weipa, Comalco's company town, did not exist at Alyangula township on Groote Eylandt. Aboriginal people were free to use all company facilities and some lived in company houses.

Before the 1980s, mining offered little to Aboriginal people. In return for the small benefits of a few on the payroll, Aboriginal communities suffered. They lost control of land, the Weipa mission being reduced from 348,000 to 120 hectares and the Yirrkala Aboriginal reserve being reduced from 35,300 to 300 hectares by the granting of mining leases. Except for Groote Eylandt, Aboriginal people were excluded from most of the benefits and entertainments of the nearby mining towns. Instead, they faced uprooting from their land and disruption to their lives caused by the invasion of men, machines, grog and Western culture. Never before had these hitherto isolated communities experienced such a cultural onslaught—for miners, unlike pastoralists, came in their hundreds in each mining area.

As Aboriginal people were pushed off pastoral properties, and failed to find work in the mining sector, their unemployment rates rose astronomically in the 1970s. Hundreds of people collected in the northern towns of Katherine, Tennant Creek, Halls Creek, Fitzroy Crossing, Broome and Derby. Government surveys in the late 1970s revealed Aboriginal unemployment rates of 50–60 per cent, ten times that of the rest of the Australian population.[62] Their misery, boredom and loss of self-esteem were bad enough, but when combined with the granting of welfare payments ('sit down money') and drinking rights in the 1960s, an explosive mix was created. To top it off, they were often far from their land and in the country of strangers. Peter Yu, who worked among his people at Fitzroy Crossing in the 1970s, recalled: 'It was a massive refugee problem, an explosion of population. There was no provision for them, no infrastructure ... People were bored, they were unable to fulfil their cultural responsibilities. They just camped in cars or iron humpies. The only organisation that helped was Community Welfare.'[63] There were no transitional arrangements between work and welfare. Few people except for the pastoralists had foreseen the consequences. Yet Pat Dodson argued in hindsight that the wage case had to happen: 'people couldn't continue to be exploited . . . But what was missing were those cultural, social elements . . . What the Government provided was assimilation, which was devastating to many Aboriginal people.'[64]

Despite the inequities, working with cattle had provided a breathing space for Aboriginal culture. Bosses did not attempt to change Aboriginal people except to make them compliant workers. They were not interested in what they believed, unlike missionaries, so long as they performed their jobs, and did not wish to educate them as this might induce cheekiness or rebellion and would cost money. Aboriginal culture was not attacked directly and in many cases it thrived as ceremonial and social life, marriage arrangements and kinship patterns remained vivid. Studies by anthropologist A.P. Elkin in the 1930s found that the Walbiri, in contact with cattle stations since the late nineteenth century, had their ceremonial life and law intact.[65] Those of mixed descent also often also adhered to tradition. George Dutton was initiated and did droving jobs along the paths of his ancestral heroes in the border country and participated in ceremonies over his life.[66] Engineer Jack Japaljarri, a Walbiri man, maintained his language and ceremonial life after 50 years of being with cattle, and was astounded that Aboriginal people in the south had not.[67] Paradoxically, cattle work, often called 'slavery', saved Aboriginal culture. Missionaries, on the other hand, as we will see, saved Aboriginal people—but not always their culture.

8

MIXED MISSIONARY BLESSINGS

INITIAL ENCOUNTERS

Missionaries were a different sort of white people and at first Aboriginal people found them hard to fathom. In 1912 the Worora people of King Sound (Derby) in the Kimberley watched silently as the Presbyterians Robert and Frances Wilson anchored their lugger and waded ashore to found Port George IV mission on Worora land. The Worora later recalled that the mission created great debate for many weeks. The people were puzzled by those who bore crosses not guns. 'Kill them,' demanded one Worora elder, Ambula, but Indamoi and others yelled 'No! They are not trying to harm us. They do not hunt our food. They have given us food and gifts. We have nothing to fear from them.'[1] The Worora soon engaged with the mission.

At other sites across northern Australia from Cape York, through Arnhem Land, to the Kimberley and into parts of the arid centre, the sails of Christian missionary luggers or mission wagons disrupted the rhythms of Aboriginal life. Churches saw missionary activity into central and northern Australia as the last chance for the Civilising Mission to help save Indigenous peoples in Australia. George Frodsham, Bishop of North Queensland, lamented in 1906:

> The Aborigines are disappearing. In the course of a generation or two, at the most, the last Australian blackfellow will have turned his face to warm mother earth . . . Missionary work then may be only smoothing the pillow of a dying race, but I think if the Lord Jesus came to Australia he would be moved with great compassion for these poor outcasts, living

by the wayside, robbed of their land, wounded by the lust and passion of a stronger race, and dying.[2]

The Anglican Roper River mission in Arnhem Land (now Ngukurr) followed in 1908. By 1920 about 25 Christian missions existed in remote Australia far from the pressures of settlement, their isolation unlike the southern missionary experience. These missions began ambivalent relationships with Aboriginal communities, which both challenged and assisted Aboriginal cultures, relations that lasted generations—some to the present day.

Aboriginal people, whose lands the missionaries had settled, knew of whites through contact with pastoralists or by news through tribal networks. They approached cautiously, assessing their intentions and strength. They were greeted with friendly gestures, gifts of tobacco, clothing, mirrors and novelties, and food. Aboriginal people were perplexed by the missionaries' lack of guns, stock and their unwillingness to accept the sexual offers made to them in exchange for food and tobacco: all behaviours so different to white stockmen. But the missionaries did seem to need labour. In 1905, many men in return for food unloaded supplies for Rev. Ernest Gribble (Rev. John Gribble's son) at the Anglican Mitchell River mission (now Kowanyama). Some distributed food only after Aboriginal visitors sat through ceremonies, which they later learned were church services. The Nyul Nyul at the Cistercian Beagle Bay mission countered such blackmail with their own, telling the Trappist monks they called 'Hail Marys' 'no more tobacco, no more h'Allelulia'.[3]

Some Aboriginal people avoided the newcomers or met them with hostility. Tiwi men helped Father Gsell establish his Catholic Bathurst Island mission in 1911, but women and children avoided the mission for many months. Some groups avoided new missions for years. The Benedictine friars settled on the Drysdale River mission (now Kalumburu) in the northern Kimberley in 1908, but the Gamberre avoided them for four years, during which time the friars hung presents and food in the trees which were silently taken. In 1913 the mission was attacked and two friars speared; it then remained a fortress rather than a mission for a further five years. In 1917 the Lardil people of Mornington Island mortally speared Rev. Robert Hall, the first Presbyterian missionary there, and held his wife and two other missionaries under siege until help arrived. At Port George IV (later Kunmunya), Robert Love almost lost his life because he insisted on camping near a certain waterhole, despite the protests of his two Aboriginal guides. It is likely that the hostility arose because the waterhole was a sacred site, rather than being a more general resentment of his intrusion on Aboriginal lands.

In time, Aboriginal people realised missionaries were spiritual people too, and to be feared and respected as they claimed powers similar to their own clever men. The newcomers related stories of miraculous creators and beings: God, the Devil, and angels, all of whom had great powers, akin to those of their great ancestors. The missionaries audaciously claimed primacy for their spiritual narratives, dismissing Aboriginal beliefs and stories, indeed defying them. Benedictine fathers, when shown a sacred sun stone which their Aboriginal informants would not touch for fear of darkening the sky, boldly picked it up and sent it to a museum—without any ill effects.[4] Missionaries applied Western medicines to sores or diseases, with miraculous results, confirming their power; the nagging skin disease yaws was later cured with a single penicillin injection. Their powers were reminiscent of Aboriginal healers, who applied medicinal plants to patients' bodies or 'extracted' stones, splinters and other matter from the body that had been placed there by malevolent clever men. Robert Wilson's hair cuttings were carefully collected by the Worora, either to share in his power or to attack him by 'singing' a piece of his body.

Aboriginal people before long included the missions in their seasonal food quest. In time, the lure of food or the need to find sanctuary from inter-tribal feuds or rapacious Europeans, brought them semi-permanently onto the missions. It was in this way that cultural changes began to unfold as the people became more sedentary.

Most missionaries were steadfast people of immense courage. They ventured unarmed and unwanted, and with few companions, into some of the most inhospitable climates. Yet they rarely faltered, even when faced by warriors brandishing spears to challenge their intrusion. Pioneering a mission involved months and years of exhausting labour with axe, hoe and saw: often to no avail. The Jesuit Daly River mission was flooded and moved three times in twelve years from 1887, before being abandoned. At Kunmunya, Wilson and Segrott waded in mud for weeks, cutting a boat channel through the mangroves. The toil, mosquitoes and the oppressive heat and humidity almost forced them to quit. The French Cistercian (Trappist) monks struggled against the heat, fires and pests to establish the Beagle Bay mission north of Broome in 1890. Daisy Bates observed of Beagle Bay in 1899: 'the condition of the mission seemed hopeless. The bark huts were dilapidated, the gardens smothered in a growth of saplings and suckers, and some of the wells had fallen in.'[5] The Cistercians tried to blend arduous pioneering with their monastic rules of silence, vegetarianism and meditation from 2 a.m. till dawn. With no experience in northern pioneering, and no training in cross-cultural work, their task was more difficult than that faced by St Paul who evangelised a people closer to his own culture and in less trying conditions. Worn out, and with no converts among the Nyul Nyul, they admitted defeat. German Pallotines were induced by Bishop Kelly of Geraldton to replace them in 1901.

The 'coming-in' of Aboriginal groups created economic problems for the missionaries. Clergy, who at home would be supported by their community, found that on missions they had to supply the food for hoped-for parishioners. Once Aboriginal people stayed in greater numbers and for longer periods, supplies ran short and then people left. The missionaries' pleas for outside support reaped little. Most congregations sent missionaries and money to exotic places in China, Africa, India or the Pacific instead. Only two of the 80 missionaries employed by the Australian Church Missionary Society between 1892 and 1907 worked in the Aboriginal mission field. Governments contributed little aid until the 1950s, as they either maintained the separation of church and state on principle, or felt unsympathetic to operations they could not readily control. The Church Missionary Society's work in Arnhem Land in the 1920s and 1930s only attracted a meagre £250 per annum from the Northern Territory administration.[6] Some missions tried commercial ventures such as beef production, but with little success. Most survived on the barest budgets and missionaries were forced to be jacks-of-all-trades, with little time for spiritual work. Many took ill under the strain and the difficult northern climate. Just as a missionary began to be trusted or mastered the local language, he or she would have to retreat to the south.

MISSION STRATEGIES

Aboriginal people who moved to missions faced efforts to control them. If these pressures became unbearable in the early years, they could simply leave for a while. This option closed as settlement became more widespread and pastoralists drove people off their runs. A return to the mission meant the people suffered the ethnocentric attitudes of missionaries who viewed Aboriginal culture as heathen, uncivilised and inferior. Reverend Ernest Gribble, an Anglican missionary all of his life, typically described Aboriginal people as 'children' who belonged to a 'degraded and depraved race'. They must be uplifted. Fundamentalist missionaries saw Aboriginal people as 'pagan' enemies who, like the forces of darkness, had to be combated and changed. The views of some were racist: one of Gribble's assistants commented more bluntly: 'niggers could not be trusted'.[7] Father (later Bishop) Gsell, who was at Bathurst Island for 26 years until 1938, claimed the Tiwi were inherently inferior: they were 'children of the Bush', and 'wild animals', who could be 'trained' to accept the gospel and civilisation, because 'in the long run, the black man will come to realize that the white is wiser and cleverer than himself'.[8] Even the more liberal-minded *The Australian Board of Missions Review* in 1923 paternalistically rated Aboriginal people 'as good as any other native'.[9]

Paternalism was inherent in the Christian tradition. Christian thought is permeated by images of fathers and sons, of shepherds and sheep, of teachers and listeners, and of hierarchies. It is about ruling, guiding and helping, which are the tenets of paternalism. Every minister (fathers in the Catholic tradition) leads his own flock of parishioners which he cares for and guides into the Christian way of life. When Christians went among 'their' black 'heathen children', to show them the 'truth and the light' they 'alone' possessed, their sense of fatherhood was dramatically intensified. Catholic orders with a strongly monastic and hierarchical regime were probably the most paternalistic. As late as 1977, Father Seraphim Sanz, Spanish Benedictine missionary at Kalumburu for over 30 years, who had a Father in Heaven, a Holy Father in Rome and a Father Abbott in New Norcia, greeted a group of middle-aged residents at Kalumburu with 'good morning boys and girls'. This denigration of grown people was followed by the work orders of the day, a directive to work hard, and a warning: 'I'll be watching you!'[10] Far from the public eye, missions, like the convict system, could be a lottery in which missionaries might be humanitarians or tyrants. Convicts could at least complain to the courts, a right Aboriginal people on missions were denied.

Some missionaries rejected paternalism. Robert Wilson at Kunmunya consulted with the Worora people over marriage law problems. His successor, Robert Love, declared: 'In this mission, we will never tolerate paternalism. These people are our equals in intelligence, and our superiors in physique. The only differences are in the colours of our skins and the fact that we have had centuries more practice at becoming civilized.'[11] Few missionaries before the 1970s shared his views, making paternalism a blot on the humanitarianism of early missionaries. Aboriginal people on missions were generally managed, protected, taught and chastised like children, which eroded their former autonomy.

Most missionaries realised conversions among adults would be few and focused their efforts on Aboriginal children. Their main strategy was to segregate children from their parents by placing the children in dormitories. Missionaries often convinced parents to leave children voluntarily in their care while they worked or travelled. Parents were often pleased to do this as nearby pastoral runs made traditional foods harder to obtain and the country a more dangerous place. However, children misunderstood their parents' motives. Dick Roughsey, a Lardil man from Mornington Island mission, recalled being left: 'Then one morning I stood wailing under the dormitory, held back only by the enclosing wire netting, while my parents, also crying, vanished into the bush on the way back home.'[12] If children were not placed voluntarily in dormitories, promises of education and threats of withdrawing rations usually worked.

Yarrabah Mission in Queensland, c. 1900. COURTESY OF THE MITCHELL COLLECTION, STATE LIBRARY OF NEW SOUTH WALES.

In the Kimberley, the missionaries at Beagle Bay collected children of mixed descent onto their mission, as they disapproved of the sexual relations between Aboriginal women and the Asian crews of the pearling luggers. The authorities, who were alarmed at such intermixing as well, but on racial more than moral grounds, supported their efforts. By 1904 Father Nicholas Emo urged that Aboriginal people around Broome be compulsorily confined to reserves and the children placed under proper control and education in his mission. He was supported by the police, and this approach was influential in the Western Australia Aborigines Act of 1905 under which the Aboriginal Protector became guardian of all Aboriginal and 'half-caste' children, with power to transfer children without parental consent to reserves or missions. In 1907 the Pallotines boasted the care of every child over seven on the whole Dampier Land Peninsula—an area of 50,000 square kilometres. By 1910 the number of children at Beagle Bay had increased fourfold to 105. The care of such a large number was made possible by the arrival of nine sisters of St John of God in 1906, an Irish order still present in the region.[13]

Dormitory life on most missions was marked by regimentation and discipline. The children—the boys in one dormitory, the girls in another—woke at six to a bell or a sprinkle of water if slow. They made their beds, rinsed any soiled linen, washed out the dormitory, and scurried to their jobs of milking goats or starting fires. Bells marked morning prayers and another bell heralded roll-call and breakfast. In some missions the children wore uniforms. The Pallotines at Beagle Bay dressed the girls in blue gingham and the boys in khaki, and this was soon extended to adults. Morning lessons followed which were rudimentary in the early years, being confined to religion and the 'three Rs'.[14] More chores including labour in the kitchen garden followed lessons, and for the older ones, training in job skills—domestic work for girls and stationhand skills for boys. Some playtime completed the day, before more prayers, dinner and bed.

The children were placed under great pressure. They were separated from their parents and kin, and in most cases saw them infrequently. Their traditional culture was eroded through lack of engagement with family and community, and by direct attacks such as being forbidden to use their own language, the most important purveyor of culture. Indeed, one United Aborigines Mission staffer at Ooldea even took photographs of sacred objects under promise of secrecy and showed them to uninitiated dormitory boys, saying: 'See what silly things these are! Just bits of old wood, that's all. Fancy anybody thinking they were important! Don't you listen to any of these old men, they're only silly old fellows that don't know anything.'[15] The dormitory routine failed to sever the bonds of traditional life completely, but its controls weakened traditional knowledge. Dormitory children were compelled to make difficult negotiations between the Aboriginal and European world.

Upon reaching the age of fourteen, young people entered the world of work on the mission. All able-bodied people had to work for their keep, for this was a key part of the Civilising Mission. People were introduced to the Western work ethic and wage system in the mission's garden, fishing, trepang or cattle enterprises. Some inmates learned skills that enabled them to go into the wider world and earn their own living. Reverend R. Schenk, who established the Mount Margaret mission in central Western Australia in 1921, imparted more skills than most missionaries. Aboriginal men learned mining, engineering, carpentry and shearing, and women learned domestic work, as well as typing and elementary nursing. Some gained work nearby in the goldfields. Most missionaries claimed to be teaching skills and habits that would make Aboriginal people independent.[16] However, missionaries were often loath to let them move into the larger world, which they believed was full of temptations and difficulties.

Independence proved elusive for Aboriginal people on missions. Few missionaries allowed the people to control their own work. Undoubtedly, supervision in new skills was necessary, but supervision remained long after the learning had stopped. Some missions created Aboriginal villages of subsistence farmers, which promised some autonomy, but paternalism and Aboriginal disinterest in non-traditional ways worked against success. In 1926 Rev. Pond commented on an 'independent' village at Kowanyama, the Mitchell River mission:

> If left alone these people, who have advanced thus far, would soon slip back to their old camp life. One realises the difficult task before the Mission when you see Mr. Chapman paying these people daily visits, telling them that it is time to clear this piece of land; asking another why he has not yet got his sweet potatoes in, and telling others that their houses are very untidy and must be cleared up.[17]

Reverend Ernest Gribble, who advocated such villages to teach 'the natives to depend on themselves', had a great reputation for being coercive and authoritarian.[18] Could such management foster independence?

Missions controlled Aboriginal people in many ways. The power of whiteness, which underpinned the title 'master', kept some in line. Occasionally, a missionary might have to show a gun, or threaten to call the police when in a tight spot. The Trappist Father Alphonse once ended a tribal fight by rushing into the fray and slapping an elder on the face. Most missionaries, however, drew the line at withdrawal of rations. The most severe was expulsion from the mission, which meant not only loss of food, but separation from family and community. Some missionaries refused to use this on principle, while others saw that it would reduce their congregation and even the amount of government subsidy.

Physical punishments were usual on some missions where Aboriginal lives were ordered by cuffs and kicks. Reverend Ernest Gribble had a suite of punishments at Yarrabah mission around 1905, including humiliation by head shaving or being forced to dress in hessian bags, standing barefoot on a hot tin roof, pack drill, withdrawal of rations and use of nearby Fitzroy Island as a place of banishment. At Forrest River mission in the 1920s, Rev. Ernest Gribble strapped inmates for impudence and bad language and lectured them continually. His authoritarian ways extended to his staff, some of whom resigned, including his son Jack Gribble and his most loyal convert James Noble. Ernest Gribble was finally dismissed in 1928 after a secret church inquiry. However, Christine Halse's biography *A Terribly Wild Man* (2002) reveals Ernest Gribble was a complex and obsessive mix of authoritarianism and a burning desire to protect Aboriginal people. This is revealed in his exposé of the Forrest River massacre in 1926. He was in the fearless tradition of his father, Rev. John Gribble, who had been run out of Western Australia for exposing abuses of Aboriginal labour in 1886.[19]

Aboriginal dependence was fostered by the thrice-daily food handouts on many missions, and the communal feeding of older people and children. Some missionaries saw the degrading nature of these food lines and ended them. George and Jessie Goldsmith of the Methodist mission on Goulburn Island introduced a cardboard money wage system in 1930 which enabled Aboriginal residents to buy the food and goods of their choice from the mission store, and to cook it themselves. The Goldsmiths, like the Presbyterian Robert Love at Kunmunya, also abolished the dormitory system in the 1930s in order to develop, not stifle, parental responsibility for their children. However, not all missions were as enlightened. At Kalumburu until 1960 the children were living in dormitories and the whole community was fed by food lines. In 1977 the older people still lined up for a dollop of food in their billy, as had their parents 50 years before. Dependence was increased by a decline in skills gathering bush tucker. This was intensified by the fact that the dormitory children received insufficient bush education from their elders due to the time-consuming demands of the Civilising Mission.

Aboriginal people suffered emotional distress and personality disorders due to the mission experience. The psychologist Geza Roheim observed that mission children in the Western Desert played sadistic games, complete with slaps and orders from 'masters' to 'victims', whereas he had never observed such sadistic play among bush children.[20] Dr J.E. Cawte, a pioneer of psychiatric studies among Aboriginal people, remarked on the number at the Benedictine Kalumburu mission in 1963 that seemed 'lost'. The mission had promoted significant changes in traditional cultural values and daily patterns of work among the mission population. Cawte believed that personality disorders and neuroses at Kalumburu were double the rates outside, adding: 'The personality disorder which permeates Kalumburu . . . is the passive-dependent variety, interwoven with passive-aggression.' He attributed this child-like dependence to the inmates' dependence on the mission and the lack of opportunity or stimulus to social action under a paternalistic regime.[21]

MISSION–ABORIGINAL RELATIONS

With few other options, Aboriginal people in the north remained as permanent inmates on over twenty missions, where their old world was ruptured and their children were increasingly confronted with new ideas. Missions were places of change because the missionaries were men and women of European culture—be it Spanish, German, French or English. Their very presence over time altered the Aboriginal world. Their food lured the people from their land, their material items changed ways, and their demands for work in return for food kept the people from their ceremonies. Missionaries were also intent on conversion. Therefore, Aboriginal people were influenced by both arms of the Civilising Mission—westernisation and Christianity. However, missionaries as a body did not agree how this Civilising Mission should be undertaken—how much of the great Aboriginal tradition should they tolerate?

The more conservative missionaries believed that Aboriginal people were pagans who needed the light of God and their old culture swept away. Some initially thought Aboriginal people lacked any spirituality, and that conversion might happen speedily. The Cistercians and the Pallotines at Beagle Bay tried to end traditional customs, which they considered were 'futile works of darkness'. (Their attitudes were softened in the 1930s by the anthropological work of their own Father Worms, who studied the ceremonies of the Yaoro near Broome. Worms was even entrusted with some sacred boards by elders.[22]) Missionaries from Mornington Island in the Gulf to Ooldea on the Nullarbor also tried to eradicate traditional culture. Reverend Schenk, who promoted progressive Aboriginal vocational training at the Mount Margaret mission, still considered Aboriginal culture to be a thing of the Devil.[23] Such conservative thinking dominated the Aboriginal mission scene until at least the 1950s, when it was modified by greater awareness of Aboriginal culture.

Liberal humanitarian missionaries, who remained in the minority until the 1950s, held a more positive view of Aboriginal culture. They saw parallels between Christianity and traditional ideas, and worked towards a blending of the two. Robert Love wrote in 1914 of a ritual cleansing and feeding ceremony practised by the Worora at Kunmunya towards Aboriginal visitors: 'When our Lord instituted the Last Supper he gave us no new observance, but took an age-old rite, sublimated it and gave it new content.'[24] Love developed a fascination

The Taylors ministering to Warnindilyaugwa children on the Groote Eylandt Anglican mission, c. 1950s. PIX MAGAZINE, COURTESY OF THE MITCHELL COLLECTION, STATE LIBRARY OF NEW SOUTH WALES.

with the beauty and complexity of the Worora language. After war service and clerical training, he returned in 1927 and focused on translating the Gospels of St Mark and St Luke into Worora. He became one of the first missionaries since colonial times—except for Carl Strehlow at Hermannsburg—to preach in an Aboriginal language.[25] Love decided to oppose sorcery because of its links with violence and death, and respect all else in Aboriginal culture. Given that sorcery explained most deaths and relations with strangers, it was still a significant cultural assault. Other liberals could not tolerate infanticide and the abandonment of decrepit people, even though they understood the traditional necessity for these practices in a semi-nomadic lifestyle.[26] In 1936 Love summed up his liberal Christian philosophy: 'I yield to none in recognizing the real intellectual ability of the Australian Aborigines. I honour their real, and indeed intense, religious sense and practices, and do not seek to overthrow these, but rather to use them as a basis for higher principles.'[27] Robert Love aimed to build Christian principles onto traditional life purely by example and education, rather than by prohibitions on tradition, which he realised would only drive it underground.

The Christian–traditional struggle, waged most fiercely by more conservative missionaries, was fought on many cultural issues, but was focused on initiation and polygamy. The former was seen by many missionaries as the ceremony that drew Aboriginal youth irrevocably into traditional life, and the latter was viewed as a moral depravity, in which older men used women and young girls as chattels.

Missionaries used their power and control of food to end initiations. Dick Roughsey recounted how missionaries at Mornington Island banned initiation in 1917, leaving the Lardil people frightened and confused. He himself escaped circumcision, somewhat to his relief.[28] Other missionaries used the dormitory system to prevent initiations and their months of preparation. The staff of the United Aborigines Mission at Ooldea used police to break up initiation ceremonies, sighing with relief: 'the devil's power and the evil spell was broken'.[29] Initiation was attacked by most missionaries, an act that threatened the thread of traditional knowledge and the core of Aboriginal religious life.

Similarly, polygamy was widely opposed. Missionaries tried to impose monogamous Christian marriage and also encouraged marriages that broke traditional kinship rules. This created feelings of guilt and fear, and also produced disruption within the community. Christine Choo, in her book *Mission Girls*, argued that control of marriage in the Kimberley 'represents the deep oppression of Aboriginal people', as it concerned 'their survival as a social and cultural group'.[30] Lazarus Lamilami recalled that his Maung people of Goulburn Island 'began to realize that if they married wrongly, it is not only for them but their children that the trouble comes'.[31] Much of the social and psychological disruption endemic on some missions was caused by such meddling. Bishop Gsell on Bathurst Island had the whole attack on polygamy down to a fine art. He purchased promised infant wives from the old Tiwi men with axes and tobacco, and placed them in the mission's dormitory to be raised as Christians. Between 1921 and 1938, Gsell bought 150 such 'wives'. Upon their maturity he easily found young Christian Tiwi men eager to marry these young women, men who might under tribal law have waited years longer for a wife.[32]

Conveying the message to Aboriginal people proved difficult as many Christian concepts simply had no equivalence in Aboriginal culture. The Dreamtime stories of great ancestors and their miraculous deeds helped people to comprehend the virgin birth, life after death and other Christian concepts. But their stories did not prepare them for sin, hell and ideas of redemption. They also lacked a sense of the geography of biblical events, and without ever seeing sheep, had no comprehension of Christian parables about flocks and good shepherds. Father Duncan McNab, who ministered around Derby, acknowledged this in 1885: 'There are simply no terms in their language fit to express our religious ideas.'[33] When shown biblical pictures, they saw a white

God, a white Jesus, white angels and a black Devil—a colour symbolism of white as good and black as evil that did not sit well with them.[34]

Language barriers also engendered difficulties. Misunderstandings caused people on one mission to sing for years, 'Jesus loves hair on the chest', instead of 'Jesus loves me'—obviously the simple mistake was made when the missionary pointed to his chest, trying to ask his informants the Aboriginal word for 'me'. Few missions early on taught in the local Aboriginal language and many resorted to pidgin English, which was a poor tool for conveying sophisticated ideas. Some, like Rev. Robert Love, refused to degrade Aboriginal intelligence by using pidgin and learned Worora instead.

Language barriers created a ludicrous situation at Yarrabah mission in 1930. C.J. Fletcher, who claimed the Ten Commandments were beyond the 'mental capacities' of the mission inmates, tried to teach these to adult baptism candidates with a combination of pidgin, actions and pictures from magazines:

> In teaching the First Commandment, I used an advertisement for Eno's Fruit Salt, representing an Eastern sitting by the roadside and holding a lemon in his hand. After blackening the face in the picture to make it appear more like that of an aborigine, the cutting was shown to the class and introduced as the illustration of a medicine man—the lemon was misrepresented as a stone which the magician had just pretended to have extracted from the organs of a patient. (This, of course, is a common trick of the native witch doctor.) In association with this picture was learned by the class, 'Only one God—no more medicine man.' . . .
>
> For the Seventh Commandment a finger was dipped in the dirt and used to dramatise, 'No think dirty, no speak dirty, no do dirty'; while the attractive properties of another digit smothered in glue were used to illustrate 'No steal'.[35]

Fletcher, who believed 'these very crude methods were successful', baptised the group. Yet, how could such crude methods possibly convey moral values, let alone subtle religious ideas? The Yarrabah people no doubt were bewildered and had a good laugh about it afterwards. It was in this fashion that some conversions 'happened'.

Many missionaries fell between the conservative and the liberal ends of the spectrum—or shifted over their lifetime as they grew closer to Aboriginal people and the world changed around them. Pastor Friedrich Albrecht, who ministered at the Lutheran Hermannsburg mission from 1926 to 1962, experienced such change. He once wrote that 'the mission wants to bring the Gospel to these heathens; the decision is theirs whether they want to take the final steps to Christianity. We never bribed anybody, and the handing out of rations never depended on their conversion.' However, he often made suggestions about cultural changes—for instance, in the marriage system. They were no more than suggestions, but of course new ideas could be alarming. One person recalled: 'They got a bit upset. How come that bloke wants to break our Law, very important Law, and it's all tied together with the land, and the tjurunga, and the promise system. And they didn't like it.'[36] However, over the years, Albrecht, his wife Minna and their children developed strong mutual bonds of affection with Aranda people. By the end of his long career, he remarked: 'When we first came here we thought we had found the only people in the world without a religion. Now we have learnt that they are among the most religious people in the world.'[37]

RESISTING MISSIONARIES

Aboriginal culture was strong and missionaries found change was generally difficult to achieve. Strict adherence to kinship avoidance rules forced the staff at some missions either to hold separate church services or place a high curtain down the aisle of the church and have two entrances. Aboriginal people sometimes argued with or secretly ridiculed missionaries. The Nyul Nyul elders at Beagle Bay, who valued fertility highly, were unimpressed by the Virgin Mary, and claimed the Sermon on the Mount simply replicated their own law of reciprocity.[38] After a baptism service at Beagle Bay in 1900, Daisy Bates observed some people mimicking Bishop Gibney's Latin incantations and blessings, to peals of laughter from the rest of the camp.[39] Others feigned compliance but practised covert resistance. As Christine Choo observed of the Kimberley: 'Aboriginal women resisted colonization by working at their own pace, escaping or running away from work, attempting to make contact with their families whom they were forbidden to contact, marrying Aboriginal, *coloured* or Asian men, learning and maintaining their languages and customs, and retaining their family contacts.'[40] They also maintained views about their relations with whites that reflected ideas of injustice.

Many elders resisted the missionaries by spiriting the young men and women away to secret initiation ceremonies, which were often hasty affairs, lest the missionaries intervene. The Cistercians at Beagle Bay, to their horror, chanced upon their altar boys in the bush smeared with ochre and blood and undergoing initiation. The boys returned to the church, donned red soutanes and white surplices and commenced Latin incantations, after which they enjoyed a mission meal.[41] By keeping secret their ongoing traditional life, the Nyul Nyul elders were maintaining tradition and enjoying the sanctuary and benefits of Beagle Bay. For the boys, it is possible that both moments were sincere cultural expressions for them—one blackfella, one whitefella.

If the balance could not be maintained, people left the mission. As time went on, and there were fewer places to go, they stayed and learned the new religion. But often this was on their terms, by a selective borrowing from the new. This is revealed by the fragments of Christian knowledge that the old Madnala people remembered in 1945 from their twelve-year association with the Jesuit missionaries on the Daly River in the 1890s. The Bible stories were not used by the Madnala to gain spiritual truth, but were arranged in their memory in traditional Aboriginal song-cycle form, to explain their predicament following white invasion. In their version of the biblical facts, God was white and Adam and Eve were black. Their expulsion from Eden explained why the Madnala had to live off bush tucker, while the whites had all the power and received all the food they needed. The Bible for them was a story of power and injustice, not of Christian revelation.[42] Pastor Albrecht also recalled: 'the question of earthly possessions and monetary gain which have a big part in the teachings of our Lord, mean little to them; native Christians have told us such passages of scripture refer to white people. They find little interest in what God said to Adam, that he should dig in the garden, that he should eat his bread in the sweat of his brow.'[43]

RELIGIOUS CHANGE

Change was inevitable as two cultures engaged and became entangled. When change came from within Aboriginal society, it was to prove enduring. The missionaries' presence—the words, suggestions and models they provided—resonated with some people. This was the liberal humanitarians' hope. In the 1930s, three Worora men at Kunmunya—Njimandum, Woondoonmoi and Albert Barungga, who daily assisted Robert Love in translating the Gospels—became leaders of some radical changes. None were professed Christians, but they were strongly influenced by their friendship with Love and his Christian principles.

Njimandum, a crewman on the mission's lugger, wanted his son Alan Mungulu to avoid the rigours of circumcision, and proposed to elders that Alan miss the cutting part of initiation. The elders were furious and refused any avoidance of this test of manhood and guarantee of adherence to tribal law. Njimandum faced their wrath alone as Love refused to support him openly, believing the Worora must decide. Njimandum held firm to his decision and Alan Mungulu only participated in part of the ceremony. Later, Njimandum refused to give his daughter in marriage to her promised older husband, who had other wives as well, arguing that on the mission this old custom must now be abandoned. Woondoonmoi, Albert Barungga and younger men supported him, and polygamy was eroded. Woondoonmoi disrupted another tradition—the law that each Worora man must place a stone under the funeral platform of a deceased person. If fluid from the corpse stained any stone, it meant that he who placed that stone was the murderer and liable to be killed. At the crucial moment in one funeral in the 1930s, Woondoonmoi declared: 'We will not put any stones!' Probably because Love was present, no man protested, and the threatening custom lapsed. Traditions were modified indirectly in other places by Aboriginal individuals who were attracted by missionary ideas or who took advantage of their presence to modify practices that they found irksome.[44]

Conversion was the core of the Civilising Mission. But Aboriginal converts were few compared to the Pacific, where whole groups converted at once, usually at the beckoning of a chief. In Aboriginal Australia, conversion was slow and piecemeal due to the strength of traditional culture. Bishop Gsell lamented tellingly of the Bathurst Island mission in 1954: 'even after thirty years of work we still could not claim one single adult convert'.[45] Conversion, when it did happen, was almost exclusively of the young. They had most exposure to Christian teachings through the dormitory, and had less to lose and more to gain from engagement with missionaries. They were also less tied to tradition. Conversion also depended on the attitude of the missionary; whether he recognised Aboriginal tentative interest, and how he defined readiness. Those who allowed Aboriginal initiative did best.

Ernest Gribble, despite his fiery and authoritarian ways and the punishments he meted out, did well at the Anglican mission at Yarrabah. Within three years of commencement in 1893, he baptised nine men and women and appointed seven male lay-readers. Despite being called 'Dadda' by the people, he gave them opportunities for leadership and respected their ability. He did not attack traditional culture, believing it would soon fade. James Noble joined Gribble at Yarrabah. He was a stockman in western Queensland who was educated in the evenings at Scone Grammar School, at the expense of his bosses. He converted to Christianity and found his way to Yarrabah, where he proved invaluable to

Gribble. James Noble married Angelina, who was rescued by police after years as a 'drover's boy' called 'Tommy' and sent to Yarrabah. James and Angelina assisted Gribble in establishing the Mitchell River mission in 1904. The Nobles pioneered the Roper River mission in 1908, accompanied Gribble to Forrest River in 1914 and then to Palm Island in 1932. After a preaching tour of eastern states, James was ordained as a deacon in 1925. He and Angelina now lie together in the Yarrabah cemetery.[46]

James and Angelina Noble with mission children, c. 1900. COURTESY OF THE MITCHELL COLLECTION, STATE LIBRARY OF NEW SOUTH WALES.

The Lutherans founded a mission in 1874 at Hermannsburg in Aranda country 140 kilometres west of Alice Springs. They enjoyed good relations with the people. Aranda children attended the missionary school, where they came under both influences—traditional and Christian. By 1887 seven Aranda teenagers requested and received baptism. A second group was baptised in 1890, including a boy named Tjalkabotta, who chose the Christian name of Moses. Moses and other baptised boys were taken by elders and circumcised and shown the sacred stones. Carl Strehlow, who arrived in 1894, had a deep anthropological and linguistic interest and did not stamp out traditional culture. After marriage in 1903 to Sofia, Moses lost his sight and became a teacher in the mission's baptism classes. More baptisms followed.

When Friedrich Albrecht arrived in 1926, he also built on traditional culture, which he did not oppose if it was not against Christian teachings. To instil responsibility, he arranged for church elders to be elected from the Aboriginal congregation. Albrecht also encouraged evangelists and soon Moses, Titus and others were spreading the Gospel independently. They spoke in settlements and cattle stations or worked permanently at Hermannsburg's western outstations, such as Haast Bluff. Albrecht gave them yearly refresher courses, but otherwise left them to it. He allowed Conrad Raberaba to take the Hermannsburg morning service from around 1950. Albrecht remarked in 1965 that Aboriginal prayer-giving revealed a deeper spirituality than he had heard from many learned European clerics. Christianity at Hermannsburg grew out of a deep Aboriginal internalisation of Christian values.[47]

Albrecht and, perhaps surprisingly, Ernest Gribble had trusted Aboriginal people to evangelise. Other missionaries remained colonial managers as well as men of God, and this mixture alienated Aboriginal people and fostered their dependency. This was evident at Kalumburu, which was under Benedictine control in 1977, when the federal government considered self-management. Superintendent Father Sanz claimed the people were 'very, very, very lazy' and 'did not see the need to work'. He believed any takeover by the residents would fail and ruin the valuable mission enterprise. The community was in a quandary, being diffident about their own abilities to manage the mission, despite the Benedictines' presence and training since 1908. Most wanted the missionaries to stay.[48] However, in June 1981 some more confident residents threatened to walk off the mission in protest at the continued paternalism of the Benedictines. The missionaries' refusal to allow a World Council of Churches investigating team to visit Kalumburu at this time added weight to the people's claims that the missionaries were autocrats.

A NEW ERA

The 1950s was a watershed for missions. New ideas were aboard in the mission field from the 1930s, and the Anglican and Methodist mission societies were outspoken on Aboriginal welfare from that time.[49] Society generally was more interested in issues of human and Aboriginal rights. New respect was emerging for Aboriginal culture, and the idea took hold that a place should be found for it, alongside the European–Christian tradition. Increasingly, missionaries learned Aboriginal languages and preached in the local tongue. There was also more thought given to Aboriginal self-reliance. Also, in 1953 the Australian government decided to finance and staff medical and educational facilities on missions. This finally ended the struggling, undercapitalised nature of most missions. However, instead of being confronted by a few missionaries, communities were now faced by teams of advisers and greater pressures from assimilation policies. Some churches encouraged self-management to give Aboriginal people a say in their future. In 1965 a Methodist Church inquiry called for more Aboriginal self-determination, and community councils quickly sprang up on Methodist missions. However, by the 1960s missions still lay along a liberal–conservative spectrum, but the balance had swung towards liberalism. A brief glance at two missions of this period will illuminate these two styles.

The Presbyterian mission established in 1937 among the Pitjantjatjara people at Ernabella in the Musgrave Ranges, Central Australia, is a gem of Australian missionary endeavour. Charles Duguid, a Scottish-born doctor, advocate for Aboriginal rights and Presbyterian Church Moderator, was the inspiration behind Ernabella. Duguid learned from the failure of others, and wanted to avoid undermining tribal traditions and authority in the quest for souls and the survival of Aboriginal people. Duguid urged that at Ernabella, 'Jesus must be lived among them before they can understand what Jesus is, and the best of their own culture must be retained. But when they have seen and experienced the best that the new civilisation brings them they will desire it. We must be content to wait till then.'[50] Ernabella also benefited from Rev. Robert Love's guidance in its formative years and his presence from 1941 to 1946 as superintendent. Children (and their parents) were not compelled to wear clothing at school, nor were the young people confined in dormitories. Duguid wrote of the children who came voluntarily to school each day from the camp: 'they arrived at the little school-house dusty with red sand and the ashes of small fires which kept them warm at night. They had great fun hosing each other down, and it was a merry sight to see the little gleaming bodies running about in the sunshine until they were warm and dry.'[51] Their parents were not made dependent on mission food and were encouraged to gather bush tucker, with their children at their side, and also to collect dingo scalps for sale. If and when they did work on the mission, they were largely unsupervised. Wages and conditions, like all important matters, were agreed upon by consultation.

The schoolchildren were taught in Pitjantjatjara but later in English as well. This was Duguid's wish and that of the first schoolteacher, Robert Trudinger, who became a clever Pitjantjatjara linguist. Tensions arose with Robert Love, who wanted English taught as well, to equip the people for the inevitable clash with the outside world. So while Trudinger taught school in the vernacular,

Love preached daily in English. It was a question of balance and a clash of wills developed between the young teacher and the older missionary. Duguid sided with Trudinger, and Love, then 57 years old, decided to step down. However, both men co-operated on translating the Gospels into the local language—with the people's tuition. The Gospels were completed and used in the 1940s, and the *Pitjantjatjara Shorter Bible* appeared in 2006, contributing to the survival of the language.[52]

The Pitjantjatjara at Ernabella (now called Pukatja) were given time to adjust to the invading European culture, with the consequence that a great deal of traditional culture, including the important ceremonies of initiation, survived. The only restrictions on traditional life at Ernabella were that no corroborees were to be held on Sundays. Those who accepted the mission's food were expected to attend the church service and at least listen to the Christian message. In the main, they enjoyed a large degree of religious free will. A church was built in 1952 by Trudinger (superintendent 1949–1957), 400 attending the opening. By 1960 a fifth of the population was baptised, church elders elected, and services at outstations were being conducted by Pitjantjatjara preachers. The number of Christian Pitjantjatjara continued to grow, yet tradition was maintained. Bill Edwards, who ministered there in the 1970s, claimed recently Pitjantjatjara Christians continue to fulfil totemic obligations as 'they see no conflict between their acceptance of these obligations and their commitments to the Christianity'. Change has been effectively managed by such incorporation of new ideas.[53]

The Apostolic Church missionaries, who established themselves at Jigalong on the western edge of the Gibson Desert in 1945, made all the errors Duguid and Love at Ernabella had avoided. They were conservative biblical fundamentalists, who had no respect for Aboriginal culture, believing 'the Law must be destroyed and replaced with a Christian way of life'. They viewed the Jigalong people 'as the children of the devil, lost in the great darkness and steeped in sin'.[54] Their regime was strict. Children were taken away from the camps and placed in dormitories where they were regimented, preached to, and beaten for misdemeanours. There was little communication between the missionaries and the Jigalong people, as the missionaries never learned their language, socialised with the people or visited their camp, which they viewed as immoral. Indeed, the missionaries' attitudes were so archaic that Aboriginal culture at Jigalong was maintained. The people had little interest in these disagreeable missionaries or their version of Christianity, which they saw as containing no love and charity, unlike their own beliefs. The Jigalong people firmly adhered to tradition and indeed revitalised it in the face of such opposition.

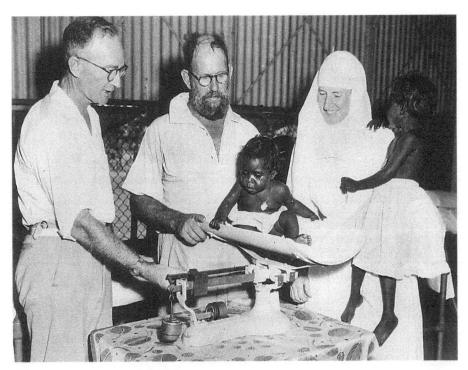

Health care on a northern mission, c. 1960. COURTESY OF THE AUSTRALIA TRAVEL INDUSTRY ASSOCIATION.

The Jigalong increasingly resisted the missionaries' intolerable actions and attitudes. They staged a walkout in 1962, which caused panic among the missionaries who were poised to lose their flock and basis for funding. In 1967 the people forced a government inquiry, which proved their allegations that the missionary superintendent had thrashed a nine-year-old girl so severely that there were welts on her legs for three months. In 1969 the Apostolic Church took the government's 'advice' and withdrew. The Jigalong mob and their traditions had survived and triumphed. As one Jigalong resident put it gleefully, 'Aboriginal law had proved too strong for Christianity'.[55]

A related case occurred at Doomadgee in the Gulf Country, where authoritarian missionaries from the Brethren Assembly formed a mission in 1931. They made some headway by the 1970s with baptisms, some 'revivals', and a minority of Aboriginal people who accepted full fellowship of the Assembly. The missionaries' conservative and ethnocentric attitudes meant they managed the mission in an authoritarian way and this fostered conflict between Christian and traditional ideas. The minority who accepted church membership shared some power with the missionaries as community councillors, which created splits with the other Aboriginal residents. Most Doomadgee residents passively tolerated the missionaries' presence, bound as they were with them in a paternal-deference relationship, retreating where possible to their own spaces for escape.[56]

It is now recognised that Aboriginal cultures had always expressed a deep spirituality—yet so often Aboriginal people had shown little interest in Christian religion. This was because Christianity in Australia was, until the 1980s, so culture-bound. The Apostolic Church and the Brethren Assembly failed because they mixed a version of Western culture—fundamentalist, puritan and ethnocentric—with the tenets of Christianity. The Christian vision was compromised in many other mission situations as well, by ethnocentrism, whiteness and also by colonialism, as most Christian church missions were funded by, or agents of, the state in twentieth-century Australia.

This nexus between colonialism and Christianity was ruptured when Aboriginal people over time internalised Christian ideas and expressed them for themselves, and sometimes used them as a way of resisting settler society—for Christianity did offer them equality before God. This had occurred in the south with scattered conversions from the 1860s. It intensified from the 1930s when Eddy Atkinson, a Yorta Yorta man from the Cummeragunja community, and then Doug Nicholls (later Sir Doug) became pastors and created vibrant Aboriginal congregations in Mooroopna and Fitzroy in Melbourne.[57] Nicholls concurrently fought vigorously for Aboriginal rights and identity. Pentecostalism was spread among the Bandjalang people of northern New South Wales by an Aboriginal pastor in the 1940s, who also used it to assert Aboriginality.[58] In the north, this embracing of Christianity occurred in several places. In 1979 on Galiwin'ku (Elcho Island), a former Methodist mission, an Aboriginal Christian revival movement emerged. Led by Rev. Djiniyini Gondarra and Kevin Rrur-rambu, it spread through Arnhem Land and as far as the Western Desert communities, including Jigalong and Ernabella. At Yarrabah in the 1980s, some in the community experienced Christian visions, which also led to a powerful revival movement.[59]

The churches, led by the Lutheran, Methodist, Anglican and the Uniting Churches, also helped sever the connection of colonialism and Christianity. This cleaving took the form of the ordination of Aboriginal clergy, which broke the nexus of white power and Christianity. James Noble was the first clergyman ordained, in 1925 but he was only made a deacon, unable to dispense the sacraments. However, in 1964 the Lutherans ordained Conrad Raberaba and Peter Bulla at Hermannsburg; the Methodists, Lazarus Lamilami at Croker Island in 1966; and the Anglicans, Patrick Brisbane in 1969. Since then there has been a stream of ordinations. Reverend Arthur Malcolm was ordained in

1978 and anointed in 1985 as an Anglican Bishop with special duties among Aboriginal people. In 1973 the Uniting Church and Anglicans formed Nungalinya College in Darwin to train Aboriginal Christian workers.[60]

By the late twentieth century, a greater proportion of Aboriginal Australians were professed and practising Christians than other Australians. A syncretism between Aboriginal and Christian cultures was emerging in the minds of many Aboriginal people, and this was gaining some ritual expression. Church iconography, orders of service, ceremonies, even architecture, have embraced Indigenous themes. The Warlpiri, for example, have developed an Easter *purlapa* or corroboree. The churches in turn have shrugged off some Western perceptions in accepting these movements. Many progressive churches, including the Catholic Church, have since the 1980s embraced social justice, forming Aboriginal and Islander congresses and other forums for their Aboriginal members to speak out. These churches have also supported land rights, reconciliation, made apologies, and have even given compensation in the form of land and property for their errors of the past.

9

CONTROLLED BY BOARDS
AND CASTE BARRIERS

In the first two-thirds of the twentieth century, Aboriginal people in southern or 'settled' Australia were controlled in two ways. First, control was exercised formally by Aboriginal Boards acting under special legislation, which incarcerated people on reserves, managed their daily lives and work, fragmented families, and denied them civil rights. Second, control was by unofficial customary discrimination—termed by observers a 'caste barrier'—against those who were deemed Aboriginal on the basis of their skin colour.

In settled Australia 20,000 Aboriginal people survived by the 1920s, a mere tenth of their number at first contact. More than half were people of mixed descent called 'half-castes' by other Australians and governments. There were perhaps 5000 in southern Queensland, 7000 in New South Wales, 500 in Victoria, less than 200 in Tasmania (mostly on Cape Barren Island), 1000 in southern South Australia and 2500 people of mixed descent in south-west Western Australia. A fifth lived on reserves, and four-fifths were in camps adjoining country towns. A handful owned farms, some lived in towns and a few in the capital cities. During the 1930s Depression, many campers were pushed back onto reserves to save paying them the dole, while others moved there to get rations. In New South Wales, reserve dwellers by 1941 rose to almost half the Aboriginal population.[1] The Second World War induced some to move to the cities. There is no neat or constant demographic pattern in 'settled' Aboriginal Australia, except to say that mobility was a key characteristic, as people moved to visit kin, find work, or at the will of—or to escape from—the authorities.

CONTROL OF RESERVES AND CHILDREN

Life on reserves in settled Australia was generally spartan, tough, and often closely controlled by regulations, although not all reserves had managers. The one reserve in Victoria after 1920 was Lake Tyers, which had a managed regime. About half the 22 reserves in New South Wales had managers, the rest being controlled haphazardly by the local police. Regulations under the Aboriginal acts in the name of 'protection' stated that, in return for food, shelter and some education, the residents had to obey the manager, submit to house inspections and were liable to have their children taken and apprenticed to Europeans as cheap labour. They had to do a 'reasonable amount of work' at a wage fixed by the manager. If they refused, they could have their rations withheld or be expelled from the reserve and thus from home and kin. Most states restricted free movement on and off the reserves. An amendment to the NSW Act in 1936 gave the Aborigines Protection Board new powers to carry out compulsory medical checks and remove people to reserves.

Life under Aborigines Protection Boards could be like a police state, although most Boards never had sufficient resources to achieve their full power. The Board in Victoria almost became defunct, being run by one part-time public servant after the 1920s. By then it refused to recognise any Aboriginal people as Indigenous, unless they resided at Lake Tyers reserve. By denying the Indigenous identity of those off reserves it sought to deny Aboriginality. Rigorous board and reserve regimes existed in New South Wales, Queensland, Western Australia and South Australia as described in great detail respectively by Heather Goodall in *Invasion to Embassy* (1996), Rosalind Kidd in *The Way We Civilise* (1997), Anna Haebich in *For Their Own Good* (1988) and Cameron Raynes in *The Last Protector* (2008).

Aboriginal Boards were run by public servants who had great power over Aboriginal people. In New South Wales Robert Donaldson for several decades shaped Aboriginal lives and removed children around the First World War. John Bleakley was Chief Protector in Queensland for over two decades and Cornelius O'Leary followed him for a similar time. In Western Australia, Auber Neville was Chief Protector for 25 years. None of these men came with skills beyond the bureaucratic for their job, but through experience they gained influence with governments. Donaldson shaped the NSW 1909 Act and its repressive amendments to remove children, making up lists of children to target. Neville perfected a bureaucratic system in the west that tracked and shaped Aboriginal lives through personal files and a web of correspondence. Neville even went beyond regulations and arranged and approved marriages.[2]

Auber Neville's administration created two settlements in the south-west of the state, Carrolup north of Albany, and Moore River at Mogumber north of Perth. These reserves segregated Aboriginal people who were mostly of mixed descent for training and eventual absorption. This was done by way of children's dormitories, which separated them from their parents, who were at a nearby camp. Aboriginal people were encouraged to move to these settlements by reducing ration relief elsewhere, and were forced by ministerial warrant. Cost-cutting in the early 1920s closed Carrolup in 1922, creating much overcrowding at Moore River where conditions deteriorated. Housing was primitive, clothing minimal and rations poor. Conditions at the adults' camp were even poorer. Little real education occurred, so people at best were fitted for low-skilled rural labouring and domestic service, for which there was always great demand. Many girls returned from domestic service pregnant to employers or their sons and workers. Moore River's regime was stern, enforced by Aboriginal trusties and black trackers, usually outsiders from the north, who did the manager's bidding. This included meting out physical punishment. The reserve had its own gaol, called the 'Boob', and those who resisted the regime got to know its interior very well.

Aboriginal memories of Moore River are often hostile, for it was not a free place. Inmate Charlie Anthill in 1923 related his impressions in staccato phrases, saying it was 'no good, no good at all. Tucker very little, no meat, little bread,

Children at the Moore River settlement in 1930. COURTESY OF THE BATTYE LIBRARY, STATE LIBRARY OF WESTERN AUSTRALIA (226011PD0).

little jam . . . Saw Boss hit boy maybe twelve years old on head and knock him down . . . Boss put him in prison one day then tie him to a tree and have him flogged . . . no good to me. I leave pretty quick.'[3] Thomas Corbett arrived there in 1920 and noted that 'the rations given us were not enough to keep body and soul together'. He spent 24 years at Moore River, and he and his wife Rose raised a family of six children. He recalled a succession of superintendents good and bad, 'but while I deferred to them, I never cowered to them'.[4] The memories of Alice Nannup (nee Barrett) from the Pilbara, who arrived at Moore River in 1925 aged fourteen, are also mixed. She recalled very poor food, stern discipline, education only to grade-three standard and lots of hard work in the store room, sewing room, the superintendent's house and kitchen. But there was some free time for bush walks, swimming and dances and special times like Christmas, when the Moore River choir 'made the ranges ring, and that's the only time Mogumber was ever beautiful'.[5] She envied those at the camp who actually ate better—having access to bush foods—and were less controlled than the dormitory children. The inmates pinched extra food and at times evaded the reserve's rules. When caught, they earned a thrashing or some public humiliation, like hair cropping and a time in the 'Boob'.[6] Playwright Jack Davis was sent to Moore River by his farming parents, not forced by the authorities, as his parents mistakenly believed he would receive a good farming education there. This did not happen but he became steeped in traditional culture, which thrived among the old at the camp. This traditional education later flowered in a wonderful series of literary writings—Moore River created some surprising legacies as well as the dismal ones.[7]

Ironically at this time of Board control, some Aboriginal men fought for the freedom of the Empire on foreign battlefields. The Defence Act (1903) allowed enlistment only of those of 'European origin or descent', and military authorities were wary of taking those of mixed descent, but some did manage to enlist. It is known that in Queensland 200 men enlisted, as Bleakley tried to control their wages under the trust account system, being successful in at least eighteen cases. In the west, five members of the Kickett family enlisted, one of them being killed in action in France. Some Cape Barren Islanders enlisted, including nine of the Mansell family, six men of the Brown family and one each from the Burgess and Fisher families.[8] In Victoria, 42 Aboriginal men of mixed descent enlisted, one in three of those eligible, mirroring the general population. Five sons of Hannah and James Lovett of Lake Condah served. The Aboriginal sacrifice was large, as 20 per cent of Aboriginal servicemen from Victoria died in action, compared with 12 per cent of all servicemen. Private William Rawlings from Purnim and Corporal Harry Thorpe of Gippsland were awarded the military medal for valour. Both later died on the same day at Vauvillers on the Somme on 8 August 1918—just three months short of the war's end. They lie in Heath Cemetery, Harbonnieres, on the Somme with their comrades—equals in war, if not in peace.[9]

•

In all states, Aboriginal Boards operated apprenticeship schemes to place teenage boys and girls into work. Boys did farm work. Young girls were placed into domestic service, where they often suffered exploitation from the double jeopardy of being Aboriginal and female. Like all domestic servants, they were overworked and underpaid, being at the beck and call of their employers for at least six days of the week. They were expected to do household chores, cooking, child-minding and even gardening. In Queensland there were about 520 Aboriginal female domestics in service in 1920, a third of them under eighteen years of age. Shurlee Robinson, who has studied the domestic service of girls in Queensland, likened their work to 'slavery'. She used this analogy because of their arduous labour for a quarter of the European wage, the use of trust accounts which held all but pocket money, the isolation, and the lack of protection from physical and sexual abuse.[10]

In Western Australia at its peak in the late 1920s about 90 girls a year were sent from Moore River to domestic service by Auber Neville, who personally arranged their placements. Again, they earned much less than white domestics, and had most of their wages held in trust accounts controlled by Neville.[11] Alice Barrett (later Nannup) was sixteen when she left Moore River to enter service. She wrote of this in her book *When the Pelican Laughed* (1992). Her account is one of long hours and hard work, mostly seven days a week, similar to the life of non-Indigenous domestic workers who had a house and children to care for, and garden or farm work to do. She learned skills of cooking and sewing not taught at Moore River—although they were supposed to be—and taught herself to write by copying jam tin labels. Alice Nannup overall gave an account which is not one of misery, partly because she was bold and resourceful enough to stand up for herself.

Alice Barrett even worked for 'Mr Neville' in his household for a time. He paid her more than the award, gave her a day off a week and spoke kindly to her—even tolerating a little outspokenness. He re-employed her after she had absconded from a pastoral property because she had not been paid. Neville's attitude is perhaps surprising, but fits with his paternalism. He arranged her marriage to Will Nannup, who had been a casual boyfriend—giving her no say—but it worked out and together they had thirteen children, rearing ten. Her account reveals an authoritarian system, but within it, individual experiences were mixed and often tolerable. Face to face, people could be reasonable—even Neville.

Working for white people under strict controls and regulations was common fare for Aboriginal people, which is detailed by Henry Reynolds in *With the White People* (1990). Most Australian children worked from the age of fourteen at low wages and some under apprenticeships, but all Aboriginal Australian children were controlled under oppressive apprenticeships. Shurlee Robinson has written a strong account of this practice in Queensland entitled *Something Like Slavery: Queensland's Aboriginal Child Workers 1842–1945* (2008). The apprenticeship system operated in similar fashion in New South Wales—and was again marked by controlled hard work, low wages, trust accounts, and much misery. Margaret Tucker left an account of her travails in *If Anyone Cared* (1977), and Victoria Haskins discussed domestic service in *One Bright Spot* (2005).

Victoria Haskins has uncovered a darker aspect to this labour trade in New South Wales. The apprenticeship system was intimately connected to the absorptionist policy, not simply by placing young women in the wider world and off reserves, but because of the alarming rate of impregnation of these girls by whites—mostly in the workplace. While the Board was to be their protector, it placed them in situations where 11 per cent of those in service between 1912 and 1928 became pregnant. Board records for other years are unavailable, but it is likely this was an underestimate of the girls' level of sexual activity. Much of it would have been forced sexual activity. Predatory practices occurred in other state jurisdictions. In a letter to the Deputy Premier in 1924, Queensland Governor Leslie Wilson put the figure at 95 per cent, perhaps with some exaggeration.[12] Claims of 'consent' were unlikely, given that a young Aboriginal servant girl was working in a controlled situation in the presence of white employers, their sons and male workers, amid a racial discourse that maintained Aboriginal women were 'easy' and 'want it'.

There were constant complaints to the New South Wales Board about these pregnancies, by both white and black people, but the Board—which was well aware of the pregnancies—publicly dismissed the claims. An Aboriginal activist of the day, Fred Maynard, wrote to one fifteen-year-old pregnant girl: 'these white robbers of our woman virtues seem to do just as they like . . . the law stands for it. There is no clause in our own Aboriginal Act which stands for principles for our Girls.'[13] The Board clearly did not show any duty of care for those it was to protect, in spite of the evidence of widespread abuse. Nor did it pursue white fathers for maintenance, even though the general law provided for this after 1904. What the Board did do was to remove mixed-descent offspring, and send the young women back into service until they were free at eighteen. Haskins concludes that, in the context of the policy of absorption, and because it ignored all the clear evidence of sexual abuse, the Board 'colluded in, condoned and indeed encouraged the systematic sexual abuse and impregnation of young Aboriginal women in domestic apprenticeships with, I contend, the ultimate aim of eradicating the Aboriginal population'.[14]

THE CASTE BARRIER AND ITS CONDITIONS

Aboriginal people living off the reserves were controlled by a colour bar or caste system that created two social worlds: one white, one black. Such a caste system assigned people opportunities on factors outside their control, and regardless of their abilities. The white settler majority created this largely unofficial barrier— based on colour—because it dominated the social and economic life of rural areas. This 'system' of customary practices, which affected most areas of life, was in place across most of settled Australia. However, it did not much operate in the capital cities, where the small number of Aboriginal residents met with far less restriction on their access to goods, services and other social opportunities.

Sometimes customary barriers found official resonances. From the 1890s until 1949, New South Wales educational authorities excluded Aboriginal children from state schools, if non-Indigenous parents objected to their presence, usually on spurious health grounds. Those excluded attended reserve schools where they received a poorer education. This did not apply in Victoria, where there was only one reserve in any case, but it did in Western Australia, where parents could request the expulsion of an Aboriginal child on grounds of health, welfare or morality. Only 1 per cent of Aboriginal children in Western Australia in the 1930s were schooled in state schools.[15] In New South Wales, Aboriginal people were not permitted to purchase or drink alcohol, although this was generally permitted in Victoria, so men in border towns crossed the Murray to quench their thirst. Aboriginal people enjoyed greater freedoms in Victoria than other places, because its government pursued an assimilation policy from 1886, and besides, its Aboriginal population was small.

The customary practices of the caste barrier meant exclusion from many shops and businesses, churches, community organisations, social and sports clubs and the town's swimming pool. Hairdressers excluded Aboriginal customers lest their white clientele raise health concerns. Town housing was often made unavailable to Aboriginal people by estate agents to keep white areas 'safe' and 'pure'. Work opportunities were confined to domestic service for women, and for men to rural manual work on properties, the local council, and the railways. Social relations between the races were frowned upon by both communities as two domains—one white, one black—arose. This was the situation in many rural towns across southern Australia. Alice Nannup experienced this in Wyalkatchem in the Western Australian wheat belt around 1930. Stranded at the railway station one evening, she was threatened by a man, who told her to go or he would kill her. In tears, she was given comfort by a white woman who explained Aboriginal people were not allowed in town at night. Alice recalled: 'Wyalkatchem was a very prejudiced town. It was a real colour bar place.' All the Aboriginal workers in the district who had to come to town for supplies headed 'straight out again. That's what it was like, not a soul allowed after dark.'[16] As much of this discrimination was unofficial, it remained entrenched long after governments adopted assimilation policies in the 1940s.[17]

The caste barrier was never total and its rigidity depended upon the specific town, individual or aspect of life. Shopkeepers often sold goods to Aboriginal people, but served them last. They could purchase food from most cafes, but usually had to consume it elsewhere. Aboriginal people could attend picture theatres, but only sit in the roped-off front seats. Those who dared sit elsewhere were thrown out and arrested for causing a disturbance. Children oblivious to prejudice and the caste barrier played together before they 'knew better'. Men mixed in the workplace but never at home. Women might be in the home together, as servant and mistress, but strict lines were drawn. One Aboriginal woman who visited a former employer was given 'a cuppa' in the kitchen while the white mistress spoke with her from the adjoining room. Social contacts were rare, except in sport, the great leveller in Australian society. Black football teams and black boxers vied against white sportsmen and sometimes joined their teams. There was sexual mixing too, but invariably in covert liaisons, which before the 1940s rarely ended in marriage unless the Aboriginal partner—invariably a woman—was fair in colour. Despite living in proximity, two separate social worlds usually existed.

This segregation blighted Aboriginal lives and gnawed away at the Aboriginal psyche. When in town, people experienced a dozen forms of rejection as they moved along footpaths, negotiated shops and encountered people. Aboriginal children learned this stigma from the first moment of name-calling or a thump from European children. Every time Aboriginal people approached a social encounter with a white Australian, they anticipated that look, that coolness, that unease, or even that overt sneer, that spelt white rejection. Indeed, Aboriginal people were victims of ambiguity as customs began to alter. Once Aboriginal children were readmitted to state schools in New South Wales after 1949, they were still banned from swimming pools in some towns. They could swim during the school's visit to the pool, but had to exit at 3 p.m., while their white colleagues could swim on. Some defied rejection, but their very defiance rested on the racial caste barrier: the fact of their blackness and its rejection in a white-dominated society.

Stereotypes that Aboriginal people were worthless, dirty or inferior were widely held and reinforced in advertising in the 1920s. Commercial brands used boomerangs and Aboriginal bodies to advertise butters, meats, and in particular paints and cleaning products, making play with black and white. 'White Way' paint was advertised by a black face declaring, 'dis will do'—a product of American 'black-face' stereotypes, as much as Australian home-grown racism. A cleanser, 'Nulla Nulla Australia's White Hope, the best Household soap', was advertised by a black-faced person being struck on the head with a nulla nulla under the caption 'knocks dirt on the head'. The word 'dirt' hung around the person's neck, imprinted on what was the unmistakable shape of a brass breast plate or gorget. These had been given to Aboriginal people over the years since Governor Macquarie first presented gorgets to 'chiefs' in 1816.[18] Jokes of the day also made racist play with supposed Aboriginal characteristics of dimwittedness and other stereotypes. These racist views persisted well into the second half of the twentieth century, as revealed in surveys conducted by Lorna Lippmann in the 1960s and by Gillian Cowlishaw in the 1970s.[19] Their endemic nature affected even the most resilient. Activist Chicka Dixon recalled of the 1940s: 'you walk down the street and you're black and the white man discriminates against you. He doesn't have to say a word to you. He steps around you, you're shit, you're nothing. And they cut you down with this sort of concept and you get that way, you feel it, you feel inferior.'[20]

White racism underpinned colonialism, which induced a cycle of poverty in Aboriginal people. Aboriginal workers congregated in low-paid, unskilled occupations and seasonal work. About a quarter were unemployed at any one time, and others were underemployed. Fruit and vegetable pickers in the Murray and Goulburn Valleys, Gippsland and the southern New South Wales coast earned good wages, especially as a family enterprise. However, living conditions were camp-style and the work only lasted eight months, even if the various

Nulla Nulla soap advertisement, c. 1920s.

harvests were followed. Aboriginal pastoral labourers, shearers or woodcutters were outside the unions, which showed them little interest, and received wages below the award. As late as the 1950s on isolated New South Wales properties, Aboriginal workers were still being paid in colonial fashion, partly in beef, flour and grog, all rated at inflated prices.[21] Aboriginal women, who did domestic work on stations, in homes in town and the local hospital, were poorly paid. Consistent wage justice only came when people worked for local councils or government departments, such as the railways, which had standardised wages. This low-paid, low-skilled cycle lasted for generations. A New South Wales survey in the mid-1960s found that 81 per cent of Aboriginal workers were unskilled, 18 per cent semi-skilled, and just 1 per cent were skilled.[22]

Meagre and irregular Aboriginal pay packets needed to meet larger demands than those of European workers, further compounding Aboriginal poverty. Aboriginal nuclear families were larger, and kinship obligations stretched Aboriginal wages further. Paid work was also missed due to kinship obligations. If a choice ever arose between attending a kin's funeral and going to work, kinship obligations always triumphed. Besides family loyalty, this was good economic sense, because the support of one's kin offered almost as much economic security as that provided by a job. Indeed, for Nyoongar rural workers in south-west Western Australia, their kinship ties even influenced 'where people worked, with whom they worked, the type of work that they did and how they shared the available resources'.[23]

Aboriginal housing reflected their low status and income. Houses on reserves were low-cost units. They were poorly maintained by authorities, and soon became as dilapidated as the home-made humpies that dotted the camps on the fringes of towns around the country. These camp humpies were conglomerations of second-hand wood, iron sheeting, hessian bags and flattened kerosene tins, perched precariously over earth floors on flood-prone riverbanks or town dumps. Such sites avoided official scrutiny, but were devoid of electricity, water and sewerage and garbage disposal. Humpies contained one or two rooms with a few beds and little furniture, much of it constructed from wooden boxes or kerosene tins. In many houses, cutlery and kitchen utensils were few and far between, enamel mugs and jam tins were often the only drinking vessels, and places to keep clothing were non-existent.

Instead of providing comfort, security and privacy as a home should, Aboriginal dwellings were places of discomfort, as they provided little resistance to heat and cold, and were flood-prone. As Aboriginal families grew in size after the 1920s, due to declining death rates, housing became overcrowded. A survey of 200 Aboriginal families in New South Wales in the mid-1960s revealed that Aboriginal dwellings contained, on average, half as many rooms and twice as many people as the average Australian home: Aboriginal houses were four times as crowded as the homes of other Australians. The survey also found that a third of the dwellings were little better than sheds.[24] Overcrowding and poor conditions placed strains on family life and disturbed sleep. Ill health spread rapidly in these conditions.[25] Such housing caused scandals among compassionate whites, as in the case of outrage about shanties in the Framlingham forest in 1933.[26] Local councils targeted these camps as 'eyesores', bulldozing camps at Mooroopna 'Flat' in 1948 and at Drouin in 1964.

Yet we should not confuse poor material conditions with unhappiness or poor parenting. Jackson's Track was an Aboriginal camping place near Drouin in Gippsland from the 1930s, where people lived rough in humpies on the edge of the forest. But Euphemia Mullett, who raised twelve children there in the 1950s, recalled great happiness, despite the deprivation. The residents enjoyed a loving extended family, bush tucker, sawmill work for the men, a school for the children, and singing and prayer meetings. Euphemia's son, Russell Mullett, added: 'we were free at Jackson's Track. Anybody could come and visit us . . . the manager of Lake Tyers couldn't hassle us.'[27] Across Aboriginal Australia, people characterised as indigent 'fringe dwellers' relished freedom from authority, but not the poor conditions. Such conditions provided ammunition for those who wished to remove children—blaming the victims, and arguing these places were unfit for families.

Young Lionel Rose, later a world champion boxer (centre back row) with friends at the Jackson's Track camp, near Drouin, Victoria, c. 1956. COURTESY OF ALICK JACKOMOS.

Material deprivation clearly contributed to Aboriginal ill health, which equalled levels of ill health experienced by European Australians a century before. Aboriginal infant mortality rates in New South Wales between 1950 and 1964 ranged from 90 to 76 deaths per 1000 live births (similar to Third World rates of one in ten). This was much better than the 143 per 1000 live births suffered by Aboriginal people in the Northern Territory, but four times greater than that of other Australians. The death rate in the second year of life for Aboriginal children in New South Wales was between sixteen and nineteen per 1000 live births, less again than the equivalent Northern Territory Aboriginal rate of 40, but eight times the rate of other Australian children.[28] There being no proof of any genetic reason for such high Aboriginal infant death rates, the answer lay in poor conditions and a lack of basic health care. Indeed, most Aboriginal infant deaths were due to gastroenteritis, pneumonia and malnutrition, the classic diseases of poverty.

Aboriginal health was impaired also by the lack of any trustworthy health service, for the Aboriginal Board had built a great dread of officialdom among Aboriginal people. People only attended clinics or took their children when illnesses had become serious, drastically reducing the chance of a speedy recovery. One country town study in 1971 revealed that Aboriginal children generally received medical attention so late that hospitalisation was necessary. Their rate of admission was ten times, and the length of their stay six times, that of other Australian children. Also, every Aboriginal child under two, and 92 per cent of those under five years old, had been hospitalised at least once in the year of the survey.[29]

Poverty led to poor eating and many survived too often on damper or bread, dipped in gravy or dripping. Meat, vegetables and fruit were luxuries in many families, although eggs, fish and milk were more common. Even those on reserves ate poorly. Chicka Dixon recalled his hunger at Lake Wallaga reserve: 'I was one of thirteen children. My father used to work one day a week for government rations. You would get government rations on Friday, it would be an all in go, and by Sunday there would be no tucker, so you'd starve till Wednesday, when he brought home some animal offal from a weekly job at the local slaughter yard.'[30] Such eating patterns created calcium, iron and vitamin deficiencies, causing anaemia. Surveys in the 1950s and 1960s found that 70 per cent and 50 per cent respectively of New South Wales Aboriginal children were anaemic—ten and twenty times the levels of anaemia in other Australian children. One medical researcher commented: 'The impact of this widespread anaemia on general health, levels of physical activity and school performance, and capacity to survive serious infection in childhood must be enormous.'[31] Other studies around 1970 revealed significant diet-related growth retardation in Aboriginal children—as much as four centimetres in height and four kilograms in weight. Consistent malnutrition can impact on intellectual ability.[32]

The school performance of Aboriginal children was undermined by many factors. Poverty and poor sanitation led to ear infections and hearing impairment in 40 per cent of Aboriginal children, ten times the community rate.[33] Aboriginal pupils considered to be poor achievers were simply poor hearers. Crowded and sometimes disruptive homes, uneducated parents and minimal money for school materials provided little help. Others performed poorly at school because of the conflict between their Aboriginal values and the European values presented there. School stressed regimentation, punctuality, individual performance and fierce competition, whereas the Aboriginal child's own background emphasised easygoing attitudes to discipline and clock-watching, and stressed co-operation. Little joy for learning could flourish in the face of the racism, and ignorance, of their fellow students and even teachers. Lessons on Australian history, which derided Aboriginal people as a 'savage', 'primitive' race, and which wrongly referred to Europeans as the 'discoverers of an unknown continent', were assaults on the self-esteem of Aboriginal children. The racial name-calling and fights that punctuated many lunchtimes and trips to and from school were also trials for Aboriginal children. Many were crushed by such an environment, in which they were usually a small minority.

The reserve schools, where most Aboriginal children were educated, were run by the Aborigines Protection Boards. Aboriginal children were considered inferior and taught accordingly. The syllabus at these schools aimed to teach Aboriginal children by the age of fourteen what state school pupils learned by the age of eight. Even after 1940, the new syllabus in New South Wales reserve schools devoted half the time to manual training, gardening and physical education, which only equipped the children for unskilled labour.[34] A survey in the mid-1960s revealed the dismal results of pre-1950 Aboriginal education in New South Wales: of those who were adults in 1965, 58 per cent had only received primary schooling, another 20 per cent had completed one or two years of high school, 2 per cent had reached intermediate and another 2 per cent had apprentice or other training. The educational background of the remaining 18 per cent was unrecorded, but was likely to be low.[35] These were rates that paralleled those of other Australians at least 50 years earlier.

ABORIGINAL RESPONSES TO THE CASTE BARRIER

Discrimination, caste barriers and white racism trapped Aboriginal people in poor education, lowly paid jobs, low esteem; and these in turn led to substandard housing, ill health, improvident habits, poverty, poor education . . . and so it went. The victim of the colonial condition, not colonialism itself, was blamed for what unfolded. How did Aboriginal people respond to this multi-causal cycle of poverty in which they were enmeshed for generations under colonialism? Put simply—and nothing is ever that simple in real life—the polarity of responses was either despair, or an attitude of defiance towards their oppressors. Many Aboriginal people exhibited both polarities over their lives, depending on circumstance, but for convenience they will be treated separately. Others had responses in-between and just got on with living and surviving.

Oscar Lewis studied the Latin American urban poor and detected alienation among them, which he called the 'culture of poverty'. Those within it were not integrated with the society at large, but rather lived on its fringes and fell apart from the mainstream. Those in the 'culture of poverty' constructed their own belief systems and networks for survival, feeling or actually being excluded from the mainstream. Lewis stated that 'the individual who grows up in this culture has a strong feeling of fatalism, helplessness, dependence and inferiority'. They had little time/work discipline, no sense of the future and instead lived for the moment.[36] Many Aboriginal people in camps and on reserves paralleled these broad forms of behaviour and exhibited the classic symptoms of alienation: anxiety, despair, low self-esteem and a sense of powerlessness. However, Aboriginal people shared such feelings not only because they were poor and powerless, but because that was the legacy of their colonial condition.

Aboriginal families in poverty, like those in Latin America, were often headed by women who managed crisis after crisis. These matriarchs provided necessary discipline in communities, which had little traditional authority remaining, and less respect for European law. Aboriginal boards and reserve managers undermined the role and status of men, and those unemployed slipped easily into aimlessness. Kevin Gilbert, a Wiradjuri man, noted a loss of dignity in certain men who cadged on their woman's child endowment, and their mother's pension. He commented of certain Aboriginal men in the 1960s in his powerful book, *Because a White Man'll Never Do It* (1973): 'A sub-cultural ethic, almost dictates that such a man does nothing but drink, fuck and fight'. Lewis had noted a similar machismo among males in the 'culture of poverty'. Gilbert added: 'There are places in New South Wales where all hell breaks out on Friday night. The entire reserve area is a shambles of drunkenness, fighting and bedlam. Children move from house to house and from bed to bed in an effort to keep clear of the drunks.'[37] Such lack of self-discipline and responsibility reflected years of forced dependence on European managers and demoralisation. A small minority played on this atmosphere of despair, lazing about, brawling, drinking and gambling and blaming it entirely on white racism. The majority who lacked discipline simply reflected confusion and a loss of purpose in their lives. Even some women fell to such despair. Gilbert remarked of some families: 'There was no regular mealtimes and often no meals as such. Everyone grabs whatever food is around when it is around . . . on many reserves, women spend a good part of their time gambling.'[38]

Alienation and loss of esteem caused some Aboriginal men to seek solace in alcoholic oblivion. Aboriginal men in Victoria could often drink in hotels, but this right was not given to those in New South Wales until 1962, unless they had a citizenship certificate or, as the people derisively termed it, a 'beer ticket'. However, prior to 1962 many obtained alcohol (admittedly at inflated prices) through illicit sources, generally white Australian middlemen, who dropped 'the grog' at a safe spot for a healthy profit. Aboriginal drinking patterns were shaped by this secretiveness. Fortified wine, which gave a quick high, was consumed rapidly in vacant allotments and on riverbanks.

Aboriginal male alcohol abuse expressed many things. Being a drinking man became a male rite of passage, and an act of defiance in order to regain some self-esteem. In a way it mirrored the ethic of hard drinking in the wider culture. It was also a way to forget problems, which were multiple for those in poverty. But it was done at great cost to family harmony and personal health and well-being. Problem drinking also diverted a quarter of the family's income into grog. One Victorian study in 1969 found that half the Aboriginal households surveyed contained at least one problem drinker.[39] Another study in Bourke, New South Wales, in 1971 revealed 53 per cent of Aboriginal men surveyed were heavy drinkers, and only 10 per cent were teetotallers. Aboriginal males in Bourke began drinking at an early age, and 36 per cent of boys aged between fourteen and nineteen years were reported to be regular drinkers. Other evidence suggests that these findings were typical of most areas in south-eastern Australia.[40] Few Aboriginal women misused alcohol, desiring to hold the family together and resenting the loss of money, neglect and violence that stemmed from alcohol abuse. However, half the Aboriginal women in Bourke in the 1971 study used 'headache' powders excessively—as did many white women—in order to feel good, and escape their problems or the boredom of reserve life.[41]

Self-hate and doubt developed within some individuals in a final collapse of morale. Gilbert recalled some people referred to themselves as 'rubbish'. In the 1950s, Ruth Fink met Aboriginal people who perceived themselves as lazier, dirtier, and bigger drinkers and gamblers than other Australians—although not all felt shame about it.[42] Such self-denigration, such 'rape of the soul', was a passing phase of the assimilation era and only occurred among some individuals; but it was real. A young Bourke woman remarked in 1971: 'I bust my guts to make everything clean and the welfare come in and make me feel dirty.' A young man in the same town said: 'We got shame. We don't know whether we're black or we're white.'[43] Every day, Aboriginal people had to make choices about where their values and identity lay.

The sources of such self-hate were many. Given that Aboriginal people experienced generations of denigration and poverty, some of them at least half-believed the slanders about them. Victims came to believe they were at fault. Others chose to emulate middle-class white Australians in their material lives and culture to escape the poverty and the daily stigma of the caste barrier. Some tried to erase the stigma of darkness and Aboriginal features through liaisons or marriages with lighter-skinned individuals or Australians of European descent.

This might raise their status and assist their offspring to slip through the caste barrier. Others used powders and whiteners to make a difference. Ida West, a Pallah woman on Cape Barren Island, recalled: 'you had to be white. At the dances you had to put on all the powder and the Pond's cream.'[44] Such attempts to reject one's Aboriginality increased alienation and self-destruction. Albert Memmi observed of this strategy:

> The colonized does not seek merely to enrich himself with the colonizer's virtues. In the name of what he hopes to become, he sets his mind on impoverishing himself, tearing himself away from his true self. The crushing of the colonized is included among the colonizer's values. As soon as the colonized adopts those values, he similarly adopts his own condemnation. In order to free himself, at least so he believes, he agrees to destroy himself.[45]

The denial of Aboriginality by some led to splits and 'class' divisions within many Aboriginal rural communities in the assimilation years from about 1940 to the 1960s.[46] This was especially the case in those states such as New South Wales, South Australia and Western Australia, where citizenship certificates were offered to Aboriginal people. However, few applied for them, as they required the adoption of European cultural mores and the rejection of Aboriginal ways. The small minority who tried to cross into mainstream Australia in the assimilation years rarely achieved their aim, and were left feeling isolated, frustrated and further alienated. Few European Australians accepted those who sought to pass, perceiving them still as Aboriginal, and most Aboriginal people shunned them as 'uppity' deniers of their true selves. The caste barrier created cleavages within Aboriginal society, based on different cultural values, income, and the conspicuous consumption of material items. Class consciousness had penetrated the Aboriginal world.

The other pole in the self-hate/defiance polarity—and the stronger and enduring one—was a resistance to white domination. Aboriginal resistance in southern Australia was rooted in five essential elements: cultural maintenance; a sense of injustice; the acting out of a sometimes negative oppositional culture; and the rebuilding of a positive Aboriginal identity. The fifth and vital part of this resistance was an Aboriginal political movement, which will be explored extensively in the next chapter.

Ceremonial life and language faded in much of southern Australia by Federation, under the pressures of the Civilising Mission and population losses

Government assimilationist propaganda, 'One People', Ministry for Territories, 1961.

of elders with knowledge. However, an unshakeable sense of being Aboriginal remained. Some anthropologists, and particularly governments, believed Aboriginal culture was 'crumbling' in settled Australia.[47] However, wiser heads realised their Aboriginality was simply somewhat different than before. Marie Reay, who studied Aboriginal people in rural New South Wales in 1949, remarked: 'Although they wear European clothing, work beside white men in the shearing shed, and have many of the accoutrements of our civilization in their homes, including the radio, the iron bedstead, the film star's photograph and the S.P. betting cards, tribal beliefs are intensely real to them.'[48] Other anthropologists recorded many survivals of traditional culture. Kinship ties, attitudes to the land, totemic and clan divisions were still recognised and often practised. Some marriages were not traditional, but most knew this and some felt guilty about it. Belief in sorcery and spirits of the dead was still particularly strong, as was adherence to traditional medicine. Some of the older people, like Jimmy Barker of Brewarrina reserve, were still bilingual or at least spoke some language, which was an amalgam of their traditional language, English and pidgin. Most practised the values of sharing and reciprocity. It was claimed there was no Aboriginal culture remaining in Bourke, but Dr Max Kamien, who advised the Aboriginal community there, in 1971 found a residual knowledge of totemism, language and sacred sites existed; a belief in sorcery and spirits of the dead was maintained; and kinship ties, traditional remedies and bush cooking were practised daily.[49] In 1969 a young Victorian Aboriginal girl remarked that being Aboriginal is 'just something we all feel—a state of mind'—vague perhaps, but intensely real.[50]

Community solidarity was also rooted in a commonly held history of injustice about past events, which were as vivid as if they occurred yesterday. Elderly people living in settled Australia had detailed accounts of frontier times and cherished histories of family survival. Family photographic albums reinforced these experiences of struggle. The first stories were set down in print from the 1950s, beginning with Margaret Tucker's *If Everyone Cared* (1997), penned originally in the early 1950s. Communities remembered massacre sites or fighting places in their region. People knew which their country was and who their kin were—and this gave them a sense of dignity and honour. Thus a shared folk history of bad times, and good, gave Aboriginal groups a strong sense of common purpose and a determination to defy other Australians over discrimination. This feeling developed into Aboriginal political movements from the 1920s, which will be treated in the next chapter.

One way to defy white ways was to create an oppositional view of so-called 'correct' behaviour. This view flourished predominantly among men at the Aboriginal end of rural towns and on the local Aboriginal reserves. However, it was not shared or practised by all, by any means.[51] Illegal drinking before 1962 and even gambling, which was illegal on the reserves, were acts of defiance against white law and also middle-class values. Drunken people knew they were shocking white respectability to which they were supposed to aspire. Aboriginal people at times played to the stereotype that whites had of them, for shock value, and many had fun doing it. Doug Young, an Aboriginal songwriter from Wilcannia, sang:

> The people in town just run around,
> They say we live on wine and beer.
> But if they'd stop and think, if we didn't drink,
> There'd be no fun around here.
> Just the other day I heard a woman say,
> We're nothing but a bunch of mugs.
> Although we fight and drink and end up in the clink
> We're going to cut a rug [get rip-roaring drunk].[52]

Similarly, the breaking of windows, doors and fences in reserve houses was done partly to shock and express rage, and also to cause work for the often-hated managers. Refusal to co-operate with managers, or defiant acts such as the walk-off from Cummeragunja reserve in 1939 (detailed in the next chapter), were other forms of oppositional behaviour. Some Aboriginal people refused to license their cars and pay the resulting fines, or pay rent for reserve houses on land they believed was theirs. White laws of all kinds, over which they had no say, were to be resisted. Acts of family negligence were sometimes defiance of welfare department values. Yet drunkenness, vandalism, family irresponsibility, even non-payment of rent leading to eviction, caused more problems than they solved. However rage, even when destructive, kept alive the Aboriginal spirit and underpinned more positive forms of resistance.

New Aboriginal identities were being built during this period, as people moved around, developing a sense of future directions for the Aboriginal community as a whole. Before the 1960s, communities across southern Australia were fragmented. For instance, in New South Wales there were 49 reserves, each with an average of 110 people. All these communities were inward-looking and often antagonistic to other groups, who were referred to as 'bad mobs' or 'thieves' or worse. Loyalties were localised, even though many reserve groups were not traditional, but amalgams of pre-contact groupings due to forced removals. These local group identities were strong, being based on kinship ties and face-to-face relations, and an ethic of mutual aid and sharing. These were traditional values, which had been reinforced by the colonial experience, and as a defence against poverty and outside interference from reserve managers, the police and governments. While mutually suspicious, Aboriginal communities reserved their greatest distrust for non-Indigenous Australians, who were definitely seen as outsiders.

Following the political activism after the interwar period and with movement to the cities, wider loyalties developed in the 1960s and additional names and identities emerged (often with variations of spelling). Those in Queensland and northern New South Wales began to call themselves 'Murries'; in Victoria 'Koories'; and in Western Australia 'Nyoongar'. White Australians in the south were often called 'Gubbas', 'Wandas' or 'Dugais', which meant 'spirits of the dead'.

Wider loyalties were also developed by the 1970s through Aboriginal heroes, mostly runners, boxers and footballers, whose fame reached beyond their local communities. Their story is told in Colin Tatz's *Aborigines in Sport* (1995). Travelling boxing tents crossed southern and eastern Australia, and young Aboriginal men journeyed with them looking for adventure and fame. Few found fame, but most earned a good and equal wage, and gained a swag of exciting stories to tell kin back home. Besides, their ring work challenged the caste barrier. Henry Collins of Cherbourg, who was ejected by police from a hotel in Casino about 1955 for not having an exemption ticket to drink, fought a policeman in the boxing tent the next day. He recalled: 'Best fight I ever had, just picked him off, chopped him over the eye, nose bled, busted his mouth, and in a sixth round just walked straight into him and knocked him cold, and spat on him.'[53] Their experience is set down in my book *Sideshow Alley* (1998). The more talented gravitated to the big city and fought professionally. Between 1930 and 1980, 30 Aboriginal boxers from settled Australia became national champions, holding 15 per cent of all Australian titles, while being only 1 per cent of the Australian population. By 1980 five were also Commonwealth champions: Ron Richards, Dave Sands, Tony Mundine, Hector Thompson and Laurie Austin. Lionel Rose, from Drouin in Victoria, held the world bantamweight title in 1968–69. Others were amateur titleholders. Geoff Dynevor from Cherbourg reserve, Queensland, won silver at the Rome Olympics in 1960 and a gold medal at the Perth Commonwealth Games.[54]

All these Aboriginal boxing champions were known across Aboriginal Australia and had cross-racial appeal as well. Champions in other sports followed, delighting Aboriginal people and other Australians. Evonne Goolagong MBE achieved great heights, winning eleven tennis Grand Slam events in the 1970s, including Wimbledon twice. Born in Griffith, she appealed to many Australians, being an exciting tennis player, a woman and a modest personality. Her biography *Home* (1993) tells of her reconnection with her Aboriginality. Footballers in three codes also achieved fame. Graham 'Polly' Farmer, who grew up in Sister Kate's orphanage in Perth, became a much-honoured star of Australian Rules in the late 1950s. Farmer revolutionised handballing before a knee injury ended his career. In Rugby League, Arthur Beetson from Roma, Queensland, is regarded as one of Australia's best League forwards. He played for the Kangaroos from 1966 to 1977, becoming their first Indigenous captain. In Rugby Union, the Ella brothers Mark, Glen and Gary, who were Wallaby players in the early 1980s, thrilled the sport. Charles Perkins excelled in the oft-forgotten but now rampant fourth code—soccer.

Some Aboriginal people quietly took the middle ground in response to the caste barrier, displaying neither despair nor defiance. They pursued their own destiny in the wider community, but not off it. Percy Pepper and his family took up a soldier settlement block at Koo-wee-rup, east of Melbourne, after his discharge from the First World War. He worked and lived alongside other returned men and made a decent living for a while. One of his sons, Phillip, who married on the eve of the Depression, survived it like some other Australians, by fruit picking, cutting timber and working in a Melbourne factory. The Peppers lived amiably with their neighbours. Phillip Pepper recalled there were good and bad Europeans, as there were good and bad Aboriginal people. Phillip Pepper remained Aboriginal in his identity and wrote a book about his Aboriginal forebears with the existential title *You Are What You Make Yourself to Be* (1980).[55]

In the 1930s, Daniel and June Atkinson left Cummeragunja to avoid their children being removed and became share farmers at Deniliquin. Daniel later worked for the Country Roads Board and funded his children through high school. Kenneth and Dulcie Stewart gained a soldier settler block at Robinvale after his service in the Second World War, which they worked successfully until their retirement.[56] In other states, a few other Aboriginal people farmed. However, in Western Australia, only three blocks were granted to Aboriginal farmers between 1915 and 1935. Joe Colbung, who applied for land at Mount Barker in 1918, was opposed by locals. They claimed his property would become 'a niggers camp with the usual collection of natives and dogs'.[57]

Pastor Bill Reid of Bourke recalled decent treatment on some pastoral properties, but discrimination on others. He thought racial separation of eating quarters on pastoral runs abhorrent. He also resented the rules and controls that existed on Aboriginal reserves. Reid earned a living by fencing, woodcutting, droving and boxing in Jimmy Sharman's tents. Many other Aboriginal families survived on woodcutting and other rural work in this unassuming manner, surviving economic and racially difficult times. A number, like Reid and Pepper, later held positions in Aboriginal welfare organisations, revealing their commitment to their identity and people.[58]

The long years of control by Protection Boards and a customary colour bar that blighted opportunity spawned various Aboriginal political movements around the country, aimed at ending discrimination and gaining equal rights for Aboriginal people.

10

FIGHTING FOR CIVIL RIGHTS

The 1930s was a time of flux in Aboriginal affairs, with opposing movements for greater control and liberation struggling for dominance. While some state and territory authorities in Aboriginal affairs were extending their control through reserve regulations, labour contracts and the removal of children, black and white activists fought for civil rights for Aboriginal people—a fight that was essentially won by the late 1960s. The anthropologist A.P. Elkin claimed in 1962 that a 'revolution for the better' had occurred in Aboriginal affairs in the previous 30 years.[1] In terms of civil rights Elkin was right, but these came with unwelcome government baggage—an assimilation policy aimed at making Aboriginal people just like other Australians.

CONTROLLING ABORIGINAL PEOPLE

The colonial folklore that Aboriginal people were not equal in ability to white Australians persisted into the 1930s. The Melbourne *Argus* typically claimed in 1938 that Australia's Indigenous people were 'a backward and lowly race', soon to be extinct. With mixed feelings of compassion, guilt and relief, most non-Indigenous Australians believed Aboriginal people would fade before so-called 'modern' civilisation. Their population decline to about 60,000 Australia-wide by 1930 seemed to prove this view. Daisy Bates's 1939 popular account of Aboriginal people was entitled *The Passing of the Aborigines*.

Aboriginal Protection Acts maintained rigid control over Aboriginal people (unless exempted), which amounted to a loss of civil rights, including the right of freedom of movement, freedom of association and marriage, the right to control one's property and earnings, and the right to vote, drink, work, carry guns and own dogs. Unless they worked off the reserves, under permits, people were confined to settlements under the control of managers, police, or bureaucrats of Protection Boards, who interpreted the Act and its regulations far from the public gaze. Charles Rowley, a social researcher, remarked of Queensland reserves: 'Aboriginal administration in these places became an issue as remote as that of gaols or asylums. The settlement has illustrated the classic ills of the institution under authoritarian management, but one more or less out of sight, as well as largely beyond the interest, of other Queenslanders.'[2]

These Aboriginal Acts reached their apogee of control with amendments in the 1930s. In the frontier jurisdictions, Acts of 1933 and 1936 in the Northern Territory, 1936 in Western Australia, 1934 and 1939 in Queensland and 1939 in South Australia extended controls. Laws governing Aboriginal marriages and sexual relations between the races were strengthened. Provisions governing their use of alcohol were tightened. The Western Australian and South Australian Acts widened the definition of 'Aboriginal', to include almost any degree of Aboriginal descent, bringing more under scrutiny. Amendments to the New South Wales Act in 1936 gave the Aborigines Protection Board power to impose compulsory medical examinations, and to remove and isolate on a reserve any Aboriginal person or individual 'apparently having an admixture of Aboriginal blood'. An unproven assertion of Aboriginality could place someone under the Act until the contrary was proven in court. The court could also decide on sight whether a person was an 'Aborigine' under the Act or not.

However, control was never total. Aboriginal people on reserves and missions found myriad ways to elude the manager's power. They secretly moved on and off reserves, maintained traditional values by hiding unauthorised kin in their houses, drank alcohol, gambled, refused to work for rations only, and refused at times to pay the rent. The Wiradjuri on Erambie mission at West Cowra were particularly militant in the 1940s, for as historian Peter Read noted, rebellion 'echoed loudest on the stations where there was a Board and a manager to hate'.[3] Others across the country refused to live on reserves or missions, preferring uncontrolled camps instead. These campers, called 'fringe dwellers', were in fact cultural warriors, refusing to surrender Aboriginal ways. During the interwar years, Tjuritja camp existed in Alice Springs, which provided labour and services and a stopover for camel trains. Tjuritja shifted about to avoid the authorities. Despite laws regulating the presence of Aboriginal people in town, the Aranda's camp also remained relatively independent. Jeff Collman, an anthropologist, remarked: 'there was no bureaucratic apparatus which attempted to regulate the camp or any official who directly administered it'.[4] Rowley observed of Aboriginal administrations in general that: 'governments had neither the funds nor often the doctrinaire heartlessness to apply these laws everywhere with equal vigour. There seem to have been many, technically within the categories, who managed to avoid some at least of the limitations on liberty.'[5]

Rigorous control was generally exercised over mixed-race children— deemed 'half-caste'. Nineteenth-century racial ideology claimed race mixing led to racial degeneration. By 1900 this shifted to the view that those of mixed descent had abilities above those of 'full blood' and needed rescuing from the conditions of 'primitive' culture. Discussion grew concerning those of mixed descent in the north. Dr Goldsmith, the Aboriginal Protector in the Territory, urged their removal to a training institution in 1898. This occurred in 1911 with the creation of the Bago reserve in Darwin. However, most desired to limit the birth of mixed-race people, as they still ascribed social inferiority to coloured skin and saw blackness as a taint to be eradicated.[6] J.W. Bleakley's 1928 report on the Northern Territory's Aboriginal administration focused on the 'half-caste question'. He differentiated between people with no racial admixture ('full bloods'), through to those of only one-eighth Aboriginal descent ('octoroons'). These gradations reflected the racist idea that people of mixed race were on a continuum between civilisation and barbarism; the lighter the skin, the more civilised and intelligent the person was claimed to be. (In Western Australia in 1952, bureaucrats determining eligibility for welfare benefits dealt in fractions as small as 1/128th Aboriginal descent.) Bleakley hoped to curb the mixed-race population. He urged tighter controls on Aboriginal females and the removal of children of mixed descent from their mothers. Their destiny was to be raised white in European orphanages or white foster homes down south.[7]

During amendments to the Aboriginal Protection Acts in Western Australia in 1936 and Queensland in 1939, similar fears about miscegenation were expressed. One Queensland parliamentarian remarked: 'We do not want any further mixing of the population. We want to keep the white race white.'[8] Two Aboriginal administrators, Dr Cecil Cook in the Northern Territory and Auber Neville in Western Australia, but not William Bleakley in Queensland, pursued aggressive policies directed at making those of mixed descent white. In what Historian Russell McGregor described as a 'perverse proposition', miscegenation would be controlled by managed miscegenation.[9]

Cecil Cook became Chief Medical Officer and also Chief Protector of Aborigines in the Northern Territory in 1927. Cook, who grew up in Queensland, became an expert in tropical medicine. He shared the prevalent nationalist anxiety that the white race might struggle to hold northern Australia against

Asian and Aboriginal influences. The major threat to the White Australia Policy was an increasing mixed-descent population in the Territory, despite the declining number of 'full bloods'. Cook believed this was a 'position of incalculable future menace to the purity of race in tropical Australia'.[10] He promoted segregation, authorising racially separate swimming pools and a segregated out-patients' clinic, and prohibited 'the mating of aboriginals with any person other than an aboriginal', especially 'alien coloured races'. He also removed mixed-descent children from their mothers where possible, stating: 'every endeavour is being made to breed out the colour by elevating female half-castes to white standard with a view to their absorption by mating into the white population'.[11] Cook believed that this controlled absorption process would take five generations and there would be no atavism; that is, no reappearance of Aboriginal physical features. Those of mixed race would be uplifted and Aboriginality would be eradicated! After 1935, Cook proposed more enlightened policies emphasising Aboriginal ability and advocating training. Neither policy was popular in the Territory. Child removals reduced the labour supply, and suggestions of educating Aboriginal people were dismissed as fancy.

Auber Neville was Chief Protector in Western Australia from 1915 to 1940. He brought a managerial style to his job and was a fervent advocate of White Australia, like most other settler Australians of his day. Neville became increasingly concerned about the growing number of people of mixed Aboriginal–European descent. In 1930 he wrote in alarmist terms that the number of 'half-castes' had doubled in two decades. Neville did not fear hybridity in the usual way, as creating racial degeneration: he was a descendant of John Rolfe, who married the Native American Pocahontas in Virginia in 1614, and brought her home to live in Norfolk, England, until her death in 1617. Neville wrote in 1930 that 'the quadroon and octoroon are scarcely distinguishable from the white. Many are handsome, even beautiful, gentle-mannered, soft-voiced girls, speaking perfectly enunciated, if somewhat abbreviated English.'[12]

Neville exerted a heavy-handed paternal protection over Aboriginal people. In 1930 three teenage mixed-descent sisters, Molly, Grace and Daisy, were removed to Moore River. Doris Pilkington, Molly's daughter, has told their story of removal and escape in *Rabbit-Proof Fence* (1996), made into a film of the same name (2002). Marriages of mixed-descent people were arranged by Neville to direct them to marrying lighter-skinned Aboriginal people or white Australians. Alice Barrett recalled: 'I got a letter from Mr Neville to say Will. [Nannup] was at Moore River and we were to get married.' She could have refused, but knew Will a little, and added: 'We got along all right, but we didn't really know each other that well because we'd never got the chance. In one way I got married to get away from the government, and I think a lot of women did that.'[13]

Neville was well read and became convinced by the claims of Herbert Basedow, the Adelaide-based anthropologist, that Aboriginal people were the 'racial brother' of Europeans, being of Caucasian stock. This was revealed by craniometric measurements by Basedow and his German mentor Professor Hermann Klaatsch, and confirmed by the so-called shallow skin pigmentation of Aboriginal people and the fair hair of some children in Central Australian tribes. Basedow argued black and white Australians could intermix successfully without fear of atavism. Basedow never foresaw how his ideas would be used to justify the removal of children. Nor did he know that fair-headedness was likely the result of endemic hookworm in Central Australian communities.[14]

During the Moseley Report hearings of 1935 in Western Australia, Neville, who also gave evidence, heard Dr Cyril Bryan pose the alternatives of creating separate populations or mixing them. Bryan stated: 'I wish to speak of the half-caste and the breeding out of the half castes, the black man whose presence irritates us ... and who is now in addition a standing menace to our dreams of a white Australia.'[15] Bryan, who was a white nationalist, urged the application of Mendelian laws to Aboriginal procreation. Following the Moseley Report, new legislation in 1936 gave Neville as Chief Protector added power to control the marriages of 'half-castes'. He increased removals of children with lighter skin for training at Moore River, followed by work in the wider world. Neville's biographer Pat Jacobs said his resolve about saving whiteness hardened in the 1930s and his earlier compassion for Aboriginal people dissolved. He came to display 'no sense of any value being placed on the maternal or familial bond'.[16]

William Penhall played a similar controlling role over 5000 Aboriginal people in South Australia in the 1940s. He became superintendent of the Point McLeay mission in 1927 and rose in the Aborigines Department when removals of children from among the 800 people of mixed descent were common. Penhall became the Chief Protector of Aborigines from 1939 to 1953, and during that time kept a low profile, neither seeking nor gaining publicity. Unlike Neville, he rarely spoke in public, even when invited. He was a strong Christian with a pessimistic view of Aboriginal people and their culture, believing 'so long as children continue to grow up in the old environment, there cannot be any radical change in the character of the people'. The South Australian Aborigines Act (1939) did not grant the Aborigines Department or the Chief Protector power to remove children from their parents, which Penhall admitted in writing in

1944 and on other occasions. However, historian Cameron Raynes discovered in the archives that Penhall quietly ignored the Act and removed children from their parents and placed them on missions or with the Children's Welfare and Public Relief Board for training. This became publicly verified in court action in 2007 when Bruce Trevorrow won his case for being illegally removed from his family beyond the authority of the Act.[17]

Auber Neville and Cecil Cook also operated beyond the Act. Their aim to 'breed out the colour', was not laid down in any Act of parliament, but it was clearly the policy that these two bureaucrats pursued in the interwar years—often with the tacit support of others in government and parliament. It was not a new aim, as absorption had been policy in Victoria in the late nineteenth century and in New South Wales after 1909. But Neville and Cook made it a systematic, racially directed policy in an attempt to erase Aboriginality and make Australia white. (It was also genocidal, for the United Nations Convention on Genocide (article 2e) refers to the forced removal of children from one group to another.) It was not explicitly sanctioned by the state, although governments must have been aware of the projects of their enthusiastic bureaucrats. These individuals, Neville, Cook and Penhall, acted out of misguided humanitarian reasons—to make Australia white and to save those of mixed descent from their 'primitive' backgrounds. Russell McGregor commented: 'the exponents of "breeding out the colour" nonetheless evinced concern for the welfare of those they sought to whiten.[18] However, it was a concern stemming from a sense of superiority and untouched by human compassion.

FORCES FOR CHANGE

The oppressive policies that blighted Aboriginal lives were countered in the interwar years by two reformist forces: a minority of white Australians who, encouraged by anthropologists, pushed for change; and Aboriginal people who formed political organisations to demand civil rights.

In the nineteenth century, scientists were often handmaidens to ideas of white racial superiority, led by the head-measurers, who formed ideas about innate ability from physical characteristics. In the 1930s, physical anthropology gave way to cultural anthropology. Eminent anthropologists such as Malinowski and Radcliffe-Brown conducted fieldwork in Australia, and new arguments about cultural difference, rather than inferiority, were framed about Aboriginal people. Radcliffe-Brown, the founding Professor of Anthropology at Sydney University in 1925, argued in the first issue of *Oceania* in 1930 that anthropology was 'a science of immediate practical value, more particularly in relation to the government and education of native peoples'.

His successor to the Chair of Anthropology in 1934, Adolphus Elkin, an anthropologist and Anglican clergyman, became expert in combining academic research and policy advice. His views and those of others began to infiltrate newspapers under paternal headlines like 'What are we to do with our Aborigines?'. By such means, some of the general public became more educated on Aboriginal affairs. Elkin urged in a pamphlet, 'Aborigines: Our National Policy' (1934), that they should receive better education and improved material conditions to match their capacity. He also wrote about the virtues of Aboriginal culture. The preface to his influential book *The Australian Aborigines* (1938), still in print in four editions after 70 years, states that Aboriginal customs were not 'noble, barbarous or amusing', but deep and complex ideas on 'law, philosophy and religion'. Elkin argued that aspects of their culture could be retained, that they did not have to be absorbed, and that other Australians might learn from them.[19]

Women's groups developed a concern for Aboriginal disadvantage in the 1920s. An umbrella body, the Australian Federation of Women Voters, and also the National Council of Women as well as other feminist groups, pushed for reforms in Aboriginal welfare by the late 1920s. The middle-class women in these organisations argued that the protection of Aboriginal women in particular was essential for Australia's claim to be a modern nation. Led by Bessie Rischbieth, a group of women representing women's organisations gave evidence to the Royal Commission into Constitutional Reform in 1927. They argued that control of Aboriginal policy should be a federal responsibility and that women should have an input. Edith Waterworth told the commission: 'as they were in possession of the land when we came here so it is the Federal Government's duty to take care of them'. Reverends W. Morley and J.S. Needham, and Auber Neville the Western Australian Protector, supported the women's calls for federalisation to inject more funds and more commonality into policy, but the commission's report rejected the idea.[20]

White activist groups specifically interested in Aboriginal affairs emerged in the 1930s, many of them led by women, as the task was viewed as philanthropic and maternal as well as political work. The Victorian Aboriginal Group (VAG) was one of many in that state. It was formed as a study circle in February 1930 by the male writers and outback researchers A.S. Kenyon and R.H. Croll in response to Bleakley's 1929 report on the Northern Territory. In 1933 two women, Valentine Leeper and Amy Brown, became its driving force for four decades. Though conservative in today's terms, the VAG and other groups lobbied the government about conditions on reserves and camps in Victoria and throughout the country.[21] Individual women made an enormous impact. Mary Bennett, who grew up on a pastoral station in Queensland, then lived in London, returned to Australia to teach on the Mount Margaret mission in Western Australia. Bennett devoted her life to pushing for Aboriginal civil rights. She penned the influential *The Australian Aboriginal as a Human Being* (1930) and other pamphlets and constantly lobbied governments.[22] Bennett and Ada Bromham, a feminist and Christian socialist, appeared before the Moseley Royal Commission into the condition of Aboriginal people. Other feminists gave evidence to the commission, including Emily Nannup, an Aboriginal woman. They lobbied on education and were especially outspoken on the removal of children.[23] Helen Baillie, a nurse in Melbourne, read Bennett's book in 1931 and also became an activist for Aboriginal causes, being noticed by ASIO, which identified her paradoxically as a 'Christian Communist'.[24]

A series of frontier incidents in the north around 1930 alarmed humanitarian groups. In 1928 two police punitive expeditions admitted to killing 31 Walbiri and Anmatyerre people—in what became known as the Coniston massacres—in retaliation for the killing of a dogger and grazier.[25] In a separate incident in 1932, five Japanese fishermen were killed by Yolgnu men at Caledon Bay in Arnhem Land. A member of an investigating police party, Constable Albert McColl, and two beachcombers were killed in 1933, allegedly at Woodah Island by Dhakiyara (Tuckiar) and one other man. An old-fashioned punitive party was averted by lobbying from humanitarian groups in southern capitals, notably the Association for the Protection of Native Races (APNR), led by Elkin. The Territory's administration asked the Church Missionary Society to investigate. Missionaries persuaded Dhakiyara and Mirera—allegedly involved in the Woodah Island murders—and the three accused over the Caledon Bay murders—Mau, Natjelma and Markaya—to come to Darwin. The men believed it was a reconciling mission, but instead they found themselves on trial. Justice Wells sentenced the three Caledon Bay accused to twenty years, with remission after three years. Dhakiyara and Mirera were acquitted on one charge of killing the beachcombers, but Dhakiyara was sentenced to death for McColl's death. Racial categories appeared to prevail here, three Japanese being worth less than one European death. Ted Egan has investigated the trials in *Justice All Their Own* (1996).

The APNR led a campaign against the confused and dubious cross-cultural 'justice' in the trials. Elkin demanded the recall of Wells, and the prisoners' release. Within two days the Prime Minister, Joe Lyons, spoke to Elkin about his allegations, as the British Dominions Office was asking questions. Australia

Dhakiyara was accused of killing Constable McColl at Caledon Bay, Arnhem Land.
COURTESY OF THE *ARGUS* COLLECTION, STATE LIBRARY OF VICTORIA (H2002.199/93).

was sensitive to outside criticism of its conduct of Aboriginal affairs, since it held the 'vital' defence area of New Guinea under a League of Nations mandate. It feared the repercussions for its control the mandate of any doubts about its guardianship over 'native' peoples. A High Court appeal in late 1934 quickly overturned Dhakiyara's conviction. Justice Wells was censured for misdirecting the jury with the view that a verdict of 'not guilty' would slander Constable McColl's memory. Dhakiyara's defence counsel was also found to be in error for not pushing for a plea of manslaughter, after Dhakiyara privately confessed to killing McColl. McColl chained himself to Djaparri, Dhakiyara's wife, but her evidence 40 years later suggests McColl did not molest her. Dhakiyara killed McColl to free her. Dhakiyara was released after the High Court decision, but disappeared. Many believe he was murdered by a Territory police officer.[26]

Such controversies stirred public concern and led to a series of inquiries: the Moseley Report on Western Australia in 1935, and Dr Donald Thomson's report on Arnhem Land in 1937. Thomson recommended that the Arnhem Land reserve and other areas be made sanctuaries, and that legislation modelled on the New Guinea Native Ordinances be introduced into the Northern Territory. Change began to emerge. In 1939 the responsible Commonwealth Minister, Jack McEwen, announced in consultation with Elkin that the aim of Aboriginal policy was 'the raising of their status so as to entitle them by right and by qualification to the ordinary rights of citizenship, and to enable them and help them to share with us the opportunities that are available in their native land'. McEwen added, however, that 'one must not think in terms of years but of generations' for citizenship to be achieved.[27] The outbreak of war in 1939 halted these hesitant white initiatives towards civil rights. More important to the cause of civil rights were the efforts of Aboriginal political movements.

The first Aboriginal political group in Australia was the Australian Aborigines Progressive Association (AAPA), formed in 1924 by an Aboriginal Sydney water-side worker, Fred Maynard. Within a year, the AAPA had eleven branches and over 500 Aboriginal members. The group pushed for the restoration of lost lands, abolition of control by the Board, an end to the removal of Aboriginal children, and demanded a royal commission into Aboriginal affairs in the state. Maynard claimed the Aboriginal Great Tradition as a civilisation equal, but different to, Western civilisation. Maynard's grandson, historian John Maynard, has found significant origins to Fred Maynard's ideas. Maynard was present when the great heavyweight champion Jack Johnson was in Sydney in 1907, and given a reception by a little-known body called the Coloured Progressive Association, formed mostly of black seamen. Maynard also was influenced by the black American leader Marcus Garvey, who headed a mass black organisation in the United States in the 1920s. Maynard's AAPA motto was 'One God, One Aim, One Destiny', the same as Garvey's. *The Negro World*, Garvey's paper, was read in Maynard's group and reported on events in Aboriginal Australia. There was also a branch of Garvey's organisation in Sydney, the Universal Negro Improvement Association—suggesting the AAPA was inspired by Garvey's black internationalism.[28]

In Western Australia in 1926 an Aboriginal farmer, William Harris, also created a movement for Aboriginal rights called the Native Union in Western Australia. It is unknown exactly what his inspiration was, beyond a desire for equality and freedom. In 1928 Harris led a deputation to the state premier, declaring: 'we want to live up to the white man's standard, but in order to be able to do this we should be exempted from the Aborigines Act, and allowed to live our lives in our own way'.[29] In 1934 the Euralian Association was formed by those of mixed descent in Port Hedland, who wished to live free of the Act. One member protested to Paul Hasluck (later Sir Paul), then a young journalist: 'You work hard but you can never get anywhere. You try to improve your place but you still can't get any of the privileges that white people get.'[30]

In Victoria, Shadrach James, son of the Cummeragunja teacher Thomas Shadrach James, gave speeches from 1929 about the extermination of 'my people'. His uncle, Yorta Yorta man William Cooper, moved to Melbourne in 1932, aged 71, and began a political movement called the Australian Aborigines' League (AAL) in 1934. Believing that the condition of Aboriginal people was a white moral problem, he created a petition to the King calling for civil rights and Aboriginal representation in federal parliament. He also wrote dozens of letters to the press over the next six years on behalf of the AAL, about many injustices. Indeed, he led a deputation to the German Embassy in 1938 to protest on behalf of the AAL, the 'cruel persecution of Jewish people by the Nazi government of Germany'.[31] His petition to the King, presented in October 1937 with 1814 signatures, was never seen by the Monarch, as the Australian government deemed it was not a matter constitutionally for the King. In 1937 William Ferguson, an Aboriginal shearer and unionist from central New South Wales, also formed a political movement called the Aborigines' Progressive Association (APA) at Dubbo in New South Wales. Like the other groups, the APA aimed at citizenship for Aboriginal people and their equality with white society. These movements for equality with whites in no way compromised their Aboriginality, of which they were invariably proud.[32]

William Cooper was an original and symbolic thinker. In 1937 he proposed a dramatic gesture to William Ferguson, Pearl Gibbs, Jack Patten and others of the APA. The 150th anniversary of the landing of the First Fleet on 26 January 1938—a day of invasion—should be marked by Aboriginal people as a Day of Mourning. Ferguson and Patten penned a manifesto entitled 'Aborigines Claim Citizenship Rights!', which they published a week before the Day of Mourning. The pamphlet opened with the startling words: 'This festival of 150 years' so called "progress" in Australia commemorates also 150 years of misery and degradation imposed upon the original native inhabitants by the white invaders of this country.' After stating that Aboriginal people were the original Australians, the manifesto continued: 'You came here only recently, and you took our land away from us by force. You have almost exterminated our people, but there are enough of us remaining to expose the humbug of your claim, as white Australians, to be a civilised, progressive, kindly and humane nation.' The Aboriginal version of Australian history was being set down publicly and starkly on paper. The manifesto asked for neither charity nor protection, but justice, citizenship rights and freedom from the constraints of the Acts—and an end to the Protection Board. There was no claim for land or money compensation, simply equality and freedom![33]

The Day of Mourning Committee held its own Australia Day meeting in the Australian Hall, Sydney, a kilometre from the government-sponsored re-enactment of Governor Phillip's landing, where obliging and unpoliticised Aboriginal performers from the far west of the state participated. The Australian Hall meeting, attended only by Aboriginal people (except for one non-Indigenous reporter and a policeman, who were allowed in), passed enthusiastic resolutions in support of Aboriginal freedom and equality. Five days later an Aboriginal delegation, led by Ferguson and Patten, met with Prime Minister Joe Lyons (another first) and presented Lyons with a ten-point program for Aboriginal equality. They sought a federal takeover of Aboriginal affairs and positive aid in the areas of education, housing, working conditions, land purchases and social welfare generally. Since the Day of Mourning, Aboriginal political activity has not stopped.[34]

In 1937 Ferguson and the APA declared war on the New South Wales Aborigines Protection Board, because of its continuing repressiveness. Together with Patten, Mark Davidson MLA, and other sympathetic black and white Australians, Ferguson forced a government inquiry into the Board in late 1937. Although this faded to an inconclusive end, it led to a closed Public Service Board inquiry into the working of the Aborigines Protection Board in 1938. Ferguson, Patten, Pearl Gibbs and others toured the state's reserves to collect evidence against the Protection Board, while Davidson hammered away at it in parliament. Pastor Bill Reid of Bourke, secretary of the APA, recalled of one trip: 'We went on a tour of northern New South Wales in an old Essex ute with a slogan slung across the back: "Citizenship for Aborigines". We didn't have any money and had to play gum leaves and sing to get some money for petrol and food. We lived on pumpkin, potatoes and stale bread.'[35] Following a visit to Cummeragunja by Patten in early 1939, the people walked off the reserve in

Jack Patten addresses the Day of Mourning Conference in Sydney, 26 January 1938. From left to right: Tom Foster, Jack Kinchela (obscured), Doug Nicholls, William Cooper. MAN MAGAZINE, MARCH 1938, COURTESY OF THE MITCHELL COLLECTION, STATE LIBRARY OF NEW SOUTH WALES.

protest at conditions, camping at Barmah across the Murray for several months, despite little help from Victorian authorities and none from New South Wales officials. They were sustained by assistance from Melbourne organised by Helen Baillie. Many never returned to the reserve, preferring the freedom on the riverbank at Shepparton and the work offered in the fruit canneries. Jack Patten was found guilty for inciting Aboriginal people to leave a reserve and placed on a bond.[36]

THE OPPORTUNITIES OF WAR

The Second World War interrupted the struggle for civil rights, but also energised it. William Cooper, who had lost a son in the First World War, wrote to Interior Minister McEwen in January 1940 urging citizenship for Aboriginal people, for 'to put us in the trenches, until we have something to fight for is not right'.[37] The Defence Act still barred those 'not substantially of European descent' from compulsory war service, and voluntary service was discouraged, but Aboriginal men of mixed descent around the country heeded the call. Once Australia faced the possibility of a Japanese invasion in late 1941, Aboriginal enlistments were accepted. Arthur Burdeau of the AAL pressed again in 1940 for the vote for Aboriginal people, but this was already covered temporarily by the Commonwealth Electoral (Wartime) Act of 1940, which gave all enlisted personnel the vote until six months after the end of hostilities. Following further pressure, this time from the RSL in 1947, the Chifley government granted all Indigenous ex-servicemen the vote in 1949.

Aboriginal men and women served in many capacities in the war. It is estimated that 3000 men and women of mixed descent served in the regular army—about one in twenty of the mixed-descent population. They were treated equally once in the forces. Reg Saunders from Portland Victoria, who served in the North African and New Guinea campaigns, was the first and only Aboriginal soldier to attain the rank of a commissioned officer in that war. Oodgeroo Noonuccal (Kath Walker) from Stradbroke Island, later a poet and activist, served as a wireless operator in the Australian Women's Army. Leonard Waters, a Kamilaroi man from northern New South Wales, was a fighter pilot flying Kittyhawks in New Guinea. About 700 Torres Strait Islanders served in the Torres Strait Light Infantry Battalion, a special force formed for the protection of that region. Over a hundred Islanders also served in the regular forces. The anthropologist Donald Thomson, then a lieutenant in the RAAF, was asked to organise a force in Arnhem Land that could act as coast watchers and fighters in case of any Japanese landing. The Yolngu willingly assisted, including— ironically—the three gaoled for killing Japanese fishermen in 1933. The Yolngu were not enlisted as uniformed and paid soldiers, but were rationed and trained. Overall, about 250 men were involved in such de facto military service in the north. Added to this were the 3000 who did civilian labour corps work in the Top End.[38]

The services gave opportunity, training and equal wages to many Aboriginal people and some wages to civilian workers in the north. It also raised their self-esteem, and gave them the vote and later, returned service benefits. Many other Aboriginal people broke free of the Protection Boards, by moving to urban areas to work in war industries, or by becoming independent in rural areas through readily available work. Full employment after the war continued this new-found freedom. In 1948 only 21 per cent of the Aboriginal population in New South Wales were on reserves and 96 per cent of Aboriginal men were in full employment.[39] Other changes during the war enlarged civil rights. In 1941 Commonwealth Child Endowment was paid to Aboriginal mothers who were not nomadic or dependent on government support. In 1942 it was extended to those on settlements, but was administered by staff, not mothers. In 1942

Victor Blanco, the famous pearl diver, in London with the Australian Imperial Forces, c. 1940.
COURTESY OF THE *ARGUS* COLLECTION, STATE LIBRARY OF VICTORIA (H99.201/71).

Commonwealth Invalid and Old Age Pensions were finally paid to those not controlled by Aboriginal Acts, leading to a move off reserves into camps by those free to do so to qualify for these benefits. These welfare pensions were not paid to all Aboriginal people until 1966.

The 1940s witnessed further exemption from Aboriginal Acts—although with odious conditions. The Western Australian Native (Citizen's Rights) Act of 1944 asked applicants—who were mostly males—to supply references of 'good character and industrious habits', and to sign a statutory declaration that 'for the two years prior to the date of the application he has dissolved tribal and native association except with respect to lineal descendants or native relations of the first degree'. A magistrate determined if the applicant was industrious and of good behaviour, whether he had 'adopted the manner and habits of civilized life', if he could speak good English, and finally whether he was free of leprosy, syphilis, granuloma or yaws. The certificate could be withdrawn if the holder failed to display habits of 'civilised' life, was convicted twice for drunkenness, or had contracted any of the above diseases. Only 1600 applied.[40] An Act to exempt people from Aboriginal legislation was introduced in New South Wales in 1948. Aboriginal people derisively called it the 'Dog Act' or the 'beer ticket'.

Only 1500 persons out of an eligible 14,000 people applied by 1964 when the system lapsed.[41] Under the Nationality and Citizenship Act (1948) Aboriginal people born in Australia were citizens, but any civil rights they enjoyed or were denied were determined by the general law, not being governed by this Act.[42]

The interwar and immediate postwar period saw other evidence of Aboriginal people making contributions to Australian society. Doug Nicholls, an ex-Fitzroy, Northcote and Victorian representative Australian Rules footballer, was mentored by William Cooper and was soon a frequent soapbox speaker on the Yarra Bank. Nicholls enlisted but was released in 1942 to lead the Aboriginal community of Fitzroy, which was in difficulty at the time. He and his wife Gladys began the Gore Street Aboriginal Chapel in 1943 and they became the driving force behind Aboriginal welfare work in Melbourne. Doug Nicholls continued the political work of the Australian Aborigines' League after Cooper's death in 1941. In 1951 the Victorian government allowed the AAL to run a highly successful Aboriginal cultural segment—'Out of the Dark'—as part of the Victorian Centenary celebrations of self-government. Nicholls commented: 'we began to realise that we should be proud of our Aboriginal culture—that we should remember we are a great people'.[43]

Aboriginal people across the country survived the dead hand of colonialism to reveal diverse talents. In 1938 Albert Namatjira, an Arrernte man of the Hermannsburg mission, held his first major painting exhibition of his 'European' style in Melbourne. He held another nine over a decade that realised well over £1000 each. By 1954, zealous purchasers almost rioted at a Sydney exhibition. In 1951 Harold Blair from the Cherbourg mission in Queensland sang at the Metropolitan in New York, marking an international career in opera. Robert Tudawali, a Waraitji man from Melville Island, starred with acclaim in the film *Jedda* (1955). However, Namatjira and others soon suffered from a new Aboriginal policy, one that was ironically a product of the movement to Aboriginal freedom. The desire for equality was translated by policymakers into a desire to make Aboriginal people just like other Australians—this began a terrible new onslaught on Aboriginal culture and identity.

ASSIMILATION POLICY

The 1937 Native Welfare conference of the heads of Aboriginal administrations across the country made a radical change in Aboriginal policy. To that date, the 'doomed race' idea had prevailed in official circles (and across society generally), but governments now decided Aboriginal people had a future and planned accordingly. The stage was dominated by experienced heads from the 'frontier' administrations. People of mixed race were the burning issue. Cecil Cook of the Northern Territory feared those of mixed descent would taint White Australia and had to be contained. John Bleakley of Queensland believed that intermixing mostly did not work and had set up the best resourced segregated reserve system in Australia. Auber Neville from Western Australia believed the two races could successfully come together over several generations. His was an optimistic view in the context of the 'doomed race' thinking, and he outwardly rejected any stigmatising of 'half-caste' people by whites; however, it was also based on a sense of cultural and racial superiority and a willingness to engineer the right outcome by controlling Aboriginal people. The racial merger he proposed was in fact a takeover, based on the disappearance of Aboriginal ways and skin tones. As Neville told the conference: 'Are we going to have 1,000,000 blacks in the Commonwealth or are we going to merge them into our white community and eventually forget that there were any Aborigines in Australia . . . I see no objection to the ultimate absorption into our own race of the whole of the Australian native race.'[44]

The conference, following Neville's view, determined: 'the destiny of the natives of aboriginal origin, but not of the full blood, lies in their ultimate absorption by the people of the Commonwealth and it therefore recommends that all the efforts be directed to that end'. The policy promised equality and cultural death at one and the same time. Administrators, who believed Aboriginal culture was 'crumbling' and inferior in any case, thought they were being progressive, and in a sense in 1937 they were. The anthropologist Adolphus Elkin, whose 'positive policy for the future centred on the elevation of primitive nomads to the status of civilisation', similarly believed in progress to civilisation represented by Western ways.[45] However, Elkin also believed that where Aboriginal culture had not 'crumbled', it should be retained, alongside this march to civilisation. His view was a minority one, but the onset of war set the whole matter to one side.

Paul Hasluck, the son of Salvation Army parents, became a journalist for the *West Australian*. In the early 1930s, he founded the Australian Aborigines Ameliorative Association with a fellow journalist. In 1934, H.D. Moseley, who was conducting a Royal Commission on Aboriginal people in Western Australia, invited Hasluck to tour the Kimberley with him. Hasluck was shocked by the conditions he saw, which stimulated him to think about policy. In 1934 he wrote a series of articles, one of which argued: 'the starting point must be that blacks are to enter the white civilisation'.[46] He completed an MA on native administration at the University of Western Australia in 1938, which was published as *Black Australians* (1942). He worked in external affairs and academia in the 1940s before becoming the Liberal member for Curtin in 1949.

In June 1950, Hasluck called on federal parliament to promote Aboriginal equality with all Australians, warning that Australia's defence of human rights in the international sphere was 'mocked by the thousands of degraded and depressed [Aboriginal] people who crouch on rubbish heaps throughout the whole of this continent'.[47] In 1951 Hasluck became Minister for Territories and immediately summonsed the September 1951 Native Welfare Conference, which reaffirmed the 1937 policy of assimilation. Hasluck told parliament in October of his vision that Australia would have 'no minorities or special classes', and Aboriginal people would move along a continuum from a 'primitive' state to one of 'civilisation'. Hasluck added: 'the blessings of civilisation are worth having'. Assimilation meant 'in practical terms, that, in the course of time, it is expected that all persons of aboriginal blood or mixed blood in Australia will live like white Australians do'.[48] Hasluck believed—and hoped—that the situation of Aboriginal people was a welfare problem, not a racial one. He emphasised that assimilation was 'a policy of opportunity. It gives to the aboriginal and to the person of mixed blood a chance to shape his own life.'[49]

His small 'l' liberal philosophy emphasised individualism and individual solutions to social problems. His view that Aboriginal society was disintegrating reinforced his belief that assimilation was to be a one-way individual journey to equality. However, it was not to be the biological absorption policy of the 1930s but a cultural one. Indeed, Hasluck claimed in October 1951 that 'assimilation does not mean the suppression of the aboriginal culture but rather that, for generation after generation, cultural adjustment will take place'.[50] However, as resistance to his vision of a classless, monocultural, unified Australian democracy grew by the late 1950s, he became more opposed to encouraging cultural difference.[51] At the 1963 Native Welfare Conference, Hasluck influenced a redefinition of assimilation to emphasise sameness, namely: 'all Aborigines and part-Aborigines will attain the same manner of living as other Australians and live as members of a single Australian community, enjoying the same rights and privileges, accepting the same responsibilities, observing the same customs and influenced by the same beliefs, hopes and loyalties as other Australians'.[52]

Administrators were steeped in prevailing Australian attitudes of conforming to a white middle-class 'Australian Way of Life'.[53] Most needed no encouragement to compel Aboriginal people 'to live like us', as Hasluck once remarked.[54] Government brochures such as 'One People' (1961) revealed smartly clothed

Aboriginal people as smiling, willing subjects, being taught how to work, cook and learn by white teachers. Assimilation was naturalised as the only path to a modern and unified Australia. Under such pressure of conformity, some Aboriginal people accepted this pathway.[55] The *Westralian Aborigine*, published by Aboriginal people of the Coolbaroo League in Perth, argued in April 1957 that for Aboriginal people to escape prejudice and demand respect they must take up a 'way of life which embraces a standard of living acceptable to the general community'. The writer urged 'cleanliness of body and property and the proper care of clothing'.[56] In practice, assimilation meant much more than soap and neat attire, for these were only symbols of deeper changes.

Assimilation in the Northern Territory occurred under the Welfare Branch, which for the first time spent significant money on Aboriginal Territorians. The Welfare Act (1953) did not mention the word 'Aborigines', for those under its care were those without the vote, deemed 'wards'. However, as Aboriginal people were the only ones without the vote, 'ward' in effect meant 'Aboriginal'. Racial nomenclature was avoided, as Hasluck claimed the Aboriginal situation was a 'welfare issue' to create the illusion of national unity. The Director of Welfare, H. Guise, had control over the movement, property, work and marriage of Aboriginal people. Many were moved onto missions, the population under control doubling to 11,000 over the period 1950–65. Communities were housed in European-style corrugated-iron units; all were rationed to create equality, and were often fed communally.

The last roaming Pintupi were brought in from Haast Bluff and other areas where Pastor Albrecht had rationed them. They were located with their kin at Papunya reserve, which was opened in 1960. The people were trucked there without their dogs, so some walked back to get them. It was a strange world without Albrecht, living in tin houses in rows, working for ration tickets that were exchanged for meals in a communal kitchen. They no longer lived on bush tucker and occasional rations, but were dependent on white rations. Their diet comprised much meat and ample sugar and fat. Most were away from country and in a powerless situation. Albrecht was replaced by welfare people. They took photographs and handprints of the people and wrote their names down— which was dangerous, for the Pintupi believed their *kurrunpa* (spirit) had been taken. Depression and other illnesses emerged from the stress of strange surroundings and living amid strange people. Of those 72 people who came to Papunya in 1963–64, 29 were dead within a year. Pinta Pinta remarked: 'in the bush we weren't in poor health, no. We weren't always sick as we went. I only became sick when I sat with the white people.'[57]

Albert and Rubina Namatjira, Frank Johnston Collection. COURTESY OF THE NATIONAL LIBRARY OF
AUSTRALIA (NLA.PIC-AN22839595).

Albert Namatjira was also destroyed by the assimilation policy. He had to
get the permission of the Welfare Branch to travel for exhibitions. His money
was controlled, he could not vote, and yet proceeds from his art sales were taxed.
He applied for an exemption to enable him to buy a block of land, but was

refused. However, administrative oversight left him off the long list of wards under the Welfare Act, giving him by default exemption from the Act. This meant he was under no restrictions, including being able to buy alcohol. However, by law he was not to give alcohol to any relatives. Namatjira, under Aboriginal law, supplied alcohol to kin living at Morris Soak. At one drinking party a teenage girl was killed. The Territory's coroner found Namatjira contributed to the death by supplying alcohol and he was gaoled. An Australia-wide protest erupted, with petitions and letters flowing from unions, Aboriginal support groups and school students. A gallup poll revealed a 95 per cent public awareness of the issue, with half supporting the law being upheld. His appeal failed, but Hasluck arranged for him to serve the six-month sentence at a reserve. Namatjira died three months later.[58]

The official assimilation policy of postwar Australia saw a more fervent round of removals of Aboriginal children of mixed descent, which had been happening since colonial times. It only slowed by the late 1960s. No overall statistic of the number removed is available, mostly due to a lack of continuous and consistent records, although searches are still being made. The controversial Human Rights and Equal Opportunity Commission's (HREOC) *Bringing Them Home* report of 1997 estimated, in the face of a lack of records, that between one in ten and one in three Aboriginal children were removed from their family across the country between 1910 and 1970. Regional studies have come up with more satisfactory numbers. Peter Read has calculated from detailed government records that about 10,000 children, or 15 per cent, were removed in New South Wales from 1899 to 1968. My research found that about 10 per cent on average were removed from 1899 to 1968 in Victoria. This was over 1000 children, but exact numbers are elusive due to the sparseness of the remaining records. The intensity of removals varied over that time, being greatest from 1940 to 1968, when the practice was stopped in Victoria. A Queensland public servant quietly claimed during the HREOC inquiry in 1996 that in Queensland over 6000 were removed since 1911, but this was quickly claimed to be an underestimate.[59] The number may prove to be in excess of 50,000 across Australia over a period of 70 years. Even though the children's material conditions and Western education may have been improved by removal, even though some removals were necessary, and even though some people were thankful for it in retrospect, overall it was a disaster. The removal of children was massive and a racially driven psychological assault on 50,000+ individuals. It was a rupturing of tens of thousands of Aboriginal families, aimed at eradicating Aboriginality from the nation in the cause of homogeneity and in fear of difference.

RESISTING ASSIMILATION

The assimilation policy did not improve Aboriginal lives as hoped, and in fact blighted them. Resistance mounted from all quarters. Elkin and others debated the policy, and especially its failures to recognise the importance of cultural groups in sustaining individuals. Aboriginal support groups criticised the policy and urged a two-way engagement of integration instead. Aboriginal people opposed assimilation publicly, consistently and vehemently. Bert Groves in 1958 condemned Australia's assimilation policy as 'simply a kind of white chauvinism: an expression of our belief that there is nothing worth preserving in Aboriginal culture and or our dislike of accepting [a] permanent national minority'.[60] Oodgeroo Noonuccal (Kath Walker) stated 'assimilation means the swallowing up by a majority group of a minority group . . . Assimilation can only bring us forward as replicas of the white race; this is not what we desire, we desire to be Aboriginals.'[61]

People on the ground across the country resisted it. The Pintupi had always been flexible in order to survive in the desert, and at Papunya they employed the same strategies. Ralph Folds, a teacher at Papunya, remarked: 'While this contact with whitefellas brought enormous upheaval, Pintupi were never grim survivors, clinging to a receding past. They already knew there was no going back to bush life . . . Pintupi seized an opportunity they saw at Papunya, and . . . its possibilities did not altogether disappoint them.'[62] They were not assimilated into white culture, but instead endured it, borrowed from it, even embraced aspects of it. They used new items of metal and glass to fashion traditional items. They moved out of the tin houses and made humpies to their own designs. They broadened their language to communicate with others and adopted European names to keep their own names secret. They adopted card games and gambled for money, which they used to fund their love affair with the car, immortalised in the television series *Bush Mechanics*. Some of the Pintupi eventually left Papunya in 1966 to live on outstations.

The policies of physical and cultural absorption of Aboriginal people had clearly failed in the face of Aboriginal resistance across the country. The long Aboriginal population decline since 1788 had bottomed at about 60,000 in the 1920s, but had risen to 106,000 in 1961. Also, Aboriginal people were increasingly moving to urban areas and the coastal cities in the postwar period, lured by employment and greater freedoms. Aboriginal capital-city communities grew in areas of cheap rents by the 1960s, including 12,000 in Sydney, 5000 in Brisbane and 2000 in Melbourne. In all, 20 per cent of Aboriginal people lived in capital cities, compared with 40 per cent of other Australians.[63]

The assimilation policy was not only challenged, but became outdated, as the world around it moved on. The United Nations, which passed the Universal Declaration of Human Rights in 1948, was busy overseeing decolonisation of colonial empires. Australia, with its trusteeship over New Guinea, had to be wary of international criticism. The Soviet government had several times voiced concerns about Australia's Aboriginal policies by way of scoring a point in Cold War politics. The student movement became concerned about racial politics in South Africa after the Sharpeville massacre in 1961 and this eventually flowed to concern over Indigenous issues closer to home. University students established ABSCHOL, an educational assistance scheme run by the National Union of Students. Postwar migration was a huge catalyst for change as the ethnic complexion of Australia shifted from exclusively Anglo-Australian, to a more diverse European mix. Ethnic groups, themselves under pressure from the assimilation policy, pushed for recognition of cultural difference. Affluence made Australians more tolerant of difference as many travelled and broadened their horizons. Asian immigration restrictions were eased in 1966. The media also played a part: its increased reportage of Aboriginal people was often negative and sensational, but some concern for Aboriginal people's situation was generated.

These changes and challenges caused the government to redefine further the definition of assimilation in 1965, namely: 'the policy of assimilation seeks that all persons of Aboriginal descent will choose to attain a similar manner and standard of living to that of other Australians and live as members of a single Australian community'.[64] The basic government aim of homogeneity remained, but it was softened by changing 'same' to 'similar' and by introducing the notion of Aboriginal choice.

COALITION POLITICS

The struggle for Aboriginal rights entered a new phase in the 1950s. New organisations emerged to fight for rights and challenge the newly renamed Welfare Boards and their assimilation policies. In most states these bodies were called advancement leagues, and were white–black coalitions. The first was founded by Dr Charles Duguid in Adelaide in 1938, but it was mostly a white affair. This was followed two decades later by the more radical Aboriginal-Australian Fellowship founded in Sydney in 1956 by two Aboriginal women,

Pearl Gibbs and Faith Bandler. Their aim was to challenge the Aborigines Welfare Board in New South Wales.[65]

To the south, Doug Nicholls, together with Gordon Bryant MHR, feminist and peace activist Doris Blackburn, and Church of Christ pastor Stan Davey, formed the Victorian Aborigines Advancement League in 1957. It emerged in response to public shame at the conditions of Aboriginal people in the Warburton Ranges—shifted there during atomic and missile testing in the late 1940s. Bill Grayden, member of the Western Australian parliament, exposed these conditions in a select committee, the book *Adam to Atoms* (1955) and the film *Warburton Ranges*. Doug Nicholls, who visited the area with Grayden, brought the film back to Melbourne and showed it widely, fostering outrage and the League's birth. When the African-American singer Paul Robeson, who was touring Australia, saw the film, he wept, then became angry, declaring: 'the indigenous people of Australia are my brothers and sisters'.[66] Advancement leagues emerged also in Perth and Brisbane, but they were less radical and less active than the Victorian Aborigines Advancement League (VAAL).

In 1960 Doug Nicholls and the VAAL fought for the return of 690 hectares of Cummeragunja land on the Murray River leased out to white farmers by the Welfare Board. The New South Wales government cancelled one lease of 80 hectares in 1962 and the VAAL stocked it with cattle. Further deputations led to the return of the remaining leased land in 1964. Cummeragunja was almost its original size, but its days as a thriving community were over. In 1963 Nicholls and the VAAL began a six-year fight to retain the Lake Tyers reserve, which the Victorian Aborigines Welfare Board wished to close in pursuit of assimilation. On 22 May 1963, Nicholls and 40 Lake Tyers residents marched to state parliament, bearing a petition demanding Lake Tyers' retention. The government was unmoved, so Nicholls increased his campaigning, even appealing to the United Nations. Finally, in 1970 the Victorian government returned Lake Tyers and Framlingham to most of their residents under land trusts with co-operative unconditional permanent title—the first such land handover in Australia.[67]

Most advancement leagues were initially led and dominated by white Australians, although the VAAL's driving force came jointly from its white secretary Stan Davey and its field officer Pastor Doug Nicholls. They did excellent work fighting for rights and developing welfare and cultural programs. These 'coalition politics' at state level formed the Federal Council for the Advancement of Aborigines (FCAA) in February 1958. It originated from a meeting of sixteen people from the state leagues, only three of whom were Indigenous: Doug Nicholls, Bert Groves and Jeff Barnes. Its first three presidents were Anglo-Australians: Dr Charles Duguid, Doris Blackburn MHR and Don Dunstan MLA.

However, at the 1960 annual conference, Aboriginal members led by Doug Nicholls requested an hour be set aside for an 'Aborigines only' discussion session. In 1961 Joe McGinness was voted the first Aboriginal president of the FCAA, a post he retained until 1973. In 1964 it was renamed the Federal Council for the Advancement of Aborigines and Torres Strait Islanders (FCAATSI) to recognise the Islanders as a distinct entity. The VAAL also became an all-black affair in 1969, the takeover being partly inspired by a visit from Bermudan MP Roosevelt Brown, a delegate of the Latin American Black Power movement. Bruce McGuiness of VAAL stated: 'it is time for the black man to emerge as his own advocate'.[68] However, longstanding local Indigenous desires for autonomy also underpinned the takeover. The VAAL was the only advancement league to survive the turmoil, and exists today as the oldest Aboriginal organisation in Australia. Even FCAATSI split over the issue of Indigenous control and faded in the early 1970s—its work done. FCAATSI's story is told in Sue Taffe's *Black and White Together* (2005).

Aboriginal people had fought for civil rights since petitioning for equal access to land and schools in the nineteenth century and in political movements beginning with Fred Maynard's organisation in 1924. In 1960 Aboriginal Acts and Boards still remained, and rights were restricted in most parts of the country, as few were exempt from the Acts. All jurisdictions except for Victoria withheld the right to drink alcohol; all but Victoria and New South Wales restricted the right to freedom of movement, to control of property and freedom of association; Queensland, Western Australia and the Northern Territory banned Aboriginal people from voting; and Queensland and Western Australia retained control over Aboriginal marriage.

CIVIL RIGHTS VICTORIES

The 1960s witnessed a dismantling of most discriminatory legislation. This was mostly due to the actions of Aboriginal people and black–white coalition Aboriginal rights bodies, as John Chesterman has argued in *Civil Rights: How Indigenous Australians Won Formal Equality* (2005).

Governments surrendered to the logic of Aboriginal claims, which were backed by arguments based on international covenants and threats of international exposure. Voting rights had been demanded since the 1930s. A Senate committee in 1961 recommended that all Aboriginal people be given the vote in federal elections immediately. Its report stated significantly that Aboriginal people must be 'integrated' (not 'assimilated'), which suggested a rejection of cultural absorption for a policy of cultural pluralism. The committee rejected the old notion of a training period, arguing that it was 'better for a right to be granted before there is a full capacity to exercise it on the part of some individuals, than that others should suffer the frustration of being denied a right that they can clearly exercise'.[69] Those under federal jurisdiction were granted the vote and logically the states had to follow suit. Other discriminations required a harder fight.

In February 1965, Charles Perkins, the first Aboriginal graduate (1964) at Sydney University, and a group of about twenty fellow students took a 'Freedom Ride' bus tour to highlight continuing discrimination in northern New South Wales. They were inspired by the freedom rides during the civil rights movement in the American South in 1961. At Moree they were confronted by ugly crowds of spitting, fruit- and rock-throwing townspeople. At Walgett, the opponents had a heated confrontation outside the RSL club, which barred Aboriginal membership. However, the angry white crowd was soon dispersed by the speech of a courageous Aboriginal woman who yelled:

Listen! You whites come down to our camp and chase our young girls around at night! You were down there last night. I know you! (pointing) I saw you last night . . . Why don't you go back and tell your wives where you've been? They're over there in the crowd! Go on, go tell 'em! You there, you're nothing but a gin jockey! Yes, and you! and you! You were there a week ago! You have been going with my sister for two years in the dark! What about tellin' your wife about her? Tell her about the little baby boy you've given her![70]

White men scurried for cover as the town's underlife was laid bare. That night the students' bus was forced into a ditch after being rammed twice by a truck. At Moree, they confronted the manager of the swimming pool who barred Aboriginal people, except when part of official school groups. After hours of confrontation, some Aboriginal children were allowed to swim. These confrontations made headlines, and forced changes. They also radicalised many Aboriginal people. Lyle Munro junior, who swam that stormy day at Moree in 1965, became an activist for Aboriginal rights, because he 'saw the power of direct action that day in Moree'.[71] Ann Curthoy's *Freedom Ride* related this story in detail.

FCAATSI led significant campaigns for civil rights in the 1960s; its work for equal wages was alluded to in Chapter 6. FCAATSI's most impressive victory was the reform of two clauses of the Constitution. One only allowed the Commonwealth to legislate for 'the people of any race other than the aboriginal race in any state' (section 51). The other determined that in any government census 'aboriginal natives shall not be reckoned' with other Australians (section 127). The Sydney-based Aboriginal-Australian Fellowship began the campaign in 1957 and it was taken up by FCAATSI in 1962. The campaign was conducted through churches, all manner of community organisations, sporting clubs, unions, political parties and with anyone who would listen. Over 90 signed petitions with 103,000 signatures were collected and presented to parliament in 1963, calling for a referendum. The conservative government led by Robert (later Sir Robert) Menzies upheld the 'one people' vision of assimilation and initially agreed to a referendum only on section 127 concerning the census.

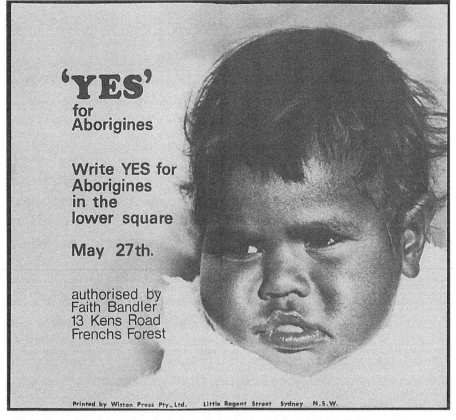

'*Vote Yes*' *poster for the 1967 Referendum*. COURTESY OF THE NATIONAL LIBRARY OF AUSTRALIA (NLA-AUS-VN3116836–1X-V).

The government's attitude shifted with Menzies' retirement in 1966. Harold Holt, his successor, agreed in February 1967, after intense pressure, to put both sections to a referendum. After a frenzied campaign which referred to Australia's need to protect its international reputation, an amazing 90.77 per cent of Australians voted for the two changes on 27 May 1967. Aboriginal people were elated, Evelyn Scott remembered: 'There was screaming when I heard it on the radio.'[72] While FCAATSI President Joe McGinness believed it 'is only a first step', it was a large symbolic stride to civil rights, and left the field clear of discrimination; except for Queensland (see below).[73] Harold Holt created the Council for Aboriginal Affairs (CAA), composed of long-time top public servant Herbert 'Nuggett' Coombs, anthropologist William Stanner, and Barrie Dexter, Director of the newly created Office of Aboriginal Affairs (OAA). The CAA gave advice on policy, which was often sympathetic to Aboriginal causes, and against the Ministry of Internal Affairs. The OAA administered new federal legislation relating to Aboriginal people and began recruiting Aboriginal public servants, including Charles Perkins in 1969.

Equality came last in Queensland, which proved particularly recalcitrant on Aboriginal rights. Queensland Aboriginal policy appeared paradoxical, but is explained by deep old-world paternalism. It offered the best housing and health facilities for Aboriginal people in Australia, but its regime was the most restrictive, and its administrators of Aboriginal affairs the most paternalistic and bureaucratic. Everything done to and for Aboriginal people was the most extreme in Queensland.

This is evident in the case of Palm Island, established in 1918 for the incarceration of 'troublemakers' from reserves across the state. In the 1950s it was run by Roy Bartlam, an ex-police officer. He ruled the island with an iron fist through compulsory saluting of whites, morning roll calls, a surveillance system of Aboriginal police and informers, violence, and a well-used lock-up. A dormitory system kept the young in check, and rationing, house inspections and oppressive work details ordered the adults. In 1957 unrest developed. On 10 June, Albie Geia was arrested for insolence in the workplace and faced deportation from his island home. The people went on strike, demanding more meat rations, better housing, higher wages and the sacking of Bartlam. Women pelted Bartlam's office with bad meat. Ivy Sam recalled: 'The money. The food. The way we were treated by the Europeans. That's what the strike was all about. And the meat . . . It was just bones.'[74] Bartlam called for twenty police from Townsville to restore order. The 1400 residents defied them by protecting the strike leaders and commandeering the rations. After five days, seven leaders were arrested in dawn raids, and led to a waiting cutter in handcuffs. Over the next few days, 47 more people were arrested and deported to Woorabinda, Cherbourg and Bamaga reserves. Another 50 were removed in the following month.

The strike, which was represented in the film *Protected* (1974), achieved change. Wages were increased, rations improved and better housing was built, but Bartlam remained. In 1958 he was sent to quell a strike at Yarrabah, and again deported the leaders to other reserves.[75] Charles Rowley, who visited Palm Island in 1964, remarked that 'the inmates were treated as rather dull "retarded" children . . . People were sent to gaol, locked up in dormitories, put to work, presumably moved through the stages of housing, all as the result of paternal decisions for their own good . . .'[76]

By 1960 almost half of Aboriginal Queenslanders were still controlled by special Acts, hangovers from the old colonial world. Reserve dwellers suffered not only the usual loss of rights, but were subject to the petty tyranny of superintendents, only found elsewhere in gaols or mental asylums. Under the Aborigines Preservation and Protection Act 1939 to 1946 (which consolidated legislative changes stretching back to 1897), the superintendent could prohibit card games, dancing and 'native' practices that might give offence; order medical inspections; and confiscate possessions that are 'likely to be the subject or cause of a disturbance of the harmony, good order, or discipline of the reserve'. Alcohol and threatening or abusive language were prohibited, as was 'any act subversive of good order and discipline'. Reserve inmates could be ordered to do 32 hours of work without payment. The superintendent, with the approval of the Director of Aboriginal Affairs, could also open mail and inflict corporal punishment. Such places of 'protection' required a permit to enter and one to leave. Conditions varied, as some managers did not enforce these rules strictly; some did not easily detect illegal behaviour; and some could not stop it, being openly defied by Aboriginal inmates. Recalcitrant people were fined or locked up for their efforts.

The reserves had their own laws, courts, police and gaols. Their superintendents were often police officer, judge and jury, at one and the same time. Court procedures varied greatly from those outside the reserves, to the detriment of the Aboriginal defendant's rights. One study by Colin Tatz in 1963 found defendants invariably pleaded 'guilty', out of ignorance or knowledge that a 'not guilty' plea would antagonise the judge, who was also the reserve superintendent. At Woorabinda reserve, of the 177 persons tried in 1956 and the 98 tried in 1962, all were found guilty by the presiding superintendent. This was surely the highest conviction rate in the world, and the equal of any 'kangaroo court'. Some offences that were tried were actually beyond the jurisdiction of these Aboriginal courts. Sentences imposed often bore little relationship to the offence allegedly committed: being asleep on the job rated more days in the lock-up than a conviction for arson. Children under sixteen years were imprisoned, though this was forbidden under the Act. Behaviour such as adultery and adult consensual sex, which were not offences in the outside world, were tried and punished on the reserves.[77]

In 1965 a new Aborigines and Torres Strait Islanders Act was passed in Queensland, but in most respects it differed little from the one it replaced. Titles changed from 'settlement' to 'community' and from 'superintendent' to 'manager', and the harshest regulations were expunged, but special courts, reserve police, lock-ups, power over Aboriginal movements, decision-making, wages and property remained. The Director and managers still made decisions for Aboriginal people under the Act and could create reserve regulations beyond the scrutiny of parliament.[78] The Act was amended in 1971, but petty controls persisted. Self-management was a distant reality for the new Aboriginal reserve councils, which could be overruled or dismissed at the Director's discretion. This Act was clearly at variance with the 1965 International Convention on the Elimination of All Forms of Racial Discrimination.

In one of the angriest books written on Aboriginal affairs, *This is Palm Island* (1978), Bill Rosser outlined the violence and despair that existed on Palm Island under the Queensland regime. On the first day of his arrival in 1974, a woman knifed her brother, a man belted his daughter over the head with a block of wood, a man shot himself in the stomach and another was shot through the arm. These incidents were outcomes of the despair of living under the Queensland Act. The Island's Aboriginal Council, which was attempting to display some independence under the leadership of Fred Clay, was sacked by the Minister. The sacking seemed suspicious as the government had just called for tenders for the development of Palm Island as a tourist resort, and the Townsville Council had tried to incorporate the island in its boundaries. The people had opposed both moves. Many suspected Aboriginal people might be manoeuvred off their land to suit commercial interests.[79]

Federal governments tried to bring Queensland into line for a decade. The Whitlam government passed the Aboriginal and Torres Strait Islanders (Queensland Discrimination Laws) Act in 1975 to override Queensland's legislation, but it was not implemented by subsequent federal authorities. In 1979 the Queensland government amended its Act under continued outside pressure, which removed some remaining discriminatory provisions. Reserve court decisions could now be appealed to higher state courts. However, award wages were not paid to reserve workers. The Premier, Joh Bjelke-Petersen, reiterated assimilationist rhetoric in 1980 when opposing self-managed Aboriginal communities: 'we don't want them set aside in some country that becomes black man's country—we want them to live exactly like we do'. However, the Act was finally scrapped in fear of a black-African boycott of the Brisbane Commonwealth Games in 1982.

The 1960s brought about a legislative sea change stimulated by Aboriginal activism, white supporters, and pressure from international covenants. From 1962, those without the vote gained it in all jurisdictions, and all were eligible to receive social welfare and equal wages after 1966. Only in Queensland was there tardiness, but Australia's signing of the 1965 International Convention on the Elimination of All Forms of Racial Discrimination made it inevitable that Queensland would finally succumb. However, conservative federal governments did not implement it, and it was left to the Whitlam government to pass the Racial Discrimination Act (1975), which put this covenant into place and prevented discrimination in employment, public places, and the supply of accommodation, goods and services. The Act does not have criminal sanctions, but works through conciliation, managed initially by a Commissioner for Community Relations. Over the years, it has proved of great value, symbolically and in real terms.

Legislation does little to change attitudes. In 1977 the Commissioner for Community Relations, Al Grassby, reported that Aboriginal people were still denied service in hotels, served last in shops, and overcharged for goods purchased. In 1978 he singled out Ceduna in South Australia as a place of regular racial discrimination and violence and in 1979 Carnarvon in Western Australia earned that title. In 1980 a certain hotel in Fitzroy, Melbourne, had allegedly banned Aboriginal people.[80] Prejudice remained long after the Acts changed and may have increased due to a backlash among some white Australians, who resented the Aboriginal elevation to equality. Claims surfaced of welfare bludging, but Aboriginal people were 66 years behind other Australians in receiving full federal entitlements!

Another barrier to full equality stemmed from the way the law was dispensed by police and the courts, which since colonial times has not been equal due to racial prejudice. An Alice Springs magistrate in 1972 allegedly retorted to a police officer, who explained how he fired warning shots over the heads of Aboriginal people on a settlement to quieten them: 'you should have given them both barrels in the legs'.[81] The majority of charges laid against Aboriginal people in the 1960s were for being drunk or disorderly, one survey revealing these two offences formed 45 per cent of all charges, compared to 15 per cent for other Australians.[82] Such offences are open to police interpretation and victimisation of those who are the poorest and most visible in a white-dominated community. Aboriginal people claimed victimisation was a daily affair. Chicka Dixon declared:

> If you're black in Redfern, Alexandria, Waterloo or Newtown and you're on that street after ten o'clock, brother, you're taking a chance. This is the procedure. Along comes the 'hurry-up wagon'.
> 'Righto-o, Rastas, in the back.'
> 'But I'm not drunk.'
> 'What do you want: Drunk? or Goods in Custody?'
> 'I'm drunk!'[83]

Once arrested, black Australians were less likely to be granted bail than other Australians, and endured a legal system that was more alien and less comprehensible to them than to most other Australians. In 1965, Aboriginal people in Western Australia, who formed less than 3 per cent of the population, were convicted of 11 per cent of the offences and made up 24 per cent of the prison population. Their percentage of prisoners rose to 32 per cent in 1971. In Australia in 1971, the Aboriginal imprisonment rate was fourteen times that of other Australians, a rate that remained steady for a decade.[84]

Civil rights were all but achieved by 1966, save for those living in Queensland, but community attitudes lagged behind. Adult white Australians alive in the 1960s had their attitudes formed in the era when it was thought Aboriginal people were an unworthy, primitive and doomed race, and the butt of jokes of those who thought themselves civilised. Adult Aboriginal Australians of the 1960s well remembered the years of no rights or few rights, and carried the psychological scars of oppression and lack of self-worth. Equality before the law was a first step, the second was to provide equality of opportunity, and the third was to provide respect for difference. By 1970 these challenges lay ahead of all Australians.

11

STRUGGLING FOR
INDIGENOUS RIGHTS

Alongside the fight for civil rights for equality with other Australians was a desire for Indigenous difference to be valued and respected. Billibellary, who developed the radical hope in the 1840s to farm like white people, did this to hold onto land that was significant to him and remain Aboriginal in the new colonial world. At the core of the continuing demand to special Indigenous rights was a claim for land. This claim, reiterated by Aboriginal people across Australia since frontier times, re-emerged in a dramatic way in the 1960s as black, and some white, voices demanded Indigenous rights.

THE CLAIM FOR LAND

In 1963 the Yolgnu people at Yirrkala Methodist mission at Gove, Arnhem Land, on the advice of Rev. E. Wells, Gordon Bryant MHR and Kim Beazley MHR, sent a petition on bark to the House of Representatives. The Yolgnu protested at the excision of 390 square kilometres of their land for bauxite mining by Nabalco. They claimed they were not consulted despite the fact that 'our occupancy of this land was lawful'.[1] They were adamant their homeland and birthplace was vital to their 'livelihood and independence'; and especially at Melville Bay, it was 'sacred to the Yirrkala people'.[2] The startling nature of the claim and its mode of delivery—on bark and written in English and the Gumatj language—forced a parliamentary investigation. The mining lease was not cancelled, but the committee recommended compensation.[3]

The Gurindji people, who walked off Wave Hill Station in 1966 after the three-year delay in granting equal wages, also claimed ownership. They petitioned the Governor-General about the Wattie Creek area: 'Our people lived here from time immemorial, and our culture, myths, dreaming and sacred places have evolved in this land. Many of our forefathers were killed in the early days while trying to retain it. Therefore we feel that morally the land is ours and should be returned to us.'[4] In 1968 public awareness of the Gurindji's struggle was highlighted by author Frank Hardy and others. FCAATSI also launched a national campaign for the return of reserve lands and compensation, supported by churches, students and unions. The Australian Council of Churches, ABSCHOL and FCAATSI published Frank Engel's *Turning Land into Hope,* which put the case for land rights.

The Methodist Commission on Aboriginal Affairs funded legal opinion about the possibility of a land case over mining at Gove and promised to underwrite such a case.[5] Following legal advice, the Yolgnu in late 1968 sought an injunction in the Supreme Court of the Northern Territory against Nabalco and the Commonwealth to prevent further mining at Gove. They also sought a declaration of their land title and compensation for damages. The Yolgnu, represented by a team led by A.E. (Ted) Woodward, over several days presented their sacred ritual objects, or *rangga,* to Justice Blackburn's court, as self-evident maps and title deeds to land.[6]

Aboriginal groups lobbied hard for land rights. The National Tribal Council, a radical splinter group from FCAATSI, issued a manifesto in September 1970 in which the Council demanded title to all traditional lands, compensation for those lost, and royalties from mining on Aboriginal lands. Its manifesto also demanded the effective protection of sacred sites. In 1971 the Aborigines Advancement League in Victoria (VAAL) made an appeal to the United Nations to support its claim for land and mineral rights, and monetary compensation from the Australian government of $6 billion.

A new political mood emerged in Aboriginal politics around 1970. The VAAL and FCAATSI were taken over by Aboriginal activists, who wanted control of these cross-racial bodies. A tiny, short-lived Black Panther Party also emerged following the tenet of the Black Panthers in the United States, and spoke of black power and black liberation. Its small membership demanded decent employment, housing, education, exemption from military service, an end to police brutality, the freeing of Aboriginal prisoners from gaols, black juries for black offenders and a United Nations plebiscite of Aboriginal people to see if they wished to remain as part of the Australian nation.[7] Two 'field marshals', Gary Foley and

Paul Coe, threatened violence, with Foley demanding: 'We want land rights now and then the black man can assimilate, integrate or live separately. But he must be able to choose for himself.'[8] Kath Walker's son Dennis was also making inflammatory statements about strategic violence. Many black and white Australians were outraged by such wild talk, which pushed Aboriginal issues onto the front page. At the Australian Labor Party conference in Hobart in 1971, leader Gough Whitlam declared that 'Australia's treatment of her Aboriginal people will be the thing upon which the rest of the world will judge Australia and Australians not just now, but in the greater perspective of history'.[9]

In 1971 Justice Blackburn delivered his decision in the Gove case. He found that the Yolgnu had traditional law, and a relationship to the land, but their native title was not recognised by the common law. The Yolgnu in a second petition of May 1971 were 'deeply shocked' at Blackburn's decision: 'The Australian Law has said that the land is not ours. This is not so. It might be right legally but morally it's wrong. The law must be changed.'[10]

Aboriginal pressure built on 26 January 1972 with the appearance of a tent on the lawn in front of Parliament House, Canberra, erected by four young New South Wales Aboriginal activists, Michael Anderson, Billy Craigie, Gary Williams and Tony Coorey. This calico tent, which Tony Coorey brilliantly dubbed the 'Aboriginal Embassy', became a centre of activity. It was soon staffed by Aboriginal activists from across the country and white supporters, and visited by those seeking dialogue, including Gough Whitlam. The tents grew in number and their defiant label of 'embassy' challenged the massive white parliamentary building opposite. It was ripped down in the middle of the night six months later on orders of the conservative Liberal–Country Party. Before this, the Aboriginal Embassy's Cabinet Committee demanded full Aboriginal control and ownership of the Northern Territory; ownership of all reserves and some city areas across Australia; preservation of all sacred lands and ownership of mineral rights; payment of $6 billion and a percentage of the yearly gross national income.[11] Demands laughable a few years earlier were being earnestly reported and debated. Everybody was talking. Younger activists with more radical ideas were willing to take to the streets to use direct action and threats.

Land claims, the Embassy and Indigenous rights galvanised many Aboriginal people across the country into a pan-Aboriginal identity. Chicka Dixon declared in 1972: 'As long as I breathe I'm black . . . of course we down south haven't got our culture, we haven't got our language, but we have the feeling that we belong . . . we're black Australians.'[12] Wesley Wagner Lanhupuy, from Galiwinku (Elcho Island) in the Northern Territory, stated at a National Land Rights conference

Aboriginal activists at the Tent Embassy, January 1972. COURTESY OF THE *CANBERRA TIMES.*

in Sydney in 1977: 'Aborigines—whether urban or tribal—who have a spiritual awareness of themselves as Aborigines and identify themselves as Aborigines are Aborigines.'[13]

Labor swept into power in December 1972 under the slogan: 'It's Time'. Aboriginal people, suffering under conservative governments and their assimilation policies for over twenty years, shared the euphoria. Prime Minister Whitlam stated on 6 April 1973 that his government's Aboriginal policy was 'to restore to the Aboriginal people of Australia their lost power of self-determination in economic, social and political affairs'. He outlined new initiatives, including an Aboriginal-elected policy advisory committee, an inquiry into land rights, and programs to revitalise Aboriginal social welfare.[14] Labor budgets increased spending in Aboriginal affairs sixfold.[15]

The Whitlam government continued to take advice from the existing Council for Aboriginal Affairs (CAA) composed of Coombs, Stanner and Dexter, and enlarged the status of Aboriginal affairs by changing the Office of Aboriginal Affairs into the Department of Aboriginal Affairs (DAA), with Dexter still as head under the Minister Gordon Bryant, the co-creator of the Aborigines

Advancement League in Victoria. The DAA began a recruiting program which sought to appoint Indigenous public servants. Charles Perkins became a leading adviser in the DAA. The government also created the National Aboriginal Consultative Committee (NACC) to give Aboriginal and Torres Strait Islander people advice on Indigenous issues.

All these bodies had difficulties. The three members of the CAA contained deep knowledge of Aboriginal affairs, but were increasingly seen by Aboriginal people as inappropriate, because they were non-Indigenous. The DAA faced the problems of a new department trying to change the culture of state governments and the community, and shifting its own culture, by slowly increasing its Aboriginal staff to about 30 per cent. The NACC had no power, was under-resourced, and met only for several weeks a year. Its 41 members, elected on large electorates by about 28,000 Aboriginal people, were never truly representative of local opinion. In this sense it was an imposition from above on a Western parliamentary model, and did not accord with Aboriginal ideas about decision-making and consensus politics. The NACC attempted to gain more power and tried to change its name to the National Aboriginal Congress, but the government resisted these moves.

The DAA, CAA and the NACC were rivals and all three were mutually suspicious. Many Aboriginal people considered them full of white and black public service 'fat cats' who were not serving their interests. Charles Perkins was torn by competing pressures and wrote: 'I found myself so isolated, not only within the Department, but it seemed virtually within Australian society.'[16] In 1974 Bobby McLeod produced an (unloaded) gun in the offices of the DAA in support of Perkins and was lucky to get off with a fine and a bond.[17] These uneasy relations persisted between the three bodies for four years while the Whitlam government held office. However, only the DAA survived. In 1976 the incoming Fraser government accepted the CAA's desire to dissolve itself, and it abolished the NACC, which was seen to be ineffective. The NACC was replaced by another elected, but advisory, body—the National Aboriginal Conference (NAC), which survived to 1985, and 'stirred the pot' by calling for a treaty.[18]

The Whitlam government created a land inquiry for the Northern Territory with, for its day, radical terms of reference. Commissioner Justice A.E. Woodward, who had put the Yirrkala's position in the Gove case, was to report on 'the appropriate means to recognise and establish the traditional rights and interests of the Aborigines in and in relation to land'. Woodward was to report on how land rights could be achieved. After consulting with twenty Aboriginal communities over six months, Woodward recommended in his interim report that two Aboriginal Land Councils be established in the Territory to promote and represent the land claims of communities. They were to be sufficiently funded to hire administrative and legal staff. He identified two problems to be resolved. Were Aboriginal 'rights in minerals and timber' full or partial rights? Should Aboriginal owners have the right to veto mining on their land?

Woodward's second report, issued in April 1974, affirmed rights to land in the Northern Territory and to sufficient financial support to allow communities to use land as they chose. Woodward recommended that reserves should be handed back as freehold title, vacant Crown land transactions should be frozen for three years to allow Aboriginal claims, and town lands should be exempt from land claims. An Aboriginal Land Fund should purchase land for urban Aboriginal housing. Aboriginal claims to land under long-term pastoral leases should be considered by an Aboriginal Land Commission, but the Aboriginal Land Fund should purchase pastoral leases for Aboriginal communities as an interim measure. Woodward also pronounced on the protection of sacred sites, the control of tourism, and legislation to incorporate Aboriginal communities, land trusts, and the two Northern Territory land councils. His proposals only related to the Northern Territory, where the federal government had jurisdiction, but Woodward hoped that state governments would follow suit.

Woodward was in considerable legal and moral conflict over the question of ownership of minerals on Aboriginal land and whether Aboriginal people had the right to prevent mining on their land. He decided that mineral ownership should remain with the Crown in accord with general practice. However, his terms of reference had asked him to decide on Aboriginal land rights 'including rights in minerals and timber', and in recognition of their traditional ownership and of past injustices, he recommended that Aboriginal people receive royalties from mining on their land. These should be negotiated by the people themselves. Government should only intervene if negotiations stalled. Government should be able to veto Aboriginal objections to mining only if 'the national interest required it'. However, Woodward stressed the word 'required', acknowledging that 'to deny Aborigines the right to prevent mining on their land is to deny the reality of their land rights'.[19] The Whitlam government had much to consider.

At the same time, the proposed Ranger Uranium Mines Pty Ltd venture at Jabiru, in the Oenpelli region, posed urgent questions. Under the assimilation policy, mining near Aboriginal communities was officially favoured, as it supposedly brought development to these regions and provided jobs. By the 1970s, this assumption was questioned. The Whitlam government appointed another commission of inquiry in July 1975, headed by Justice R.W. Fox, to inquire into the Jabiru proposal. The inquiry was to consider the mining of uranium and also the impact of mining on Aboriginal people. The commissioners brought down an interim report on the principle of uranium sales, recommending that in the context of an energy-hungry world and with certain imposed safeguards, uranium mining and export by Australia should proceed.

The commissioners then examined the question of the specific proposal for mining the Oenpelli region, where 1000 Aboriginal people still resided in a largely traditional manner. Mining at Jabiru would proceed from two open-cut 100-hectare pits up to 190 metres deep, which would create a dirt mound half as large. The uranium ore would be crushed, dissolved in sulphuric acid, the uranium extracted and the slurry piped to a huge 125-hectare tailings dam with 30-metre walls. Sulphuric acid was made on site from imported sulphur; lime would be imported to neutralise the tailings; and fuels, chemicals, explosives and building materials trucked in. The report found that this activity, plus the building of a town for a thousand people, made for a significant environmental impact. Mining dust, sulphur dioxide fumes and possible seepage of radioactive water from the tailings dam brought recommendations for modifications to the tailings dam and that the pits be filled once mining ceased.

The report found that mining would significantly affect the Oenpelli people themselves. Blasting threatened sacred sites at Djidbidjidbi and Dadbe on the Mt Brockman escarpment, three kilometres from the Number One pit site, and several hundred metres from possible future pits. The blasting would not physically damage sites, but it would alarm Aboriginal people as the Rainbow Snake resided at Mt Brockman. The commissioners doubted any benefits of employment, health and education that the company claimed mining would bring to the Oenpelli people—and with good reason. Past mining projects had so far failed to produce significant benefits for local Indigenous owners.

Although they included only one Aboriginal witness in their 415-page report—Silas Roberts, Chairperson of the Northern Land Council—it was clear that most Aboriginal people opposed the mine. Roberts told the inquiry:

We in the Northern Territory seem to be the only ones who have kept our culture. We are worried that we are losing a little bit, all of the time . . . We are very worried that the results of this Inquiry will open the doors to other companies who also want to dig up uranium on our sacred lands . . . We think that if they all get in there and start digging we'll have towns all over the place and we'll be pushed into the sea. We want a fair go to develop. We are human beings, we want to live properly and grow strong. We see white men as always pushing.[20]

The commissioners acknowledged past evidence that rapid development adjoining Aboriginal communities 'caused the breakdown of the traditional culture and the generation of intense social and psychological stresses within the Aboriginals'. They added: 'There is no evidence which convincingly demonstrates that the result in the Region will be different, although the recognition of Aboriginal land rights is a uniquely favourable factor in this regard.'[21] Despite these findings, the commissioners recommended that mining (with modifications) be allowed to proceed at Jabiru and that Aboriginal opposition to mining 'should not be allowed to prevail'. No doubt the attraction of the estimated profits—ranging from \$574 million to \$3591 million, which would 'provide high rates of return on capital invested'—was too powerful to allow 1000 people to stand in the way of development.

In an endeavour to lessen the impact of mining, the commissioners proposed a number of safeguards, including: restrictions on the sale of alcohol; the upgrading of Aboriginal welfare services; sequential development to soften the impact of mining; modifications to the mining proposals; and limiting the size of the company town to protect the environment. Land rights were also suggested, but of course with no power to stop the mining. In spite of all the contrary evidence, the commissioners convinced themselves that these safeguards offered 'a chance of ensuring a satisfactory relationship between white and black people, and of improving the general happiness and prosperity of all people in the region'.[22]

The Fraser Liberal–Country Party government, in power by the time the Ranger inquiry was completed, sanctioned a start at Jabiru on 25 August 1977. The safeguards proposed by the Ranger report were accepted, except for sequential development. Prime Minister Fraser focused his comments on issues of nuclear waste disposal and the potential for nuclear terrorism, devoting less time to the mine's Aboriginal neighbours. Land rights would be granted, the nearby Kakadu National Park phased in, and the Oenpelli people encouraged to work as park rangers. The government pledged to adopt special measures to advance Aboriginal well-being in the region and to temper the effect of mining. Fraser glibly concluded that 'Aborigines will have new opportunities to control the use of their traditional lands and to protect their interests'; yet they held few cards, and mining companies controlled the game.[23] Aboriginal control did not include the power to stop mining and the invasion of their land by over 4000

European workers. Most involved were insensitive to the disruptive potential to traditional communities, one mining company official stating: 'every Aboriginal reserve should have a mine next door'.[24]

The Whitlam government presented a Land Rights Bill based on Woodward's report in 1975, but it lapsed when the government was dismissed in a constitutional crisis in November 1975. In 1976 the Fraser government passed its own Aboriginal Land Rights (N.T.) Act. It was weaker than the Whitlam government's bill, and perpetuated the limitations of both Whitlam's bill and the Woodward report. However, the Act went a considerable way towards fulfilling Aboriginal claims for justice in the Northern Territory. It was remarkable that a conservative government, partly representing landholders and mining companies, went as far as it did, which was evidence of community pressure for Aboriginal justice. However, it was the last moment of party consensus on land rights issues for the next generation.

The Land Rights Act established a mechanism for granting land rights, but only in the Northern Territory, and only to Aboriginal reserves or vacant Crown lands to which traditional and ongoing attachment could be proven. The needs of town dwellers, and people alienated from traditional lands, were not met. The Act established two Land Councils to represent the claims and rights of the various communities and created an Aboriginal Lands Commissioner to adjudicate claims. It contained clauses that protected sacred sites, stopped unauthorised entry to Aboriginal land and prevented the Territory government (usually controlled by pastoralists) from resuming Aboriginal land. Aboriginal communities could prohibit mining on their land, unless it was judged in the 'national interest'. This overriding power could be objected to by either house of Parliament within fifteen days of proclamation of the 'national interest' provision. Aboriginal people could negotiate directly with mining companies over mining royalties, which were to be at their disposal.

Despite offering Aboriginal people radical gains in land ownership, the Act still had major deficiencies. Only vacant and Crown land could be claimed and by those who could demonstrate a continuous traditional use. The veto was overridden by a 'national interest' clause, which included the Ranger uranium project, and all exploration licences taken out before the bill was first presented on 4 June 1976. If negotiations over mining contracts stalled between a land council and a mining company, the Aboriginal Affairs Minister could appoint an arbitrator whose decision was final.

These weaknesses for Aboriginal people were soon revealed once the Oenpelli people began negotiating mining contracts with Ranger Uranium

Mines Pty Ltd over the Jabiru mine. The people, under advice from Steven Zorn, who had American experience, demanded 36 per cent of profits. The chief Aboriginal negotiator, Northern Lands Council (NLC), was chaired by Galarrwuy Yunupingu, a very capable 29-year-old from the Gumatj group at Gove. Yunupingu was strongly traditional despite his Christian education. He stated in March 1978: 'up here we still have our land and that gives us our strength and our pride!' He had witnessed the upheaval of Nabalco's explorations at Gove in the mid-1960s, even though the Nabalco mine there never proceeded. Yunupingu was determined that the people would be well compensated for upheavals at the Jabiru site. The NLC insisted that the pits be filled in after mining had ended, despite company complaints that this would cost $100 million. After months of hard talking, the NLC negotiators initialled a draft agreement in late August 1978, granting the Oenpelli people $7 million in a lump sum and 4.25 per cent of the royalties or an estimated $13 million a year at full production. This was far below the 18–25 per cent that Native American groups had received, and less than one-eighth of their original demand, but Ranger and the government were determined not to pay more.

The Australian press claimed the Oenpelli people would be 'stone age millionaires'. This was derogatory and clearly wrong, for under the Act, part of mining royalties went to all Aboriginal Territorians. Based on the then current price of uranium, the Oenpelli people would receive about $6500 each in royalties per year, small compensation for threats to their land and culture. Besides, the people's aim was not money, but protection of their heritage, which soon became clear.

As negotiations were about to be concluded, the Fraser government enraged the people by allowing another mining company, Pancontinental, to extend the road to its Jabiluka exploration lease (30 kilometres north of Ranger), despite Aboriginal opposition to mining there. On 9 September 1978, Yunupingu claimed that 'we've been pushed right through—and now we are being pushed to sign the papers'. Under such pressure the NLC split: six Aboriginal communities placed a court injunction on the NLC's ratification of the draft agreement, claiming that they had not been fully consulted. Under pressure of being dethroned as NLC chairperson, and of creating Aboriginal disunity in the face of common enemies, Yunupingu and the NLC agreed to further consultation. The government claimed that the Labor Party and the anti-uranium lobby were manipulating the NLC to wreck the negotiations. Aboriginal Affairs Minister Ian Viner made veiled threats about appointing a negotiator and thus circumventing the NLC.

The Oenpelli traditional owners rejected the draft agreement, believing it did not protect their land and sacred sites. However, at a closed session, the NLC, pressured by Yunupingu (who was also under great government duress), agreed to sign if the Oenpelli people signed. At a secret meeting at Oenpelli attended by Viner, Yunupingu and the NLC, but allegedly only three of the traditional Oenpelli owners, the Ranger agreement was signed. It was a sorry tale of pressure and manipulation by the federal government and ultimately the mining companies. The NLC had exercised some muscle and delayed events, but was powerless beyond a certain point. Prime Minister Fraser's claim in August 1977 that Aboriginal people could 'protect their interests' proved hollow.[25]

During this turmoil, Justice Toohey, the Aboriginal Land Commissioner, was quietly assessing traditional land claims in the Territory under the Land Rights Act. In open-air court sessions on traditional lands, claimants sang and danced their religious affiliations to their land. The Walbiri and Kartanangaruru-Kurintji people claimed 95,000 square kilometres of land south of Wave Hill, which Toohey granted, reversing an exodus from this land that began after massacres by whites in 1928.[26] Assessing the Alyawarra and Kaititja claim to 1540 square kilometres of land north of Alice Springs, Toohey remarked: 'The obvious enthusiasm of those people for their country and the disclosure of important places and sacred objects was compelling.'[27] He granted their claim. Toohey wrote: 'there are some objective criteria by which to measure but in the end the assessment must reflect a large element of the subjective, an attempt to understand the feelings and attitudes of people, an attempt to see things as they see them.'[28]

Aboriginal Territorians were fortunate Toohey had such empathy. During his tenure, they gained 30 per cent of the Territory's lands by about 1980. However, claims on Uluru (Ayers Rock) and Kata Tjutu (the Olgas) were not possible, as they were national parks and not eligible for claim under the Act. The Larrakia's application for land around Darwin was also thwarted by the Darwin town council, which in 1979 enlarged the size of Darwin's boundaries (population 50,000) to four times that of London (population 14,000,000). This was done as the Act prevented claims on town lands. Land was also set aside at Tennant Creek for future public use, smack in the middle of an Aboriginal land claim. However, in 1985 the High Court ruled these attempts to manipulate the Act were illegal, for the excisions were not made for town planning purposes, but to defeat the terms of the Aboriginal Land Rights Act.[29]

LAND: SUCCESSES, FAILURES AND BACKLASH

The Pitjantjatjara people in South Australia doubled their ownership of land to 20 per cent of the state's lands in 1982 in an unwilling decision by the conservative Tonkin government. The previous Dunstan Labor government had introduced a land rights bill, but it lapsed when it lost office in 1978. The incoming Tonkin Liberal government demurred over land rights, before opening 30,000 square kilometres of Pitjantjatjara claimed land for mineral exploration without consulting Aboriginal people. Public outrage forced the Tonkin government to pass its own Land Rights Act. Although it did not contain an Aboriginal right of veto over mining on Aboriginal land (unlike the previous Dunstan government's bill), it allowed Aboriginal people to negotiate directly with mining companies, and receive royalties. Any deadlock went before an impartial arbitrator, whose terms of reference stressed the rights of Aboriginal people, as well as 'the economic and other significance of the operations to the State and Australia'.[30]

By 1980, the Queensland and Western Australian governments still refused to recognise any Aboriginal claims to land, traditional or otherwise. They even blocked legitimate purchases of pastoral properties by the Aboriginal Land Fund, on the irrelevant and discriminatory argument that Aboriginal people would not use the land 'productively'. The Queensland government's view on land fund purchases was overruled in 1982 following a three-year court battle. The High Court ruled, in *Koowarta vs Bjelke-Petersen*, that such a view was discriminatory under the Racial Discrimination Act of 1975. During the lead-up to the Brisbane Commonwealth Games of 1982, the Queensland government was under pressure from international threats of a black Games boycott. It passed a Land Act, which granted Aboriginal reserve lands to occupiers, under a Deed of Grant in Trust. However, Aboriginal people could not veto a development or claim compensation, and the grants could be revoked without reason at any time. A supporting Reserve Management Act gave government the right to dismiss reserve councillors. These Acts were widely condemned. The Fraser government criticised the Queensland Land Act, as a Deed of Grant in Trust did not meet its four land rights principles of security of tenure, integrity of boundaries, self-management and full consultation. Land rights beyond reserves were not even considered. The 'Friendly Games' were marred by the arrest of 400 land rights protesters, including the Governor-General's daughter Ann Stephen, using special draconian powers.[31]

Charlie Carter accepts the title of Lake Tyers reserve from the Governor of Victoria, Sir Rohan Delacombe, in July 1971. This was the first land handover in Australia, but little else in Victoria was handed back. COURTESY OF THE ALICK JACKOMOS COLLECTION.

Aboriginal people in New South Wales owned a mere 3500 hectares, or 0.005 per cent of the state, by 1980. However, a state parliamentary committee in July 1980 recommended that ways be found for non-traditional Aboriginal people to have access to urban land for housing or community centres and projects. The Wran Labor Government passed a Land Rights Act in 1983, which gave inalienable freehold title over 4300 hectares of reserve land; 7.5 per cent of the state's land tax for fifteen years to purchase land; and the right to claim vacant Crown land, except land set aside for essential purposes. Aboriginal people were angered that the Act also retrospectively validated resumptions of 10,000 hectares of reserve land made between 1909 and 1969.

The story was worse elsewhere. The community at Wreck Bay reserve in the Australian Capital Territory was negotiating over 405 hectares of land in 1980. Two small groups of Aboriginal Victorians owned a mere 1821 hectares, or 0.0008 per cent of Victoria. In 1980 the Framlingham community was fighting for a further 1400 hectares of former reserve land. A Victorian Aboriginal Land Council was seeking further former reserve lands. The Pallawah in Tasmania had no land at all by 1980. In June 1981, the National Aboriginal Conference demanded that Crown land transactions throughout Australia be frozen until all Aboriginal land claims were registered and settled.[32]

In 1981 the Territory's conservative government, acting for pastoral interests, lobbied fellow conservatives in the Fraser government to amend the 1976 Land Rights Act. White pastoralists opposed the right of Aboriginal groups to convert Aboriginal-held pastoral leases to freehold title and make claims over stock routes. Aboriginal people sought parts of stock routes, as the Act prevented small claims for Aboriginal living excisions from white pastoral leases. People who had been turned off pastoral properties after losing their jobs in an industry restructuring wanted living areas on or near their traditional lands. Although road transport had rendered most stock routes useless, the pastoralists challenged such claims. After several High Court battles in the 1980s, the Territory government, under federal pressure, created a tribunal in 1989 to consider small excisions.

The mining provisions of the 1976 Act were also attacked. The Australian Mining Industry Council (AMIC) and the Territory government urged abolition of the veto and a reduced royalty.[33] Barry Tuxworth, the Chief Minister, stated in November 1993 that the Act had 'failed' and imposed a federal brake on the Territory's development.[34] AMIC and Tuxworth argued that the veto and royalty rights were inequitable, as they were not rights shared by other Australians. However, they ignored special Aboriginal needs arising from their unique contact history, their special relationship with the land, and the impact of mining on isolated Aboriginal communities. In 1984 a report entitled *Aborigines and Mining* strongly condemned mining for creating 'disunity, neurosis, a sense of struggle, drinking, stress, hostility, of being drowned in new laws, agencies and agendas'.[35] Murabuda Warramarrba of Groote Eylandt, where Gemco had mined for 25 years, declared in 1990: 'we are losing a generation. These kids sniff petrol and lose any ambitions and end up not being able to have kids themselves. When they've had it in the mind, they don't think twice before they break and enter.'[36] Justice Woodward, whose report shaped the 1976 Act, stated that land rights only had a reality if accompanied by a veto on mining—that is, a brake on the onslaught of modernity. Royalties compensated communities which chose mining. The veto gave rights; royalties gave a chance of independence.

In November 1981, the Territory government also sought to alter its Aboriginal Sacred Sites Act, to enable Cabinet and not the Aboriginal Sacred Site Authority to determine which sacred sites could halt development. A dispute arose over development and sacred sites in the Sadadeen Valley adjoining Alice Springs. In 1982 the government sanctioned the bulldozing of part of the Injalka Caterpillar Dreaming Track, allegedly to force a test case on the definition of a sacred site under the Act.[37]

After intense pastoral lobbying, the Fraser government in June 1982 announced changes to the 1976 Act to prevent Aboriginal pastoral leases being converted to freehold, and to stop claims on stock routes, national parks and land designated for public use.[38] The Labor Opposition and the Democrats declared they would block these amendments in the Senate. The Territory government launched a propaganda campaign in support of the changes, while the Uniting Church and Aboriginal Land Councils issued booklets opposing the amendments. The fall of the Fraser government in 1983 ended the matter.

The Territory government legally opposed each Aboriginal land claim, causing massive delays and legal costs to Aboriginal land councils. The Gurindji's 1976 claim for 3293 square kilometres at Daguraga Station was only achieved in 1983.[39] The Warlpiri waited a decade for their 2600 square kilometres claim at Chilla Well to be finalised. The Marranunggu's claim on the Finniss River was delayed for fourteen years before 12.5 square kilometres (and later more) was granted in May 1992. Only two of the elders who first made this claim were still alive. April Bright, the community's spokesperson, said: 'It is a new and stressful experience for them to be fighting in European courts and facing alien laws to have to prove they are the people of this country! . . . This country was, still is and will always be the land of our people . . . They are keepers of this land. To protect its sacred sites and to live, eat and drink off this land.'[40]

Clyde Holding, the federal Minister for Aboriginal Affairs in the new Hawke government, announced a bold land rights program in March 1983. The states would have to conform to Labor's policy and grant Aboriginal landowners mining royalties and a veto over mining.[41] Holding also promised to pressure Territory pastoralists to provide living excisions of land to Aboriginal people, to pass legislation for sacred sites and to set minimum uniform standards for land rights. He also promised compensation for landless urban Aborigines and justice for Maralinga people injured in the 1950s atomic tests, and he welcomed suggestions concerning a handover and leaseback arrangement for Uluru.[42] Holding courageously declared, in a ministerial statement of 8 December 1983, that human rights were above state's rights. He also foreshadowed parliamentary recognition of Aboriginal people as the 'original owners and prior occupiers' of Australia, who through colonisation had become 'as a group, the most dis-advantaged in Australian society'. He predicted opposition from beer-swilling 'rednecks', but hoped for great progress by the Bicentenary in 1988. Charles Perkins, the chairperson of the Aboriginal Development Commission, optimis-tically hailed the statement as incorporating all the principles for which Aboriginal people had struggled.[43]

Conservatives were startled and mounted a public fear campaign. In May 1982, the historian Geoffrey Blainey, posing as prophet and not recorder of past events, suggested Aboriginal people may slow the Territory's development. He mischievously speculated that if they became a majority of the Territory's population, they might side with a foreign Asian power against Australia.[44] Two years later, Hugh Morgan, Director of Western Mining Corporation, characterised traditional Aboriginal culture as vengeful and cannibalistic, and claimed land rights would destroy mining.[45] Geoff Stewart, head of North Flinders Mines, contradicted Morgan, pointing to his company's amiable goldmining venture with local Aboriginal landowners.[46] His voice was lost in the swelling hatreds of minorities that emerged from the controversy over Asian immigration. This was sparked by Geoffrey Blainey's comments on allegedly unwise high levels of Asian immigration. The National Farmers' Federation joined the mining lobby's campaign. Victorian RSL leader, Bruce Ruxton, termed land rights 'discrimination against white people'. Liberal Opposition leaders in three states also attacked land rights: Jeffrey Kennett in Victoria found the issue 'divisive', Bill Hassell in Western Australia thought them 'a serious threat to the security and future of Australia', while Nick Greiner stated the issue was irrelevant as 'there are no tribal Aborigines in NSW and clearly no link to tribal land'. Andrew Peacock, Liberal leader in the federal sphere, regretted the passage of the 1976 Act.[47]

The Western Australian Chamber of Mines, representing local and overseas mining corporations, initiated a powerful media campaign against land rights in 1984. One television advertisement portrayed black hands building a wall across a map of the state and posting the sign: 'Keep Out—this land is part of Western Australia under Aboriginal claim'. The slick and emotive campaign argued that land rights, which gave special rights to Aboriginal people, would end freedom of access to the land and halt mining development, the backbone of Australia. Aboriginal people and their sympathisers argued back. Dr H. ('Nuggett') Coombs retorted that the mining industry provided few jobs, largely sent its profits overseas, received preferential tax treatment, had a poor record in Aboriginal rights, and falsely claimed Aboriginal people had slowed mining in the Territory.[48] However, these voices were ineffectual against mass advertising. The Labor Cabinet was shocked when an ANOP survey showed only 18 per cent supported land rights, while 30 per cent opposed and 52 per cent were suspicious of them.[49] In 1987 Rod Cameron, Director of Australian National Opinion Polls (ANOP), said this campaign against land rights was the 'most brilliant public relations effort' of the decade. At its close, soft and hard-line opposition to land rights had grown from 35 per cent to 75 per cent.[50] Generosity to Aboriginal people also declined. In 1964, 75 per cent of those surveyed in an ANOP questionnaire agreed that Aboriginal people should have a little or a lot more welfare assistance. By 1976 and 1981, the affirmative response had dropped to 50 per cent, and plummeted to 32 per cent by 1983–84.[51]

Pollster Rod Cameron rightly described the campaign 'as a total success in WA'. In late 1984, Paul Seaman QC reported on land rights to the Burke Labor government in the west, recommending the right to claim former reserves, vacant Crown land, mission lands and national parks. He saw 'no compelling reason' why Aboriginal people should not control mining on their land. Premier Burke, bowing to mining companies and fearful of lost votes, immediately opposed much of Seaman's report. Burke rejected any veto on mining, despite the veto being approved of in his own party's platform.[52] When in Perth three weeks later, Prime Minister Hawke also dumped his commitment to a veto, saying: 'there are other ways of ensuring the proper protection of the rights of Aborigines than by the exercise of a veto'. Hawke indicated the much-vaunted national uniform land rights legislation could be limited to a set of principles.[53] Aboriginal people and the Labor caucus were outraged. Burke's bill, drafted with the help of mining groups, contained no veto, no compensation rights, no hunting rights on mineral leases, and no mechanism to prevent Aboriginal reserves from being excised for public or mining purposes.[54] The federal government agreed to it, retreating further on its principles, but the conservative upper house in Western Australia defeated even this pro-mining bill.

Clyde Holding produced modified uniform proposals, advocating a 'South-Australian-style' tribunal to adjudicate on disputes over mining between companies and Aboriginal communities. In the face of conservative fury, there were hopes that the handover and leaseback of Uluru (Ayers Rock) in October 1985 would pacify Aboriginal people and the Labor caucus.[55] A month later, Holding introduced the long-awaited amendments to the 1976 Land Rights Act, ending any chance of Aboriginal claims on stock routes and limiting the Aboriginal veto over mining to five years. Further Aboriginal outrage, backed by a caucus revolt, caused the amendments to be shelved.[56] In March 1986, federal Cabinet agreed to Burke's minimalist plan to give Aboriginal people in Western Australia merely long leases on reserves and a five-year $100 million package of federal money.[57] In 1987 sixteen million hectares of Aboriginal reserve land (7 per cent of the state) was handed back to Western Desert people on 50 or 99 year leases.[58] Uniform land rights with a veto, royalty rights and compensation for the urban landless were dead and Aboriginal people felt betrayed.

Indigenous rights had made some headway, most notably in the Northern Territory, but uniform land rights—the hope of Justice Woodward in his 1974 report, the pledge of the Hawke government in 1983, and the goal of pan-Aboriginal activists—were unfulfilled. Only limited gains were made in the 1980s. The Tasmanian government handed back only two square kilometres to Pallawah. A bill to restore Mutton Bird Island, some rock art sites and Oyster Bay passed the lower house, but failed in the upper house. The Wreck Bay Community in the Australian Capital Territory finally gained 405 hectares in 1987. In Victoria, a conservative backlash and upper house opposition meant Victoria's 1987 Land Rights Act to return the Framlingham forest was passed by federal parliament using its external affairs powers. The New South Wales Act of 1983 promised gains, but by 1990, 60 per cent of claims were rejected, and only 348 square kilometres of land transferred, mostly under freehold. After 1983, Aboriginal land councils in New South Wales purchased sheep properties, retail outlets and franchises with Land Fund moneys to provide employment. The Land Fund, created from 7.5 per cent of land tax revenues until 1998, promised to realise a further $400–500 million for future buy-back schemes. In Western Australia, 7 per cent of the state's Western Desert was handed back under long leases. There were gains in Queensland, when a 1991 Act converted former reserve lands held under Deeds of Grant in Trust to communal freehold. Aboriginal people could also claim vacant Crown land outside towns and cities not needed for public purposes, but such lands amount to only 2 per cent of the state. There was no land fund, no compensation, no protection of sacred sites, and no final veto over mining on Aboriginal land in Queensland, but there were some royalty equivalent payments. Across Australia, progress on land rights was patchy and mostly disappointing for Aboriginal people.

ABORIGINAL NATIONALISM

Indigenous rights in the form of land rights had become a powerful force in politicising Aboriginal people and binding disparate groups into a national movement. An Aboriginal flag designed in 1971 by Harold Thomas, a Lutitja man from Alice Springs, with red and black halves emblazoned with a yellow disc symbolising the unity of sun, land and people, was raised all over the country. The fight for land rights emboldened Aboriginal people and gave them confidence through a shared sense of injustice. Land formed the basis of a growing sense of common feeling that for the first time overlaid parochial traditional loyalties. Russell McGregor has termed this an Aboriginal nationalism.[59]

People across the country marched, occupied sites, formed committees and petitioned parliaments. Around 1980, the Groote Eylandt people demanded that Gemco renegotiate the mining contracts it offered them in the 1960s. They banned miners from moving beyond the mining camp on weekends to force Gemco to the table. In late November 1980, some Gunditjmara women claimed and occupied a sacred place on the site of the proposed Alcoa aluminium smelter at Portland to prevent site desecration. Appeals were made to the United Nations from 1970 onwards. In 1980 a National Aboriginal Conference delegation met the United Nations sub-commission on the rights of minorities to discuss the Noonkanbah people's plight, who since 1976 had been resisting mining of their land by the Amax Petroleum Corporation.

Aboriginal people forged links with groups overseas, which deepened their justifications for Indigenous rights and developed emerging ideas of Aboriginal sovereignty. Aboriginal delegates visited China, Africa and Europe in the 1970s.[60] Indigenous global networks emerged in the 1970s and ideas were exchanged to improve Indigenous lives worldwide. Aboriginal people were schooled in international human rights, such as the International Labor Organization's Indigenous and Tribal Populations Convention and Recommendation, 1957 (C107), and other such conventions which justified Indigenous rights. NACC representatives were at the preparatory meeting at Port Alberni, Canada, for the inaugural World Council of Indigenous Peoples (WCIP) meeting in 1975. The WCIP was granted NGO status at the United Nations and drew support from numerous groups, including the World Council of Churches. Aboriginal representatives attended subsequent congresses, hosting the 1981 conference in Canberra.[61] Meetings occurred between Aboriginal activists and Canadian, Maori and other First Nation peoples. Aboriginal support groups developed in Europe and an Aboriginal information centre was established in Geneva. Indigenous

The Aboriginal flag flies at Noonkanbah, Western Australia, 1980.
COURTESY OF WESTERN AUSTRALIAN NEWSPAPERS LTD.

leaders visited from other countries, beginning in 1971 with the arrival of George Manuel of the Shushwap tribe, British Columbia, Canada. The WCIP's Declaration outlined the commonly perceived and shared exploitive history of colonialism, vowing 'to control again our own destiny and recover our complete humanity and pride in being Indigenous People'.[62] Transnational Indigenous identities developed from these WCIP links and the agendas of Aboriginal organisations followed Indigenous rights—land, sovereignty and treaties—from the 1970s onwards, partly influenced by these international conversations.

The idea of a treaty between Aboriginal people and the Australian government emerged when Stewart Harris, a Canberra journalist, proposed in 1976 that 40 per cent of resource royalties go to Aboriginal people. 'Nuggett' Coombs developed the idea in 1978 and called a meeting of an Aboriginal Treaty Committee (ATC) in April 1979. Eight eminent white Australians published a 'call for a treaty, within Australia, between Australians' and a book was published by Harris, called *Its Coming Yet* (1979). In the same month, the newly created National Aboriginal Conference (NAC), which succeeded the NACC, endorsed the idea. The NAC campaigned for a *makaratta*, a Yolngu word for thigh, connected to the ritual of dispute settlement by leg spearing. It was not only a symbolically important Aboriginal word, but was more palatable for the conservative Fraser government, which worried that a treaty worked against the idea of a united Australia. The ATC and the NAC pursued their own discussions across the country. It was a novel expression of Indigenous rights and sovereignty, but Aboriginal people were divided on the question. Some were deeply suspicious about what a *makaratta* might contain, how it would be negotiated, and who would speak for Aboriginal people. Kevin Gilbert and Michael Mansell argued that a *makaratta* could only be between 'two equal sovereign peoples' and that was not currently the situation in Australia. The Senate Standing Committee on Constitutional and Legal Affairs discussed a *makaratta* from 1981 to 1983. The idea was lost amid a sea of debate, splits within Aboriginal groups, and the demise of the ATC in 1983.[63]

CULTURAL REVIVAL

The Land Rights Act or the hope of land rights, combined with unemployment in the north after the equal wages case of 1965, stimulated a return to the land by many traditionally orientated people. Family groups moved from towns and settlements to small, isolated outstations, where they lived off bush tucker, supplemented by European foods, and supported by educational and medical facilities. Here they were freed from the pressure of European advisers and the turmoil of large-scale communal living on reserves. These outstations provided opportunities for cultural revival and the time and space to regain control over their lives. By 1980 there were 40 outstations in Arnhem Land, containing over 30 per cent of the reserve population, and 65 in Central Australia. Others existed in the far north of Queensland and Western Australia.[64]

The federal government provided each group with basic transport, shelter and health facilities, at the minimal cost of $10,000 per group. In 1978 it directed its departments to be more flexible in adapting their services to alternative Aboriginal lifestyles. The Turnbull report into outstations in 1979 found that the cost of supporting people on outstations was one-tenth of the amount needed to support them on settlements.[65] Turnbull revealed that outstation people produced more in the way of saleable handicrafts than those on settlements, and were largely self-supporting due to their traditional food-gathering activities. Not all Aboriginal people preferred the isolation and rough living at outstations, but those who did worked hard at being their own boss on their own land. On one station, 80 kilometres east of Oenpelli, an old man and two younger men, equipped only with shovels and crowbars, surveyed and built an airstrip to receive supplies. It took them six months at only the cost of their food, whereas a construction team with bulldozers would have cost tens of thousands of dollars.

Cultural revival also occurred on settlements where art and craft work proliferated. One of the most amazing stories occurred at Papunya in 1971. A teacher, Geoffrey Bardon, encouraged painting to refurbish traditional culture, which had been damaged in the assimilation era. Men painted Dreaming story murals on the school walls and doors, including the Honey Ant Dreaming by Long Jack Phillipus Tjakamarra and Billy Stockman Tjapaltjarri. This created controversy among the people and related groups, for some of the material was secret-sacred. Out of this evolved a new dot style of painting that obscured secret meanings from outsiders. During the 1980s, the fame of the group spread, fuelled by the showing of their work in the 'Dreamings' exhibition at the Asia Society Gallery in New York in 1988. Books and films document their work, producing both pride and income from art sales to galleries and individuals. Other art movements arose elsewhere in the north.

The cultural revival in the north was echoed by Aboriginal people in the south, who used cultural activities to regain their self-esteem and control over their own lives. This had begun with a rejection of assimilation and a reassertion of Aboriginal identity in the 1960s. Paul Coe, the Director of the new Aboriginal Legal Service in Sydney, argued around 1972:

We've never been a part of the white Australian mainstream of life. Every time we've tried to join it, we've been shunted off. The only way we could join it is by becoming imitation white men. And I think that if a man has to almost prostitute himself in order to join something, he's better off without joining and by maintaining his own separate identity. The people should be in a position to make and implement their own laws and live by them, rather than have other laws forced on them.[66]

Generations of experience under Protection Board control, decades of avoiding the welfare who removed children, and years of suffering the racism of service providers encouraged Aboriginal people to create their own service organisations to circumvent the mainstream. These constructive efforts were forged by young black activists, often associated in the public mind with 'destructive' black power. With the help of the sixfold funding boost from the Whitlam government, these organisations mushroomed in the 1970s. Aboriginal communities in capital cities and some regional centres created their own housing, health, legal and other services. They were modelled on the Aboriginal Legal Service and the Aboriginal Medical Service founded in Sydney in 1970 and 1971. They created informal and accessible services that aimed at community control, despite initial reliance on white professionals. Government funding placed them at the mercy of insensitive white and black bureaucrats, which made the assertion of community control a long battle. However, the struggle for control was important for these organisations (mostly incorporated bodies), which gave Aboriginal people jobs and a sense of achievement. Given Indigenous people still formed about 1 per cent of the population, wider political power was beyond them, but service organisations developed leadership and some control over their own lives.

The Victorian Aboriginal Health Service (VAHS) founded in 1974 was staffed by Aboriginal people and white medical staff. It fostered Aboriginal identity and autonomy, and also treated their clients' ailments, recognising that health and pride were interrelated. Its services were well used and 200 clients attended its 1979 annual general meeting. One Aboriginal client remarked: 'It's a home away from home'; 'It's a focal point. It is a point where people can sit down and talk and not just about sickness and medicine. It's a community place.'[67] It also ran a funeral fund, child-care centre and a craft room. The VAHS, however, competed with a better funded government-run Aboriginal service. Early in 1979, VAHS staff worked for a month without pay, as most federal health funds went to the government body. This was an Australia-wide pattern. In 1979, $18 million was spent on Aboriginal health in Australia, but only $4 million of this was channelled through Aboriginal-controlled services. However, this situation gradually changed as the Aboriginal-run services proved themselves. Two studies in 1980, one government and one independent, found that the government health service in Victoria failed to reach Aboriginal people.[68]

The same assertion of pride and identity occurred in country communities. Significant changes were forged within a dispirited Aboriginal community in isolated Bourke, New South Wales, when it formed an Aboriginal Advancement Association in 1972. The Association organised picnics, film evenings, a newsletter, a play group and working bees. The community also established a housing co-operative. Both bodies experienced the usual difficulties with government departments, but made progress. Dr Max Kamien, who worked with the community, summed up what happened in Bourke, which applied to co-operatives across the country:

> The AAA became the power base of the Bourke Aborigines from which they could get access to federal, state, and through them to local government bodies . . . To be taken notice of instead of being ignored or ridiculed, to succeed occasionally instead of always to fail, allowed for the development of an increased personal status in the Aboriginal which in turn led in some to a new found dignity. In addition, the fact of having to run their own affairs led some members to learn the skills of negotiation, compromise and pressure needed to succeed in a white man's world.[69]

While self-management promised immense benefits for Aboriginal self-esteem, it was often overridden by governments.[70] This was nowhere clearer than in the tragic Aurukun and Mornington Island affair of 1978. A weak federal government promised much but was out-manoeuvred by the Bjelke-Petersen Queensland government, which, by making these reserves local government areas, avoided federal intervention.[71]

The cultural expressions of Indigeneity grew exponentially in the 1970s. These expressions developed Indigenous pride and spread awareness of Indigenous cultures throughout the Australian community. Indigenous cultural expressions ranged from art, writing, music and dance to sport and religion. Aboriginal art, such as the Papunya Tula movement, grew in stature. Indigenous poets and writers matured in the 1970s, including Oodgeroo Noonuccal (Kath Walker), who wrote five books from 1964 to 1981, Mudrooroo (Colin Johnson), who has written at least ten books since 1965, Jack Davis, who wrote seven plays and three books of poetry from 1972 to the 1980s, Kevin Gilbert, author of two books, and others. Life stories, stimulated by Black Writers' conferences, were published sometimes in collaboration with white academics. The magazine *Identity* was founded in 1971 and soon claimed 10,000 readers. Its editors included Jack Davis and John Newfong. *Identity* promoted Aboriginal and Torres

Young Indigenous dancers, 1980. COURTESY OF THE ABORIGINAL ISLANDER DANCE THEATRE.

Strait Islander identity and talents, and also reported on Aboriginal politics, before closing in 1982. At least a dozen other black-produced magazines emerged in the 1970s to express Aboriginal viewpoints.

Other arts flourished. A Black Theatre group was formed in Sydney in 1971 which ran until 1976. A dance group established in Sydney in 1972 became the Aboriginal Islander Dance Theatre in 1976. It trained performers as well, and by 1980 30 students were enrolled in its three-year course. The company performed widely, including overseas, and its graduates established the Bangarra Dance Theatre in 1989, which still thrives. European-style artists flourished as well, notably the Victorians Ronald Bull and Lin Onus. Bull was mentored by landscape master Hans Heysen; Onus developed a style that blended European forms with Aboriginal political themes and techniques to form a seamless originality. Aboriginal people began to make films, such as Essie Coffey's *My Survival as an Aboriginal* (1978). Other Australians, such as Phillip Noyce, made films with black actors, Gary Foley starring in *Backroads* (1977). Foley toured Europe with thirteen films on black Australia in 1978, with some acclaim at Cannes.[72]

Music was perhaps central to this cultural revival. It could be performed anywhere and everywhere, and on a shoestring. Aboriginal people had earlier embraced church music, minstrel music and modern music whenever they encountered it. This interest continued in the postwar world, especially focused on country music. Clinton Walker remarked 'before anything else, country music gave Aboriginal people a voice in modern Australia'.[73] Walker argued that as rural dwellers, Aboriginal people were exposed mostly to country music; it was a music of stories and tales of the land and was played on cheap, portable guitars. Jimmy Little, a Yorta Yorta man from Cummeragunja, was an early exponent of country music in the mid-1950s. Jimmy Little has remained in the business ever since, achieving two gold records and a gold album. A host of others sang, including boxing champions George Bracken and Lionel Rose. The first song written by Bob Randall, a Pitjantjatjara man who had been removed as a child, was 'Brown Skin Baby'. It was about a mother's attempt to protect her child. He sang it at the first National Aboriginal Country Music Festival in 1976. Randall remarked of country music: 'they were story songs about sad experiences . . . we could relate to that, because we'd lost everything'.[74] The dominance of country was toppled by rock in the 1980s, led by bands such as No Fixed Address, Warumpi Band and Coloured Stone, who all played music with a strong resistance theme.

Politics and culture intermixed. Aboriginal and Torres Strait Islander performers attended the South Pacific Festival in 1976 in New Zealand, along with 22 other Pacific nations. The following year, performers attended the Second Black and African World Festival of Arts and Culture in Lagos, Nigeria. The trip was funded by the Aboriginal Arts Board, which was headed by Yolgnu man Wandjuk Marika. A conference associated with the festival heard papers, including several from Australia, on 'world black civilisation'.[75] Indigenous gatherings invariably turned to talk of Indigenous rights. It was no coincidence that, amid the Ranger Mining controversy, over 1000 people assembled for a festival at Groote Eylandt in September 1978. Similarly, political meetings have cultural consequences. Aboriginal people from 26 Pilbara and Kimberley communities, who assembled at Noonkanbah in April 1980 to help protect the Goanna spirit sacred site from mining, also held extensive corroborees. People and the land are one, so politics and culture merge. Banjo Woorunmurra declared at Noonkanbah: 'We don't want money, we want our land. Our spirits are in our land. Our old people are still in the land, our motherland, our dusty old land.'[76]

Black studies units were offered in 1970 by Bruce McGuiness and other Aboriginal activists in Melbourne to instil pride in young Aboriginal people. Their model was partly the black pride movement among militants in the United States. But McGuiness, who promoted the use of the term 'Koori' from 1969, drew on Aboriginal tradition as his source of pride. One student of McGuiness, Jill Johnson, wrote:

> Before the white man came to this country our wise men were greater than the world's best scientists, our tribesmen survived in the most harsh conditions. We have to show the Europeans that we are as good as they are, even better. But we can be proud of our past and our people . . . Watch out, white man, Aborigines are stepping out.[77]

Student radicals took an interest in Aboriginal history and historians did likewise. Aboriginal history emerged as a discipline in the early 1970s, with its own academic journal of that name in 1977. The first formal unit in Aboriginal history was taught by John Hirst at La Trobe University in 1974.

Significant gains were made in Indigenous rights by 1990. Land had been won in some places and Aboriginal and Islander culture was resurgent. There was also much greater respect for Aboriginal culture. Indigenous tourism emerged in the 1970s, led by the growing popularity of the Uluru–Kata Tjuta

National Park as a Year 12 rite-of-passage trip and a destination for tourists. The popularity of Uluru and some other sites around the country revealed that Australians and travellers from overseas were increasingly influenced by Aboriginal ideas of land. They began to connect modern Australian identity with its ancient Indigenous culture. But gains in civil and Indigenous rights did not mean that equality was being achieved.

12

HOPING FOR EQUALITY

By the 1980s, Aboriginal people held the radical hope that they could be equal with other Australians and respected for their difference. Civil rights had been won, the assimilation policy had given way to multiculturalism, and the first Indigenous rights to land had been granted. However, the legacies of the past were strong. Colonialism moulds the colonised into 'have-nots' as land and resources are expropriated by colonisers. A continuing cycle of individual poverty developed due to a lack of education and training, the absence of equal opportunities, low wages and few assets to pass onto children. Aboriginal communities also faced development problems due to their undercapitalisation, remoteness and lack of resources. Colonial legacies of racial discrimination and violence also continued despite being outlawed after 1975. Finally, a history of removal of children and control by governments left many ill-equipped to manage their own lives.

ABORIGINAL PEOPLE AND THE ECONOMY

By the 1980s, Aboriginal groups in remote Australia saw mining royalties as a way out of the welfare trap and white control—to achieve 'true independence', as Galarrwuy Yunupingu remarked.[1] However, mining royalties need to be seen in perspective. They did not produce great wealth, despite Queensland Premier Joh Bjelke-Petersen's claim that Aboriginal people would become 'very wealthy people—like the sheiks of the Middle East'.[2] It was estimated in the mid-1980s that, by the year 2000, Aboriginal people whose land was mined would earn $3413 per annum and those in other parts of the Territory, $750 yearly. While royalties could provide some capital for development, royalties at the rate then awarded were insufficient to provide economic independence.[3]

Also, negotiations over mining royalties did not always proceed smoothly. Despite initial unease, traditional owners agreed in 1982 to uranium mining by Pancontinental at Jabiluka.[4] The deal offered $10 million and 4.5 per cent royalties over a decade. The people at Koongarra were initially more enthusiastic. Ironically, both agreements collapsed once the Hawke Labor government blocked new uranium mines on environmental grounds. The NLC's head, Galarrwuy Yunupingu, declared the traditional owners were being denied the chance to 'get themselves off the dole'.[5] In 1988 the Koongarra people again unsuccessfully lobbied the ALP National Conference for permission to mine, and to gain royalties for housing, health and education projects.[6]

However, the right to negotiate over mines and royalties gave Aboriginal communities a sense of new-found power. When the Mereenie gas pipeline agreement was signed in 1984, Pat Dodson, head of the Central Land Council (CLC), said: 'Aboriginal people have exercised with complete responsibility their right of control over whether and how the pipeline development could go ahead'.[7] In the 1980s, other traditional owners formed joint ventures to mine gas, gold, copper and aluminium with Australian and international companies, including de Beers, a South African company strongly linked with apartheid.[8]

Royalties were also good for the Northern Territory's economy. In 1983–84, 90 per cent of the Territory's mining was on Aboriginal land and this created a stimulus to the economy, as people with few resources spend any new income on essentials in the local region. In 1984–85 there was a $25 million boost for the Territory's economy through the payment of mining royalties to Aboriginal communities.[9] Despite claims that mining was the Territory's salvation, a study revealed that only 11 per cent of total payments by the mining industry went directly to the Territory through taxes, charges, revenues and wages, compared with over 35 per cent locally at the Bougainville copper project in Papua New Guinea. However, of this 11 per cent, almost half came from payments to Aboriginal people under the 1976 Land Rights Act.[10] Far from being a 'failed' Act as conservative critics asserted, this Act not only gave Aboriginal people land, dignity and some income, but also helped to retain mining income in the Territory.

Royalties of course have to be used wisely. The Gagudju Association of Oenpelli near Kakadu made significant gains from mining. Gagudju, a close-knit community of landholders and kinfolk, distributed 13 per cent of its royalty income from 1979 to 1985 equally to all, including children, amounting to $1000 each per annum. This very modest sum raised their low per capita income by almost half. The remainder of the royalties were spent on housing and outstation services, investments in a motel, a hotel, store, service station, a contracting business, a new school and employment of a doctor. The school and doctor were soon funded by government—as was appropriate. Most ventures were well managed and returned a profit.[11] So assertive was Gagudju that in 1985 the community took the government to the High Court to force a renegotiation of mining royalties and more stringent environmental safeguards. It argued government duress in the original negotiations of 1978 and a breach of trust towards Aboriginal people under the Land Rights Act.[12]

However, the Kunwinjka Association just 70 kilometres away at Narbarlek frittered its royalties away through administrative negligence, poor investments and large payments to favoured individuals and groups, who bought vehicles that were soon wrecks from misuse and the hard terrain.[13] Such financial failings were lessened by the Act, which directs only 30 per cent of royalties to local owners. Another 40 per cent went to the regional land councils, which have generally used these royalties effectively, although much of it is eaten up by administration—which of course pays people a living—and court battles. The other 30 per cent is paid to the Aboriginal Benefits Trust Fund for the benefit of Indigenous people across the Territory. However, a report in 1985 accused the Territory government of using the Trust fund for projects that should have been financed from the government's own Aboriginal affairs budget.[14]

Besides royalties, mining promised employment opportunities. After the passage of the Racial Discrimination Act (1975), companies were obliged to treat Aboriginal people equally. However, while mining companies allowed Aboriginal people access to facilities at mining townships, in the 1980s they remained on the fringe. After surveying mining in northern Australia, David Cousins and John Nieuwenhuysen concluded that 'the employment impact of mining has been limited and employment unstable'. Despite some benefits, and Aboriginal desire for controlled mining, they warned that mining created a 'decline in traditional authority patterns and adverse effects on morale and community discipline'.[15] In the 1990s, mining companies offered more to Aboriginal people, despite the traumas of the native title wrangles. Companies routinely employed Aboriginal liaison officers, worked more with communities, and often provided scholarships and other funding. In 1996 Rio Tinto created an Aboriginal Fund to form partnerships with Aboriginal people on education, health, cultural and leadership projects, earmarking a modest $17 million over ten years for such projects.

However, most Territory Aboriginal landowning communities did not have a mine close by from which to earn royalties or wage payments. Indeed, in the mid-1980s only 10 per cent were affected by mining. However, all communities in the Territory received some benefits from the 30 per cent of royalties that flowed to the Aboriginal Benefits Trust Fund—that is, when they were passed on by government.

From the 1980s it became clear that the key to Aboriginal autonomy was not simply land rights but economic self-sufficiency. However, this was difficult to achieve. Many commercial enterprises were tried—cattle stations, mining ventures, crocodile, emu and fish farms, horticultural projects, retail stores and tourist operations—but most failed, reinforcing white stereotypes of Aboriginal incompetency. However, most failed for the reasons other Territory small businesses failed: lack of capital, problems of materials and transport, and especially the smallness of the local market and isolation from larger ones. Colonial reasons existed as well, including a lack of education, business training and experience. There were also Aboriginal cultural reasons for failure—the power of kinship, lack of the Western work ethic, and absence of the individual acquisitive instinct—which often opposed commercial success. Failure was inherent in enterprises that began as training programs but were later expected to be profitable. Others failed because they were top-down impositions by white bureaucrats.[16]

Studies in the mid-1980s of the Yuendumu community of 1200 Warlpiri and Anmatyerre people, 300 kilometres north-west of Alice Springs, illustrated the typical problems of Aboriginal economic self-sufficiency. Yuendumu had a cattle enterprise on 2500 square kilometres, which began in 1958 as a training project. The community gained freehold over Yuendumu in 1979 and formed the Ngarkyikirlangu Cattle Company. However, the poorly watered and marginal nature of the land kept cattle numbers below 3000 head. The workforce, managed by a European couple, hovered between only ten and 25 people depending on the season. The company, unable to return a profit, was sustained by government grants. However, it still supplemented community pride and employment at Yuendumu and trained young people in pastoral skills. The Yuendumu Social Club formed a community store in 1959 that evolved into a modern supermarket with a $2 million turnover, yet only half of the dozen staff were Aboriginal and the manager was non-Indigenous, so the store administrators were torn between making a profit and serving the community. A copper mining company established by the Yuendumu Council in 1964 failed to make commercial finds. The council in the 1980s employed seven people, four of them Indigenous, and returned profits from its gravel pit, service station-workshop and retail store. The health and housing services and the school were the other major employers, half of the workforce being non-Indigenous, because their skills were needed. All this activity generated jobs for fewer than 50 Aboriginal people at Yuendumu— perhaps an eighth of the potential workforce.

Then, in the mid-1980s, Yuendumu burst onto the art scene after school doors painted by elders to 'brighten them up' attracted media attention. The Warlukurlangu Artists Association was formed and made $2 million in 1985 and 1986 alone. Half was shared between a hundred artists—which gave them a very modest $1000 per annum each—while the association received 15 per cent. The remainder covered costs.

All these efforts at Yuendumu depended on government grants from numerous departments and schemes within three tiers of government, demanding financial expertise, often non-Indigenous at this stage, to access these grants. In 1986 only a third of the Yuendumu labour force was employed, and three-quarters of those with jobs were in government-funded agencies or enterprises. Even the commercial enterprises that employed the other quarter needed occasional government help. A research team generalised from the Yuendumu study that: 'there are only limited opportunities for Aboriginal controlled economic enterprises of the profit-making market oriented kind in Aboriginal communities'. Remoteness, a blessing for those wishing to avoid outside contact, can be a curse for those wanting self-sufficiency and development.[17]

Yuendumu and many of the hundreds of remote Aboriginal communities around Australia resembled underdeveloped countries in their low standard of living. With only 22 per cent of the Territory's population and 2 per cent of the Australian population in the 1980s, Aboriginal people were outvoted and subjected to internal economic control. They could not employ the strategies of the Third World to control foreigners through the ballot box, migration controls and investment legislation.[18] The 1976 Act gave many in the Territory land, but they remained income-poor. One economist estimated in the mid-1980s that the Tiwi community of about 1000 people needed $10 million in capital to sustain their per capita income in the face of population growth. This was a large sum for a small community, but not so large for Australian governments seeking to reconcile themselves with Aboriginal communities and get Aboriginal people off welfare.[19]

One economic salvation of the 1980s was the homelands movement, where the subsistence sector flourished. In 1987 an inquiry counted almost 700 homelands in the north, containing over 10,000 people.[20] Of the 1200 people at Yuendumu in 1986, 687 lived at the central settlement, 150 at Nyirrpi (a subsidiary settlement), and a further 400 at fourteen outstations up to 200 kilometres away. Outstation residents can be very productive, if their unwaged work in development and craft projects is counted. They also produced much food, using rifles, machetes, crowbars and four-wheel drives to get bush tucker. Returns depend on traditional skills and whether their land is in 'good heart'. Case studies at this time of Arnhem Land and East Kimberley outstations revealed that three-quarters of the residents' diet came from bush tucker, although in arid Central Australia the proportion was between a tenth and a third. The latter still provided significant economic gains to people on low incomes, as well as cultural benefits.[21]

However, the grim fact was that most Aboriginal people in remote areas had insufficient employment opportunities and depended on social security benefits. This perpetuated white control. One bright spot was the Community Development Employment Project (CDEP) scheme devised in 1977 by the Fraser government, after Aboriginal communities requested work for the dole—which other Australian welfare recipients did not at that time perform for their payments. Aboriginal people wanted payments to go to communities, not individuals, to boost development funds. A trial began at Barunga in 1977 and was soon extended to other places. Communities converted these individual payments to a government development grant with attractive on-costs and recurrent funds. Projects managed by communities avoided the disastrous outcomes of earlier imposed programs, of which the failed Wiluna agricultural project in Western Australia was such a depressing example.[22] After 1987, non-remote Aboriginal communities became eligible for CDEP grants as well. In Victoria a CDEP brick-making plant at Lake Tyers employed people, and soon nurseries, landscaping and craft businesses were operating. In 1991, 166 communities with 18,266 Aboriginal workers received $189 million under the scheme. By 1993–94, CDEPs existed in 279 communities, totalling approximately 28,000 participants, with a budget of $361 million.

Some have criticised the CDEP for substituting white bosses for black, as communities have to manage funds, according to government rules and accountability. Aboriginal communities now reflect the values of white bureaucrats in a new form of welfare colonialism.[23] However, the CDEP scheme clearly provided work where there was none, contributed to real development needs and restored Aboriginal dignity. Despite the requirement of Western accountability, and the government being the source of the funding, CDEPs empowered the community.[24] It was not a scheme of pooled unemployment benefits, but an income support scheme that enabled Aboriginal people to work, to learn skills, to be self-reliant and independent, and to escape the 'sit-down money' of social security. Communities are accountable for CDEP money, and should be, but were not subjected to the close fortnightly management under it, like that experienced by those on the dole which is the alternative in many places to CDEP. For instance, Wathaurong Glass in north Geelong began in 1998 as a CDEP project of the Wathawurrung people aided by technical advice from RMIT University. It soon produced beautiful glassware objects and panels with traditional designs. The business prospered. CDEP paid a third of the wages of nine Indigenous employees, providing meaningful work for these nine at a federal cost of just $70,000.[25] The CDEP is not perfect, but like mining royalties, offered significant autonomy through self-sufficiency.

During the 1970s and 1980s, many Indigenous people still experienced serious levels of social inequality and discrimination. Between 1976 and 1986, the average real annual incomes of Indigenous people remained unchanged, and at half the level of other Australians.[26] Declining incomes due to rising unemployment were offset somewhat by universal access to social security payments from 1966. However, it took decades for all those eligible to gain benefits due to intercultural communication problems. By 1986, over 50 per cent of Indigenous income came from social security benefits compared to 28 per cent for other Australians.[27] Aboriginal people also benefited from housing, health, education and other grants that had been increased by 80 per cent in real terms during the 1980s.[28] However, all these were accompanied by bureaucratic surveillance. Also, the Cass report in 1998 found a significant minority still did not have access to payments for which they were eligible.

It is significant that Aboriginal people in the 1980s were less well off in their own society than African Americans and Native Americans in theirs. In 1981 Aboriginal and Torres Strait Islander people were employed at only 58 per cent of the rate of other Australians, whereas African Americans and Native Americans were employed at 93 and 84 per cent the rate of other Americans. Aboriginal median family incomes were at 54 per cent of the total rate, compared to 60 and 66 per cent for African and Native Americans respectively. The narrower gap on income and employment experienced between these minorities reflected the higher unskilled wages and better social welfare in Australia than the United States.[29] There is reason to believe these Australian–American comparisons have altered little since.

Employment was harder to find in the 1980s. Workplace restructuring in the pastoral, agricultural and industrial sectors increased Aboriginal

Railway track repair team, Hughenden, Queensland, 1979. COURTESY OF PHOTOGRAPHER RAYMOND DE BERQUELLE AND THE NATIONAL LIBRARY OF AUSTRALIA (NLA.PIC-AN24912943).

unemployment from a negligible 5 per cent in the 1950s to 25 per cent in 1981, and 35 per cent in 1986—over four times the Australian rate. Unofficial regional unemployment estimates in the late 1980s ranged between 55 and 76 per cent for Aboriginal men, and 23 and 65 per cent for Aboriginal women.[30] These were averages, with unemployment being worst in rural areas and among the young. For instance, in 1986 official figures showed Aboriginal unemployment rates for those aged 25 to 60 years at between 20 and 35 per cent, dependent on the precise age group, whereas youths under 20 had a rate of 51 per cent.[31] Unemployment in formal work on remote communities could affect up to three-quarters of working-age adults.

These high Indigenous unemployment rates also stemmed from inadequate education, low skills and remote living. In the Torres Strait Islands, standard employment opportunities have been limited since the collapse of pearling in the 1940s. And despite admirable training programs of some mining companies, like Comalco at Weipa in the 1980s, Aboriginal employment in mining remained low by 1990 at about 1 per cent of the mining workforce.[32] One study has shown that if such factors as education and qualifications, age, location, marital status and job history are taken into account, the unemployment rate of Aboriginal youth in 1986 should have been about 22 per cent for males and 20 per cent for Aboriginal females. However, they were actually much higher than predicted, at 57 and 45 per cent respectively, the difference being accounted for by either discrimination against Aboriginal workers or Aboriginal attitudes to work.

Studies in the 1980s revealed many Aboriginal people worked hard and productively and that the Aboriginal unemployed wished to work. A survey undertaken in 1986 of 100 Aboriginal households in north coast New South Wales found a strong interest in work, strong satisfaction with work, and stable work histories among the 19 per cent of working age Indigenous people who had jobs.[33] A 1985 study of the Darwin Aboriginal workforce found Aboriginal workers had similar or lower rates of labour turnover and absenteeism as other workers. Interviews with Aboriginal workers revealed a preference for work, a liking for work, and a desire for promotion.[34] This satisfaction was perhaps more remarkable given that Aboriginal workers in 1986 were three times as likely to be in unskilled work, and half as likely to be in professional, paraprofessional or administrative positions as other Australians.[35] Most of those on outstations work productively, but this is rarely classed as formal work because it is in the unpaid, informal economy of food collection, property maintenance and production for exchange, not sale.[36] A survey of 293 Aboriginal residents of Katherine in 1985 by Peter Loveday concluded: 'most Aborigines want work . . . The attractions of work appear to be far greater than the attractions of life on the dole.'[37]

Therefore, white discriminatory attitudes to Indigenous people, more than Aboriginal work attitudes, compounded industry restructure, poor education, training and remote living to create high Aboriginal unemployment. This had serious implications for black–white relations as well as Aboriginal well-being. Whereas in the past the two groups regularly met through work, unemployment from the 1970s separated them, reinforcing the unfavourable stereotypes each had of the other.

ABORIGINAL HEALTH

Although Indigenous people by the early 1990s were better off in some respects and enjoyed more freedoms, their hospitalisation and death rates were still four times higher, their infant mortality was three times higher, and their life expectancy was about twenty years lower than other Australians. Adult Indigenous deaths stemmed from high rates of heart, respiratory and diabetic diseases.[38] A study of Aboriginal children in Sydney around 1990 found that 28 per cent needed hearing aids as a result of constant ear infections.[39] A Darwin study in 1993 found half the children in the area malnourished, ten times the rate of the general population.[40] A study at impoverished Yalata in 1989 found all Aboriginal children malnourished and their growth rate a year behind the normal body size for age, due to poor diet and persistent diarrhoea caused by bacterial infections.[41] Some Aboriginal parents who abused alcohol were at fault, but poor health stemmed mostly from appalling material conditions, often beyond Aboriginal control. A comprehensive overview of Aboriginal health in the 1980s is to be found in Sherry Saggers and Dennis Gray's *Aboriginal Health and Society* (1991). Such research prompted the federal government to outlay $232 million in 1990 for improved Aboriginal child health.[42]

Health issues flared again in 1994. The federal Health Minister, Senator Graham Richardson, visited remote communities in the Northern Territory and Western Australia and, clearly shaken, remarked: 'I saw things out at Bulman and Weemol yesterday that would barely be tolerated in a war-ravaged African nation, let alone here.' The showers, toilets and the sleeping accommodation horrified him. 'That cannot be tolerated in 1990s Australia. I suspect that it should not have been tolerated in 1890s Australia,' he said, adding that the National Aboriginal Health Strategy of 1990 was totally inadequate.[43] The Senate Parliamentary Sub-committee on Human Rights described Aboriginal health rates as 'third world'. Its Chairperson, Stephen Loosley, reported that at 'Pigeon Hole' on the Victoria River Downs, up to ten people lived in each one-roomed shack, the area became a sea of raw sewage when it rained, and the community had poor access to doctors. Richardson and Loosley both witnessed the massive difficulties of service delivery to remote Aboriginal homelands.[44]

A proposed $800 million grant was halved due to budget cuts, but further surveys increased pressure for more funds. One based on Perth Aboriginal families revealed poor dietary practices, high rates of obesity and diabetes, and ill-health rates higher than in Bangladesh. An ANU study, 'Morbidity and Mortality 1979–1991', found an alarming deterioration in Aboriginal health over two decades, and increased rates of cancer, diabetes and heart–lung disease among Aboriginal women. A further study by Dr Paul Torzillo and others of 14,500 Aboriginal people in Central Australia found rates of pneumonia 60 times higher than in the United States for children under two; and rates eleven times the local non-Aboriginal population for those less than five years old. Poor housing, washing and hygiene facilities and poor service delivery were the causes. Aboriginal health was going backwards! A report on health administration by ANU researchers Ben Bartlett and David Legge, 'Beyond the Maze', revealed governments were spending less on health for Aboriginal Australians than for other Australians. Aboriginal people were again victims of federalism as governments shifted their responsibility to other agencies. The researchers called for a new Commonwealth–State agreement to make spending equitable.[45] The new Health Minister, Carmen Lawrence, added $200 million for Aboriginal health over four years in the May 1995 budget.

Such disadvantage induced stress and emotional problems. These were compounded by alcoholism and substance abuse, cultural change and a breakdown in traditional values among some people. In 1990 the Queensland Aboriginal Coordinating Council reported certain Aboriginal communities had very high rates of domestic violence, an alarming use of pornographic mail-order videos leading to sexual abuse of children, and rates of assault, rape and homicide 50 times higher than the average Queensland rate. The report, authored by Barbara Miller, the Council's Director and psychologist, referred to 'the appalling physical and mental health of Aboriginal people which leads to . . . the rapidly increasing breakdown in the whole fabric of Aboriginal society and culture'.[46]

DISCRIMINATION AND VIOLENCE

Toomelah in northern New South Wales revealed the flesh and bones of Aboriginal disadvantage. This settlement of 500 people near Boggabilla suffered 50 years of paternal rule before being handed over to Aboriginal control, without training, in 1977. Toomelah hit the headlines when nineteen of its residents were arrested after a racial brawl with whites in Goondiwindi's main street on 10 January 1987. The fledgling Human Rights and Equal Opportunity Commission (HREOC) appointed Justice Marcus Einfeld to investigate conditions at Toomelah and community relations in the region. Einfeld found two-thirds of the 40 houses were substandard, lacking glazed windows, watertight roofing, proper drainage and adequate bathrooms. A housing shortage meant that each contained twenty people on average. The water supply was rationed to half an hour a day, forcing people to bucket water from the nearby Macintyre River. Consequently eye, ear and skin diseases were chronic, leaving half the children with ear infections. An unrepaired septic system caused sewage to surface, adding to the 'barren and stark' surroundings. Toomelah was neglected by local authorities and the Department of Aboriginal Affairs.

Relations between Toomelah's residents and white townspeople were poor. Evidence given to Justice Einfeld indicated strong racism in the school and streets where Aboriginal people were called 'coons' and 'niggers'; young Aboriginal

women were verbally abused and propositioned; and young Aboriginal footballers, much sought after by local teams, were never invited into white houses.[47]
Bill Lee, Goondiwindi's mayor, encapsulated the more printable local attitudes
when he said of Aboriginal troublemakers: 'they all drive cars. Do you know
how a darkie gets a car? He buys it on hire purchase, makes a couple of payments
then says he can't pay and some government agency pays the rest.'[48] Was it any
wonder that Justice Einfeld publicly wept over the situation at Toomelah? All
the more remarkable, then, that $1 million in community services, an involvement
in the CDEP scheme and new-found community pride created an Aboriginal
resurgence at Toomelah by late 1990.[49]

In the last years of the twentieth century there were many 'Toomelahs'
around Australia. The 1986 Census revealed Aboriginal Australians were four
times more likely than other Australians to live in substandard or impoverished
accommodation. A 1988 estimate showed a massive 15,674 shortfall in Aboriginal
housing units.[50] At Swan Hill in 1990, 70 per cent of Aboriginal residents lived
in overcrowded housing and twenty families were forced to live in cars or hessian
shacks on the riverbank. Outside Cairns, a shanty town among mangroves near
the tip housed 40 Indigenous people, who quite liked the place because of the
freedom from control. In Western Australia in 1993 over 700 people lived on
the fringe of air-conditioned mining towns. On Nanny Goat Hill outside
Kalgoorlie, people lived in fibro and tin two-roomed houses with concrete floors,
no water, electricity, fireplaces or furniture. In 30 months, 33 of the town's 90
Aboriginal inhabitants died of respiratory disease, alcohol abuse, violence or
burns from campfires.[51]

Poor conditions bred hopelessness and violence. In a damning study of
violence on Queensland reserves, Paul Wilson in 1982 estimated that assaults,
both reported and hidden, occurred at fifteen times the Queensland rate and
homicides at ten times the Queensland and Australian rates. People also slashed
and shot their own bodies, smashed their hands through windows and even
poured petrol on themselves. Wilson remarked that 'frustration and anger were
the underlying causes of self-mutilation'. Violence was shaped by alcohol abuse
but also by anger at paternal controls that were hard to escape.[52] Irene Moss,
investigating policing at Mornington Island in 1993, called the administration
'neo-colonial', adding: 'all key positions of power, decision-making and
administration are held in non-Aboriginal hands'.[53]

The riot at Goondiwindi by Toomelah residents in 1987 was one racial
incident among many. At Moree in November 1982, an Aboriginal male was
shot dead in a fight; over 100 brawled at Mt Magnet in July 1984; and 200 rioted

at Mullewa in August 1985 after a friend was killed in a hotel bar. Many incidents occurred when Aboriginal people challenged the unofficial colour bars imposed in country hotels by local convention. There were also large riots in Roebourne (October 1983) and Geraldton (August 1988) after Aboriginal men died in police custody. These incidents were merely the spectacular eruptions from an atmosphere of mutual suspicion and indifference, tinged with racism and racial violence that extended from the country to the suburbs.[54] The National Inquiry into Racist Violence reported in 1991 that 'racism permeates the day-to-day lives of Aboriginal people either through direct acts of violence, intimidation and racist abuse, or through more insidious processes of discrimination'.[55] The national inquiry described scores of violent incidents and listed 115 cases reported to the inquiry, two-thirds allegedly committed by police.

The National Inquiry into Racist Violence stated that Aboriginal people 'regularly experience racist violence, intimidation and harassment at the hands of the police'.[56] It detailed harassment and gross over-policing of Indigenous people. While the police–population ratio of New South Wales was 1:459, in the following outback 'Aboriginal towns' the ratios were: Brewarrina 1:145, Bourke 1:113, Walgett 1:96, and Wilcannia 1:73—that is, between three and six times the state's average rate. Aboriginal people felt under siege.[57] This is certainly the case in Redfern, where Aboriginal–police relations have been poor since a two-hour battle involving hundreds of people in November 1983. Relations reached rock bottom in February 1990 when 135 police from the special force, including the Tactical Response Group in riot gear, stormed Everleigh Street, Redfern, supposedly searching for drugs.[58]

Over-policing fell most heavily on Aboriginal youth. A study for the national inquiry found that 85 per cent of 171 youths surveyed in three states had been hit, punched, stabbed or kicked by police.[59] Over-policing and racial bias in the judiciary meant Aboriginal people had a high rate of arrest and imprisonment.[60] In 1987–1988 the national inquiry found they formed 29 per cent of those in custody and 15 per cent of those in prisons throughout Australia, while being only 1.5 per cent of the population.[61]

It was unclear from this inquiry whether racism and racist violence was waxing or waning. However, it was clear that open discrimination practised widely in the past was declining due to legislation and penalties. The Commission for Community Relations set up under the federal Racial Discrimination Act (1975) was only able to conciliate, embarrass and reprimand. However, it settled almost all of the thousands of complaints of discrimination before it by conciliation during its seven-year existence.[62] It was superseded by the Human Rights

Commission in 1982, itself replaced by the HREOC in late 1986, which has the power to impose penalties and to initiate inquiries such as the one into Toomelah. Four states also introduced anti-discrimination legislation: New South Wales (1977), Victoria (1984), South Australia (1984) and Western Australia (1984). The HREOC operates through these state's commissions. These Acts cover racial discrimination in employment, accommodation, access to public places, and the provision of goods and services. New South Wales also passed a Racial Vilification Act (1989) making it an offence 'to incite hatred towards, serious contempt for, or severe ridicule of' a person or group because of their race. Other jurisdictions followed.

Such legislation made employers, real estate agents, providers of services and others more wary. In March 1992 Mandawuy Yunupingu, Australian of the Year (1992) and leader of the Aboriginal band Yothu Yindi, was refused service at the Catani Bar in St Kilda. The club's manager quickly claimed it was due to the state's complex eat and drink licensing laws, not racial discrimination. Premier Joan Kirner, the *Age* newspaper and protesters outside the club were sceptical. Yunupingu, with typical Aboriginal grace, accepted the owner's apology rather than suing, before leaving to collect five prizes at the Australian Record Industry Awards.[63] In August 1993 Murray Bull was awarded $20,700 in damages by the HREOC for the humiliation, distress and loss of personal dignity caused by being refused the rental of a caravan in Sale, Victoria, in 1991, because he was Aboriginal. The owner, Mrs Robyn Kuch, made matters worse for herself in court before Commissioner Ron Castan by saying: 'I have got great admiration for a lot of Aborigines, as I have for a lot of other non-Australian people.'[64] In her mental world, there were Australians and there were those others also living in Australia. However, anti-discrimination cuts both ways. In January 1994, Commissioner Castan ordered Harry Brandy, an Aboriginal employee in 1990 of the then Aboriginal Affairs Department, to pay damages to John Bell, a white Australian co-worker, for threats and racial abuse.[65]

Discrimination and racism were also being reined in by community sentiment. Racial slurs have long been a fact of life in sport. Aboriginal footballers Maurice Rioli, the Krakouer brothers, Chris Lewis and a host of others experienced racist heat from players and crowds in the 1980s. In April 1993, St Kilda's Nicky Winmar fought back. Lifting his shirt before taunting Collingwood supporters and pointing to his bared chest, he yelled: 'I'm black, and I'm proud to be black.' The press and others supported his stand. The President of the Collingwood Club, Allan McAlister, publically opposed racism in sport, but added that 'as long as they [Aboriginal players] conduct themselves like white people, well, on

Cartoonist Peter Nicholson's interpretation of Nicky Winmar's declaration to Collingwood supporters in April 1993: 'I'm black, and I'm proud to be black.' COURTESY OF PETER NICHOLSON AND THE *AGE*.

and off the field, everyone will admire and respect them.' He quickly corrected himself, saying: 'as long as they conduct themselves like human beings', but the damage was done.[66] A chastened McAlister told his players that racial taunts were unacceptable—but Collingwood supporters still gave St Kilda player Gilbert McAdam a racial 'serve' four weeks later. In an interesting twist, in July 1993, McAdam was appointed as an AFL promotional officer charged with developing a code of conduct to stamp out racist remarks on and off the field. In that same year, Aboriginal footballers asserted themselves by deed, Gavin Wanganeen taking the Brownlow Medal and Michael Long the Norm Smith Medal and the federal government launched a 'Racism Sux' campaign. The Western Australian Amateur Football League introduced fines for racial taunts on the field and in club rooms in May 1994, preceding the AFL, whose code emerged in June 1996.[67]

BICENTENARY DISRUPTIONS

Once the Bicentenary celebration of white settlement was mooted in the early 1980s it was bound for controversy: some Aboriginal people condemned it outright as a gross insult while others saw it as a great opportunity to make political capital. As the event unfolded, it became a more eventful time than anyone ever imagined.

The first disruption concerned Aboriginal deaths in custody. The issue had seethed within the Aboriginal community, especially after the death of John Pat in the Roebourne lock-up in 1983, and the deaths in 1984 of Charles Michael and Robert Williams.[68] Deepening anger in late 1986 led the families of five men who died in custody in the west to embark on a national speaking tour. They were supported by the National Committee to Defend Black Rights, formed after five police were acquitted over John Pat's death. An alarming series of sixteen deaths in eight months caused the federal government in early 1987 to consider a parliamentary inquiry. The Royal Commission into Aboriginal Deaths in Custody (RCIADIC) was announced in August, allegedly after United Nations' disquiet.[69] Justice James Muirhead, appointed to investigate 44 deaths, was soon investigating more than 100, as further deaths occurred and the National Committee to Defend Black Rights unearthed more. The RCIADIC began work in January 1988 as the Bicentenary commenced. By April it faced 28 demands from the Committee to Defend Black Rights, which alleged a cover-up and unwillingness by the RCIADIC to press charges. As the Bicentenary unfolded, Australians faced the weekly embarrassment of headlines about the RCIADIC's proceedings. Justice Muirhead's interim report in December 1988 recommended changes to sentencing practices, police, prison and coronial procedures, and the use of preventive cell architecture to stop the deaths.[70]

The second disruption was the issue of a treaty between Aboriginal and other Australians. In April 1979 the Aboriginal Treaty Committee led by 'Nuggett' Coombs and the National Aboriginal Commission (NAC) had both suggested one. A Senate Committee discussed it but the matter lapsed in 1983.[71] Charles Perkins, Galarrwuy Yunupingu and others resurrected it in mid-1987. Prime Minister Bob Hawke, looking for the right Bicentenary gesture, and wary of likely Aboriginal protests and international embarrassment, suggested a compact. It was to be in the form of a preamble to the bill to create a new Aboriginal commission to replace the now defunct NAC. Perkins attacked this as inadequate because Acts can be repealed. He said Indigenous people in Australia wanted a treaty, and one to cover issues of land, compensation, recognition of prior ownership, Aboriginal law, languages and sacred sites. Joh Bjelke-Petersen, the Queensland Premier, with characteristic hyperbole, declared a compact could create 'civil war'. The federal Opposition opposed the idea, and Aboriginal radicals agreed, wanting nothing less than a recognition of Aboriginal sovereignty.[72]

In an opinion poll, 58 per cent supported a compact, 41 per cent supported recognition of prior ownership, 44 per cent supported giving Aboriginal people more land, and only 27 per cent supported cash compensation. Strongest support came from Labor voters and those in southern states.[73]

The government proceeded with its idea of a preamble in the Aboriginal and Torres Strait Islander Bill. A draft contained ten 'and whereas' clauses, notably: 'AND WHEREAS they were dispossessed of their land by subsequent European occupation and have no recognised rights over it other than those granted by the Crown'. Some saw it as a great moral statement, others as a threat to white landholders. Aboriginal commentators were concerned that it could damage their land claims. While it challenged the notion of Australia as waste, 'terra nullius' and open to claim in 1788 (upheld by Justice Blackburn in 1971), it also threatened Aboriginal claims that native title had never been ceded or extinguished. The word 'recognised' might avoid that threat but they were uneasy.[74] The Opposition opposed the wording and rejected a compromise proposed by the heads of fourteen churches. The Labor government's majority carried the bill in August 1988, with a significant preamble that stated: 'Aborigines and Torres Strait Islanders suffered dispossession and dispersal upon acquisition of their traditional lands by the British Crown'. It acknowledged their entitlement to 'self-management and self-determination subject to the Constitution and the laws of the Commonwealth'. The Opposition failed in its bid to insert the words, 'in common with all other Australians', after 'self-determination', to prevent its fears of separate development.[75]

The third disruption to the Bicentenary stemmed from Aboriginal efforts to embarrass Australia internationally. Activists planned a monster protest rally in Sydney on Australia Day to expose Australian racism. The Aboriginal poet Oodgeroo Noonuccal returned her MBE in a personal protest. On 26 January in Sydney, between 15,000 and 50,000 people (estimates varied) rallied in protest behind their banners, 'White Australia has a Black History—Don't Celebrate 88'. Another two million people (a Bicentenary Authority estimate) gathered a few kilometres away to celebrate on the harbour foreshores. Far away on the sands of Dover, Burnum Burnum (Harry Penrith) planted the Aboriginal flag and claimed Britain on behalf of Aboriginal people.[76]

Questions of sovereignty also arose in several other spheres. Two weeks before, the (Torres Strait) Islander Coordinating Council (ICC) dropped a bombshell by demanding independence, or at least autonomy, from Australia. It also foreshadowed a $1 billion lawsuit for loss of land and resources. The ICC Chairperson, George Mye, said Islanders had been neglected by governments, and received no royalties from its fishery or an imminent goldmine. Mye claimed gold and fishing royalties, tourism, shipping and a possible United States naval and air base there could sustain an independent Islander economy. Hawke dismissed the idea but promised a meeting to discuss any legitimate concerns. The Islanders were angry at being fobbed off and threatened to seek UN and international support. The Minister for Aboriginal Affairs, Gerry Hand, flew to meet with them on the eve of the Bicentenary celebrations, calmed them, but did not end their resolve for independence.[77] In the Torres Strait an anti-independence group emerged, led by Ted Loban, claiming to have the support of 80 per cent of Islanders. Loban declared 'we are Australians living in Australia and enjoying the privileges of Australians'.[78] Many Islanders also enjoyed and valued the protection of Australia against illegal immigration from the north. The ICC pushed for modifications to their place in the Aboriginal and Torres Strait Islander Commission (ATSIC), accepted assurances on more funding, and shelved independence.[79]

At the Top End's Barunga Festival in June 1988, Prime Minister Hawke optimistically promised a treaty by 1990 before 10,000 Aboriginal people. They had gathered to 'show Australia and the world that our traditions and our lore are alive and strong here in our country', said Cyril McCartney, head of the Barunga–Wugularr Council. Galarrwuy Yunupingu, Chairperson of the Northern Land Council, presented the Prime Minister with the Barunga Statement, a claim of Aboriginal rights framed by a bark painting to guide the government's thinking about a treaty. It opened confidently: 'We, the indigenous owners and occupiers of Australia, call on the Australian Government and people to recognise our rights.' The statement then set these down and listed all the UN conventions on human rights that underpinned these claims. These were Aboriginal demands in universal terms.[80]

A more radical document—a draft treaty—drawn up by Kevin Gilbert was also in circulation. It claimed Aboriginal people were a sovereign people whose sovereignty was not extinguished by time, invasion or act of cession. This draft treaty claimed all Crown lands in Australia as Aboriginal state lands with inalienable title. It demanded Aboriginal autonomy in community government, development, culture and law. It also demanded compensation of $1 billion up front, and 7 per cent of gross national product paid yearly, reducing to 2.5 per cent after twenty years in perpetuity. This document received little publicity and no official recognition.[81]

The treaty debate split between those on the Left who argued it would finally unite Australia, and those on the Right who claimed it would divide the

Galurrwuy Yunupingu, head of the Northern Land Council, presents Prime Minister Bob Hawke with a statement of Indigenous rights at the Barunga Festival, June 1988. COURTESY OF THE *AGE*.

country.[82] The Opposition leader, John Howard, rejected it as divisive and absurd, as a nation could not make a treaty with itself. A new opinion poll in July revealed only 45 per cent were now in favour of a treaty, and 53 per cent thought it would create greater division.[83] The issue dragged on and in 1990 the Hawke government set the Centenary of Federation in 2001 as a new possible date for a treaty.

The fourth disruption to the Bicentenary was the bitterness and sadness surrounding the sacking of Charles Perkins, Australia's top Aboriginal bureaucrat and Head of the Department of Aboriginal Affairs since 1984. Trouble erupted in October 1988 in the Senate Estimates Committee, when Liberal–National Party members led by Senator Tambling from the Northern Territory grilled Perkins with over 400 questions about his department's finances. There were innuendos about maladministration, nepotism and corruption. Matters finally focused on the approval of a department loan of $300,000 to a Canberra Aboriginal Social Club, for money to buy poker machines. Perkins's Minister, Gerry Hand, also came under fire in parliament, straining relations between the two. Perkins was forced to stand aside for eight months until he was completely and unreservedly exonerated by six separate inquiries. Hand refused to reappoint him, so Perkins retired, embittered, to become a public consultant. He stated: 'the message for the 1990s is that it is up to us'—a theme he followed since working for his people as Chairperson of the Arrernte Council of Central Australia.[84] Thus the departmental career of Australia's top Aboriginal public servant ended. It had been a long journey and rise by a boy who, aged seven, was given up by his Aboriginal mother to be educated in an Adelaide church hostel.

The RCIADIC continued to hear evidence and revealed to those who followed its proceedings in 1988 the frequency of the removal of Aboriginal children from their families, a fact then little known to most Australians. In 1983 an historian, Peter Read, had estimated that over 5000, or about one in seven, Aboriginal children had been taken in New South Wales between 1909 and 1969.[85] His work initially had little impact due to its obscure publication by a government department. The event that publicised these official acts of cultural genocide—the attempted remaking of Aboriginal children in a white image—was the trial of James Savage in late 1989, for the rape and murder of a woman in Florida in the United States.

James Savage, born Russell Moore, was given up by his mother in January 1963 and adopted by a Salvation Army couple, the Savages, who moved to America when Moore was five. Years of cultural confusion in America over his origins and identity encouraged antisocial behaviour, drug addiction and finally actions of theft, rape and murder. Russell Moore's predicament became known to his birth mother, Beverly Whyman, who was fifteen at the time of his birth. She claimed, rightly, that she was coerced by the Welfare Board into giving up her son four days after his birth.[86] She had later searched for him in vain. With Russell Savage now on trial for his life, the federal government, under great public pressure, funded eight witnesses to appear at his trial in his defence. Savage was found guilty and sentenced to death, but on appeal was sentenced to life in prison.[87] The episode was a news sensation, especially with television footage of Whyman recounting harrowing details of her baby's loss. In June 1993, another bureaucratic victim, Joy Williams, applied to the New South Wales Supreme Court to extend the Statute of Limitations to allow her to sue for being removed from her family.[88]

The RCIADIC report was completed in April 1991 after three and a half years of prodigious work. Its massive five-volume report containing 339 recommendations was based on case reports of 99 deaths, 84 specially prepared papers on statistics, social indicator reports, background papers prepared by a team of historians, and scores of submissions from the public. The task of synthesising all these papers and reports was completed by five commissioners, led by Elliot Johnson QC and including Aboriginal community leader Patrick Dodson, at a cost of $30 million.[89] The pity was so few copies were ever printed, but the report is now available on the Internet.

The commission found the 99 deaths were not due to deliberate violence or brutality by police or prison officers, but that a poor standard of care by officers and defects in the custodial system contributed to the deaths. The common thread was the deceased's Aboriginality.[90] It recommended many reforms to the custodial system and also specific ways of creating equity and justice for Aboriginal people. The empowerment of Aboriginal people and their right to self-determination was the central issue of the report. The commission identified three essential prerequisites to achieve this: that Aboriginal people must take control of their own lives; that the broader society and governments must allow and assist them to achieve this; and assistance must be given without creating welfare dependence. The funding of Aboriginal organisations that not only gave them power but also helped, rather than hindered black–white relations, was a key strategy. It also recommended that Aboriginal Justice Advisory committees be created in each state to monitor the implementation of the commission's 339 recommendations.[91]

The commission reported on each death within its familial, social, cultural and historical context. As microcosms of colonial outcomes, each case history makes for disturbing reading. One of them is found in the Prologue to this book. Each of the state social issues papers is also enlightening. The one for the Northern Territory, 'Too Much Sorry Business', is a chilling account of the problems of alcohol and substance abuse, the problems of living with two laws, and the difficulties of over-policing. There was hope too in this detailed report— details of a community fightback against grog and petrol-sniffing, and ways of improving Aboriginal–police relations.[92] While other Australians had a higher rate of death in custody than Aboriginal Australians, the reason there were so many Aboriginal deaths was that there were so many Aboriginal people in custody. This reflected their over-policing in Australia and ultimately the impact of dispossession, colonialism and racism on Aboriginal people. The commission found that Indigenous people throughout Australia in August 1988 were on average 27 times more likely than other Australians to be in custody. The multiples of Aboriginal imprisonment over other Australians for individual states in ascending order were: Tas. × 5; ACT × 11; NT × 11; Vic. × 13; NSW × 15; Qld × 17; and SA × 26. Aboriginal people in WA were a massive 43 times more likely to be imprisoned than others in that state.[93]

The details of the 99 people who died in custody are revealing: 88 were men, their average age was 32 years; 40 had not been educated beyond primary level; 77 were unskilled, 83 were unemployed at the time of their detention; 43 had been removed from their families by the state; 60 came from urban areas, and 21 from Aboriginal communities. Seventy-four of them had been in trouble with the law before the age of 20, 35 had been detained for drunkenness just prior to their death; and 59 of them died in either Western Australia or Queensland, 63 while in police custody, and the rest while in prison. Thirty-seven had died from natural causes, 30 by hanging, nine from drug overdose, twelve from head injuries, four from gunshots and seven from other external trauma.[94] Commissioner Johnson, in his hard-hitting report, argued that it was the burden of history that underpinned Aboriginal disadvantage and the deaths in custody. He rehearsed the policies of dispossession, protection, removal and control that had left Aboriginal people as disadvantaged, dependent people: 'legacies of the history of two centuries of European domination of Aboriginal people'. He concluded: 'the whole thrust of this report is directed towards the empowerment of Aboriginal people on the basis of their deeply held desire, their demonstrated capacity, and their democratic right to exercise, according to circumstances, maximum control over their own lives and that of their communities'.[95]

Reactions to the RCIADIC report were mixed. The National Committee to Defend Black Rights slammed it for not recommending that charges be laid. Paul Coe, representing Aboriginal legal services, the ATSIC Board, and the Aboriginal community in general, approved of the report. The conservative Institute of Public Affairs attacked its alleged inconsistencies, assumptions and stress on racism in Australian society.[96] After digesting it for a year, the Keating Labor government announced a $150 million package in June 1992 to implement the law, justice and drug rehabilitation measures of the RCIADC report. Two months later, a $250 million package to cover employment and development programs was announced.

In February 1994 the first two-volume annual report into the Implementation of the Recommendations of the RCIADIC detailed the expenditure of $400 million since the royal commission, but found little improvement in black death rates and no improvement in Aboriginal imprisonment rates. The House of Representatives Standing Committee on Aboriginal and Torres Strait Islander Affairs was asked to inquire into this report. Its 394-page report, *Justice under Scrutiny*, made 90 recommendations concerning grossly inadequate responses to the RCIADIC. It recommended that the Office of the Aboriginal and Torres

Cartoonist Steve O'Brien captures the grim tally of deaths encountered by Social Justice Commissioner Michael Dodson while reviewing the implementation of the RCIADIC report. COURTESY OF STEVE O'BRIEN AND THE *COURIER MAIL*.

Strait Islander Social Justice Commissioner of the HREOC take control of monitoring the implementation for five years.[97]

In late 1996 the Commissioner, Mick Dodson, angrily launched his report, exclaiming: 'Where has the $400 million gone? Where the bloody hell is it? What did you do with it? Why are our people still dying?' The report found that Aboriginal gaol rates were still 17.3 times—and death-in-custody rates 16.5 times—that of other Australians. The 536-page report revealed that none of the RCIADIC's key ideas were in place, namely custody as a last resort; JP involvement in sentencing; decriminalisation of public drunkenness; and custodial health and safety rules.[98] Despite three critical reports in three years, improvements remained elusive. In 2001, the tenth anniversary of the RCIADIC, statistics revealed that Aboriginal deaths in custody were greater in the 1990s than in the 1980s, there being 115 deaths from 1990 to 1999 compared to 110 from 1980 to 1989. Deaths in police lock-ups had declined, but increased in prisons. Imprisonment rates increased, due to new and controversial mandatory sentencing laws in Western Australia and the Northern Territory, which went against the intent of the royal commission's recommendations. Aboriginal imprisonment rates remained fifteen times higher than for other Australians. In 2001 ATSIC's Chair, Geoff Clark, again called for imprisonment only as a last resort. The *Age* remarked that the deaths would keep occurring while 'entrenched inequality continues'.[99]

There were two significant and disturbing personal reactions to the RCIADIC. In September 1989, two white Bourke policemen attended a charity function in tiny Eromanga, 600 kilometres north of Bourke. They blackened their upper bodies and faces, placed nooses around their necks, and exclaimed amid laughter: 'I'm Lloyd Boney' and 'I'm David Gundy'—two Aboriginal men who had died in custody. Someone videoed the scene and it was handed to ABC television and screened in March 1992. Aboriginal people were outraged, decent people throughout the nation were shocked, and Prime Minister Keating called it a 'national disgrace'. With great emotion he called for this moment to be a watershed in Australia's racism.[100] Two months later, Alice Dixon, a leader in the creation of the RCIADIC and mother of nineteen-year-old Kingsley Dixon who died in custody, committed suicide. She hanged herself as did her son, telling her family shortly before her death that there were too many problems: 'I can only go so far.'[101]

CULTURAL EXPRESSIONS

Others remained undaunted. Members of the Victorian Aboriginal community, for instance, fought for custody over Aboriginal relics. In October 1983, 92 Aboriginal relics were seized from Leonard Joel Auctioneers under the state's Archaeological and Aboriginal Relics Preservation Act (1972). After a failed prosecution and an amendment of the Act making it illegal to buy, sell or display Aboriginal relics without the Minister's approval, Jim Berg, an Aboriginal warden under the Act, audaciously impounded Melbourne University's Murray Black collection. It contained the remains of over 800 individuals between 300 and 14,000 years old, collected by a Gippsland grazier, Murray Black, who had stripped Aboriginal graves along the Murray Valley during the 1940s. The Supreme Court of Victoria ruled in 1984 that the collection must be transferred to the Museum of Victoria. Jim Berg astounded local and international archaeological circles by saying the remains should be reburied. In June 1988, the Victorian government gave Aboriginal communities control over the remains.

The Australian Archaeological Association acquiesced to Aboriginal custodianship and reburial, but not of the 33 unique Coobool Creek skulls that bore evidence of ancient head-binding. Despite the protests, 1240 remains, including more Murray Black material from Canberra, were handed to six Aboriginal communities for reburial.[102] The important Kow Swamp material was also reburied in August 1990. In 1992 the Australian National University handed back for reburial the 27,000-year-old Mungo Woman remains, the world's oldest known cremation. Aboriginal protesters have also regained skeletal evidence from British and other European museums—a process that continues.[103] Aboriginal people now have more say on such matters, backed by state and federal legislation. Controversy will continue between those who see skeletal remains as part of human heritage to be studied scientifically, and those who see remains as part of Aboriginal heritage to be returned to mother earth.

Struggles for equality were led by a growing body of Aboriginal activists, community workers and professionals. As former leaders passed on—educationalist Hyllus Marus (1986), community leaders Sir Doug Nicholls (1988), Stewart Murray (1989), the poet Oodgeroo Noonuccal (1993) and writer and activist Kevin Gilbert (1993), younger ones stepped forward. By the early 1990s there were several Aboriginal politicians, scores of Aboriginal solicitors and barristers, doctors and academics, over 1000 Aboriginal university graduates, and over 5000 Aboriginal professionals, including teachers, nurses, health workers, managers, architects and engineers—many of them working in the hundreds of community organisations throughout Australia. Another 10,000 Aboriginal and Torres Strait Islander people have gained other vocational qualifications. Some have attained public office. Pat O'Shane, Charles Perkins, Lowitja O'Donoghue and Shirley McPherson have headed government departments or bodies, the former is now a magistrate. Patrick Dodson, a former Catholic priest and Commissioner of the RCIADIC, became head of the Council for Aboriginal Reconciliation. His brother Michael, a barrister, became the HREOC's Commissioner for Social Justice. Aboriginal people have also received honours. Lowitja O'Donoghue (1984) and Mandawuy Yunupingu (1992) were made Australian of the Year, joining earlier holders of that title: Lionel Rose (1968), Evonne Goolagong (Cawley) (1971), Galarrwuy Yunupingu (1978) and Neville Bonner (1979). Cathy Freeman received the award in 1998. Lowitja O'Donoghue, the chair of ATSIC, was being touted in the early 1990s as a possible future governor-general.

Respect for Aboriginal arts and Aboriginal people in the arts strengthened. In July 1993, a satellite videoconferencing system linked 300 cognoscenti of the

European art world to 30 Aboriginal artists from the Warlukurlangu Artists Cooperative at Yuendumu for a symposium on Aboriginal art.[104] Aboriginal writing increased with the publication of more life stories and creative works, glimpsed in such anthologies as *Inside Black Australia* (1985) and *Aboriginal Writing Today* (1985). The David Unaipon Award for Aboriginal writing annually unearthed new talents, and state literary awards introduced Indigenous writing prizes. In 2000, Boori Monty Pryor and Meme McDonald won the NSW Premier's Young People's literature award for *The Binna Binna Man*, and Kim Scott the Miles Franklin award for *Benang*. Aboriginal theatre strengthened in the 1990s and fine plays were staged. Of note was the series of six plays, *Black Inside*, staged in the Malthouse in Melbourne in 2002. It included Richard Frankland's moving autobiographical *Conversations with the Dead*, played brilliantly by Aboriginal actor Aaron Pederson, which recounted Frankland's time investigating deaths for the RCIADIC. Traditional Aboriginal music and dance has struggled for wider audiences, but Aboriginal interpretations of Western dance and music have succeeded. By 1990, Archie Roach, Kevin Carmody, Tiddas, Christine Anu and Yothu Yindi, who performed using Aboriginal themes or instruments in soul, country or rock mediums, had won wide acclaim and music awards. Maroochy Barambah, the Aboriginal opera singer, shone in the leading role of Maria in *Porgy and Bess* at the Sydney Opera House in 1996. Originally from Cherbourg and educated in Melbourne, she came to prominence in the acclaimed opera, *Black River* (1989), and in the first Aboriginal musical *Bran Nue Dae* (1990).[105] Aboriginal film-makers in the 1990s were still to make an impression, but Aboriginal producers did in other media.

Indigenous radio and television made a big impact by the late 1980s. The first Aboriginal radio program was broadcast on Melbourne's 3CR in 1976. By 1981, the Central Australian Aboriginal Media Association (CAAMA) broadcast in several Aboriginal languages through the ABC's transmitters. It began its own radio station, 8KIN, in Alice Springs in 1985. In 1993 there were 30 Aboriginal radio programs on the 100 community radio stations across the country, broadcasting 500 hours per week.[106] In 1986 the Australian Broadcasting Tribunal made the momentous decision to award Central Australia's first commercial television licence to Imparja, an Aboriginal organisation backed by CAAMA and government finance. It began broadcasting to over 60,000 viewers in Aboriginal languages and English programs. At last, Aboriginal people could choose television programs in their own image. However, the Northern Territory conservative backbencher Paul Everingham deemed it 'the final chapter in a shoddy story of a Labor Government carrying out social engineering experiments at taxpayers' expense.[107]

The 1991 Census counted 265,459 Australians who identified as Aboriginal or Torres Strait Islander people. This was still a quarter of the generally accepted pre-contact population.[108] These people lived in diverse geographic, economic and social situations throughout Australia. Though they shared a pan-Aboriginal identity, they exhibited probably greater cultural diversity than the 500 Aboriginal language groups which had inhabited the continent in 1788, displaying 500 variations on a common Aboriginal theme. In 1991, this Aboriginal diversity ranged from suburban professionals to people on outstations living partly off the land in more traditional style. All of them in their own way were remaking Indigenous cultures.

The census count is based on a self-definition of group identity. It asks: 'Is the person of Aboriginal or Torres Strait Islander origin?' Some people of mixed descent have answered this question in differing ways according to the climate of tolerance of the day. By the 1990s, more who believed they were Aboriginal or Islander were identifying as such. Also, the rage for genealogy uncovered more about people's pasts. Even the leading historian Henry Reynolds found some Aboriginal ancestry, as outlined in his book on mixed descent, *Nowhere People* (2005). Others have made such a discovery and the responses among them and their children are mixed. Some embrace it, others shun it and yet others are confused. If they have Indigenous heritage, does it make them Indigenous, should they make this claim, what does it all mean? The responses from their friends are mixed, ranging from disbelief, fascination, and thinking they might be after a welfare rort. The search for self became an important one for people making these discoveries, beautifully told in Sally Morgan's *My Place* (1987). Many by this time, like Morgan, had married non-Indigenous Australians. The meanings of Aboriginality were shifting, being reinvented as people shaped Indigenous culture in new ways.

In south-eastern Australia, Aboriginal Victorians, many of whom embrace the name 'Koori', as well as a local name such as Yorta Yorta, Kurnai, Wotjobaluk and Gunditjmara, still adhered to customary values of community and family. They worked hard revitalising their communities. In 1990, at Echuca, an Aboriginal co-operative ran several businesses: a clothing factory designing and making sportswear, a construction firm and a museum. It also operated a pre-school centre, 'Berrimba', given to them by the Uniting Church, which conducted night classes for older school students and classes in Aboriginal culture. Sue Saunders, a co-operative employee, remarked of these culture classes: 'we want them to feel proud of their heritage so that when they go to school they can cope with the taunts and the insults about them being black'.[109]

In the north-west of Australia, the Warang Ngari Association of the Ngarinyin people of the Kimberley was funded under an employment program in 1986 to teach twelve young people to repaint the badly faded Wandjina rock paintings. Despite claims that the young people were poorly trained and were using house paint, the repainting was done with traditional materials, methods and storytelling. As David Mowljarlai and Cyril Peck explained:

> Mostly the figures were re-painted just as they were . . . but sometimes where the earlier work was faded we put in our own idea of what had been there before . . . New figures were added at two sites. A yellow snake was done by the custodian at Low . . . several other figures at Low and Ngornjar 2 are in areas which had no earlier paintings or had paintings that were so badly faded that the earlier figures could not be seen easily . . . In some places non-Aboriginal ways of preserving the art were used. At two sites silicone drip lines were put in to keep water away from the painted areas, and at four sites fences were put up to keep animals away from the paintings . . . We know we are on the right track and believe the work done has brought our culture one step closer to survival.[110]

As with all reworkings of culture, there was tradition, invention and borrowing, but above all, there was continuity and a sense of belonging.

13

UNDER SIEGE

From the moment of European colonisation in Australia, land was at the centre of the struggle between settlers and Indigenous owners. The European myth that Australia was 'waste' and its Indigenous owners had no rights to land reigned supreme, until five Murray Islanders made a fatal challenge to this notion. Turmoil was unleashed as the Keating Labor government recognised this decision in legislation and commenced other initiatives to extend justice to Aboriginal people. After an electoral victory in 1996, conservatives under John Howard attempted to wind back gains in Indigenous affairs. It ushered in the most tumultuous fifteen years in black–white encounters since the frontier wars. The turmoil was fuelled by other debates, including the truth of tradition, the truth of the stolen children, and the truth of history itself. Aboriginal people felt under siege. Only a reconciliation movement that gathered grassroots momentum in the late 1990s countered these tensions.

THE MABO CASE

In 1982 Eddie Mabo and fellow Murray Islanders of the Torres Strait—Father Paul Passi, Sam Passi, Celuia Mapo Salee and James Rice—challenged the Queensland government over land. They claimed: 'since time immemorial the Torres Strait Islands of Mer (known as Murray), Danar and Waier and their surrounding seas, seabeds, fringing reefs and adjacent islets have been continuously inhabited by people called the Meriam people'. It was the most significant claim since the three Marika brothers lost their case against Nabalco in 1971. Justice Blackburn had ruled in that case that traditionally 'the clan belongs to the land [rather] than the land belongs to the clan', therefore Australia had been 'terra nullius' (no-man's land) and thus open to claim by the British Crown. He also ruled that native communal title did not form, and had never formed, any part of the law of Australia. Faced with the Murray Island claim, a nervous Queensland government passed the Queensland Coast Islands Declaratory Act 1985, which stated that all Torres Strait Islanders' rights and claims were extinguished at the moment of annexation of the islands in 1879. However, the High Court ruled in 1989 that this 1985 Act contravened the Racial Discrimination Act (1975), further attesting to the importance of this 1975 legislation of the Whitlam government.

The Mabo case, as it came to be known, now came before the High Court. The claimants argued their title had never been extinguished, despite Governor Bligh's declaration of possession in 1797, and Queensland's annexation. They maintained their ongoing traditions and belief in Malo, the human-octopus ancestral hero. The Queensland government, in a modern version of the 'white man's burden', argued Torres Strait Islanders were saved from barbarism by annexation, and that the Crown assumed all rights to land upon annexation. It was a flawed argument, as the Queensland government purchased land for a police station from the Islanders in 1913, and also created a land court to adjudicate Islander claims. Both actions tacitly recognised native title. In February 1992, Eddie Mabo died muttering to his last, through a cancer-drug haze: 'land claim!'. His barrister, Bryan Keon-Cohen, in his eulogy said: 'He was in the best sense a fighter for equal rights; a rebel; a free-thinker; a restless spirit; a reformer, who saw far into the future and into the past.'[1]

On 3 June 1992, the High Court ruled six to one for the claimants, saying: 'the Meriam people are entitled as against the whole world, to possession, occupation, use and enjoyment of the lands of the Murray Islands'. Justice Brennan argued against Blackburn of 1971, that 'native title survives the Crown's acquisition of sovereignty'. Brennan added: 'the common law of this country would perpetuate injustice if it were to continue to embrace the enlarged notion of terra nullius and to persist in characterising the indigenous inhabitants of the Australian colonies as people too low in the scale of social organization to be acknowledged as possessing rights and interests in land'.[2] Communal native title was now part of the common law of Australia. Prime Minister Paul Keating saw it in wider terms, exclaiming in his December 1992 Redfern speech, which launched the International Year of Indigenous People: 'Mabo is an historic decision—we can make it an historic turning point, the basis of a new relationship between indigenous and non-Aboriginal Australians.'[3]

The Mabo judgment, which overturned 200 years of understandings about ownership, caused fifteen months of fear and turmoil. Western Mining's Chief

Eddie Mabo, whose claim with four other Murray Islanders changed the status of native title in the common law of Australia. COURTESY OF THE AGE.

Executive, Hugh Morgan, called on the Liberal–National Party Opposition to repeal the Racial Discrimination Act (1975) and overrule the Mabo decision if they won government. His wish was denied, as against the odds Keating's government retained power in 1993. Morgan declared that Aboriginal people could claim vast tracts of Australia under the Mabo decision.[4] Banking and investment analysts predicted massive disinvestment in mining and rural development if uncertainty over land titles continued, which in the fullness of time proved alarmist. One London analyst wailed: 'Australia would go back to being a Stone Age culture of 200,000 people living on witchetty grubs'.[5] The Northern Territory's Chief Minister, Marshall Perron, claimed Aboriginal people 'really are centuries behind us in their cultural attitudes'. Sir John Gorton, a former Prime Minister of the 1960s, blurted out that Aboriginal people were 'inferior' and 'not as good as the white people'.[6] Abuse mounted, encouraged by leading conservatives. Charles Perkins was run off the road while in his car near Alice Springs, and Aboriginal youths in Melbourne claimed they were bashed by police, one of whom said: 'you won't get Mabo'.[7] Victorian Premier Jeffrey Kennett avoided denigration, but maliciously feared that suburban backyards could be claimed.[8]

Such absurdities were fed by irresponsible Aboriginal ambit claims. In December 1992, some Mullenjarli claimed the Brisbane CBD, although other group members and ATSIC officials condemned the claim as untenable, and it was withdrawn. Other large claims followed, some clearly ambit, others serious. Kimberley people claimed 0.25 million square kilometres, the Wiradjuri demanded most of central New South Wales (later since overruled as a political claim), and the Yorta Yorta claimed the Barmah Forest on the Murray. Others claimed the ACT and the Snowy Mountains region, half of Tasmania, Queensland's Sunshine Coast and Burnett District, large areas of Cape York, and the Martu people claimed 0.2 million square kilometres of the east Pilbara.

Fear and uncertainty were fuelled by conservative attacks on the High Court. Hugh Morgan declared it had divided the country by 'major indeed revolutionary constitutional change without any deference to the role of Parliament or the authority of the people'. He asserted the judges 'seemed to be ashamed to be Australians'.[9] Sir Anthony Mason, head of the High Court, countered that 'far from being an adventure on the part of the High Court, the decision [to reject 'terra nullius' and acknowledge continuing native title] reflects what has happened in the great common law jurisdictions of the world and in the International Court, except that in the case of Australia it had happened later than it has happened elsewhere. In New Zealand it happened almost 150 years ago.'[10] Geoffrey Blainey renewed the attack in November 1993, alleging the judges had a flawed view of history, and demanded the historical evidence for their judgment. Blainey renewed his claims that land rights would divide Australia and stifle mineral development. Historian Henry Reynolds disputed Blainey's views, noting the British government recognised native title in the Waste Lands Act (1848–).[11]

Federal Cabinet and Aboriginal leaders called for rational debate. ATSIC's acting-chairperson Sol Bellear calmly quelled conservative fears. First, most of

Australia was not open to Aboriginal claim because only vacant Crown land could be claimed, and only by those able to prove a traditional and continuous link to that land. Second, Australia's minerals would not be locked up because Aboriginal people were not against development. Third, Indigenous people would not receive more rights than other Australians under Mabo. There was to be no compensation for land lost before the 1975 Racial Discrimination Act. He might have added that native title was an inferior form of title to freehold; being communal, it could not be sold or money borrowed against it. It was also more easily extinguished or overridden by leases than freehold.[12] Rick Farley, the Executive Director of the National Farmers' Federation, and ATSIC officials both lashed out at white conservative hysteria and Aboriginal ambit claims. Good sense prevailed and the public became educated. A *Time* poll in April 1993 found 69 per cent of those polled had not seen, heard or read about the Mabo decision, but by August 1993, 88 per cent of 1000 voters polled knew Aboriginal people could only claim vacant Crown land to which they had a continuous relationship. Fifty-five per cent agreed Mabo was likely to damage Australia's economic development, but 51 per cent said Aboriginal people should have the right to veto mining on native title land holdings.[13]

Behind the scenes, federal and state bureaucrats, miners, pastoralists and Aboriginal leaders engaged in complex, tortuous and tough negotiations. There were constant reports over fifteen months that created bewilderment about the intricacies of land laws and titles. The federal Opposition was paralysed into inaction by internal divisions over Mabo. The federal government's position paper in May 1993 recommended tribunals to adjudicate claims, proposals over compensation, and the validation of titles issued since 1975, but left uncertain by the Racial Discrimination Act (1975). Aboriginal negotiator Noel Pearson called it a 'slimy' document.[14] This stung Prime Minister Keating, who saw Mabo legislation as creating a moral basis for reconciliation as well as establishing land rights. The federal government's attempt to forge a national approach was rejected by the conservative-governed states, led by Victoria and Western Australia, which rejected federal tribunals, Aboriginal vetoes over development, and a proposal that native title would revive after mining and pastoral leases expired.[15]

In August a representative gathering of Aboriginal leaders at Eva Valley, Katherine, also rejected the proposals, especially the lack of a veto over development, claiming there was a lack of consultation.[16] New negotiations produced a greater say for Aboriginal native title holders over development, and better compensation, but no veto power. Further trouble flared in August with the Queensland government over the Wik people's claim to large areas near Weipa, which threatened a $1.75 billion mining development by Comalco. After intense posturing by Queensland and federal leaders, the federal government, desperate for votes, jobs and export earnings, agreed to validate all pre-1975 leases threatened by native title.[17]

Aboriginal negotiators publicly rejected the proposals on 5 October, before intense negotiations hammered out a final agreement that balanced the interests of existing landholders, Aboriginal claimants and the states in complex ways. All land titles issued before 30 June 1993, when negotiations over the new Act began, were to be validated. Pastoral leases could be renewed with limitations, but native title could be revived once mining leases expired. Aboriginal people with traditional links to vacant Crown land or who held pastoral leases could seek communal native title over that land. They could negotiate over development on native title land, but had no power of veto. (In this sense, it was inferior to the 1976 Land Rights Act.) A land acquisition fund for unsuccessful claimants and those ineligible to claim would assist them to gain land, and a social justice package was promised. The states retained power over land titles and development, if they followed non-discriminatory principles. A National Native Title Tribunal was established for claimants who chose not to use state tribunals.[18] Paul Keating announced on 18 October: 'As Mabo was an historic judgment, this is historic legislation, recognising in law the fiction of terra nullius and the fact of native title. With that alone, the foundation of reconciliation is laid—because after 200 years, we will at last be building on the truth.'[19] But the proposal first had to pass through federal parliament.

Western Australia immediately rejected the agreement and passed its own bill, which extinguished native title and replaced it with more inferior user rights, providing little control over mining and development. The Kimberley Land Council claimed it was discriminatory in the High Court the next day.[20] The Liberal–National Opposition supported Western Australia and state's rights over land titles and management, opposing Keating's Mabo bill. The Australian Mining Industry Council also opposed the agreement—but within a month, it announced mining profits were up 7 per cent, exploration was steady and mining investment was increasing, suggesting fears about Mabo's impact on mining were unfounded.[21] The Northern Territory Land Rights Act (1976) was also attacked, especially its veto and royalty provisions, which gave Aboriginal people more powers than under the Mabo bill and more power than other Australians had over development.

With federal parliament polarised, the Mabo bill's fate rested with two Green Party senators, Christabel Chamarette and Dee Margetts, who held the balance of power in the Senate. The Greens secured amendments that had Aboriginal approval. Six days of emotion-charged debates followed as the Opposition filibustered, the Greens horse-traded with the government over 200 amendments, and the Keating government threatened to sit till Christmas to pass the bill before 1994. On 21 December, the Native Title Act was passed at 11.58 p.m. to ringing applause from government, Green and Democrat members and a packed public gallery, after the longest debate in the Senate's history. Paul Keating's 'historic turning point' was law; the High Court's momentous decision over land was now a political reality. The Liberal–National Opposition was stunned, but next day vowed to fight the next election on the Mabo Act.[22]

The Mabo turmoil between conservatives symbolised by Geoffrey Blainey and Hugh Morgan, and small 'l' liberals or progressives like Henry Reynolds and 'Nuggett' Coombs, reflected different views about division and unity in Australian society. The conservatives, in pessimistic and fearful tones, claimed a united Australia was being divided by legislation that supported Indigenous rights: land, culture and special welfare programs. Progressives optimistically argued that Australia was already divided, but could be united by Indigenous rights and positive discrimination to extend justice and equality of opportunity to Aboriginal people. The progressive position was closer to the facts of history than the conservatives. Australia's history reveals black and white Australians were divided by colonialism, white power and racial ideology, discriminatory legislation, and by the Constitution itself, which was indifferent to Aboriginal people and their rights. While civil rights were gained in the 1960s, Indigenous rights were still in the process of fulfilment, and equality of opportunity and reconciliation were fledgling movements. National unity cannot exist without equality and respect for difference.

Conservatives continued to resist the Mabo decision and the Native Title Act. In February 1994, Richard Court's Western Australian government challenged the Native Title Act in the High Court. Premier Court argued that his state, with 90 per cent of Australia's Crown land and a large mining sector, would lose much from native title claims. His government argued the Native Title Act was unconstitutional as it undermined the state's own sovereign land law passed in 1993, to extinguish native title in favour of a weaker statutory right to traditional land use. He also argued it discriminated against non-Indigenous Western Australians.[23] The High Court accepted the case, concurrently with two challenges to the state's 1993 land law, from the Worora people and the Biljabu.

Alexander Downer, the new leader of the federal Opposition, vowed in August 1994 to repeal the Native Title Act—if elected. He also opposed the

Keating government's Land Fund bill with 122 stonewalling amendments before backing down under threat of a politically unfavourable double dissolution. The subsequent Act provided $1.46 billion over ten years for an independently run Indigenous Land Corporation, to assist land acquisition by the great majority of Aboriginal people unable to claim land under the Native Title Act.[24] Within days of this Land Fund victory, the High Court ruled unanimously that the Western Australian Land Act 1993 was invalid, as it contravened the Racial Discrimination Act (1975). Prime Minister Keating hailed the ruling as 'historic'. The conservative attack on native title was momentarily in tatters.

John Howard, who succeeded Downer as Coalition leader, announced he would amend rather than repeal the Native Title Act—if he was elected.[25]

Aboriginal communities were busy filing claims to Crown lands and national parks with the Native Title Tribunal. The Yorta Yorta people claimed 4000 square kilometres of Crown land near Echuca. The Dieri Mithi Corporation claimed 120,000 square kilometres centred on Lake Eyre; the Dagaman people filed for land between Bowen and Proserpine and the Whitsunday Group of islands; other groups lodged claims near Yarrabah, Cairns and North Stradbroke Island. The Gabi Gabi people claimed the Glass House Mountains, promising a magnificent national park, to protect its cultural and natural heritage. The local federal member, Peter Slipper, thought this 'outrageous', adding somewhat irrelevantly: 'a lot of people are concerned at the millions being squandered in the area of Aboriginal affairs'.[26] Some applications were ambit, even mischievous, like those in 1992 over the Brisbane CBD and central New South Wales. Some claims clashed: the Adnyamathanha claim over the Flinders Ranges conflicted with three other applications. Paul Seaman of the Native Title Tribunal noted overlapping claims were natural, as 'Aboriginal people have never had occasion over the last 100 years or so to work out boundaries'.[27] Claims were also made over the sea to protect sacred sites and marine resources and to assert ownership. The Murray Islanders claimed their encircling waters, clans in Arnhem Land applied for the seas off Croker Island, while others considered a claim to 500,000 square kilometres of the Arafura Sea.

In 1996 the Cape York Aboriginal Land Council and the Cattlemen's Union, together with the Wilderness Society and the Australian Conservation Foundation, forged a remarkable agreement outside the Native Title Tribunal's jurisdiction, covering the huge area of Cape York. After two years of negotiations and eleven drafts between former antagonists, the pastoralists in the region guaranteed Aboriginal access to pastoral properties for hunting and cultural/religious activities, in return for an end to native title claims on the Peninsula (there had been

eighteen to that time). The Keating government promised $40 million to pur-
chase properties in sensitive conservation areas. The agreement was a model of
good will for other negotiated settlements outside the Native Title Tribunal and
the courts. It was also the model supported by the National Indigenous Working
Group on Native Title.[28]

STOLEN CHILDREN AND DISPUTED TRADITION

Colonialism had meant not only loss of land but loss of children. In October
1994 the 'Going Home' Darwin Conference organised by Barbara Cummings,
who was raised in the Darwin Baptist Rhetta Dixon home, brought together
500 people also removed and raised in Territory institutions. An exhibition,
'Between Two Worlds', travelled the country to tell their story. Six people, headed
by Alec Kruger and aided by Ron Merkel QC, launched a landmark High Court
case for compensation in April 1995. They alleged that the federal government
breached the Australian Constitution, and also the United Nations' Convention
on Genocide (1948), which had been ratified by the Australian government.
Joy Williams also took the New South Wales government to court, after first
successfully applying to the state's Supreme Court in 1993 to extend the Statute
of Limitations to allow her to make a case. With the prospect of additional
claims, the Keating government expanded the terms of reference of its inquiry
into the removal of children. The inquiry by the Human Rights and Equal
Opportunity Commission (HREOC), which opened in August 1995, was headed
by Sir Ronald Wilson. It was also to consider the question of compensation and
report within a year. It took almost two.

The public was soon confronted by the unfamiliar story of children
removed; of childhoods and families lost. Disagreement was rife. When the
inquiry heard evidence in Brisbane in June 1996, one Queensland government
spokesman said 6082 children were removed in Queensland since 1911. An
archivist, Kathy Franklin, who sorted government records for two years, claimed
it was a 'gross underestimation'. A former senior Queensland bureaucrat, who
was summonsed and asked that his name be suppressed, denied there were
any removals: 'that did not take place in Queensland in any shape or form'.
Jackie Huggins, HREOC Commissioner and an Aboriginal Queenslander,
incredulously exclaimed: 'he seems to have had a temporary case of amnesia;
to claim these things didn't happen just flies in the face of the facts established
through testimony and government archives'. This unnamed official also
claimed of his state's Aboriginal policy, in true assimilationist style: 'One of

the greatest achievements has been giving the silent majority of people of Aboriginal and Torres Strait Islander origin conventional lives in [an] urban situation and participating in life in the fullness of all social structures.'[29] As the inquiry traversed Australia, the battle-lines emerged over removal and assimilation. Was it a policy of genocide, or a benign effort to give equality to Aboriginal people?

Plans to build a bridge at Goolwa in South Australia, bringing development to Hindmarsh Island (Kumarangk) of $175 million, were stymied in 1994 after two years of controversy. Twenty-five Ngarrindjeri women claimed the bridge would destroy sacred sites and their fertility. The Minister for Aboriginal Affairs, Robert Tickner, on expert advice and in accord with the Aboriginal and Torres Strait Islander Heritage Protection Act, banned the bridge for 25 years. A ten-year Hindmarsh Island Bridge affair unfolded that had more legal turns than a lawyers' car rally, and became hopelessly enmeshed in party politics. It produced a remarkable sequence of events. These included a Federal Court appeal that overturned Tickner's decision; a South Australian royal commission that found against the women claiming sacredness; a special Act of parliament to allow the building of the bridge; and a High Court decision that after four years upheld the Act. The developers built the bridge, which was finally opened in March 2001, and sued the federal government for $20 million. However, they lost the case in the Federal Court, as Justice John von Doussa in August 2001 concluded: 'I am not satisfied that the restricted women's knowledge was fabricated or that it was not part of genuine Aboriginal tradition.'[30] A Liberal shadow minister was forced to resign after misusing confidential documents aligned to the case and misleading parliament, and a conservative High Court judge stood aside due to conflict of interest. The Ngarrindjeri were also hopelessly split between those who upheld tradition and those who said it was invented. The sensational episode has been narrated by Margaret Simons in *The Meeting of the Waters* (2003).

The case centred on the authenticity of Aboriginal tradition in contemporary Australia. This issue also underpinned the question of mining at Coronation Hill in the Northern Territory in 1991; the Hawke government banning it to protect the spirit of Bula, an ancestral spirit of the Jawoyn people.[31] However, the Hindmarsh Island affair was different as it involved Ngarrindjeri people in the south, who appeared less traditionally minded. It also followed the Mabo legislation, through which traditional connections and native title were seen to threaten property holders and development. It was clear Ngarrindjeri women were divided between those who wished to follow tradition, and those who did

Ngarrindjeri custodian Muriel Vandenberg reveals her refusal to speak to the South Australian royal commission into the Kamarangk/Hindmarsh Island 'secret women's business', July 1995.
COURTESY OF PHOTOGRAPHER BRYAN CHARLTON AND THE *AGE.*

not; between those who learned particular Hindmarsh Island (Kumarangk) stories from their elders, and those who did not. These matters are explored in Diane Bell's detailed anthropological study *Ngarrindjeri Wurruwarrin* (1998).[32] This disagreement was manipulated politically in a battle over development at Goolwa, and by those who wished to discredit Aboriginal custodial claims in native title deliberations. It revealed the continuing gulf between Western and Aboriginal systems of knowledge and belief, and the politics and manipulations that flourish in that gap.

The public, who were bewildered by the conflicting claims of the Ngarrindjeri, the developers, anthropologists, politicians and several inquiries, probably followed their instincts or prejudices. Those sympathetic to the Aboriginal cause believed the secrets were true, while those who were unsympathetic believed it was a case of mere fabrications preventing legitimate development. Despite Justice Doussa's vindication of the probable truth of tradition in the compensation case, Aboriginal cultural claims across the country were harmed by the case. The Leader of the Opposition, John Howard, tacitly supported the Ngarrindjeri dissenters, observing: 'from now until the end of time, whenever Aboriginals legitimately raise something about their culture, people will say: "Oh this is another put-up job"'.[33]

HOWARD'S ASCENDANCE

There was a clear party divide on Aboriginal issues in the March 1996 election. Prime Minister Paul Keating had spoken passionately at Redfern on 10 December 1992 about the wrongs of the past, including killings, loss of land, the removal of children and lack of care of Aboriginal people due to 'our failure to imagine these things being done to us'. This address was voted by one Internet Sydney poll in 2007 as the third most memorable speech of all time.[34] Keating shaped the Native Title Act (1993), implemented the recommendations of the Royal Commission into Aboriginal Deaths in Custody (RCIADIC), created a Reconciliation Commission, and encouraged the HREOC inquiry into the removal of children. However, the Leader of the Opposition, John Howard, was committed to changing the Native Title Act. He also promised to empower Aboriginal people to be self-reliant and to escape paternalism.[35] The policy sounded enlightened, but after the Howard Coalition government took power it proved illusory. There was an unstated agenda to reverse much of what had been achieved in Aboriginal affairs towards Indigenous rights; particularly to curb land rights, ATSIC's power, and reintroduce the mainstreaming of services to Aboriginal people. This reflected the strong belief among conservatives for national homogeneity and a neo-assimilation policy.

During the campaign, Pauline Hanson, a small businesswoman and the Liberal candidate for Ipswich, was disendorsed for allegedly racist remarks. Hanson told the *Courier Mail* that governments gave Aboriginal people too much. Ipswich conservatives returned her to federal parliament as the Independent member for Ipswich. John Leslie, of the National Aboriginal and Islander Legal Services, called on the new Prime Minister, John Howard, to reject Hanson's views and 'speak out loudly against the cowardliness of attacking the victim'. John Howard remained silent.[36]

Hanson's maiden speech in Parliament on 10 September 1996 inflamed the political landscape with a blatant public attack on Aboriginal people. She stated: 'I am fed up to the back teeth with the inequalities that are being promoted by the Government and paid for by the taxpayer under the assumption that Aboriginals are the most disadvantaged people in Australia.' In what some have termed the 'politics of envy', Hanson made other attacks, including a claim that 'we are in danger of being swamped by Asians'.[37] It was a dangerous moment in Australian politics, which the media highlighted, giving Hanson's allegations prominence. Two weeks later, Prime Minister Howard defended free speech. In an address to the Queensland Liberal Party, which gave Hanson tacit support, he stated: 'I welcome the fact that people can now talk about certain things without living in fear of being branded a bigot or as a racist or any of the other expressions that have been too carelessly flung around in this country whenever somebody has disagreed with what somebody has said.'[38] While Howard scorned her claim in October that there could be civil war in Australia, he said little else. The Prime Minister only repudiated Hanson in May 1997, once foreign relations and trade with Asia were threatened, finally branding her views as 'simplistic nonsense'.[39]

The Aboriginal and Torres Strait Islander Commission (ATSIC), which replaced the NAC as the Indigenous voice, became an early Howard government target. The Coalition had opposed its existence since its creation in 1990, but it also had other detractors. Some criticised its 35 elected regional councils, which voted in seventeen commissioners, as too bureaucratic. ATSIC oversaw $1 billion in grants annually, each application passing through local, regional, state and federal processes. Peter Yu, Director of the Kimberley Land Council, asked: 'why is there a necessity to have this convoluted way of dealing with things?'[40] Many Aboriginal people were ambivalent, and with non-compulsory voting in ATSIC'S elections of 1990 and 1994, voter turnouts were around 30 per cent. The Keating government earlier had its own doubts during the Aboriginal health crisis of 1994, and took over the health budget from ATSIC.

These real concerns paled before the Howard government's probe into ATSIC. Within weeks of the election, it initiated a review of legal services receiving ATSIC funding. Some Aboriginal people, notably consultant Sharon Firebrace and Magistrate Pat O'Shane, cheered. Firebrace claimed 'mismanagement, theft, cronyism and nepotism [have] become wholesale practice in Aboriginal organisations. Only a royal commission can get to the length and breadth of it.'[41] Professor Hal Wootten QC, RCIADIC commissioner and co-founder of the NSW Aboriginal Legal Service, said cronyism in the legal service was 'a betrayal of all those who worked idealistically for the Aboriginal cause'. He added that the Legal Service's cry of 'racism' to avoid an investigation was 'shameful'.[42] Pressure mounted for greater accountability and the government ordered an external audit of ATSIC'S 6000 grants to more than 1000 Aboriginal organisations. It also introduced a bill aimed at restructuring the commission and giving the federal government power to appoint ATSIC's head and an administrator if necessary. It was an extraordinary move for a party claiming to end white paternalism in Aboriginal affairs. Senator Herron directed ATSIC not to fund any Aboriginal organisation not deemed 'fit and proper' to receive public moneys. The NSW Aboriginal Legal Service challenged this direction, which was upheld by the Federal Court in September 1996, as Herron had acted beyond his power under the ATSIC Act and against the intention of the Act to 'promote the development of self-management and self-sufficiency'. Tensions eased once Howard invited Aboriginal leaders to talk. Lowitja O'Donoghue, ATSIC's Chairperson, stated that Aboriginal people felt 'under siege since the election of the Government'.[43]

Despite claims of Aboriginal corruption, the audit process found most bodies guilty of mismanagement rather than fraud. The auditor remarked that most staff in the 1122 Aboriginal community organisations he investigated lacked skills and training in management and bookkeeping. He found that only 60 bodies, or 5 per cent, were 'not fit and proper'—the NSW Aboriginal Legal Service, which had misused $1 million, being one. Prosecutions followed. Of the remainder, 937 had breached funding conditions in some way, and 125 were certified correct.[44] The audit revealed the failure of long-term paternalism, which left Aboriginal people inadequately trained for 'self-management' and survival in the complicated world of grant-based community development projects.

The government pressed ahead with amending legislation. However, Senate opposition modified the ATSIC Amendment bill by barring the power to sack commissioners and appoint an administrator. The government also agreed to an elected chairperson after 1999. Until then, Senator Herron appointed Gatjil Djerrkura, a tertiary-qualified Yolngu elder from Yirrkala. He was a former conservative political candidate, who the government hoped would be a moderate and compliant. But by 1998, Djerrkura, a temperate man, widely admired for his imposing and calming manner, became disillusioned by the government's attitude to native title and the removal of children, claiming that Howard lacked 'leadership' and Herron was 'paternalistic'.[45]

THE WIK CASE: NATIVE TITLE CONSTRAINED

Prior to the Howard government's election, the Wik people lost a longstanding native title case in the Federal Court, which dated back to 1993. In January 1996, Justice Drummond ruled that a pastoral lease near the Gulf of Carpentaria extinguished their claim to native title. This confirmed Paul Keating's opinion during the Native Title bill debate in 1993, echoed in the preamble to the Act, that like freehold title, pastoral leases extinguished native title. The Wik people appealed to the High Court. Pastoralists urged the Howard government to legislate to extinguish native title on pastoral leases to provide certainty. The government waited for the High Court's decision on Wik, fearing legislation might contravene the Racial Discrimination Act and invite compensation claims, endless litigation, and international condemnation. It also feared that the Senate, which the government did not control, was likely to oppose such legislation.[46] The government proposed restricting Aboriginal negotiating rights under native title instead. The National Farmers Federation, led by the tough-talking Donald McGauchie, rejected this proposal and predicted a long halt to development and mining investment.

The Wik appeal was heard over three days in June, involving submissions running into thousands of pages. Both sides predicted doom as the High Court reserved its decision. The Council for Aboriginal Reconciliation brokered talks in September between Aboriginal, mining and pastoral representatives on changes to the Act. In October the government announced draft changes. In an allusion to the protracted negotiations and native title claim between the Waanyi and CRA over the Century zinc mine, the draft allowed the government to override native title negotiations if a project of major national significance was in jeopardy. There was also a proposed ministerial override on public infrastructure leading to private developments, to overcome the native title claim over a proposed gas pipeline in Queensland. All awaited the Wik decision. The Native Title Act, and most opinion, stated that leaseholds in the common law extinguished native title, giving leaseholders 'exclusive possession'.

A chill rippled through conservative Australia and pastoral leaseholders once the Wik decision was announced two days before Christmas 1996. The High Court ruled that the pastoral lease issued on Wik land did *not* extinguish native title. The Court found that Australian pastoral leases of the nineteenth century often included Aboriginal rights to land, a fact often ignored or overlooked since. This was the forgotten gift of Earl Grey, British Secretary to the Colonies, to Indigenous people in the Waste Land Act of 1848. The Court said the two forms of title, leasehold and native title, co-existed. However, the Court refused to establish a general principle as dozens of different kinds of leaseholds existed in Australia. Each case would have to be decided individually. Thus the decision did not deliver certainty over pastoral leases, which covered 40 per cent of Australia, and which formed about two-thirds of those lands under native title claims. Furthermore, any law to deliver certainty could be challenged under the Racial Discrimination Act.[47]

Leaseholders and conservative premiers demanded legislation, despite the Coalition's pre-election promise not to legislate away native title or make changes to the Racial Discrimination Act. Prime Minister Howard was soon considering both, claiming his promises were based on the now baseless view that pastoral titles were believed to extinguish native title. This news caused a furious response from Aboriginal groups. Wild talk followed. Pastoralists claimed land values in Queensland were halved, the Queensland government froze the issuing of mining leases, and Howard echoed the exaggeration that 70 per cent of Australia's lands were affected. The deputy leader of the Coalition, Tim Fischer, toured the bush calling for 'buckets full of extinguishment' and urged state premiers to lobby Howard. A *Bulletin*-Morgan poll found that 56 per cent of 530 people sampled disapproved of the Wik judgment, with the percentage in Queensland topping 72 per cent. Sixty-four per cent approved of legislation to extinguish native title on pastoral leaseholds.[48]

A bitter eighteen-month struggle followed, which overshadowed even the invective of the Mabo wrangle. Conservative state premiers astonishingly called for changes to the High Court, which was simply acting on what others had conveniently forgotten: the Waste Land Act of 1848. Rob Borbidge, the Queensland Premier, wanted to prevent judges acting like 'some sort of magical circle like kings and queens of old to invent laws that were contrary to conventions and legal precedent'.[49] The Coalition threatened to split as the National Party wanted extinguishment. Others like John Purchell of the Cattlemen's Union, who had been involved in the Cape York deal, called for negotiation but to no avail. ATSIC also tried to educate the public, but fear and ignorance reignited. A series of summits were held over the next few months, as Aboriginal people, miners, farmers and premiers met separately to determine their position. Prime Minister Howard sought a decision in four weeks, but this quickly proved impossible.

While Howard rejected extinguishment as politically and constitutionally unworkable, he favoured a severe curtailment of the right to make native title claims, which became known as the 'ten-point plan'. The Prime Minister stated: 'I clearly believe that my model is the better way, the fairer way, the way more likely to deliver an early sense of security and stability than the alternatives that have been urged on me. Extinguishment may look a simple, easy option but it has a number of drawbacks.' These drawbacks included compensation claims, High Court challenges—and a point he did not mention—the political implications of legislating away the rights of one group.[50] Deputy Prime Minister Fischer, Premier Borbidge of Queensland and the Farmers Federation all felt 'betrayed', while Aboriginal leaders feared the 'ten-point plan' was de facto extinguishment.

The details of the plan revealed that Indigenous people were right to be fearful, as it favoured pastoral interests and curtailed rights of Aboriginal native title holders, despite Howard's claims of a 'fair' compromise. The ten points are more fully examined in Michael Bachelard's *The Great Land Grab* (1997). In brief, they proposed:

- Validation of all mining leases granted by state governments on pastoral leases between the Native Title Act (1994) and the Wik decision (1996).
- Extinguishment of native title on all land with 'exclusive tenure', including pastoral leases that were intended to be 'exclusive'.
- Native title to give way to the provision of essential services infrastructure.
- Confirmation of the primacy of pastoral leases over native title, definition of valid activities to be undertaken on a pastoralist's land, ability of states to upgrade pastoral leases (upon payment) to perpetual, exclusive or freehold leases, and the reduction of the Aboriginal right to negotiate on activities on pastoral leases to normal state grievance procedures.
- Definition of access rights of native title holders to pastoral lands, but only if they already had such access.
- Control of mining leases on pastoral land to pass to the states, the Commonwealth to pay 75 per cent of any compensation over native title.
- Provision of rights for governments to buy land for commercial purposes or infrastructure purposes, with modified or no rights of Aboriginal people to negotiate, depending on the land in question.
- Denial of native title over waters or airspace.
- A sunset clause giving a six-year deadline for title or compensation claims to be made.
- Recognition of voluntary agreements as binding and immune from challenge.

In May, John Howard faced angry pastoralists at Longreach in Queensland, who wanted nothing less than 'buckets full' of extinguishment. Over 90 per cent of them voted against his plan, despite its very favourable terms for them. Expressing the fears of the bush, the *Sunday Mail* in Brisbane published a map to show that while Aboriginal people currently owned 14.5 per cent of Australia, a further 44 per cent was under native title claim.[51] Lawyers and the ALP raised doubts about whether Howard's plan was constitutional. The Hindmarsh Island case, then before the High Court, promised to determine if only beneficial race-specific laws could be made without contravening the Racial Discrimination Act. (In fact it determined the opposite.)

By September 1997, the struggle had moved into parliament where the Labor Opposition proposed 350 amendments, most of which the government rejected. An Aboriginal delegation travelled to South Africa to seek support, causing Nelson Mandela to offer mediation, an offer firmly but diplomatically declined by the government. Bitterness mostly prevailed outside as a chorus of opposition arose. The Australian Law Reform Commission pronounced the bill as racially discriminatory. Paul Keating and the leader of the federal Opposition, Kim Beazley, agreed. Noel Pearson described conservative politicians as 'racist scum'.[52] A 'Stick with Wik' Coalition emerged, patronised by some leading Australian entertainers. A group called 'DON'T' (Defenders of Native Title) became active at the suburban level. Prime Minister Howard attacked church leaders who spoke against the bill, saying they did not have a 'superior ownership of moral issues'.[53] The Governor-General, Sir William Deane, obliquely observed that 'the very suggestion that church leaders aren't qualified to talk about disadvantage is an insult to the people who are asked to swallow it', causing Premier Jeff Kennett to criticise Sir William for political comment.[54] Ex-Prime Minister Gorton, aged 86, as he did in the Mabo debate, implied that Aboriginal people were primitive and a 'people who had no concept of private property . . . [and who] had never grown or farmed any crops'.[55] Ex-Prime Minister Malcolm Fraser and some eminent Australians signed a statement against racism. Joseph Guttnick, mining entrepreneur, spoke out against the mining industry's 'bully' tactics on Wik.

Fear and ignorance assisted the resurgence of Pauline Hanson. Ex-Prime Minister Bob Hawke organised a communiqué from former prime ministers to condemn her, but Howard refused to sign. Pundits predicted an imminent 'race-election'. Rick Farley of the Council for Aboriginal Reconciliation (CAR) stated anxiously: 'in my view this is a defining moment for the Australian nation. We have two choices, a divided nation or a shot at a more harmonious outcome. I don't want my legacy to my kids to be a divided nation.'[56] Farley called for a national summit on Wik. Instead, Prime Minister Howard spoke on television, hoping to sway the nation. However, Howard failed to move even the moderate Evelyn Scott who, in her trademark black hat, had replaced the bearded Patrick Dodson as Head of the CAR. Scott declared: 'Wik is not negotiable' and accused the government of 'lying by claiming that suburban backyards were at risk from native title'.[57]

The Wik bill returned to the House of Representatives in April 1998. The government was pessimistic about the outcome, as the Senate had already rejected it twice. Many feared a 'race-based election', following a deadlock and a double dissolution of parliament. The government fiercely denied the issue was one of race and that it was racist. However, Ian Viner, a former Liberal Minister for Aboriginal Affairs, and now a member of the CAR, disputed this.

Senator Brian Harradine dances with elder Gladys Tybingoompa and other Wik people in a moment of unity, April 1998, which quickly failed in the face of a political deal.
COURTESY OF PHOTOGRAPHER ANDREW MEARES AND THE *AGE*.

Viner wrote: 'Mr Howard will say native title is not a race issue, but of course it is, because his amendment bill has the single purpose of reducing the legal rights of a specific race of people.'[58] Senator Harradine, the Independent from Tasmania who held the balance of power in the Senate, flip-flopped on the issue. He danced an impromptu dance, bare-foot in shirt and tie, with bare-breasted and ritually painted Wik elder Gladys Tybingoompa, on the lawn of Parliament House. This appeared to signal his solidarity with Aboriginal people. However, he seemed more drawn to an exotic moment, as he explained: 'I hadn't intended to dance . . . I felt as if I was doing something uniquely Australian . . . There was something stirring in my memory from childhood.'[59] The next day he sought a compromise to avoid a double dissolution, then changed his vote twice in two days on the 'sunset' clause.

Pauline Hanson chose her moment to address the lower house of parliament on the United Nations' Draft Declaration on the Rights of Indigenous Peoples, giving it an extraordinary conspiratorial interpretation. John Howard finally attacked her outright, many thought two years too late. He termed her speech 'not only a dishonest, inaccurate speech, but it verges on the deranged in various places'.[60] The pressure was intense and increased by the Queensland election, in which Hanson's right-wing One Nation Party shocked the nation by capturing 23 per cent of the primary vote—way above the expected 5–10 per cent.

Harradine immediately offered a Wik compromise to avoid a double dissolution, which would likely herald his own loss of a Senate power base to One Nation. The Prime Minister could barely believe his good fortune after eighteen months of struggle on Wik. Aboriginal rights were horse-traded by Howard and Harradine in secret discussions. Gladys Tybingoompa arrived at Harradine's office and demanded her ochre-coloured pandanus armband back, which she had given him as a symbol of trust. The Native Title Amendment bill passed in July 1998 with the vote of Harradine. The disgraced Labor rebel Senator Colston, who was facing possible fraud charges only to have them dropped due to ill-health, also supported the bill. Harradine had made some gains, ending the threat of a six-year sunset clause on claims, and ensuring that governments acted within the Racial Discrimination Act. But he failed to gain for Aboriginal people the right to negotiate with mining companies on pastoral leases. Father Frank Brennan of the Jesuit Social Justice Centre believed fellow-Catholic Harradine had done his best, 'given the political constraints'.

The legislation had been formed without Aboriginal involvement in the negotiations. The Aboriginal public intellectual Noel Pearson concluded that 'Howard has managed to rip the heart out of the original native title legislation'.[61] Pearson pointed to just two of the provisions. The upgrading of pastoral leases to full primary production leases meant that pastoralists could undertake even forestry and tourism on their leases, without consulting the Aboriginal native title holders. Also, the Act included a list of specific leaseholds which, in the opinion of the government, extinguished native title. This was an arbitrary political decision, which the courts should have made on a case-by-case basis. After the enabling state legislation was passed, native title was eventually lost on almost 7 per cent of Australia's lands and in particular on 22 per cent of Queensland's land.[62]

LAND VICTORIES

Despite the agonies of Wik, there were some ecstasies over land, gained by different mechanisms, including consensual agreements, tribunal cases, land use agreements and purchase. But progress was slow, as applications under the Native Title Act clogged the Native Title Tribunal due to legal complexities, opposition to claims and the under-resourced state of the Tribunal. A confidential report to ATSIC in early 1998 identified 700 claims before the Tribunal, with the number set to rise.[63]

The first successful consensual determination was over 12.4 hectares at Crescent Head in October 1996. The Dunghutti people held native title for six hours before exchanging it under agreement for $738,000 in compensation. Twelve more consensual claims were finalised before the National Native Title Tribunal by the end of 2000. In 2000, the Western Australian government and the Ngaanyatjarra Council or Spinifex group reached consent over their native title to 50,000 square kilometres in the Great Victoria Desert. This gave them the right of possession, hunting and occupation, and the right to make decisions over its use.[64]

The first native title land case that was successful came in November 1998 when the Miriuwung Gajerrong people gained title over 7900 square kilometres, which contained the Argyle diamond mine, the Ord River irrigation lands and pastoral lands. After four years, a marathon 83 days in court and millions in costs, Justice Lee of the Federal Court granted claimants the right to 'possess, occupy, use and enjoy the land, including the power to decide how it was used', and 'the right to receive a portion of any resources taken by others'.[65] An appeal followed, and in 2000, the full bench of the Federal Court overruled Lee's decision as it conflicted with some High Court decisions. After appeal to the High Court, it ruled in August 2002 that the people had native title rights, which were coexistent with pastoral and mining leases, but of a non-exclusive kind. The people had no rights over minerals or petroleum. Elder Ben Ward was frustrated by a 'vague' decision after eight years of cases and vowed to take no further legal action.[66] The Meriam people gained title to Dauar and Waier Islands in June 2001 (excluded from the Mabo decision due to leasing complications), ending a twenty-year struggle. Betty Mabo Tekahika, daughter of Eddie Mabo, exclaimed his spirit was singing; 'this is what I want for the Meriam people. It is happy now.'[67]

The first native title sea case was won in the Federal Court in July 1998 when people were awarded native title to 3300 square kilometres of the sea and seabed around Croker Island but with a 'non-exclusive' use provision and subject to Commonwealth or Territory laws. The decision was appealed, but the Court upheld both provisions, thus allowing commercial fishing, tourism and mining in the area. The Croker Island decision was as significant as the Mabo and Wik findings, opening the way to the resolution of 120 other sea claims then pending. In 2007 the High Court upheld a Federal Court ruling which gave the traditional owners of 80 per cent of the Northern Territory's coastline the right to control access and fishing from the shoreline by permit. However, non-Indigenous fishermen vowed to reject permits even though they were to be free.[68]

Development was generally freed up despite the pessimism over native title. Indigenous Land Use Agreements were negotiated, which protected the interests of native title claimants, while developers gained legal status and certainty for their projects.[69] The Queensland government in August 2001 reached agreement with the Queensland Indigenous Working Group on a mechanism by which mining companies could negotiate directly with regional Indigenous groups to fast-track exploration permits. If minerals are found then the normal native title negotiations would follow. The agreement promised to free up 1200 exploration permits in limbo since the Wik decision.

Aboriginal people gained land in other ways. The Indigenous Land Corporation purchased 127 properties for Aboriginal people by 2000, 73 being divested to Aboriginal corporations. Aboriginal economic development on this land is vital to ameliorate the problems of unemployment, substance abuse, imprisonment, poor education and ill health. Land Enterprises Australia Pty Ltd assisted in the management of Indigenous owned and managed properties created by the Indigenous Land Corporation's purchase. In 2000 alone, it mentored the development of six pastoral properties and explored requests to assist with horticultural enterprises in Central Australia, an abalone project at Point Pearce and more pastoral properties.[70]

Even those in despair experienced some bright spots. In December 1998, the Yorta Yorta case over the Barmah region on the Murray River ended after four years, 114 sitting days, 201 witnesses and over 11,000 pages of transcript. Justice Olney of the Federal Court rejected the claim, saying the 'tide of history has indeed washed away any real acknowledgement of their traditional laws and any real observance of their traditional customs'. He added that 'not withstanding the genuine efforts of the members of the claimant group to revive the lost culture of their ancestors, native title rights and interests once lost are not capable of revival'.[71] The Yorta Yorta people, who had strong claims to continuity of connection through Maloga (1874) and Cummeragunja (1888) reserves, were deemed by Justice Olney to have lost their culture. Olney's reliance on the writing of white settlers of the nineteenth century led him to adopt a static view of culture. If people did not practise a traditional economy and perform ritual as it was observed 150 years ago, they did not possess 'Aboriginal culture', despite their maintenance of kinship, a group identity and other cultural ideas. Olney also decided that 1880s petitions for land by the Yorta Yorta 'to cultivate and raise stock' were evidence of a lack of continuity.

Native title litigation is a fraught business. The Yorta Yorta appealed to the full bench of the Federal Court and lost. They appealed to the High Court and lost again in December 2002. The High Court ruled five to two against them, Justices Michael Kirby and Mary Gaudron dissenting. The latter two argued traditional culture did not have to be continuous, as long as identification with the community was continuous.[72] In late 2000, the Indigenous Land Corporation purchased 259 hectares of Murray River farmland for the Yorta Yorta, and in May 2004 the Victorian government designated them as 'original owners', and gave them a say in managing the region.

The Yorta Yorta case revealed the difficulty of achieving native title in settled Australia, even by agreement, as was achieved by the Wotjobaluk. Through long negotiation the Wotjobaluk gained recognition as 'original owners'; 45 hectares of freehold; management rights and 'non-exclusive' rights to hunt, fish and camp along the Wimmera River.[73] Scholars have criticised the Native Title Act for its 'repressive authenticity', which makes claims by people who are disconnected from land and culture impossible. Patrick Wolfe, who coined the term 'repressive authenticity', has argued that by defining native title so narrowly—living continuously on land in a traditional way—the land rights of the remainder have been eliminated. Wolfe added that despite the gains some make under native title, Mabo was not a break with the colonial past, but a continuation of the settler logic of elimination of the native.[74]

Aboriginal people are jaundiced about native title as well, for it caused splits within communities, and endless meetings and litigation. On the tenth anniversary of the Mabo decision, Noel Pearson wrote that while the High Court's decision recognised native title, its recognition rested on coexistence and compromise, and three principles: 'whitefellas can keep what is now theirs; the blackfellas get what is left over; and both black and white titles coexist on pastoral leases, and if there is conflict in the coexistence, then the Crown title prevails over the native title'. The process of gaining native title had been bogged down in legal delays and 'meanness'. He declared: 'my message to new Australians is you have received your share of the Mabo compromise, now help Indigenous Australians receive theirs'.[75]

Native title claims are perilous, taking years. Inevitably, any victory is appealed right up the line to the High Court. The Ngaanyatjarra people's win in June 2005 over 188,000 square kilometres of remote Western Australian desert,

The Federal Court of Australia recognised the Ngarla people's claim to about 4655 square kilometres of land near Port Hedland in May 2007. Ngarla representatives Charlie Coppin (left) and Stephen Stewart are either side of Tribunal case manager Gerry Putland. COURTESY OF THE NATIONAL NATIVE TITLE TRIBUNAL.

the largest win to date, took twenty years from their first moves for land rights. In 2008 the Native Title Tribunal reported that it had received 1774 applications since 1994, of which two-thirds had been resolved, most in Western Australia. Those finalised in the previous year by consent had taken on average almost six years; those by litigation seven years; and those determined unopposed took one year. The tribunal estimated that it would take a further 30 years to resolve all current and anticipated native title claims at the current rate of clearance.[76]

CULTURAL EXPRESSIONS

Traditional cultural expression reflected the new respect many Australians showed for Aboriginal land. In 1997 the Australia Council ratified the first Aboriginal and Torres Strait Islander arts policy, governed by principles of respect, authority, rights, responsibility and diversity. The Council helped Indigenous artists to travel internationally, including members of Brisbane's Kooemba Jdarra Theatre Company, who performed in London, and Sydney's Bangarra Dance Theatre, whose members appeared at the Edinburgh Festival. The Council's manager, Michael Lynch, justified the move, stating that Indigenous arts constituted a third of Australia's cultural exports. In 1999–2000, one of the Council's sub-committees, the Aboriginal and Torres Strait Islander Arts Board, supported the artistic endeavours of over 120 Indigenous communities and artists with $4.3 million out of a total Council budget of $49.9 million.[77] In September 2001, the Centenary of Federation National Council funded the Yeperenye (Caterpillar Dreaming) Festival in Alice Springs, attended by 26,000 people. Over 4000 Indigenous performers played music and danced on the red earth beneath the MacDonnell Ranges, testimony to the vitality of Indigenous cultures. There are now dozens of Indigenous festivals annually, one of the biggest being the Gama festival of the Yolgnu people.

Aboriginal traditional art and its purchase flourished in the 1990s and beyond. Foreign visitors in the mid-1990s spent close to $50 million per year on Aboriginal art and craft works, and this interest continued.[78] In 1995 Clifford Possum Tjapaltjarri, a former stockman from Central Australia, set a new record of $50,000 for his huge 1970s Papunya painting *Warlugulong*. It had originally been bought for $1200 by the Commonwealth Bank and hung at Mornington Island in its canteen before its sale in 1995. Two years later, Johnny Warangkula Tjupurrula's *Water Dreaming at Kalipinya* sold for $206,000. The price of this painting climbed to $486,500 in 2000, but was surpassed in July 2001 when the National Gallery of Australia paid $786,625 for a Rover Thomas work, *All That Big Rain Coming from Top Side*. The late Emily Kame Kngwarreye's massive *Earth's Creation* sold for $1.05 million in May 2007, bought by Mbantua Gallery in Alice Springs for permanent display. This was surpassed by the late Clifford Possum Tjapaltjarri's *Warlugulong*, which sold for $2.4m in July 2007.[79]

These fabulous payments existed alongside the abject poverty in Central Australia of their creators. Indeed, critics pointed to gross exploitation of the artists by some unscrupulous art buyers. These people allegedly furnished the artists with canvases and paint and encouraged them to create for paltry sums: providing only living or 'grog money', amounting to less than a tenth of the eventual retail sale price. Johnny Warangkula Tjupurrula, who sold *Water Dreaming* in the 1970s for $150, existed on the pension in 1997. His request for 4 per cent of the sale price in 1997 was refused.[80] Clifford Possum Tjapaltjarri was in the same financial predicament, caught between grasping white art dealers and an Aboriginal ethic of sharing.

Emily Kame Kngwarreye from the Simpson Desert was an Aboriginal pastoral worker and later a batik artist, before she turned to acrylics in 1989 when aged 80. Her luminous colours and diverse and bold abstract styles made her an instant success with the art world. She painted furiously, producing a phenomenal 3000 works in the eight years before her death, an average of one a day. This kept her kin at Utopia in supplies and vehicles. Some claim art dealers worked her to the point of exhaustion. Art curator Judith Ryan commented:

> She was an elderly woman and the amount of pressure she was under was immense. There were a lot of different dealers coming to take her to different places to paint, but she seemed to be able to tailor what she painted to their demands. That takes an immense amount of ingenuity, and she did it without compromising her integrity.[81]

It was little wonder that *Earth's Creation* fetched over a million dollars.

Some criticise the rage for Aboriginal art, seeing it as parallel to the nineteenth-century museum fever for the exotic. The art itself has been Westernised, as it was originally painted on bodies and in sand, and has become portable and saleable. Some works have been misused. In the late 1990s, instances of Kathleen Petyarre and Ginger Riley fakes surfaced, other frauds and the constant misuse of copyright shook the art world—but not the prices. A work by Yolngu artist Banduk Marika, entitled *Djanda and the Sacred Waterhole*, meant to educate on a museum wall, to her great distress became a carpet design. Fortunately, Marika won a court case for damages. However, power and influence runs both ways. Aboriginal people have always wanted to show their art to establish a claim for country which it represents.[82] However, they are expert at keeping secret material from outside eyes, by 'blacking out', and due to the esoteric and hidden meanings of their work. The money they have earned (paltry as it often is), and the respect they have gained in international forums, reveals a new-found power amid all the exploitation.

Protection has finally been extended to Indigenous artists. In November 1999, the National Indigenous Arts Advocacy Association introduced a trademark of authenticity for Aboriginal art and pledged to educate artists about contracts and copyright.[83] In 2008, legislation was finally promised to give all Australian artists a five per cent royalty each time their work priced at over $1000 is resold during their lifetime, and for 70 years thereafter.[84]

One curious footnote to this adulation was the case of Elizabeth Durack, who grew up with Aboriginal people on the Durack's Kimberley pastoral empire in the 1920s. Durack held 50 solo exhibitions of her paintings over 50 years, becoming strongly influenced by Aboriginal techniques. In the mid-1990s, she entered Aboriginal-style paintings in competitions under the name of 'Eddie Burrup'. When she admitted her deception, Aboriginal groups were furious, claiming 'cultural exploitation'. Durack remained unrepentant before her death in May 2000, saying 'culture is something flowing through the world. Eddie Burrup is very much a conduit of stored knowledge.'[85] Certainly, the Heidelberg School of Australian painting borrowed in admiration from French Impressionism, to create something unique. Perhaps Durack's *The Big Sorry*, on the death of Princess Diana, was the same.

Torres Strait Islander communities pressed for autonomy in 1988, partly on the basis of a cultural resurgence. Their desire stemmed from their isolation, the belief that their interests are sometimes swamped by those of Aboriginal people, but also the strength of their culture known as 'Ailan Kastom'. Their recent history and culture are outlined in Jeremy Beckett's *Torres Strait Islanders* (1989) and Nonie Sharp's *Stars of Tagai* (1993). By 2001 there were 6000 Torres Strait Islanders living on eighteen island homelands (forming 80 per cent of the population there), and over 33,000 living on the Australian mainland (a third of whom claim mixed Aboriginal and Torres Strait Islander descent). In 1996 the people gained their own federal budget allocation, separate from ATSIC. The House of Representatives Standing Committee on Aboriginal and Torres Strait Islander Affairs investigated their status and recommended in 1998 that a new, democratically elected Torres Strait Regional Assembly replace three existing administrative bodies, and that this Assembly control government block funding. It also recommended the establishment of a Cultural Council to nourish 'Ailan Kastom'. The Committee called on the Queensland and federal governments to foster the fishing industry and generally to stimulate employment and training in the region. It also recommended ways that ATSIC could more efficiently and equitably deliver services and cultural programs to mainland Torres Strait Islander people.[86] In 2000 the Torres Strait Regional Authority funded community consultation to determine the principles underpinning autonomy. Tommy Waia, the Authority's Chairperson, declared in September 2000 that 'we can focus on our long term goals with the clear support of the people'.[87]

REMOVED CHILDREN, NEW ASSIMILATIONISM AND CULTURE WARS

During the Howard government's first year in 1996, the HREOC's 'National Inquiry into the Separation of Aboriginal and Torres Strait Islander Children from their Families', headed by clergyman Sir Ronald Wilson, gathered evidence. Most Australians discussed the issue and splits developed, even within government ranks. Senator John Herron, Minister for Aboriginal Affairs, argued in October

that Aboriginal children had benefited by removal. Michael Wooldridge, Minister
for Health, retorted that the removal of about 60,000 children was a 'big scar
on the conscience of Australia'.[88] The government's submission to the inquiry
was unequivocal, denying responsibility for the actions of previous governments
and rejecting the possibility of compensation for victims.

The inquiry's 689-page report, *Bringing Them Home*, was tabled in April
1997. In the face of incomplete records, it estimated between one in three and
one in ten Indigenous children were removed in Australia from 1910 to 1970.
The report traced the history of removal in each state, and through individual
testimony, the consequences for the children and their families. Most extended
families were affected and it made for harrowing reading. Regarding compensation,
the report examined three United Nations international declarations, all of
which had been ratified by the Australian government. These were: the 1945
United Nations Charter, which outlawed racial discrimination; the 1948 Universal
Declaration of Human Rights, which declared that 'all human beings are born
free and equal in dignity and rights'; and the 1948 Convention on the Prevention
and Punishment of the Crime of Genocide, which in part defined genocide as
'forcibly transferring children of the group to another group'.[89] The report made
53 detailed recommendations in four key areas: methods of making reparation,
apologies and monetary compensation; methods of future treatment of
government records; ways of assisting families to be traced and reunited; and
funds and services to be established for counselling those affected. Recommendation
Ten stated that 'the Commonwealth legislate to implement the Genocide
Convention with full domestic effect'.[90]

The Howard government branded the report as 'flawed', claiming governments
at the time were well intentioned. It rejected compensation or any apology for
the removals.[91] The report was tabled during the Wik debate and during Pauline
Hanson's ascendance. Her book *The Truth* (1997), containing writings of other
One Nation supporters, made outrageous and bizarre claims about Aboriginal
culture, immigrants, and alleged United Nations control of Australia. It was
widely condemned for going beyond acceptable comment in Australian political
debate.[92] In December 1997, the Howard government announced its response
to *Bringing Them Home*, which offered a package of $63 million over four years
to provide counselling and family link-up services; family support; language
maintenance programs; and archival and oral history projects. There was to be
no legislated compensation and no apology.[93]

Some Aboriginal people sought redress in the courts. In August 1997, the
High Court found adversely in the Kruger case. It ruled that governments had

not acted unconstitutionally by removing children, nor was there anything in Northern Territory ordinances that authorised the destruction of a group.[94] Massive court costs hampered further cases. In August 1999, Joy Williams finally lost her compensation case against the New South Wales Government for being removed. In March 1999, Lorna Cubillo and Peter Gunner sued the Commonwealth for damages over being removed at the age of seven around 1950. About 700 other claimants were poised, awaiting the outcome. Cubillo and Gunner alleged cruel treatment and sexual abuse in church-run homes in Darwin. In August 2000, Justice O'Loughlin accepted their evidence of mistreatment, but dismissed their claim for damages. In Cubillo's case there were insufficient documents to judge whether the Native Affairs Branch had failed to perform its statutory duty of care. In Gunner's case, his mother's thumbprint was found on a document indicating her 'consent' to his removal. O'Loughlin was careful to state that his judgment in no way denied the existence of a 'stolen generation'.[95] Gunner and Cubillo's appeal to the full Federal Court was rejected in August 2001, and their application to appeal to the High Court was refused in May 2002 due to a lack of living witnesses.

Public debate raged in 1998 over the truth of claims in the *Bringing Them Home* report. The attack on the report was led by the conservative *Quadrant* magazine after Robert Manne was removed from the editorship in November 1997. The magazine's management believed Manne had shifted Left on Aboriginal issues. Peter Howson, a former conservative Minister of Aboriginal Affairs (1971–72) argued in *Quadrant* that Aboriginal children were not 'stolen', but rather 'rescued',[96] although Ron Brunton, an anthropologist with the conservative Institute of Public Affairs, argued that neither 'stolen' or 'rescued' fitted the complexity of events. 'Rescued' was the argument put for the Commonwealth by Douglas Meagher QC in the Gunner–Cubillo case. Robert Manne (and others) put the opposing view in the press and later in his book *In Denial* (2001).[97] Both sides of the debate were pushed to extremes—children were either stolen or rescued. There was no sense that both might have operated in reality and that child removal was a benign genocide, such as practised by Auber Neville in the 1930s.[98]

The government appeared before the Senate inquiry into the report's implementation. Senator Herron, the Minister for Aboriginal Affairs, again opposed compensation, as removal was 'essentially lawful and benign in intent'. He claimed on ABC radio there was no 'stolen generation': 'we're arguing it's not a generation if it was 10 per cent. If it was a generation, it means the whole generation, so we think it is a misnomer.'[99] Coalition backbenchers and even the conservative Western Australian Premier, Richard Court, insisted there was a 'stolen generation'. Prime Minister Howard stated the government's submission was an 'honest attempt to put some facts on the table'. Outrage bubbled from Aboriginal leaders who predicted trouble at the Sydney Olympics. Historian Janet McCalman slammed Herron's semantics. 'Yes, Senator Herron, there wasn't a "stolen generation", there were stolen generations . . . Neither does the toll have to be "100 per cent" to qualify as a generation: indeed, only 50 per cent of men of military age went to World War I.' She concluded: 'Forced assimilation meant the destruction of Aboriginality; the ceasing to be of the people as a distinctive, historical, community. In other words, the planned extinguishment of a people, a genocide'.[100] Anna Haebich, in her impressive 726-page history of the removal of Aboriginal children in Australia, *Broken Circles* (2000), concluded the policy was part of the long colonial struggle for control of Australia, writing: 'possession of the children indicated ownership of the future'.[101]

Following the Gunner–Cubillo decision, Peter Howson also claimed: 'Australia has no stolen generation. Sir Ronald's report has been discredited by Judge O'Loughlin's decision.' He urged an end to the 'separatism of the past 30 years'.[102] Aboriginal supporters attacked O'Loughlin's failure to see that the policy was racist, rather than not well-intentioned, as children were removed because they were Aboriginal, not because they were 'neglected'. Malcolm Fraser claimed the government of the day had failed in its 'duty of care' to Cubillo and Gunner. He called for an end to expensive litigation by the Commonwealth, costing over $11 million in this case alone, and advocated the creation of a healing fund.[103] John McDonnell (a white Australian, and son of the Director of Welfare in the Northern Territory), who attended primary school with Cubillo and others from the Rhetta Dixon Home, claimed (with no evidence beyond individual memory) that 'in my experience, Rhetta Dixon children were not removed to be assimilated into a European environment'.[104]

The personal cost of removal was clear and was inter-generational. Dayne Childs was removed from his nineteen-year-old unmarried Aboriginal mother, four days after his birth in Brisbane in 1972. The facts of her consent, whether it was given or not, and in what circumstances, are unclear. The Childs family, who later moved to London, fostered him from the age of three. In October 1996, Dayne was reunited with his family in Brisbane: his natural mother, activist Cheryl Buchanan; his six half-siblings; and his natural father—former black power advocate Dennis Walker, then in gaol for assault. Cheryl Buchanan and her parents had tracked Dayne down after the adoption laws changed in 1991. Dayne Childs met his extended family and was welcomed into the Wacka Wacka and Kabi Kabi people before he returned to Norwich, England, where he lived with his partner Kirsten Milton and their baby, Hollie.[105] Dayne, who had always been told he was Aboriginal, still became depressed back in Norwich, torn by two heritages and the enormity of his situation. In August 1998, after sitting beside the A11 motorway at Norwich, he simply walked into the traffic and was killed. A court case ensued over his body, which ruled he should be buried in England. Justice Brenda Hale remarked that in October 1996 Childs was troubled by the *Courier Mail*'s headline: 'Tears as stolen child comes home after 24 years'. His friends in Norwich said he had changed. 'He was no longer the cool and collected young man as before.' His foster family agreed not to cremate his body as intended, out of respect for the wishes of his Aboriginal family. His natural mother viewed his body before burial in Norwich.[106]

The 'stolen generations' debate did not allow for much subtlety. In March 2001, the Melbourne *Herald-Sun* introduced an interview with Lowitja O'Donoghue by Andrew Bolt with the words: 'Aboriginal leader's shock admission'. Bolt's interview was headlined 'I Wasn't Stolen', because O'Donoghue chose to use the term 'removed' to explain her personal situation. Bolt concluded: 'the "stolen generation" push now threatens to become an even greater disaster for the Aboriginal cause than the fabricated Hindmarsh Island "secret

Cartoonist John Spooner's comment on the attempt to deny the term 'stolen generation'.
COURTESY OF JOHN SPOONER AND THE *AGE*.

women's" [business]'.[107] Questioned on ABC TV's *Stateline* about the existence of a 'stolen generation', Bolt affirmed: 'no. There is no firm evidence to suggest this at all'. Even though Bolt's interview with O'Donoghue was conducted on the telephone, the paper printed a picture of a tearful O'Donoghue, suggesting her remorse at the interview.

Prime Minister Howard quickly commented that the story was 'highly significant', implying he agreed with Bolt on the stolen generations being fabricated. O'Donoghue, the highly respected former chairperson of ATSIC, was extremely distraught at being 'taken out of context and distorted' in what she described as a 'manipulative' interview. She explained that her Irish father had placed her, aged two, with four siblings in the Colebrook mission in Quorn, South Australia. O'Donoghue's mother, who she found 30 years later, had grieved endlessly. In her press release, O'Donoghue stated: 'I know that my Aboriginal mother would have had no legal recourse, nor any moral support, in resisting our removal. I also know that her grief was unbearable.'[108] Bolt and Howard had caused renewed suffering for O'Donoghue and other Aboriginal people. The Prime Minister, who denied genocide, declared: 'It is time we stopped this business about who was to blame for what may or may not have happened in the past.'[109] In John Howard's 'comfortable' Australia, memories were to be shelved, unless they were about positive things.

'Removed', 'stolen', 'signed away' or 'given up' by young, frightened Aboriginal mothers in the face of white bureaucratic power; the final truth for Peter Gunner, Dayne Childs, Lowitja O'Donoghue and thousands of others is that the choice of these words is irrelevant. Governments led by white men, who 'knew' what was best for black mothers, engineered the situation so that those mothers would not raise their children. They thought they were giving their children a better life. They thought they were rescuing them from depravity. They thought Aboriginal people, especially women, were inferior and their views were of no account. They thought separation would create a brave new Australia, where all people were white and the same, and Aboriginality was washed away from the 'Australian Way of Life'. The fact that decision-makers thought all these things can be shown from the historical record. By stealing, by coerced consent and, in some cases, willing consent, Aboriginal children, deemed of mixed descent, were denied parental nurturing and often the proper 'duty of care' from the State that oversaw and encouraged their separation. Few of them learned how to be parents in state institutions and some even experienced abuse. Thus the cycle of misery descended to the next generation and the next. Profound bewilderment—even self-destruction—resulted in the minds of Dayne Childs and others about why it had happened. This is the ongoing legacy of removal.

There have been a few gains in this sorry business. In 2006 the Tasmanian government apologised and instituted a compensation scheme whereby those removed—or if deceased—their children, could receive $5000 or $20,000 maximum per family. Other states rejected the idea. In August 2007, in the first case of its kind which took nine years to resolve, the South Australian Supreme Court awarded Bruce Trevorrow $525,000 for being removed from his mother in 1957 when aged 13 months.[110]

It is an issue over which the Coalition government led by John Howard never apologised. Since 1997, many Australians, the powerful and the not-so-powerful, wanted him to do so as his government was a successor government to those which separated children from their families. Churches, trade unions, police departments and state governments have apologised; in annual 'Sorry Days' since 1997, tens of thousands of Australians have done so. But Prime Minister Howard steadfastly refused in an official capacity. Commentators pondered his reasons. Was it prejudice, racism, insensitivity, a fear of compensation claims?

Howard did actually make a vague personal apology at the 30th-anniversary conference of the 1967 Referendum in May 1997, saying: 'personally, I feel deep sorrow for those of my fellow Australians who suffered injustices under the practices of past generations towards indigenous peoples'. Delegates were unmoved. As Howard unwisely went on to defend his Wik 'ten-point plan', hundreds of Aboriginal delegates yelled abuse and turned their backs on the remainder of his speech.[111] His expression of regret and his determination in the face of such pressure were admired by the 43 per cent of Australians who supported him for not apologising in a poll in November 2000.[112] His only concession, after a year of wrangling with the National Sorry Day Committee, was to agree in June 2003 to permit a memorial to be built in Reconciliation Place, Canberra. The wrangle was over the words 'stolen generation', but the Committee said this was non-negotiable and the government uncharacteristically relented.[113]

Prime Minister Howard and the hardliners of his party denied the 'stolen generation' and yearned for the assimilation policy of the 1950s. Distrusting Aboriginal culture, they claimed Aboriginal autonomy had failed.[114] *Quadrant*, and a new 'think tank' devoted to Indigenous issues called the Bennelong Society, launched in May 2001 and headed by John Herron, both promoted this view. Peter Howson in *Quadrant* overlooked successful Aboriginal communities to highlight the economic problems, poor education and domestic violence evident in some others, to assert a general state of chaos. He claimed, with gross exaggeration, the existence of a 'state of barbarism which is now ubiquitous in every remote Aboriginal community in Australia', and paralleled this to the alleged savagery of the state of nature asserted by the seventeenth-century English philosopher Thomas Hobbes in his *Leviathan* (1651). Howson quoted Hobbes, who concluded that in a state of nature, marked by no arts, no letters, no account of time, 'the life of man, (is) solitary, poore, nasty, brutish, and short'. Howson concluded 'Australian civilisation' had more to offer than the hunter-gatherer ways of their forebears: 'The key to participation in this civilisation is becoming absorbed in the mores of that civilisation; in manners, in going to school, in reading and writing English, in carrying out the responsibilities of a job, in soberness and in the enjoyment of the unrivalled pleasures of domestic life.'[115]

The subtext was the same as the 1950s or even the 1850s: the successful Aboriginal person was the Europeanised one. It was the Civilising Mission in late twentieth century guise. Education, employment, sobriety and good health are extremely vital to modern life but they do not have to come at the cost of Aboriginality, or necessarily, by moving from one's homeland.

The Culture Wars became the History Wars. John Howard, who grew up in the 1940s, the twilight years of British Australia, claimed that Australia's past has been unnecessarily blackened by many recent historians, who dwelt on the negatives and obscure the positive legacies of Australia's European heritage. He followed the lead of Geoffrey Blainey, who termed such writing 'black-armband history'. Howard took the view with Aboriginal matters that we should forget the past and look to the future.[116] However, he was always happy to dwell on and celebrate Australia's past white glories, such as Anzac, Federation, or Don Bradman.

New Right assimilationists attacked so-called 'black armband' accounts of frontier violence written by historians over the previous 30 years. Keith Windschuttle, a novice to Aboriginal history, led a vitriolic attack, claiming historians had 'fabricated' frontier history.[117] The 'History Wars' raged white-hot for five years at great personal cost, as some on both sides experienced extraordinary abuse. It led to millions of words in the press, history journals and books; claims and counter-claims of plagiarism; and attempts to embarrass by hoaxes. It still simmers. Those wishing to revisit this bitter debate can be guided by Stuart Macintyre and Anna Clark's *The History Wars* (2003), Bain Attwood's *Telling the Truth about Aboriginal History* (2005), and compilations of often tendentious opinion edited by Robert Manne, *Whitewash* (2003), and John Dawson, *Washout* (2004).

RECONCILIATION AND 'CORROBOREE 2000'

The Council for Aboriginal Reconciliation (CAR) proceeded to a planned Declaration of Reconciliation by 2000, which was sorely needed, but unlikely amid such vitriol. The Howard government proved unhelpful, in November 1997 edging out its widely respected head, Patrick Dodson, noted for his full beard and bush hat. The CAR had developed significant grassroots support which was not to be denied. This was aided by former Prime Minister Malcolm Fraser, a social justice advocate, and that great Australian, Sir William Deane, who used his term as Governor-General to promote the cause at every opportunity. Both showed the statesmanship their Prime Minister lacked. In his Australia Day speech of 1998, Sir William called for 'a true, just and lasting reconciliation by 2001 . . . if we are not to enter our second century as a diminished nation'.[118] In November 1998, Howard called for an inspirational document minus an apology. By 1999, Council member and author Jackie Huggins, together with celebrated author David Malouf, created a draft document with an indirect apology.[119] Arguments for and against making an apology raged, as the Council, led by Evelyn Scott, talked up Reconciliation.

Since Corroboree 2000 reconciliation has burgeoned, giving a new spirit to Australia Day. Here are some unidentified young Indigenous Australian performers in the Botanic Gardens, Sydney, on Australia Day in 2009. COURTESY OF PHOTOGRAPHER DAVID BROOME.

Hopes were raised in a concurrent debate over the wording of a proposed preamble to the Constitution to be put to a referendum. This was resolved in August when Aboriginal Democrat Senator Aden Ridgeway negotiated a compromise with John Howard, who wanted his own version (co-authored with poet Les Murray) to be accepted.[120] In early 2000, John Howard dug his heels in over an apology and baulked at a December 2000 document. An opinion poll commissioned by the CAR in February revealed that 80 per cent of Australians supported the reconciliation process and 84 per cent a recognition of Aboriginal people as the original owners. However, only 40 per cent supported an apology, which Howard was quick to point out. Allegations arose in parliament in April that the government had imposed other questions on the poll to elicit negative outcomes. Thus in the same poll, 80 per cent believed there was too little to show for moneys spent in Aboriginal affairs and 61 per cent believed Aboriginal people received too much special assistance; the implication being compensation for the 'stolen children' was out.[121]

The Declaration of Reconciliation was the product of compromise. However, in as many words as Abraham Lincoln's Gettysburg Address, it retained a nobility of aspiration and hope that fell not too far short of Lincoln's inspirational moment. The Declaration managed to retain an indirect apology and reference to customary law and self-determination. Howard opposed parts of it, even though he was to receive it on behalf of the government at 'Corroboree 2000' in May.[122] Charles Perkins, fiery as ever, demanded that Howard resign as he had 'blown reconciliation out of the water'.[123] Indigenous leaders met with Howard and gained his support at least for the process of reconciliation, but no apology. However, Prime Minister Howard refused to join the Reconciliation March across the Harbour Bridge on 28 May with over 200,000 Sydneysiders, claiming it was a people's march. He also forbade his cabinet ministers from marching. Similar large marches occurred around the country, revealing grassroots support for a better future with Aboriginal and Torres Strait Islander people.

In his speech at 'Corroboree 2000', Social Justice Commissioner Mick Dodson (brother of Pat) expressed honest anger. Dodson outlined the discrimination, the removals of children and the forced assimilation that occurred in his own lifetime, which also happened to be in the lifetime of the Prime Minister. His point to Howard sitting uncomfortably beside him on the dais, was that these things were not in the past but in a present inhabited by Howard and all living Australians, and for which they were responsible. He added very pointedly: 'let us smash the mould of assimilation that afflicts my generation of politicians'.[124] In his following speech, Geoff Clark, head of ATSIC, called for a treaty, as the unfinished business of reconciliation. Clark argued: 'true reconciliation means recognising we possess distinct rights. They arise from our status as first peoples, our relationships with our territories and waters, and our own systems of law and governance. Our right to self-determination is a core principle.' Howard told a press conference, as he did fifteen years earlier, 'a nation, an undivided united nation, does not make a treaty with itself'.[125]

The Sydney Olympics created strong good-will as the nation basked in the adulation of the world over the staging of this big event, and in particular the opening ceremony with its significant Indigenous themes. Most notable was the lighting of the Olympic Cauldron by Cathy Freeman in a moment that thrilled the world. She then went on to win the 400 metres gold medal. At Monte Carlo in May 2001, she was voted World Sportswoman for the Year 2000 and in June was one of ten to receive the Silver Olympic Order for achievements of 'remarkable merit'. Many Aboriginal people continued to express their talent through sport. Top End and Tiwi Island footballers now attracted the eye of talent scouts. Aboriginal footballers formed over 10 per cent of the AFL list by the early part of the twenty-first century, exciting fans across the country. A former Rugby League star, Anthony 'the man' Mundine began boxing in 2000 and won the world middleweight title in 2003. He also made music recordings and caused controversy with outspoken political comment following his conversion to Islam.

It was fitting that Charles Perkins, who broke through racism because of his ability in soccer, saw Freeman's victory before he died aged 64 in October 2000. A flood of tributes and a state funeral in Sydney farewelled this Arrernte man and top public servant, who achieved more than any other person to change the face of modern Aboriginal Australia.[126] In a November poll, support for reconciliation was now 78 per cent and 53 per cent favoured a treaty, up from 43 per cent at the time of 'Corroboree 2000'.[127] Michelle Grattan's book *Reconciliation: Essays on Australian Reconciliation* (2000) contains diverse perspectives on this movement. The CAR backed future negotiations for a treaty in its final report in December 2000, before handing over to a new body, Reconciliation Australia. The Prime Minister mellowed his support for reconciliation but, ever the pragmatic politician, called for 'practical reconciliation' to end Aboriginal material disadvantage.[128] Just what that would mean was soon to unfold.

14

CRISIS, INTERVENTION
AND APOLOGY

In June 2007, the Howard government began a dramatic intervention into the lives of Aboriginal people in the Northern Territory. It was said to be in response to a new crisis within Aboriginal communities that required unprecedented action. However, the new 'crisis' was in the Coalition's electoral position, as it was facing defeat after four terms in office. The alleged new crisis within Aboriginal communities in the Territory was actually at least twenty years old, but had been largely ignored by successive governments, despite many warnings. Howard's solution of a dramatic, blanket and unilateral intervention to make him appear a decisive and caring leader was controversial. However, such action was not actually new, as it implemented one more round of close management aimed at assimilation, similar to that imposed on Aboriginal people since colonial times. What *was* new was that it was again being tried—despite the failures of previous imposed programs.

ABORIGINAL COMMUNITIES AND THEIR SUCCESSES

The needs of Indigenous Australians increased as their numbers rose in census data at the turn of the twenty-first century: 265,371 in 1991; 352,970 in 1996; 410,003 in 2001; 455,028 in 2006. Under-counting led the Bureau of Census and Statistics to estimate there were almost 520,000 Indigenous people in Australia in 2006: 2.5 per cent of the population. Ninety per cent were Aboriginal, 6 per cent Torres Strait Islander and the rest of mixed Aboriginal–Islander descent.

The number of Indigenous people in Australia jumped an amazing 33 per cent from the 1991 to 1996 census, with increases of 16 per cent and 10 per cent between the later censuses of 2001 and 2006. These rapid increases were caused by three factors. First, the birth rate of the Indigenous population was strong, being currently 2.1 births per Indigenous female, compared to 1.7 for other Australian women. Second, identification as Indigenous is almost universal among those with a claim due to growing pride in Indigenous identity in the face of stronger community acceptance. Also, most children of mixed Indigenous and non-Indigenous couples identify themselves as Indigenous and the percentage of intermixed couples is increasing. Of couples with an Aboriginal member, 46 per cent were mixed in 1986, 51 per cent in 1991, and 69 per cent in 2001.[1] This bodes well for ongoing reconciliation. Third, in country and remote areas, in particular, under-counting is a problem and each census has varying success at obtaining an accurate count. In 2008 it was estimated by John Taylor and Nicholas Biddle of an Australian National University team that in the remote Aboriginal communities in the Northern Territory and north-west, population under-counting was between 19 and 24 per cent.[2]

The growing desire to identify as Indigenous has enriched the lives of many individuals. In 2007 Jonathon Griffin, a young ruckman at the Adelaide Football Club, confided in mates about his Aboriginal heritage, after they met his darker-skinned grandfather. He had been shy and diffident about it, especially being so fair-skinned himself, but once he 'came out' he felt a 'sense of belonging'. Answers to questions began to flow, especially once he discovered his Bibbulman forebears were good footballers. In February 2009, Griffin proudly lined up with the Indigenous All-stars in the biennial match in Darwin against an AFL club—which they won, beating Griffin's regular club Adelaide.[3]

However, the desire to identify has led to small numbers of fraudulent claims, especially in Southern Australia. Pallawah activist Michael Mansell challenged the Aboriginality of eleven Tasmanian Aboriginal and Torres Strait Islander Commission (ATSIC) candidates in the Federal Court in 1998, which barred the candidacy of two. He made the astonishing allegation that of the 16,000 Tasmanians claiming Aboriginal ancestry in the 1996 census, almost 10,000 lacked any Aboriginal connection.[4] ATSIC Tasmanian commissioner Ted Stevenson believed some wanted dollars in a 'track-back-a-black' racket, which would reduce resources to people who were genuinely Indigenous.[5] However, some simply wanted to identify with what they admire: an ATSIC commissioner for Victoria, who had changed his name to give it an Aboriginal ring, was asked to resign in 1995 because he was not Indigenous.[6] The label 'Aboriginal' clearly has lost its former sense of otherness for many Australians.

By the early twentieth century, the well-being of Indigenous people, especially those in remote locations, was still below that of other Australians and little better than a decade or so earlier. The 2007 report *Overcoming Indigenous Disadvantage in Australia*, by Garry Banks, Chairperson of the Productivity Commission of Australia, found that Indigenous disadvantage was 'inter-generational'. Their unemployment rate was four times that of other Australians, and their labour force participation rate only three-quarters of other Australians. They were still twice as likely to be in the lowest income bracket. Their rates of chronic disease, diabetes and kidney illness were three times higher than other Australians and their life expectancy seventeen years lower, with those in their middle years dying at a rate six times that of other Australians. Their educational achievements were below other Australians, lagging in reading, writing and numeracy from grade three, with an increasing gap as schooling progressed. Their completion rate from secondary school was half that of other Australians. A quarter of Indigenous people lived in overcrowded housing, increasing to almost two-thirds in remote areas. After adjusting for age differences between Indigenous and other Australians, Indigenous adults were thirteen times more likely to be imprisoned and youths 23 times more likely to be in detention.[7]

Aboriginal disadvantage is stark, but given Indigenous people make up less than 3 per cent of the Australian population, it is a challenge within the capability of an affluent country to meet. Difficulties are created by the fact that 50 per cent of Indigenous Australians, as opposed to 10 per cent of other Australians, live outside the capital and regional centres, where services are poorer. Also, the Indigenous population is younger than the total population, creating greater needs for early childhood, education and housing services. However, disadvantage is not universal and many community success stories exist.

In 1991 the Jawoyn people at Katherine in the Northern Territory gained control of their lives. In that year they stopped the mining of Coronation Hill, a sacred site, but negotiated a goldmining agreement for the non-sacred Mt Todd area, exchanging their native title claim for employment and training opportunities at the mine. Their organisation, the Jawoyn Association Aboriginal Corporation (JAAC) based in the Katherine region, won the second National Indigenous Business Award in 1995. The JAAC, with good management, grew from a small business to a turnover of $10 million in just five years. The association, chaired by Robert Lee, is the principal ore extraction contractor to the Mt Todd goldmine, runs caravan parks, operates Nitmiluk tours to the

Katherine Gorge, and is paid royalties by the Northern Territory government and tourist operators on the Gorge.[8]

Indigenous governance awards were initiated by Reconciliation Australia with the support of BHP Billiton in 2005. The first winner was the Koori Heritage Trust in Melbourne, which is an overarching cultural body for Aboriginal Victorians. In 2006 Gannambarra Enterprises, which runs a pottery and car-detailing enterprise in Wagga Wagga, won the award. In 2008 there were 37 nominees in two categories: under and over ten years of operation. The eight finalists in both categories included several cultural centres, a theatre group, a credit union, a health centre and a service for early intervention for Indigenous youth at risk. In reality, all nominees were winners. However, the judges chose Warakurna Artists, which was established in 2004 to support the creation and sale of Indigenous art of Western Australia, and the Traditional Credit Union, created at Milingibi in 1994, which now provides services to 13,000 Indigenous members across twelve branches in the Northern Territory.[9]

At Mooroopna in Central Victoria, the Rumbalara Football and Netball Club maintains a proud Yorta Yorta tradition of sports performance since the 1890s when Cummeragunja teams won district sporting competitions. Many Indigenous youth develop confidence and skills through membership of this dynamic club, which continues to win pennants in regional leagues despite residual prejudice against the club. In 2005 the club partnered with the University of Melbourne to form the Academy of Sport, Health and Education (ASHE). The program offered three levels of certificates in sport and community recreation, followed by employment placement programs and professional development courses. Partnerships have been developed with the ANZ Bank, Microsoft and Victorian government departments. George Briggs found that the ASHE program 'gave me confidence to try new things because I was exposed to new things every day I went to ASHE'. In 2007 he enrolled in a Bachelor of Education degree.[10] Rumbalara Aboriginal Cooperative, the mother organisation of the club, also runs successful community programs in health and elderly care.

Harry and John Watson lead the Jardmadangah Burra Aboriginal Corporation in the Kimberley, formed by the Nyikina people of the Fitzroy River and the Mangala people of the Great Sandy Desert country. They run the 150,000 hectare Mount Anderson Station bought by the Aboriginal Land Commission in 1983. This community of 80 people contains a primary school, clinic, community store, community arts centre, and runs the Nyikina Cattle Company and recently the Purely Unreal Kimberley Dreamtime Adventure Tours. The community enjoys fresh and frozen foods fortnightly from Derby 150 kilometres away and locally killed beef and bush foods, including fish from the nearby Fitzroy River. Until recently the Community Development Employment Project (CDEP) supplemented incomes. Some of the young people receive TAFE training in Broome; others visit town for a break. Their land ownership, the alcohol-free rule, the ordered buildings with air-conditioned housing, the schooling with breakfast program, and the confident stance of the people as they show outsiders their land and culture reveal a people in control of their situation.[11] There are

Harry Watson, community leader of Jardmadangah, Mount Anderson, Kimberley.
COURTESY OF LEON MEAD AND JARDMADANGAH BURRA ABORIGINAL CORPORATION.

many such Jardmadangahs around Australia, which will feature in Indigenous Business and Governance awards in the future.

Other remote community outstations, also called homelands, continued to manage with a combination of bush tucker, CDEP payments and income from art and craft work.[12] The Guugu Yimidhirr people of Hopevale, Cooktown, formed a partnership with the Body Shop lifestyle chain to supply tea-tree oil for cosmetics from an outstation, and the first harvest was made in 1996. The agreement included making the area 'green', as the community had just gained the return of the Lakefield National Park from the Queensland Aboriginal Land Tribunal. Other communities ran cattle stations and, increasingly in the Top End, ecotourism businesses, as surveys showed that 70 per cent of in-bound tourists wanted to experience Indigenous cultures. In Queensland, thousands of tourists visited Pajinka Wilderness Lodge, run by the Injinoo in northern Cape York, and the Aboriginal Dreamtime Centre in Rockhampton. Tens of thousands visited yearly the Tjapukai Aboriginal Cultural Park in Cairns, which emerged from the Tjapukai Dance Theatre begun a decade earlier. The $9 million Cultural Park is 51 per cent owned by the community and the great majority of its 120 staff are Tjapukai. It exhibits an ancient tradition in a spectacular sound-and-light-show format.[13]

There are hundreds of commercial and cultural ventures across Australia that build Indigenous pride and esteem. The problem is how to promote development on Aboriginal lands, especially as northern Aboriginal population growth is concentrated there. The conservative view is that the people must leave communities and move into the market economy—and some have done that—but many do not wish to do so. Academic Jon Altman points out that communities resident on Aboriginal lands are in reality a mixed economy: a small market economy, often just a store; a state economy composed of government services and CDEP payments; and a customary one of bush food and craft industry, which is not quantified in monetary terms. One issue is how to ascribe a monetary value to the latter, which has value for land care, biodiversity and the environment generally. Indeed, if conservation and species diversity is valued, Aboriginal communities might be paid to do such work, offsetting the costs to government of remote living.[14] Barrie Pittock, former CSIRO scientist, has also suggested that renewable energy, solar, wind power, tidal installations and geothermal, which is abundant on Aboriginal lands, might be developed in partnership with business to feed into an expanded national direct power electrical grid.[15]

COMMUNITIES IN CRISIS

These recent successes have won through despite fierce obstacles, for colonialism created 'have-nots' by expropriating the resources of first Australians. There is no doubt there are some Aboriginal communities which are in grave difficulties today from the fallout of colonial dispossession: a loss of control over their lives; funding shortages; severe infrastructure problems; growing populations; and leadership difficulties. However, it should be realised that the way such communities catch the headlines forms part of a long series of moral panics created by settler Australians, concerning the health and morality of Indigenous Australians—perceived as Other. Those currently most talked about are in remote areas, which comprise a minority of Aboriginal communities. Indeed, only 15 per cent of Indigenous people live in remote townships in the north and 8 per cent in remote outstations. The townships, not outstations, experience the major problems. Thus those communities that hit the headlines are drawn from less than 15 per cent of all Indigenous Australians. This is not to say that the other three-quarters are without difficulty, but it illustrates how we need to keep the following discussion in perspective.

This situation of communities in crisis is not new. Researchers Paul Wilson and Bill Rosser noted violence and dysfunction on some Queensland reserves in the 1970s, as did black activist Kevin Gilbert on New South Wales reserves. The Royal Commission into Aboriginal Deaths in Custody (RCIADIC) inquiry in the late 1980s found inordinate drinking and substance abuse in some communities, which led to violence and occasionally death. The commission's regional reports for the Northern Territory and Queensland contained much about Aboriginal drinking cultures. Information prepared for the Queensland report concluded that, while there was much retention of traditional knowledge concerning leadership and authority, in some communities it was no longer applied, due to the impact of missions and colonial administration, and new structures had not gained sufficient authority to curb antisocial behaviour.[16] While violence and dysfunction is multi-causal, the tendency has always been to blame the victim rather than the colonial condition. But some personal responsibility should also be shouldered for antisocial or violent behaviour. In many communities, Aboriginal people do not ascribe sufficient shame to drunken behaviour, or hold people accountable for their actions when drunk, describing them simply as 'mad'.[17] This is clearly an unhelpful attitude in terms of modifying behaviour.

Numerous studies and inquiries have revealed dysfunction among some remote Aboriginal communities. David McKnight, an anthropologist who did fieldwork on Mornington Island in the Gulf of Carpentaria in the late 1960s, noted daily arguments and fights, and most months a melee of a hundred people fighting. Some were mock or controlled disputes, others were not. While McKnight observed no deaths in the three years, there were many cuts, bruises and broken bones. He also saw fighting on other reserves. This was not new, dating from traditional times, and was mostly acted out for traditional reasons. However, new reasons had emerged. The Civilising Mission and the assimilation policy pushed people together in conveniently large administrative units. At Mornington Island, the community, originally a Presbyterian mission, became a super camp of all the Lardil, plus other groups, totalling 600 by the 1960s. McKnight argued that each person had 600 relationships, but through the kinship system, 359,400 kin relations enmesh the community in total. In a traditional camp of 30 people, total relationships would be merely 870. When groups of 30 people went camping on holidays, McKnight observed there was rarely conflict as the groups were small, and they were people of the one clan. Thus large concentrations of mixed tribal and clan groups at Mornington Island, created by colonial policy, increased the 'social burden', leading to conflict.[18] Other large settlements were prone to such dysfunction, especially those where large numbers of diverse tribal groups were placed after removal from their home country, notably Palm Island, Cherbourg and Woorabinda.

Palm Island, the penal island where rebellious Aboriginal people from other parts of Queensland were placed, experienced magnified problems of under-development, violence and despair. Its population of over 3000 by the 1990s came from several rival cultural–linguistic groups. It suffered from drastic underemployment, a severe housing shortage, and inadequate water, sewerage and electricity services. The Queensland government increased funding in 1995, but the fourfold home-building increase that year (to 32 houses) still left a five-year building backlog, even if this higher rate was sustained.[19] While only a quarter to a third of the island's population consumed alcohol, all were affected by the violence and ill health that stemmed from heavy alcohol abuse. About 90 per cent of all crimes were alcohol-related, and most violence was domestic in nature. Rape was drastically under-reported and violence against women was a daily occurrence. Professor Paul Wilson, who researched the island's crime rate in the 1980s and found it the highest in the developed world, saw no change in 1994, commenting: 'It is one of the most depressing sagas in my experience of crime. No longer is it just a black issue, it is an issue of people dying.' Researcher James Barber commented that 'intoxication provides a brief, albeit artificial, experience of what has been denied Palm Islanders throughout their history . . .

a desire for freedom.' However, freedom has its responsibilities.[20] When nine women ran for the island's council in 1994, on a ticket to close the 'wet' canteen, they were defeated.

Youth and drug abuse problems, essentially among men, existed on other large or mixed Queensland settlements, including Woorabinda, Cherbourg and Doomadgee, each with a population of close to 1000 people. In December 1996, Woorabinda was in the news, following a mass arrest and strip search by 21 police of 65 Woorabinda residents for unpaid parking and minor crime fines. This caused Aboriginal anger at over-policing and a call for a police apology. Conditions at the settlement were glimpsed during the incident as Nora Fitzgibbon, a Catholic Sister of Mercy at the 1500-strong community, stated: 'there are no future prospects for the people. Unless we build some employment base for this community, the people have nowhere to go.' Fitzgibbon added that unemployment was at 90 per cent, education standards were low, and truancy rates were at around 70 per cent. 'The spirit of the people was so low.'[21] A community submission a month earlier pleaded: 'we are sick and tired of training programs, which lead nowhere'.[22]

Despair ran deep in remote Aboriginal Australia, where unemployment, lack of education, alcohol abuse and related domestic violence were and remain key problems. These are legacies of colonialism. However, they are also now issues of personal and community discipline which must be faced. These are difficult issues to discuss, as they are also key white racist stereotypes of blacks. How can these be faced without strengthening old myths? This has been particularly the case since politics were racialised by land rights in the post-Mabo era, the History Wars, and the Howard government's use of race issues to drive a wedge between voters.

SUBSTANCE ABUSE AND DOMESTIC VIOLENCE

It should be noted at the outset that recent data from the Australian Bureau of Statistics revealed that proportionately fewer Aboriginal Australians drank alcohol than other Australians. This has been a long-term trend. A National Drug Survey report found in 1994 that, while 45 per cent of the general population were regular drinkers, only 33 per cent of Indigenous people were. However, whereas only 12 per cent of the total Australian drinkers consumed to harmful levels, 80 per cent of Aboriginal drinkers did so. While most Aboriginal people abstained, most of the minority of Aboriginal people who drank, did so heavily and publicly. This often resulted in violence to family and the wider community.

In the early 1990s, Aboriginal people sustained seventeen times the hospitalisation rates of other Australians from interpersonal violence.[23]

David McKnight analyses alcohol abuse in *From Hunting to Drinking* (2002). His study is based on five years of fieldwork at Mornington Island and Doomadgee from 1985. The residents were first able to drink in 1976 and did so out of conviviality and because it is the Australian way. They began to drink more heavily out of boredom and because it expressed the frustrations they experienced of being 'have-nots', without much power under a quasi-colonial rule. Drinking soon consumed almost half their income, as drinkers on average had five cans a day, a medically harmful level. McKnight found a quarter of hospital cases were alcohol-related, with many people suffering from diabetes, heart disease, kidney and liver failure. Since drinking rights were granted in 1976 there have been fifteen homicides, almost all alcohol-related, whereas in the previous 60 years there was one. The homicide rate was 25 times that of Queensland generally. There have been 26 suicides since 1983, 22 of them from 1996 to 2000—34 times the Queensland rate. There have also been eighteen attempted suicides since drinking began. McKnight commented, 'men and women are literally drinking themselves to death and in the process community life is destroyed'.[24]

In 1978 the Queensland government evaded federal control of the former missions of Mornington Island and Aurukun by gazetting it as a shire, which by nature continued to give it full access to a liquor canteen. Since then, the community's Council has been run by Aboriginal people, who are themselves heavy drinkers interested in maintaining access to beer. The Council is advised by white bureaucrats who also have no interest in reducing drinking. Indeed, the shire now owns the canteen and survives on its liquor profits, which come from the misery of the people. Yet it is claimed the canteen's profits are for the 'good of the community'. The government could have closed the canteen, if it chose, but has not. At Doomadgee a new non-drinking female-dominated Council in 1991 banned alcohol sales. But this was reversed in 1995 by male Aboriginal councillors, much to the anguish of female residents.[25] McKnight, after much thought, was dismal about any solution for a group whose world and conversation now surrounds the canteen, and concluded that if they ever did stop drinking they 'will discover that only a dim shadow of their traditional culture remains'.[26]

However, other Aboriginal communities have banned or modified the sale of alcohol on community property. The Human Rights and Equal Opportunity Commission (HREOC) in July 1995 upheld this in a landmark decision, when it ruled that individual rights to buy alcohol had to give way to community desires for restriction.[27] Of course, community decisions could be overturned, as at Doomadgee, with a change in leadership. Bans also do not stop sly grog selling, sometimes by the white taxi driver from a nearby town. Nor do they stop drinking in town. Alice Springs, which is surrounded by 'dry' Aboriginal communities, has an alcohol problem that caused ATSIC Deputy Chairperson Charles Perkins to despair in late 1995: 'it's just out of control. It's something we have to face up to—it's not safe to be in Alice Springs at the moment ... Alcohol is affecting the economy, it's affecting the lifestyle, it heightened race relations tensions.'[28] He added that Alice Springs had 70 liquor outlets, perhaps more per capita than any other place in Australia.

Perkins applauded the Julalikari Aboriginal Council of Tennant Creek led by David Curtis, which devised another strategy. The council convinced the Northern Territory Liquor Commission in March 1996 to restrict sales permanently in Tennant Creek after a successful trial. All alcohol sales in hotels and outlets are banned on Thursday—social security payment day—and the sale of wine casks is limited to two-litre casks, and one per person per outlet per day. Taxi drivers are forbidden to buy alcohol for others. The local publicans were unhappy, but during the trial, police attendance at incidents and criminal damage cases fell by 50 per cent each, the number of women attending casualty declined by 58 per cent, and there was a 23 per cent fall in 'sickies' taken by the Council workforce. Sales of cask wine fell by 54 per cent and lower-strength beer was up 7 per cent. Two-thirds of the town approved of the outcomes. The Julalikari Council, which employs 200 people in a recycling project and construction business, is optimistic.[29]

The HREOC approved an Aboriginal request in 1996 that the Club Hotel in Wiluna, Western Australia, restrict sales of packaged alcohol to Aboriginal locals to 2 p.m. to 7 p.m. weekdays for a one-year trial. People were also banned from drinking spirits or wine at the hotel outside of those hours.[30] In December 1997, a ban on all sales to Aboriginal people at the Curtin Springs Hotel, near Uluru, was imposed with the support of the Pitjantjatjara communities, the HREOC and the hotel's management. The irony was the hotel's owner had agreed to this a decade before, but was taken to court by the federal government for discrimination.[31] The ending of alcohol abuse is a long road for both black and white.

Another alarming problem since the 1980s is the incidence of petrol sniffing among Aboriginal youths, especially in central and southern Australia. Social researcher Maggie Brady has shown that the practice spread in the 1970s after isolated reports of sniffing in the 1950s. It was taken up by youths on reserves, who 'share social groups' and had access to petrol supplies.[32] Petrol sniffing induces lead and hydrocarbon poisoning, which attacks the protective membrane surrounding the nerve endings of the brain, leading to anorexia, fatigue, headache, depression, hallucinations, brain impairment, lung disease and even death. Brady recorded at least 35 deaths from 1981 to 1988, but deaths recorded as due to lung diseases may disguise a higher tally. Users claim they sniff to realise personal autonomy, to resist convention and to lose weight. One remarkable finding was that former cattle station communities had a low incidence of sniffing. Brady attributes this to a productive life of pride and self-esteem, so that young people have not 'sought to express their personal autonomy through the act of petrol sniffing'.[33] In 1992 she reported that little was being done, as action had 'fallen victim to federal–state and interdepartmental rivalries'.[34]

In August 2000 there were twenty sniffers at Papunya out of a community of 300, and perhaps 250 in the communities west of Alice Springs. At Yuendumu the abusers had claimed they sniffed out of boredom. It was a situation akin to an outbreak of glue sniffing in rural Victoria at the same time by bored white youth. At Yuendumu the community rebuilt the youth centre, complete with games rooms and videos in 1999, which almost ended the sniffing. Yuendumu and other communities also developed 'drying-out' areas at outstations, which had considerable success. However, at Yuendumu a remaining small, hard-core group of sniffers smashed up the youth centre in early 2000 to assert themselves and attract more fellow-sniffers. Outback communities are hampered by a lack of funds to deal with the problem.[35] OPAL fuel, which does not give a 'high', contains the same octane as unleaded petrol (91) but has a much lower percentage of aromatics (five instead of 25). It was first produced by BP Australia in 2005. By 2006, 52 communities in the Top End had supplies with the help of a federal government grant of $20 million over four years. However, Alice Springs and many communities were still waiting for the roll-out of OPAL to reach them. Meanwhile, lives continue to be wasted, as revealed in the film *Samson & Delilah* (2009), directed by Aboriginal film-maker, Warwick Thornton.

While petrol sniffing is largely practised by youths, alcohol, which is abused mostly by adult men, more often results in domestic violence. Northern Territory Aboriginal women surveyed by Audrey Bolger in 1991 for the Commissioner of Police 'believe that abuse of alcohol is the main cause of violence in their communities and families and are adamant that the sort of violence levelled at women today has no counterpart in traditional practices'.[36] Bolger herself believed in a multiplicity of causes, particularly the misuse of male power, and the fact that violent Aboriginal men claimed falsely that their actions were sanctioned by tradition. After careful investigation, assessing all the problems of statistics and non-reportage, she believed a third of Aboriginal women were assaulted each year in the Territory.[37] Violence against Aboriginal women is a long-term, but undiscussed issue, although it was raised in RCIADIC reports in the late 1980s. The Australian Bureau of Statistics reported in 1999 that Aboriginal people were five times more likely to be attacked or threatened, while Aboriginal women suffered 45 times the rate of domestic violence and ten times the rate of death at the hands of a partner than other Australians.[38]

The issue was highlighted again in Queensland in 1998 after repeated efforts by Aboriginal women over a decade to raise awareness of domestic violence and child abuse. Mrs Jonny of Doomadgee said: 'ever since [1987] I have been to meetings we have been talking, talking about domestic violence all the time . . . I would like to see action.'[39] A Brisbane journalist, Tony Koch, took up the campaign in feature articles about a horrendous sexual assault on a seventeen-month-old Aboriginal girl at the Kowanyama community at Cape York in 1996. Her assailant, who had a history of alcohol abuse, was sentenced to life, while the girl carried physical and emotional scars. Police and Aboriginal activists called for an inquiry. Aboriginal leader Jackie Huggins likened some places to 'war zones' and linked alcohol abuse to family violence, calling alcohol 'genocidal' in its outcomes. She added: 'Aboriginal women have said to me it is good that finally the issues we have known about for years are coming out.'[40]

The Queensland government finally bowed to calls for an inquiry, and instituted an Indigenous women's taskforce headed by Aboriginal academic Boni Robertson. The taskforce found colonialism and dispossession, as well as the poor state of reserves, were central to the violence. This touched every family and led to many youth suicides, seventeen on one reserve in a year not being an isolated case. Indigenous domestic violence offences increased from 664 in 1994 to 1075 in 1998. The report found 'appalling acts of physical brutality and sexual violence are being perpetrated within some families and across Communities to a degree previously unknown in Indigenous life'.[41] Indigenous and non-Indigenous men perpetrated an almost equal proportion of attacks, while the remaining 17 per cent of attacks were pack rapes. The report recommended in general: a whole-of-government approach with Indigenous participation in decision-making; economic and social development of Aboriginal people and communities; effective policing of alcohol use and rehabilitation measures; and health, housing and educational initiatives to improve lives. In 2001, reports emerged of domestic and sexual violence and child abuse in Victoria. In May,

Aboriginal family services coordinator Sally Jo Scherger spoke out, saying: 'sexual abuse is rife and there is a type of collusion within the Koori community that is hard to break down. I'd be hard pressed to find a Koori girl in this community that hasn't been sexually abused.'[42] There was little public discussion.

However, public debate erupted about explosive rape allegations in high places, concerning Geoff Clark, the prominent Chairperson of ATSIC. In 2000 Clark avoided conviction of pack raping a cousin in 1971 due to lack of evidence. He claimed there was a political vendetta against him.[43] Certainly, his own Framlingham Aboriginal Community was bitterly divided between pro- and anti-Clark forces. In June 2001, the Melbourne *Age* sensationally published unproven allegations of rape against Clark, under a large front-page headline: 'Geoff Clark: Power and Rape', urging Clark to sue if he dared.[44] The ATSIC Board closed ranks around Clark, who claimed it was 'trial by media' and an 'anti-Aboriginal attack'. Magistrate Pat O'Shane, who had inquired into domestic violence against Aboriginal women for the New South Wales government in 1991, to the dismay of some feminists, defended Clark, saying 'a lot of women manufacture a lot of stories' about rape.[45] Evelyn Scott, former Chairperson of the Council for Aboriginal Reconciliation, tearfully confided that her three daughters had been sexually assaulted as children by a family acquaintance, while she was at work as a single mother. She called for Aboriginal women, once silent, to speak out on this human rights issue. Courageously, her son Sam Backo, a former Rugby League international, stated to her and the nation that he had also been sexually abused when seven years old by a family member.[46]

Gatjil Djerrkura, a former ATSIC chairperson, called on Clark to step aside while the matter was resolved, as did some ATSIC Board members. Others defended him and his right to stay until charged. Debate raged. Clark was found guilty in March 2003 of obstructing police in a Warrnambool hotel fracas, and the Howard government suspended him as ATSIC chairperson during his appeal. His sentence was reduced to a $750 fine in December, but the government refused to reinstate him as more clouds hung over him.[47] In August 2004, the Federal Court ruled his suspension from ATSIC was racially discriminatory. By then, both political parties signalled their intention to disband ATSIC after the coming election, a decision ATSIC took to the High Court.[48] Even though the Victoria Police declined to prosecute Clark for rape, two Aboriginal women through court action in June 2003 and January 2004 gained the right to take civil action against Clark beyond the statute of limitations, which was upheld in 2006 by the High Court. In February 2007, a jury found that Clark had twice led a pack rape against Carol Stingel in 1971. The court awarded her $20,000 in compensation and ordered Clark to pay her costs of $70,000.[49] Clark appealed the decision, which was rejected by the full bench of the Victorian Court of Appeal in December 2007.

Calls continued, both from within and outside the Aboriginal community, for action and a national approach to Aboriginal domestic violence. Brisbane journalist Tony Koch continued to discuss violence against women and children in Queensland Aboriginal communities. As pressure mounted, the Queensland government in late June 2001 announced an inquiry by Tony Fitzgerald into criminal justice processes in communities on Cape York. Noel Pearson called for some 'dry time' on reserves there, to break the cycle of alcohol abuse.[50] ICAM, the Indigenous Cultural Affairs Magazine, took up the issue on SBS Television. The ABC's *Four Corners* also aired a program in September 2001 on Aboriginal domestic and sexual violence against women and children. In the program, leaders of the Kimberley, Central Australian and Perth Aboriginal communities spoke of the suffering, life-long trauma and venereal disease caused by attacks. Ted Wilkes, Director of the Western Australian Aboriginal Health Service, stated: 'It affects all families. If you continue to abuse the women, the mothers of Aboriginal people, the future of Aboriginal people in this country is a stake.'[51]

It was a sorry time but no federal-government-initiated national action followed, unlike that on gun control after the Port Arthur massacre. The Howard government had been distracted by controversy over land rights, stolen children, the History Wars, the apology and reconciliation in its first two terms. John Howard had promised 'practical reconciliation' in 2000, by which he meant an improvement in material life—albeit through mainstream services, which smacked of an assimilationist philosophy. Little action on 'practical reconciliation' emerged amid further distractions following the extraordinary events of the second half of 2001. The World Trade Center in New York was destroyed by terrorist-controlled aircraft on 9/11 (11 September), while John Howard was in the United States. The attack made a deep impression on him. A federal election followed in November, in which the fear of terrorism and false claims about children being thrown overboard by refugee parents on the *Tampa* delivered victory to Howard.

The crisis in some Aboriginal communities deepened arguments about Aboriginal policy. Autonomy and assimilation were bandied about by Left and Right politicians. Indigenous leaders wanted to strengthen Indigenous culture and seek development, but differed about how to do it. In mid-2001, Patrick Dodson spoke in America and at home about his fear for the future of Aboriginal culture in the face of social disintegration, substance abuse, domestic violence and the results of the assimilation policies. He called for a treaty to gain agreement on how to end Aboriginal physical and cultural disintegration.[52] Aboriginal public intellectual Noel Pearson, who was on the Left on land rights, shifted to the Right on welfare dependency, which he claimed had reached 'genocidal proportions'. Unless a change occurred, said Pearson, who was now Director of the Cape York Institute for Policy and Leadership, 'we might end up with enclaves permanently illiterate, permanently outside the real economy, paralysed by drugs, kept alive with minimal government support and conveniently remote from mainstream Australia. Outside these enclaves Aboriginal Australia would be just a dark shade in the skin of part of the underclass—and a small group in the middle class.' Pearson wanted community development partnerships instead, which would be negotiated, run and responsible at the local level, with holistic (not fragmented) government support.[53] His emphasis on Aboriginal responsibility and rejection of welfare dependency caught the ear of the Prime Minister.

MAINSTREAMING

The Howard government, in its third term from 2001, began to pursue 'practical' reconciliation'. This had been Howard's 2000 response to calls for an apology. This approach eschewed a rights agenda with symbolic gestures such as apologies, treaties and bills of rights, and focused instead on improvements in services and life chances. While the latter was to be applauded, any government could pursue both—if it chose. The government's intentions were made clear as ATSIC lost control of its $1.1 billion service delivery funding in April 2003, which was placed in the hands of Aboriginal and Torres Strait Islander Services, answerable only to the Minister. Another $1.6 billion for Aboriginal programs was already under the control of government.[54] Services were not to be delivered through Aboriginal agencies, but as Howard pithily stated, 'in a mainstream way'.[55] ATSIC was under investigation before finally being abandoned in November 2004. It was replaced by a fourteen-member government-appointed advisory body, the National Indigenous Council.

'Practical reconciliation' took a new turn during the Howard government's fourth term in office from late 2004. It was inspired by the thinking of Noel Pearson, who argued for the need for Aboriginal responsibility, and sought partnerships with government and business to lift Aboriginal communities. The government soon issued radical policies to induce personal responsibility among Aboriginal people, which echoed the stress on individual and moral development in the assimilation policy of the 1950s.

Cartoonist John Spooner portrays Prime Minister John Howard's low aspirations for reconciliation. COURTESY OF JOHN SPOONER AND THE AGE.

In November 2004 'mutual obligation' was devised by bureaucrats led by Peter Shergold, Howard's top public servant. Aboriginal communities and governments would make contracts in which funding, often for basic services, would be given in return for undertakings. If these were broken, penalties would apply.[56] Home ownership strategies were soon mooted and the CDEP itself was soon under scrutiny. Programs were obliged to demonstrate whether CDEP jobs fitted into the marketplace or were just of benefit to communities. The aim was to contract some jobs to private business, such as garbage collection, and also to ensure that youths in CDEP do some TAFE training that would lead to a 'real' job.[57] In November 2006, the government scrapped the CDEP in urban areas but retained it in remote areas.

The Mulan community in the Western Desert was the first to sign a 'mutual obligation' agreement, promising to attend to their children's hygiene and school attendance in return for money for a petrol bowser. Controversy arose within Mulan, as some parents said they did all this already. Noel Pearson and Pat Dodson argued parents should be expected to do this without a benefit. Both added that such agreements undermined the concept of parental responsibilities and trivialised the concept of 'mutual obligation'. Others argued CDEP work-for-the-dole schemes, introduced at the behest of Aboriginal people in 1977, were already a form of mutual obligation and nothing more was required.[58]

'Mutual obligation' agreements were signed at other communities, including Emu Point where vegetables were to be grown in exchange for funding a crèche; Yalata, where school attendance was traded for funding a scout troop; and Bonya, where an end to littering, vandalism and use of credit was promised in return for a new community store. In April 2005 Prime Minister Howard visited Wadeye in the Territory, a sprawling reserve of 2500 people with many development problems. Community leaders caught in third-world conditions wanted to open Wadeye to participation in Australia's society and economy. By May 2005, 52 'mutual agreements' were in place.[59]

Land rights came under reconsideration as well. At Wadeye, Prime Minister Howard expressed the view that Aboriginal people should be able to aspire to owning a home and a business. 'Having title to something is the key to your sense of individuality, it's the key to your capacity to achieve and to care for your family and I don't believe Indigenous Australians should be treated differently in this respect.' Howard assumed by privileging individuality and home ownership that Aboriginal Australians were identical, culturally, to other Australians— and shared the Australian Dream. Michelle Grattan, who reported the Prime Minister's words, pointed out that the push on this came from the Northern Territory Labor government and Warren Mundine, the Indigenous National Vice-President of the ALP. They advocated voluntary 99-year leases of Aboriginal land with annual payments in return. This would allow sub-leasing for homes or businesses. Party lines on policy had become blurred in the face of radical ideas. However, David Ross, Director of the Central Land Council, said that average incomes on reserves were so low, at $9000 per year, that home ownership was beyond most people.[60] Galarrwuy Yunupingu, former head of the Northern Land Council, saw the idea of leases as an attack on Aboriginal communal title, which he believed had underpinned the flowering of Aboriginal culture and Aboriginal development in the Territory. Most careful observers believed that third-world conditions on Aboriginal communities stemmed from generations of government neglect, not communal title or Aboriginal culture.[61]

In July 2005, Noel Pearson presented his ideas to the Treasurer, Peter Costello, whom he escorted around Cape York. Pearson urged a radical scheme whereby parents who gambled or drank away family welfare payments would have them diverted to more responsible family members, such as grandmothers. Attacked as racist, as it only applied to Indigenous communities, Pearson retorted: 'I don't want to wait for reform in my communities until the rest of the country is ready to move on welfare reform.'[62]

Lowitja O'Donoghue attacked Pearson's idea as paternalism. He replied that 'in left-liberal and progressive discourse the words "patronising" and "paternalistic" have become hot buttons that stifle thought'. Pearson added he was not opposed to O'Donoghue's views, but was merely rebalancing the rights of parents and children. He pointed to the illogical situation that children can be removed from parents for abuse, but parents' income could not be managed when their unwise spending caused prolonged abuse through poor environments for their children. He rejected agreements that rewarded parents for normal parental behaviour, but supported those that 'enable us to reach families and children in great trouble'.[63] In October 2005, he addressed the Centre for Independent Studies in Sydney and stated: 'the only way to break this vicious cycle of disadvantage and dysfunction is to build capability through economic and social development based on engagement with the real economy'. Development depended on balancing communal title, which was integral to Aboriginal culture, and individual property rights, which were conducive to development.[64]

Violence and sexual abuse continued in some communities. Governments failed to act, as they had continually neglected to act since the 1980s. In June 2003, Mick Dodson addressed the National Press Club on the issue. He warned of a crisis, stating 90 per cent of Indigenous families were affected and Aboriginal women were 45 times more likely to be subjected to violence than other Australian women. In July 2003, John Howard finally held a national summit on domestic violence with fifteen prominent Aboriginal leaders. Indigenous participants concurred with Mick Dodson, who reiterated that violence and abuse of children was 'beyond comprehension'. Noel Pearson, who lamented the lack of a national policy, advocated controls on substance abuse, development and partnerships. Howard promised action.[65]

Howard visited Pearson's pilot programs at Napranum in Cape York a few weeks later. Tania Major, the youngest ATSIC councillor, and later Young Australian of the Year (2007), spoke of her community at Kowanyama, its poor record in education and health, and the sexual abuse of girls and women hidden under a 'blanket of shame'. Howard was moved and again promised action, but spoke instead of an Aboriginal credit union and real jobs.[66] A still functioning ATSIC proposed its own program against sexual abuse in late July 2003, promising a mix of education, rehabilitation programs, night patrols, and Aboriginal police aids.[67] Howard's promises took eighteen months to make any headway as the Council of Australian Governments (COAG) meeting expired in 2004 before any discussion, although a commitment was made finally in 2005. ATSIC's plan faded once it was disbanded.

In June 2006—fully three years after Howard's summit on domestic violence—the new Minister for Indigenous Affairs, Mal Brough, promised a national summit on the crisis in Aboriginal communities. Clare Martin, the Territory's Chief Minister, rejected another talk fest, and Aboriginal people again recalled inaction following the 2003 Summit. On 21 June 2006, Dr Geoff Stewart alleged on ABC's *Lateline* that a paedophile was buying sex with petrol for sniffing from the boot of a Commonwealth car at Mutitjulu near Uluru. Despite informing the Territory's child protection services, nothing was done. Stewart reported other instances of abuse and high rates of sexually transmitted diseases among young girls in some communities. The Northern Territory government, showing some decisiveness, immediately instituted an inquiry by Rex Wild QC and Pat Anderson. Brough created his own audit of communities. Three Aboriginal intellectuals who formed the Lingiari Policy Centre—Noel Pearson, Mick Dodson and Marcia Langton—urged a long-term holistic and national approach, accountable to a body like the Productivity Commission. Pearson said that so far a one-year combined federal–state government trial had only managed to tackle one community in each state, whereas 200 communities Australia-wide needed some action.[68]

At the June 2006 summit, Brough presented a take-it-or-leave-it package of $130 million over four years, involving extra police, drug rehabilitation, safe houses, a truancy unit and network of Indigenous women. State ministers baulked at the scrapping of customary law, while Marion Scrymgour, the Territory's Minster for Women's Affairs, and the only Indigenous person at the summit, attacked Brough's law-and-order approach and the neglect of underlying issues such as housing and education.[69] Again, little action followed. An academic paper delivered in August argued that Indigenous youth suicide in the Kimberley was linked to sexual abuse, further expounding the nature of the problem.[70]

In mid-June 2007, Wild and Anderson's explosive report for the Northern Territory government entitled *Little Children are Sacred* was made public. It was a comprehensive 313 pages, reflecting eight months of investigation in 45 Territory communities. Wild and Anderson predicted a looming disaster unless governments worked together over a fifteen-year period to counter a deep-seated and multidimensional problem. They made 97 recommendations, covering government services, family, health, housing, education, substance rehabilitation, the regulation of alcohol, gambling and pornography. The report reiterated that all this had been said before, but governments had failed to act. It documented a 'breakdown of peace, good order and traditional customs and laws' and an alarming amount of substance abuse, violence and sexual abuse. Wild and Anderson pointed out that the perpetrators were both Indigenous and non-Indigenous, and were only a minority of all men on those communities. The abuse did not stem from tradition as some had claimed, but from colonisation and learned behaviour from films, videos and some individuals. The abuse created a cycle of offending where the abused became the abuser.[71]

The Territory's Martin government promised action. Brough called for strong action and greater emphasis on policing, as this was 'a national emergency'. He said he had well-developed ideas that he would soon put to Cabinet. Brough felt deeply and genuinely about the issue, and had just visited Kalumburu, where elders spoke of the problem of sexual abuse at the settlement.[72] At the same time, he praised a report by Noel Pearson entitled *From Hand Out to Hand Up*, which set out the problems of passive welfare dependency and outlined his Cape York model of creating 'moral norms' of responsibility in parents by withholding welfare payments.[73]

THE NORTHERN TERRITORY EMERGENCY RESPONSE

Just two days later, on 21 June 2007, Prime Minister Howard announced 'a national emergency'—the same phrase as used by Brough—and a range of extraordinary measures to combat the sexual abuse of Indigenous children in the Territory. The impositions included a five-year control of communities by government, through managers, police and the army; the end of permits to enter Aboriginal community land; compulsory health checks for children; the quarantining of 50 per cent of all welfare payments by Centrelink to ensure payments were spent on food, with further money possibly docked for non school attendance; and forcing welfare recipients to clean homes and streets. There was also to be a six-month ban on alcohol in all Aboriginal communities and the banning of X-rated pornography. The response was heavy-handed, as the majority of innocent and well-meaning parents were treated the same as the negligent and criminal. It was also discriminatory as it only applied to Aboriginal people. The Prime Minister had brilliantly seized the moral high ground, for who did not want to protect children? Yet why did it come a full four years after Howard's summit on domestic violence in Aboriginal communities? Just six months out from an election, and at a time when the polls were moving against him, this decision made him a man of moral action. Like terrorism, domestic violence created a 'national emergency', which was electorally good for the Prime Minister.[74]

Responses were mixed, despite all commentators being in favour of some action after years of inaction. The Opposition Leader Kevin Rudd naturally fell into line, as did the government-appointed National Indigenous Council. A *Herald Sun* poll in Melbourne found 97.1 per cent support for an alcohol and pornography ban in Aboriginal communities. Readers were not asked whether they would want it imposed on themselves or what they thought of compulsory checks on health, domestic and street cleanliness, and income management. Indigenous leaders thought it authoritarian. Mick Dodson labelled it 'paternalistic', and attention to a problem eleven years overdue. Lowitja O'Donoghue commented it was 'just Brough and Howard doing their sergeant major routine'. Lyn Allison of the Democrats thought it 'an outrageous, authoritarian crackdown', and Bob Brown of the Greens termed it an inordinate 'pre-election push'. Former Prime Minster Malcolm Fraser slammed Howard for paternalism and a failure to consult. Sixty Aboriginal, community and church organisations mounted an open letter against the plan.[75]

Protesters converge in Canberra to rally against the Northern Territory Intervention, 12 February 2008. COURTESY OF LOUISE WHELAN AND THE NATIONAL LIBRARY OF AUSTRALIA (NLA.PIC-VN4491987-V).

Howard defended his plan in a speech at the Sydney Institute. Likening the situation to a 'Hobbesian nightmare' and to the devastation of Hurricane Katrina in New Orleans, he called for 'urgent action' and a 'highly prescriptive' response, one better than in the United States. 'As the generation we're supposed to save sinks further into the abyss . . . We have our Katrina, here and now. That it has unfolded more slowly and absent the hand of God should make us humbler still.'[76]

Criticism continued of what was now simply called 'the Intervention'. Muriel Bamblett, Chairperson of the Secretariat of National Aboriginal and Islander Child Care, wrote an open letter to John Howard. 'Your own "old way" of dealing with Aboriginal people is to disregard our voices. We have been trying to talk to you for years about the lack of services for health, education and child protection.'[77] Paul Briggs, a Yorta Yorta leader from Shepparton, also attacked the absence of any true dialogue between Indigenous and other Australians. He outlined the pressures of Aboriginal disadvantage and of maintaining culture against the dominance of Western culture. Briggs believed the Intervention, intended or not, had 'an aggressive subliminal message that lays all blame at the feet of Indigenous people and legitimises the view of Indigenous dependency'. Pat Turner, the former top Indigenous public servant, led a delegation to Canberra of church and Aboriginal groups. She alleged that 'the Government is using child sexual abuse as the Trojan horse to resume total control of our lands'.[78] Even Noel Pearson warned about penalising good parents in a blanket approach.

As the survey teams, including army personnel, approached Mutitjulu near Uluru, families reportedly fled, fearing their children would be taken. A community member, Mario Giuseppe, said: 'they have long memories, they remember this from years ago'. Another elder, Vince Forrester, declared 'you don't bring an army into a community. This is intimidation.'[79] Brough, a former army reservist, rejected this, saying the army was there to assist in communications and the survey teams. The Mutitjulu community met the taskforce with dignity. Soldiers played kick-to-kick football with children. Discussions ensued amid Aboriginal cynicism that the community's problems, especially their lack of basic services, had been focused around one thing: exaggerated claims of child abuse. Some felt shame, others were angry. Elder Daisy Walkabout muttered politely that government promises had all been heard before and 'might as well have been written on toilet paper'.[80]

As the surveys continued amid a shortage of doctors and police to staff the effort, the government softened its stance a little. First, it announced that others besides Indigenous Australians would face welfare quarantining or cuts if they were judged irresponsible towards their children. Second, that health checks would be voluntary and would not routinely include invasive examinations for sexual abuse. Hilary Tyler of Alice Springs reiterated the land grab claim, saying the *Little Children are Sacred* report did not mention land, and the Howard government had only taken up three of its 97 recommendations. The government also announced the end of the CDEP, which had still operated in remote areas, to end 'passive welfare' and allow Indigenous people to get 'real' jobs after education and training.[81] Many wondered where sufficient 'real jobs' were to be found in remote areas; people would have to leave reserves, which was a long-term Coalition aim. It was universally acknowledged that rapid action was needed, but many considered that the Howard government had trampled people's rights and mixed the need to protect children with its agenda to move Aboriginal communities into the mainstream. By mid-July, the Territory government and the Northern Land Council announced a legal challenge to the Intervention.[82]

In early August, the Howard government presented the House of Representatives with a 500-page bill to implement its Intervention into 73 Territory communities, requesting that it be passed within a day, and by the Senate within a week. It provided $587 million over five years, but included some tough new provisions. Aboriginal land could be taken over for five years with no guarantee of compensation on 'just terms', including the Alice Springs town camps which had defied regulation. The appeal rights of those under income management were removed. Territory courts could no longer take into account customary law when assessing bail or passing sentence. The new Act would be exempt from provisions of the Racial Discrimination Act (1975). The Labor Opposition opposed some provisions, especially the last. However, with an election imminent, and in the face of Brough's claims that it 'would not have the guts' to carry the Intervention through, Labor supported the bill. Criticism forced a one-day Senate review which pushed for compensation on 'just terms' for any land takeover. The bill was through in ten days.[83]

Within a week, the Northern Territory government announced its own response to the *Little Children are Sacred* report, with $286 million over five years to employ 220 more staff, including a children's commissioner, child protection workers, family and child specialists, family violence support workers, teachers and a permanent child-abuse taskforce. It also established an Indigenous Council to advise government. The Martin government also stated it would work with the federal Intervention.[84] It was a response clearly directed at implementing the report and preventing child abuse, which critics claimed the federal Intervention did not.

John Howard made a dramatic gesture. In a speech to the Sydney Institute in October 2007 he proposed a referendum within eighteen months, if re-elected, to recognise Indigenous Australians in the Constitution. He said he now saw the need for 'symbolic' as well as 'practical reconciliation', but he would still not issue an apology. He admitted he had struggled over reconciliation and said his personal failures were partly due to the context of his birth—although other Australians of his age had escaped their context and thought differently to him. Howard stated: 'The challenge I have faced around indigenous identity politics is in part an artefact of who I am and the time in which I grew up.' Marcia Langton graciously applauded his shift, but Lowitja O'Donoghue was cynical, saying: 'he wants to keep breaking our hearts. He has had 11 years and he has failed us.'[85] The Melbourne *Age* called it 'however heartfelt, an election face-saver'. Certainly, the Howard government on 13 September 2007, together with three other former white settler nations (the United States, New Zealand and Canada), had voted against 143 countries which adopted the United Nations Declaration on the Rights of Indigenous Peoples.

The Intervention continued to worry Indigenous communities. Harry Jakamarra Nelson told a big meeting of Warlpiri people at Yuendumu that, while they strongly supported action on child abuse, 'this intervention has hit us like a ton of bricks. There has been no consultation with us . . . We don't know what is expected of us and we really believe that our future is under threat.' Labor Member of the House of Representatives, Warren Snowden, speaking at the same meeting, said he had heard similar complaints in twenty other communities and promised to wind back parts of the Intervention if Labor was elected.[86] A month later, John Howard lost the election in a landslide victory to Kevin Rudd's Labor Party. He became only the second incumbent Australian prime minister to lose his own seat, that of Bennelong in leafy Sydney.

Labor continued the Intervention as promised, but quickly restored the CDEP. In June 2008, a year on from the Intervention, it was revealed that 773 or 65 per cent of children in 73 communities had had health checks revealing 42 cases of neglect and fourteen cases of abuse notification. Few charges had been laid. It was not quite a 'national emergency', but even one case was too many. Child welfare referrals were no higher than in previous years but an Australian Crime Commission investigation found that white truck drivers were buying sex from under-age Aboriginal girls in north-west New South Wales and other states.[87] Sixty per cent of residents had welfare payments quarantined; about 1900 CDEP jobs had gone, due to the previous government's phase-out, and only 1147 'real' jobs created. Sue Gordon, who stepped down as head of the Intervention in June 2008, said the situation was still at a critical point, and billions would need to be spent over the long term, especially in housing. She called for a revamp of service provision. It should be managed by Aboriginal people, and that it should go hand-in-hand with an end to the CDEP.[88]

After a year, the Rudd government instituted a Review Board to give a progress report on the Intervention. In late September, Aboriginal representatives from many Territory communities met at Alice Springs to urge the end of the Intervention as being harmful, non-consultative and for failing to deliver services. An *Australian* journalist published drafts of the Review Board's report, claiming they differed from the final version which was watered down. He claimed the government pressured the Board, which Jenny Macklin, Minister for Indigenous Affairs, denied.[89] The review said the Intervention could improve the lives of Aboriginal people, but its implementation had negated much of this potential good. The exemption from the Racial Discrimination Act breached human rights and 'humiliated and shamed' people, suggesting they were less worthy than other Australians. The review called for a new relationship so that government and communities could have a 'genuine engagement' over community development. It also stated that 'unmet service needs and infrastructure backlogs in remote Indigenous communities' had to be addressed 'as a matter of urgency'. Finally, it urged new efforts 'to enhance Indigenous governance' to enable communities to achieve their goals. On the controversial issues of income management, restoration of permits and the acquisition of land, it urged changes, but after an 'intermediate' transition period.[90]

In October 2008, Jenny Macklin announced that the Intervention would continue for another year. Influenced by Indigenous women at Wadeye and elsewhere who had welcomed welfare quarantining, Macklin said quarantining would also continue and might be extended to non-Indigenous people. The CDEP would also be reviewed.[91] In November 2008, the government committed $647 million to 750 new houses and 2500 refurbishments in the Territory, but insisted that communities sign long leases for land on which new housing was built to allow an independent agency to manage rent and maintenance—thus subverting the role of Aboriginal housing co-operatives.[92] By early 2009 the government had promised $4.6 billion to 'Close the Gap' in housing, health, education and other services to end the difference in life chances between Indigenous and other Australians.

In February 2009, the High Court decided by six votes to one that the Intervention was not unconstitutional. A Territory group, the Prescribed Areas People's Alliance (PAPA), immediately lodged a claim with the United Nations

Committee on the Elimination of Racial Discrimination. A spokesperson for PAPA, Barbara Shaw, said: 'my people are suffering because of these terrible racist laws. Anyone who experiences this discrimination knows it is wrong and we need urgent action. Everyday we face segregation in Centrelink and in shops because of the welfare quarantine regime. We are going hungry because of this system and my people are again being dispossessed of our land and our assets thorough discriminatory intervention powers.'[93]

The future of the Intervention is unclear, although the government assured a United Nations Committee that it would end the suspension of the Racial Discrimination Act in spring 2009.[94] However, hopes that the Intervention might end are fading. The Productivity Commission in July 2009 released its fourth biennial report on Indigenous affairs, *Overcoming Indigenous Disadvantage. Key Indicators 2009*. This detailed report, covering all social indicators, found little improvement over the past two years. On the matter of child protection it found that Australia wide between 1999 and 2008, the reported incidence of Indigenous child abuse—physical, emotional and sexual—and neglect in the Northern Territory had doubled from 16.4 to 35.3 per 1000. This massive increase to six times the non-Indigenous rate, which was 5.5, was probably due to more accurate reporting during the Intervention. Protection orders were 41 per 1000 and 5.3 per 1000 respectively. However, it is disturbing that the problem stretched beyond the Northern Territory, which also undermined the view that the Northern Territory was different and needing special intervention. The Western Australian premier Colin Barnett revealed in response to the Productivity Commission's report that extra police surveillance in the Kimberly had resulted in 500 charges being laid there for sexual abuse in the last two years. Significantly, while the rate of Indigenous children below 17 years under protection orders in the Northern Territory was 14.6 per 1000 in 2008, it was an appalling 51.9 in New South Wales and 55 per 1000 in Victoria among Indigenous children. The rate for the general population was 5.3 per 1000 children.[95]

The Productivity Commission attributes this high incidence of abuse and neglect of Indigenous children to poverty, unemployment, substance abuse, mental ill health, cultural loss and stress within the Aboriginal community. The blame must also be sheeted home to the legacy of colonialism, which has reshaped the Aboriginal family since 1788. While the Aboriginal family was never perfect—for violence and gender abuse is part of the human spectrum— colonialism has often reduced it to a tangle of confusion, anger and self-destruction. But does the fault end here? Clearly not all Aboriginal people, particularly men, are violent and abusive to women and children—otherwise the incidence of abuse would be even higher. Most men act out their protective role and most resist the corrosive forces of colonialism, poverty and despair. However, some individual Aboriginal men, along with the colonial legacy and poverty, are to blame. Governments must spend more to end poverty; governments must act to devise ways to give Aboriginal people more autonomy; but it is also time for some errant Aboriginal men to step up, to be moral beings, to be strong and find ways to shrug off this terrible shame.

There were some glimmers of hope. The government announced its intention to support the United Nations Declaration of the Rights of Indigenous Peoples (2007). The Declaration, which the previous Howard government refused to endorse in September 2007, cannot be signed in retrospect. However, the Rudd government conveyed a statement of support to the United Nations in May 2009, albeit with some qualifying statements on the Intervention, which contravenes some of the Convention's articles.[96] The Rudd government also announced it was considering a suggestion by High Court Chief Justice Robert French that the burden of proof be shifted in native title cases from claimants to states and others. Federal Attorney General Robert McClelland commented: 'if someone is the occupier of premises, you assume they have title to those premises'. He stated the government would also consider recognition of an association with land below that of native title.[97] In August 2009 the government received favourably a report to create a new Indigenous body to succeed ATSIC. It is to be a research, policy and advisory body without a service role. The report advised the new body be elected by Indigenous organisations and individuals, and that there be equal numbers of male and female members.[98]

THE APOLOGY

The election of Kevin Rudd's Labor government in November 2007 broke a number of impasses in Indigenous affairs, not least the willingness to apologise to the stolen generations. The Australian churches had done it, state governments had apologised, even the Pope followed suit, but John Howard steadfastly refused. But within three days of his win Kevin Rudd declared: 'we will say sorry'.[99]

Huge crowds converged on Parliament House in Canberra on Wednesday, 13 February 2008. Indigenous people travelled from across the country to pack into parliament and outside. Across the country, tens of thousands of Indigenous people gathered at cultural centres to view the televised coverage. Former prime ministers, but not John Howard who was absent, gathered together with Indigenous leaders. Much of the nation stopped, and tuned in, as only happens

A smoking ceremony to mark the Apology to the Stolen Generations, Parliament House, Canberra, 13 February 2008. COURTESY OF CRAIG MCKENZIE AND THE NATIONAL LIBRARY OF AUSTRALIA (NLA INT-NL39844-CM18-V).

for a Melbourne Cup race. Many wept or were deeply moved as Rudd spoke clearly and strongly:

> Today we honour the Indigenous peoples of this land, the oldest continuing cultures in human history. We reflect on their past mistreatment. We reflect in particular on the mistreatment of those who were stolen generations—this blemished chapter of our nation's history. The time has now come for the nation to turn a new page in Australia's history by righting the wrongs of the past and so moving forward with confidence to the future. We apologise for the laws and policies of successive parliaments and governments that have inflicted profound grief, suffering and loss on these our fellow Australians. We apologise especially for the removal of Aboriginal and Torres Strait Islander children from their

families, their communities and their country. For the pain, suffering and hurt of these stolen generations, their descendants and for their families left behind, we say sorry. To the mothers and the fathers, the brothers and the sisters, for the breaking up of families and communities, we say sorry. And for the indignity and degradation inflicted on a proud people and a proud culture, we say sorry . . .

Prime Minister Rudd promised a future free of injustice and inequality for Indigenous Australians, and one based on 'mutual respect, mutual resolve and mutual responsibility', in which they will be equal partners with equal opportunities.[100] In particular he promised to 'close the gap' on Indigenous housing, education, health and mortality rates. Yet he refused to consider the issue of compensation, although for how long it can be avoided is a question for the future.

The reaction from Indigenous Australians was gracious, and a dignified acceptance. Even though 36 per cent of Australians still did not agree with the need to make an apology, it created the most positive mood in Indigenous affairs in living memory. In July 2008 at Yirrkala, Prime Minister Rudd met with Galarrwuy Yunupingu and promised a Referendum on Constitutional

The crowd listening to the Apology outside Parliament House, Canberra, 13 February 2008.
COURTESY OF PHOTOGRAPHER CRAIG MCKENZIE AND THE NATIONAL LIBRARY OF AUSTRALIA (NL.INT-NL39844-CM13-V).

recognition of Indigenous Australians. Yunupingu presented him with a bark petition calling for economic independence and cultural recognition for Indigenous Australians.[101] One year on, some Indigenous Australians felt not much had happened, but others admitted Indigenous disadvantage could not be turned around quickly, and were patient. In December 2008, the government appointed Father/Professor Frank Brennan to report on whether Australia should have a bill of rights.

Mick Dodson AM was named 'Australian of the Year' in January 2009. Mick Dodson's honour is symbolic of a new mood in modern Australia. He was the eighth Indigenous Australian to win this award since it was instituted in 1960, a rate six times the expected rate for the Indigenous proportion of the population.[102] Many Australians are showing growing respect for Indigeneity in other ways. In the last decade, acknowledgement of traditional owners and their elders is made at civic and public ceremonies without demur. Aboriginal actors and personalities grace the television screen more often, and Aboriginal footballers, 10 per cent of the AFL player total, power across screens every weekend. Crowds marvel at their deeds and the old tendency to abuse is muted. Aboriginal singers like Garrumul Yunupingu entrance listeners and Aboriginal paintings continue to sell for top prices.

In myriad ways, Indigenous Australians are making their presence felt in entertainment, sport and teaching, but also there is a muted, but growing presence too, in business and the professions. Other Australians encounter Indigenous Australians as never before, normalising relations between them and raising the level of respect for difference. The fact that two-thirds of couples with an Indigenous partner are mixed relationships testifies to a powerful grassroots transformation that has been building for several decades. Despite the current problems of some Aboriginal communities facing Intervention, a spirit of reconciliation generally prevails. The true meaning of 'practical reconciliation' is not the provision of services instead of symbolic gestures, but both things at once— and Australians getting on in face-to-face meetings. A new dawn will break over Australia when Indigenous people assume positions of wider community leadership.

In a time of optimism, Indigenous leaders and their communities can again entertain the radical hope that Billibellary, the *ngurungaeta* or elder of early Melbourne, imagined: to be both Indigenous and part of the new world—forging an Indigenous way as a fully equal and accepted partner in the coming Australia.

NOTES

PROLOGUE: ENDINGS AND BEGINNINGS

1 J.H. Wooten, 'Report of the Inquiry into the Death of Malcolm Smith', *Royal Commission into Aboriginal Deaths in Custody Reports*, AGPS, Canberra, 1989.

2 A. Memmi, *The Colonizer and the Colonized*, Beacon Press, Boston, 1967; F. Fanon, *Black Skin, White Masks*, Grove Press Inc., New York, 1967.

3 P. Wolfe, 'Nation and Miscegenation: Discursive continuity in the post-Mabo era', *Social Analysis*, no. 36, October 1994, p. 99.

4 R. Broome, 'Why Use Koori?', *La Trobe Library Journal*, special issue: 'Sources for Aboriginal Studies in the State Library of Victoria', vol. 11, no. 43, Autumn 1989, p. 5.

CHAPTER 1: REFLECTIONS ON A GREAT TRADITION

1 This set of reflections is based on reading a number of texts. For further reading, see: J. Mulvaney and J. Kamminga, *The Prehistory of Australia*, Allen & Unwin, Sydney, 1999; J. Flood, *Archaeology of the Dreamtime*, Collins, Sydney, 1999; J. Flood, *The Riches of Ancient Australia*, University of Queensland Press, Brisbane, 1990; T. Flannery, 'The Fate of Empire in Low and High-energy Ecosystems', in T. Griffiths and L. Robin (eds), *Ecology and Empire: Environmental History of Settler Societies*, Melbourne University Press, Melbourne, 1997, pp. 46–59; J. Diamond, *Guns, Germs and Steel: A Short History of Everybody for the Last 13,000 Years*, Vintage, London, 1998; M. Sahlins, *Stone Age Economics* (1974), Routledge, London, 2004; H. Lourandos, *Continent of Hunter Gatherers: New Perspectives in Australian Prehistory*, Cambridge University Press, New York, 1997; C. Macknight, *The Voyage to Marege: Macassan Trepangers in Northern Australia*, Melbourne University Press, Melbourne, 1976; C. Macknight, 'Macassans and the Aboriginal Past', *Archaeology in Oceania*, vol. 21, no. 1, April 1986, pp. 69–74; J. Campbell, *Invisible Invaders: Smallpox and Other Diseases in Aboriginal Australia 1780–1880*, Melbourne University Press, Melbourne, 2002; For Lieutenant James Cook's impressions, see M. Clark (ed.), *Sources of Australian History*, Oxford University Press, London, 1957, pp. 52–4.

CHAPTER 2: THE EORA CONFRONT THE BRITISH

1 J.L. Kohen and R. Lampert, 'Hunters and Fishers in the Sydney Region', in D.J. Mulvaney and J. Peter White (eds), *Australians to 1788*, Fairfax, Syme and Weldon Associates, Sydney, 1987, pp. 342–67.

2 A. McGrath, 'The White Man's Looking Glass: Aboriginal–colonial gender relations at Port Jackson', *Australian Historical Studies*, vol. 24, no. 95, October 1990, pp. 189–206; W.E.H. Stanner, 'The History of Indifference Thus Begins', *Aboriginal History*, vol. 1, pt 1, pp. 3–26.

3 N. Baudin, *The Journal of Post Captain Nicholas Baudin*, trans. C. Cornell, Libraries Board of South Australia, Adelaide, 1974; M. Blackman (ed.), *Australian Aborigines and the French*, University of New South Wales, Sydney, 1988.

4 Cook's Instructions and his summary remarks of 23 August 1770, M. Clark (ed.), *Sources of Australian History*, Oxford University Press, London, 1957, pp. 39, 52.

5 W. Dampier, *A New Voyage around the World*, London, 1698, vol. 1, p. 462, quoted in Clark, ibid., p. 25.

6 See H. Reynolds, *The Law of the Land*, Penguin, Melbourne, 1987, chap. 1.

7 On exclusive right, see F. Huggett, *The Land Question and European Society*, Thames and Hudson, London, 1975, chap. 3; H. Reynolds, *Frontier: Aborigines, Settlers and Land*, Allen & Unwin, Sydney, 1987, pp. 182–96.

8 W.J. Jordan, *The White Man's Burden: Historical Origins of Racism in the United States*, Oxford University Press, London, 1974, chap. 1; H. White, 'The Forms of Wildness', in E. Dudley and M. Novak, *The Wild Man Within: An Image in Western Thought from the Renaissance to Romanticism*, University of Pittsburgh Press, Pittsburgh, 1972, pp. 3–38.

9 T.B. Clark, *Omai: First Polynesian Ambassador to England*, University of Hawaii Press, Honolulu, 1969.

10 M.B. and C.B. Schedvin, 'The Nomadic Tribes of Urban Britain: A prelude to Botany Bay', *Historical Studies*, vol. 18, no. 71, October 1978, pp. 254–76.

11 Phillip's instructions quoted in S. Stone, *Aborigines in White Australia: A Documentary History of Attitudes Affecting Official Policy and the Australian Aborigine, 1697–1973*, Heinemann, Melbourne, 1974, p. 19.

12 W.E.H. Stanner, 'The History of Indifference thus Begins', *Aboriginal History*, vol. 1, pt 1, pp. 18–20; I. Clendinnen, 'Spearing the Governor', *Australian Historical Studies*, no. 118, 2002, pp. 157–74.

13 W. Tench, *Sydney's First Four Years* [1789–1793], ed. L.F. Fitzhardinge, Library of Australian History, Sydney, 1979, pp. 207–15.

14 A. McGrath, 'Birthplaces' in P. Grimshaw, M. Lake, A. McGrath and M. Quartly (eds), *Creating a Nation*, McPhee Gribble, Melbourne, 1994, chap. 1.

15 J.J. Auchmuty (ed.), *The Voyage of Governor Phillip to Botany Bay*, Angus & Robertson, Sydney, 1970, p. 58.

16 Tench, *Sydney's First Four Years*, p. 280.

17 ibid., p. 281.

18 C. Turnbull, *The Black War: The Extermination of the Tasmanian Aborigines*, Sun Books, Melbourne, 1974, p. 62.

19 *Historical Records of Australia*, vol. 1, p. 500.

20 R. Broome, 'Pemulwoy', *New Dictionary of National Biography*; K. Willey, *When the Sky Fell Down: The Destruction of the Tribes of the Sydney Region 1788–1850s*, Collins, Sydney, chaps. 8–9; Macquarie's proclamation in Stone, *Aborigines in White Australia*, pp. 33–6.

21 D. Day, *Conquest: A New History of the Modern World*, HarperCollins, Sydney, 2005, pp. 1–14.

22 A. Memmi, *The Colonizer and the Colonized*, Beacon Press, Boston, 1967, pp. 52–3.

23 T. Watling quoted in B. Smith, *European Vision and the South Pacific 1768–1850*, Oxford University Press, London, 1960, p. 135.

24 Tench, *Sydney's First Four Years*, p. 294; M. Banton, 'Environmentalism', in E. Cashmore et al. (eds), *Dictionary of Race and Ethnic Relations*, Routledge, London, 1994, pp. 96–7.

25 Tench, *Sydney's First Four Years*, p. 294.

26 Auchmuty, *The Voyage of Governor Phillip to Botany Bay*, p. 79.

27 John Campbell issuing Macquarie's rules and regulations, 10 December 1814, quoted in J. Brook and J. Kohen, *The Parramatta Native Institution and the Black Town*, University of New South Wales Press, Sydney, 1991, pp. 60–2; P. van den Berghe, 'Paternalism', in Cashmore, *Dictionary of Race and Ethnic Relations*, pp. 236–7.

28 Cited in *Sydney Gazette*, 4 January 1817.

29 Cited in J. Woolmington (ed.), *Aborigines in Colonial Society, 1788–1850*, Cassell, Melbourne, 1973, p. 17.

30 Brook and Kohen, *The Parramatta Native Institution and the Black Town*, chap. 12.

31 Cited in B. Bridges, 'The Aborigines and the Land Question: New South Wales in the period of imperial responsibility', *Journal of the Royal Australian Historical Society*, vol. 56, pt 2, June 1970, p. 97.

32 N. Gunson (ed.), *Australian Reminiscences and Papers of L.E. Threlkeld, Missionary to the Aborigines 1824–1259*, Australian Institute of Aboriginal Studies, Canberra, 1974, vol. 2, p. 187. See also J. Harris, *One Blood. 200 Years of Aboriginal Encounter with Christianity: A Story of Hope*, Albatross Books, Sydney, 1990, chap. 1; R. Broome, *Aboriginal Victorians: A History since 1800*, Allen & Unwin, Sydney, chap. 3.

33 Cited in Woolmington, *Aborigines in Colonial Society*, p. 17.

34 Harris, *One Blood*, p. 72.

35 Cited in Woolmington, *Aborigines in Colonial Society*, p. 97.

36 Cited in ibid., p. 95.

37 R. Reece, *Aborigines and Colonists: Aborigines and Colonial Society in New South Wales in the 1830s and 1840s*, Sydney University Press, Sydney, 1974, pp. 6–7.

38 J. Brook, 'The Forlorn Hope: Bennelong and Yemmerrawannie go to England', *Australian Aboriginal Studies*, 2001, no. 1, pp. 36–47.

39 Cited in K.V. Smith, *King Bungaree: A Sydney Aborigine Meets the Great South Pacific Explorers, 1799–1830*, Kangaroo Press, Sydney, 1992; see also K.V. Smith, *Bennelong*, Kangaroo Press, Sydney, 2001; M. Nugent, *Botany Bay: Where Histories Meet*, Allen & Unwin, Sydney, 2005.

40 Evidence of Mahroot, in 'Report from the Select Committee on the Condition of the Aborigines', in *New South Wales Legislative Council Papers*, 1845, pp. 1–5.

41 Cited in R.H.W. Reece, 'Feasts and Blankets: The history of some early attempts to establish relations with the Aborigines of New South Wales 1814–1846', *Archaeology and Physical Anthropology in Oceania*, vol. 7, no. 3, October 1967, p. 205.

42 Cited in 'Report from the Select Committee on the Condition of the Aborigines', Q 139.

CHAPTER 3: RESISTING THE INVADERS

 1 Henry Reynolds, *The Other Side of the Frontier: An Interpretation of the Aboriginal Response to the Invasion and Settlement of Australia*, History Department, James Cook University, Townsville, 1981, chap. 1; J. Urry, 'Beyond the Frontier: European influence, Aborigines and the concept of traditional culture', *Journal of Australian Studies*, no. 5, 1979, pp. 2–16.

 2 T.L. Mitchell, *Three Expeditions into the Interior of Eastern Australia*, vol. 2, T.W. Boone, London, 1839, p. 159.

3 Cited in A.S. Kenyon, 'The Aboriginal Protectorate of Port Phillip', *The Victorian Historical Magazine*, vol. 12, no. 3, March 1928, p. 158; E.M. Curr, *Recollections of Squatting in Victoria*, Melbourne University Press, Melbourne, 1965, pp. 80–1.

4 T.H. Irving, '1850–70', in F.K. Crowley (ed.), *A New History of Australia*, Heinemann, Melbourne, 1974, p. 154.

5 R. Ward, *The Australian Legend*, Oxford University Press, London, 1959, pp. 72, 94 and 96.

6 R. Boldrewood, *Old Melbourne Memories*, Heinemann, Melbourne, 1969, p. 48.

7 A. Crosby, *Ecological Imperialism: The Biological Expansion of Europe, 900–1900*, Cambridge University Press, New York, 1985, p. 186.

8 Cited in R. Evans et al., *Exclusion, Exploitation and Extermination: Race Relations in Colonial Queensland*, Australian and New Zealand Book Co., Sydney, 1975, pp. 380–1.

9 W. Clarke in T.F. Bride (ed.), *Letters from Victorian Pioneers*, Heinemann, Melbourne, 1969, p. 279. See also H. Reynolds, 'The Other Side of the Frontier: Early Aboriginal reactions to pastoral settlement in Queensland and Northern New South Wales', *Historical Studies*, vol. 17, no. 56, April 1976, pp. 51–4.

10 Cited in R. Boldrewood, *Old Melbourne Memories*, p. 58.

11 Cited in R. Evans et al., *Exclusion, Exploitation and Extermination*, p. 30.

12 R. Broome, 'The Struggle for Australia: Aboriginal–European warfare, 1770–1930', *Australia, Two Centuries of War & Peace*, Australian War Memorial and Allen & Unwin, Sydney, 1988, pp. 97–100.

13 Cited in S. Stone (ed.), *Aborigines in White Australia*, Heinemann, Melbourne, 1974, p. 87.

14 Cited in Curr, *Recollections of Squatting in Victoria*, p. 53.

15 C. Turnbull, *Black War: The Extermination of the Tasmanian Aborigines*, pp. 39–40.

16 N. Gunson (ed.), *Australian Reminiscences and Papers of L.E. Threlkeld, Missionary to the Aborigines 1824–1859*, p. 91.

17 Cited in Gunson, *Australian Reminiscences and Papers of L.E. Threlkeld*, p. 40. See also K. Fry, *Beyond the Barrier: Class Formation in a Pastoral Society, Bathurst 1818–1848*, Crawford House Press, Bathurst, 1993, chap. 2.

18 *Van Diemen's Land. Copies of all correspondence between Lieutenant-Governor Arthur and his Majesty's Secretary of State for the Colonies on the subject of military operations lately carried out against the Aboriginal inhabitants of Van Diemen's Land*, 1831, reprinted Hobart, 1971, p. 11.

19 Cited in L. Ryan, *The Aboriginal Tasmanians*, 2nd edn, Allen & Unwin, Sydney, 1996, pp. 121–2.

20 J. Connor, 'British Frontier Warfare Logistics and the "Black Line" Van Diemen's Land, 1830' (Tasmania), *War in History*, vol. 9, no. 2, 2002, pp. 143–58.

21 Ryan, *The Aboriginal Australians*, chaps 6–8.

22 H. Reynolds, *Fate of a Free People*, Penguin, Melbourne, 1995, chap. 5.

23 H. Reynolds, 'Genocide in Tasmania', in A. Dirk Moses (ed.), *Genocide and Settler Society*, Berghahn Books, New York, 2005, p. 147. See also Reynolds, *Fate of a Free People*, chaps 2–4.

24 Cited in P. Hasluck, *Black Australians: A Survey of Native Policy in Western Australia 1829–1897*, Melbourne University Press, Melbourne, 1942, p. 48.

25 R.W.H. Reece, 'Inventing Aborigines', *Aboriginal History*, vol. 11, pt 1, 1987, pp. 14–23.

26 Cited in W. McNair and H. Rumley, *Pioneer Aboriginal Mission: The Work of Wesleyan Missionary John Smithies in the Swan River Colony, 1840–1855*, University of Western Australia Press, Perth, 1981, p. 9.

27 A. Hasluck, 'Yagan (–1833), *Australian Dictionary of Biography Online*; P. Turnbull, '"Outlawed Subjects": The procurement and scientific uses of Australia Aboriginal heads,

ca.1803–1835', *Eighteenth Century Life*, vol. 22, no. 1, 1998, pp. 156–71; *West Australian*, 17 September 2008.

28 Cited in Bride, *Letters from Victorian Pioneers*, pp. 211–12.

29 T.L. Mitchell, *Journal of an Expedition into the Interior of Tropical Australia* (1848), repr. Greenwood, New York, 1969, p. 25.

30 H. Reynolds and N. Loos, 'Aboriginal Resistance in Queensland', in *Australian Journal of Politics and History*, vol. 22, no. 2, August 1976, p. 221.

31 Cited in 'Report of the Select Committee of the Legislative Council on the Aborigines', *Votes and Proceedings of the Victorian Legislative Council, 1858–1859*, D8, p. 69; Broome, 'Struggle for Australia', pp. 112–13.

32 J. Bassett, 'The Faithful Massacre at the Broken River, 1838', *Journal of Australian Studies*, no. 24, 1989, pp. 18–34.

33 Bride, *Letters from Victorian Pioneers*, pp. 219–20.

34 *Port Phillip Gazette*, 2 June 1841.

35 A. Atkinson and M. Aveling (eds), 'At the Boundaries', *Australians 1838*, Fairfax, Syme and Weldon, Sydney, 1988, pp. 55–61; M. Sturma, 'Myall Creek and the Psychology of Mass Murder', *Journal of Australian Studies*, no. 16, May 1985, pp. 62–70.

36 Jane Lydon, '"No Moral Doubt . . .": Aboriginal evidence and the Kangaroo Creek poisoning, 1847–1849', *Aboriginal History*, vol. 20, 1996, pp. 151–75.

37 H. Meyrick, *Life in the Bush (1840–1847): A Memoir of Henry Howard Meyrick*, Thomas Nelson and Sons, London, 1849, p. 137.

38 Ian Clark, *Scars on the Landscape: A Register of Massacre Sites in Western Victoria, 1803–1859*, Aboriginal Studies Press, Canberra, 1995.

39 For the Aboriginal resistance, see M. Christie, *Aborigines in Colonial Victoria 1835–86*, Sydney University Press, Sydney, 1979, chap. 3; R.H.W. Reece, *Aborigines and Colonists*, chap. l; Bride, *Letters from Victorian Pioneers*; F. Robinson and B. York, *The Black Resistance*, Widescope, Melbourne, 1977; J. Critchett, *A Distant Field of Murder: Western District Frontiers, 1834–1848*, Melbourne University Press, Melbourne, 1990.

40 Reynolds, *The Other Side of the Frontier*, chaps 3–4; Ryan, *The Aboriginal Tasmanians*, p. 139.

41 M. Fels, *Good Men and True: The Aboriginal Police of the Port Phillip District, 1837–1853*, University of Melbourne Press, Melbourne, 1988.

42 Cited in R. Boldrewood, *Old Melbourne Memories*, p. 68.

43 For Victoria, see B. Blaskett, 'The Level of Violence: Europeans and Aborigines in Port Phillip', *Historical Studies*, vol. 19, no. 77, October 1981, p. 540; for Queensland, see J. Richard's *The Secret War: A True History of Queensland's Native Police*, University of Queensland Press, Brisbane, 2008, pp. 71–4.

44 P. Berger, *Invitation to Sociology*, Penguin, Melbourne, 1963, p. 115.

45 See especially B. Bridges, 'The Native Police Corps, Port Phillip District and Victoria 1837–1853', *Journal of the Royal Australian Historical Society*, vol. 57, part 2, June 1971, pp. 113–42; R. Evans et al., *Exclusion, Exploitation and Extermination*, chap. 4; A.J. Boyd, *Old Colonials*, Sydney University Press, Sydney, 1974, pp. 191–211.

46 Report by Rev. Threlkeld in Gunson, *Australian Reminiscences and Papers of L.E. Threlkeld*, p. 49.

47 Cited in J. Woolmington (ed.), *Aborigines in Colonial Society: 1788–1850*, Cassell, Melbourne, 1973, p. 16.

48 Cited in P. Cunningham, *Two Years in New South Wales* (1827), Libraries Board of South Australia, Adelaide, 1966, vol. 2, p. 46.

49 Neil Black to Gladstone, 9 September 1840, Neil Black Papers, State Library of Victoria, LT MS 8996.

50 Cited in Bride, *Letters from Victorian Pioneers*, p. 78.
51 Curr, *Recollections of Squatting in Victoria*, pp. 103–47; G. Jenkin, *Conquest of the Ngarrindjeri*, Rigby, Adelaide, 1979, pp. 46–50; and the many squatters' accounts of the frontier in Bride, *Letters from Victorian Pioneers*.
52 Report from the Select Committee on Aborigines (British Settlements) House of Commons, 26 June 1837, *Historical Records of Victoria*, M. Cannon (ed.), vol. 2A, pp. 61–74.
53 Cited in B. Blaskett, 'The Aboriginal Response to White Settlement in the Port Phillip District 1835–1850', M.A. thesis, University of Melbourne, 1979, p. 238.
54 See Christie, *Aborigines in Colonial Victoria 1835–86*, chaps 4 and 5; Symmons cited in Hasluck, *Black Australians*, p. 78.
55 Despatch from the Right Honourable Earl Grey, Downing Street London, 11 February 1848 to Governor Sir Charles A. Fitzroy.
56 Broome, 'Struggle for Australia', 1988, pp. 116–20; Reynolds, *The Other Side of the Frontier*, pp. 98–101; Reynolds, *Frontier: Aborigines, Settlers and Land*, Allen & Unwin, Sydney, 1987, pp. 29–30, 53.
57 K. Windschuttle, 'The Myths of Frontier Massacres in Australian History. Part II: The Fabrication of the Aboriginal Death Toll', in *Quadrant*, November 2000, p. 21; K. Windschuttle, *The Fabrication of Aboriginal History, Volume One, Van Diemen's Land, 1803–1847*, McLeay Press, Sydney, 2002.
58 B. Attwood and S.G. Foster, *Frontier Conflict: The Australia Experience*, National Museum of Australia, Canberra, 2003.
59 E. Kneebone, Notes to the Exhibition 'Bones of Contention' 2005, La Trobe University Gallery, July–August 2008.
60 Cited in A. Markus (ed.), *From the Barrel of a Gun: The Oppression of the Aborigines, 1860–1900*, Victorian Historical Association, Melbourne, 1974, p. 66.
61 Cited in C.D. Rowley, *The Destruction of Aboriginal Society*, Penguin, Melbourne, 1970, p. 158.

CHAPTER 4: CULTURAL RESISTANCE AMID DESTRUCTION

1 *South Australian Government Gazette*, 3 November 1838.
2 A. Hamilton, 'Blacks and Whites: The relationships of change', *Arena*, no. 30, 1972, p. 41.
3 B. Blaskett, 'The Aboriginal Response to White Settlement in the Port Phillip District 1835–1850', M.A. thesis, University of Melbourne, 1979, p. 188.
4 P. Read and Engineer Jack Japaljarri, 'The Price of Tobacco: The journey of the Warlmala to Wave Hill, 1928', *Aboriginal History*, vol. 2, part 2, 1978, p. 143.
5 W.E.H. Stanner, 'The Dreaming' in *White Man Got No Dreaming: Essays 1938–1973*, Australian National University Press, Canberra, 1979, pp. 48–9.
6 E.M. Curr, *Recollections of Squatting in Victoria*, Melbourne University Press, Melbourne, 1965, p. 127.
7 William Taylor in T.F. Bride (ed.), *Letters from Victorian Pioneers*, Heinemann, Melbourne, 1969, p. 311.
8 Curr, *Recollections*, p. 137.
9 N. Gunson (ed.), *Australian Reminiscences and Papers of L.E. Threlkeld, Missionary to the Aborigines 1824–1859*, p. 167; for Encounter Bay, see G. Jenkin, *Conquest of the Ngarrindjeri*, Rigby, Adelaide, 1979, p. 50.
10 Martin Gibbs, 'Nebinyan's Songs: An Aboriginal whaler of Western Australia', *Aboriginal History*, vol. 27, 2003, pp. 1–16.
11 Cited in D. Bairstow, 'With the Best Will in the World: The demise of the Gampignal on the AA Company's estate at Port Stephens', *Aboriginal History*, vol. 17, p. 10.

12 R. Broome, 'Aboriginal Workers on South-Eastern Frontiers', *Australian Historical Studies*, vol. 26, no. 103, October 1994, pp. 202–20; A. Pope, 'Aboriginal Adaption to Early Colonial Labour Markets: The South Australian experience, *Labour History*, no. 54, 1988, pp. 1–15.

13 Joseph Watson, evidence to 'Royal Commission on the Aborigines' 1877, *Victorian Parliamentary Papers*, no. 76, p. 110.

14 Hugh McLeod, ibid., p. 108.

15 James Dawson, ibid., p. 100.

16 G. Aiston, 'The Aboriginal Narcotic Pitcheri', *Oceania*, vol. 7, no. 3, March 1937, pp. 372–7; J. Mulvaney, 'The Chain of Connection', in N. Peterson (ed.), *Tribes and Boundaries in Australia*, Australian Institute of Aboriginal Studies, Canberra, 1976, pp. 72–94.

17 Curr, *Recollections*, p. 109.

18 Julie McIntyre, 'Bannelong sat down to dinner with Governor Phillip, and drank his wine and coffee as usual', *History Australia*, vol. 5, no. 2, pp. 39.1–39.14.

19 Gunson, *Australian Reminiscences and Papers of L.E. Threlkeld*, p. 54.

20 Cited in R.M. and C.H. Berndt, *From Black to White in South Australia*, Cheshire, Melbourne, 1951, p. 85.

21 See Noel Butlin, *Our Original Aggression: Aboriginal Populations of Southeastern Australia 1788–1850*, Allen & Unwin, Sydney, 1983; Judy Campbell, *Invisible Invaders: Smallpox and Other Diseases in Aboriginal Australia 1780–1880*, Melbourne University Press, Melbourne, 2002, chap. 5; A. Frost, *Botany Bay Mirages*, Melbourne University Press, Melbourne, 1994, chap. 10; and Christopher Warren, 'Could First Fleet Smallpox Infect Aborigines?—A note', *Aboriginal History*, vol. 31, 2007, pp. 152–164.

22 Cited in H. Reynolds (ed.), *Aborigines and Settlers*, Cassell, Sydney, 1972, p. 72.

23 Bride, *Letters from Victorian Pioneers*, p. 181; R. Evans et al., *Exclusion, Exploitation and Extermination*, Australian & New Zealand Book Co. Sydney, 1975, pp. 98–101, respectively.

24 R. Broome, *Aboriginal Victorians: A History Since 1800*, Allen & Unwin, Sydney, 2005, pp. 87–9.

25 Cited in Berndt, *From Black to White in South Australia*, p. 84.

26 B. Blaskett, 'The Level of Violence: Europeans and Aborigines in Port Phillip', *Historical Studies*, vol. 19, no. 77, October, 1981, p. 536.

27 William Thomas in Bride, *Letters from Victorian Pioneers*, pp. 425–7; H. Reynolds, *The Other Side of the Frontier*, James Cook University, Townsville, 1981, p. 47.

28 Daniel Bunce, *Travels with Dr Leichhardt*, first pub. 1859, Oxford University Press, Melbourne, 1979, pp. 75–6.

29 Thomas quarterly report, February–August 1840, Victorian Public Records Series 10, unit 6.

30 R.H.W. Reece, *Aborigines and Colonists: Aborigines and Colonial Society in New South Wales in the 1830s and 1840s*, Sydney University Press, Sydney, 1974, p. 188.

31 L. Ryan, *The Aboriginal Tasmanians*, Allen & Unwin, Sydney, 1981, pp. 66–71; Reynolds, *The Other Side of the Frontier*, p. 37.

32 Peter Beveridge, *The Aborigines of Victoria and Riverina*, Hutchinson, Melbourne, 1889, p. 70.

33 L. Sharp, 'Steel Axes for Stone Age Australians' in E.H. Spicer (ed.), *Human Problems in Technological Change*, Russell Sage Foundation, New York, 1952, pp. 69–92; and J. Taylor, 'Goods and Gods: A follow-up study of "Steel axes for stone age australians"', in T. Swain and D. Bird Rose (eds), *Aboriginal Australians and Christian Missions*, Australian Association for the Study of Religions, Adelaide, 1988, pp. 438–51.

34 Cited in Reynolds, *Aborigines and Settlers*, pp. 54, 53.

35 See Broome, *Aboriginal Victorians*, pp. 116–18.

36 H. Reynolds, 'The Land, the Explorers and the Aborigines', *Historical Studies*, vol. 19, no. 75, October 1980, pp. 213–26.

37 Cited in George Mackaness, *George Augustus Robinson's Journey into South-Eastern Australia, 1844 with George Henry Haydon's Narrative of Part of the Same Journey*, by author, Sydney, 1941, pp. 50–1.

38 Cited in Gunson, *Australian Reminiscences and Papers of L.E. Threlkeld*, p. 46.

39 Beveridge, *Aborigines of Victoria and Riverina*, p. 94.

40 Cited in J. Woolmington (ed.), *Aborigines in Colonial Society, 1788–1850*, Cassell, Melbourne, 1973, p. 71.

41 Bride, *Letters from Victorian Pioneers*, p. 380.

42 Woolmington, *Aborigines in Colonial Society*, p. 102.

43 A. McMahon, 'Tasmanian Aboriginal Women as Slaves', *Tasmanian Historical Research Association*, vol. 23, no. 4, December 1976, pp. 44–9.

44 L. Ryan, 'The Struggle for Recognition: Part-Aborigines in Tasmania in the nineteenth century', *Aboriginal History*, vol. 1, pt 1, 1977, pp. 27–52.

45 Ryan, *Aboriginal Tasmanians*, chaps 12–13.

46 Cited in H. Reynolds, *Fate of a Free People*, Penguin, Melbourne, 1995, pp. 7–8.

47 Ryan, *Aboriginal Tasmanians*, chap. 14.

48 Cited in Reece, *Aborigines and Colonists*, p. 12.

49 C.D. Rowley, *The Destruction of Aboriginal Society*, Penguin, Melbourne, 1972, p. 203; Bride, *Letters from Victorian Pioneers*, p. 132 and 187; Curr, *Recollections*, p. 106.

50 Cited in E. Morrison, *Early Days in the Loddon Valley: Memoirs of Edward Stone Parker*, Daylesford, 1966, p. 52.

51 Thomas quarterly report, June–August, September–December 1846.

52 See Blaskett, 'The Aboriginal Response to White Settlement', p. 328.

53 Bride, *Letters from Victorian Pioneers*, pp. 430–3.

54 C.E. Sayers (ed.), John Morgan, *The Life and Adventures of William Buckley*, Heinemann, London, 1967, chap. 2.

55 Ryan, *Aboriginal Tasmanians*, p. 149; Blaskett, 'The Aboriginal Response to White Settlement', p. 356; Bride, *Letters from Victorian Pioneers*, p. 359; M. Christie, *Aborigines in Colonial Victoria 1835–86*, University of Sydney Press, Sydney, 1979, pp. 78–9.

56 Blaskett, 'The Aboriginal Response to White Settlement', pp. 394–5.

57 Butlin, *Our Original Aggression*, pp. 143–4.

58 For a recent discussion of the Victorian figures, see Broome, *Aboriginal Victorians*, pp. 90–3.

59 'Reports on the Diseases of Aborigines', BPA, *Annual Report*, 1st, 1861, appendix 3.

60 For a discussion, see Broome, *Aboriginal Victorians*, pp. 63–5.

61 Cited in Blaskett, 'The Aboriginal Response to White Settlement', pp. 288–9.

62 S. Hallam, 'Aboriginal Women as Providers: The 1830s on the Swan', *Aboriginal History*, vol. 15, 1991, p. 52; M. Taylor, D. Schmitt and P. Roy, 'Undermining the Social Foundations: The impact of colonisation on the traditional family structure of the Goulburn tribes', *Aboriginal History*, vol. 27, 2003, pp. 208–23.

63 Cited in Berndt, *From Black to White in South Australia*, p. 89.

64 J. Lear, *Radical Hope: Ethics in the Face of Cultural Devastation*, Harvard University Press, Harvard, 2007.

65 Cited in Thomas quarterly reports September–December 1843, VPRS 4410, unit 3.

CHAPTER 5: RADICAL HOPE QUASHED

1 J. Lear, *Radical Hope: Ethics in the Face of Cultural Devastation*, Harvard University Press, Harvard, 2007.

2 Cited in Diane Barwick, *Rebellion at Coranderrk*, L.E. Barwick and R.E. Barwick (eds), Aboriginal History Monograph 5, Canberra, 1998, p. 40.

3 *Argus*, 8 March 1859.
4 'Report of the Select Committee of the Legislative Council on the Aborigines', 1859, *Victorian Parliamentary Papers, Legislative Council*, 1858–59, Da, p. iii.
5 Cited in S. Lucas, 'A History of Coranderrk Aboriginal Station, 1859–1882', B.A. Honours thesis, La Trobe University, 1976, p. 12.
6 Cited in D. Barwick, 'Coranderrk and Cumeroogunga: Pioneers and Policy' in T. Scarlett Epstein and D.H. Penny (eds), *Opportunity and Response: Case Studies in Economic Development*, C. Hurst and Co., London, 1972, p. 23.
7 Barwick, *Rebellion*, p. 66.
8 Cited in Barwick, *Rebellion*, p. 74.
9 For a pioneering account of Coranderrk, see D. Barwick, 'Coranderrk and Cumeroogunga'.
10 Cited in D. Barwick, 'And the Lubras are Ladies Now', in F. Gale (ed.), *Woman's Role in Aboriginal Society*, Australian Institute of Aboriginal Studies, Canberra, 1974, p. 54.
11 Cited in Barwick, *Rebellion*, p. 75.
12 Cited in Barwick, 'The Lubras are Ladies Now', p. 57.
13 ibid.
14 D. Barwick, 'Changes in the Aboriginal Population of Victoria, 1863–1966', in D.J. Mulvaney and J. Golson (eds), *Aboriginal Man and Environment in Australia*, Australian National University Press, Canberra, 1971, p. 313.
15 G. Jenkin, *Conquest of the Ngarrindjeri: The Story of the Lower Murray Lakes Tribes*, Rigby, Adelaide, 1979, chaps 4–7.
16 N. Cato, *Mister Maloga: Daniel Matthews and his Mission, Murray River, 1864–1902*, University of Queensland Press, St Lucia, Queensland, 1976, p. 112.
17 Barwick, *Rebellion*, p. 255.
18 ibid., p. 387.
19 ibid., p. 339.
20 Cited in H. Goodall, *Invasion to Embassy: Land in Aboriginal Politics in New South Wales, 1770–1972*, Allen & Unwin, Sydney, 1996, p. 78.
21 Barwick, 'Coranderrk and Cumeroogunga', pp. 50–4.
22 M.T. Clark, *Pastor Doug: The Story of Sir Douglas Nicholls Aboriginal Leader*, Rigby, Adelaide, 1975, chap. 3; M. Tucker, *If Everyone Cared: Autobiography of Margaret Tucker M.B.E.*, Ure Smith, Sydney, 1977, chaps 1–4.
23 Jenkin, *Conquest of the Ngarrindjeri*, pp. 205–21.
24 ibid., pp. 215, 275; P. Brock and D. Kartinyeri, *Poonindie: The Rise and Destruction of an Aboriginal Agricultural Community*, South Australian Government Printer, Adelaide, 1989.
25 Lucas, 'A History of Coranderrk Aboriginal Station, 1859–1882,' p. 44.
26 J. Critchett, *Untold Stories: Memories and Lives of Victorian Kooris*, Melbourne University Press, Melbourne, 1998, chap. 9.
27 ibid., p. 56.
28 *Leader*, 15 July 1882, cited in S. Stone (ed.), *Aborigines in White Australia*, Heinemann, Melbourne, 1974, p. 98.
29 On Barak's art, see A. Sayers, 'Barak and the Affirmation of Tradition', in A. Sayers (ed.), *Aboriginal Artists of the Nineteenth Century*, Oxford University Press, Melbourne, 1994, pp. 13–26.
30 'Coranderrk Aboriginal Station. Report of the Board Appointed to Inquire into, and Report upon, the Present Condition and Management of the Coranderrk Aboriginal Station, Together with the Minutes of Evidence', *VPP*, 1882, no. 5, p. 98.
31 For a very detailed account, see Barwick, *Rebellion*. For a briefer account, see M. Christie, *Aborigines in Colonial Victoria 1835–86*, pp. 181–91; Broome, *Aboriginal Victorians*, chap. 9.

32 Barwick, 'Coranderrk and Cumeroogunga', pp. 52–4.
33 A. Massola, *Coranderrk: A History of the Aboriginal Station,* Lowden Publishing Co., Kilmore, 1975, pp. 34–5.
34 Barwick, 'Coranderrk and Cumeroogunga', p. 43.
35 Letter from Shadrach James to Board Protection of the Aborigines, 18 February 1948, National Archives of Australia, B314/5 box 1, item 8.
36 H. Goodall, *Invasion to Embassy: Land in Aboriginal Politics in New South Wales, 1770–1972,* Allen & Unwin/Black Books, Sydney, 1996, p. 137; see also her chap. 11.
37 Barwick, 'Coranderrk and Cumeroogunga', p. 64; C.D. Rowley, *Outcasts in White Australia,* Penguin, Ringwood, Vic., 1972, p. 90.
38 L. Smith, J. McCalman, I. Anderson, S. Smith. J. Evans, G. McCarthy, and J. Beer, 'Fractional Identities: The political arithmetic of Aboriginal Victorians', *Journal of Interdisciplinary History,* vol. xxxviii, no. 4, Spring, 2008, pp. 533–51.
39 R. Van Krieken, *Children and the State,* Allen & Unwin, Sydney, 1992, chap. 5.
40 P. Read, 'The Stolen Generations: The removal of Aboriginal Children in NSW 1883 to 1969', NSW Ministry of Aboriginal Affairs, Occasional Paper No. 1, 1983; see also P. Read, *A Rape of the Soul so Profound: The Return of the Stolen Generations,* Allen & Unwin, Sydney, 1999, chap. 3.
41 Ogilvie to F.R. Godfrey, 10 April 1877, reprinted in 'Royal Commission on the Aborigines', *VPP,* 1877, no. 76, p. 2. See his testimony, pp. 2–9.
42 Clark, *Pastor Doug,* p. 40.
43 Tucker, *If Everyone Cared,* p. 94.
44 ibid., chaps 8–11.
45 J. Barker, *The Two Worlds of Jimmie Barker: The Life of an Australian Aboriginal 1900–1972, as told to J. Matthews,* Australian Institute of Aboriginal Studies, Canberra, 1977, p. 93.
46 ibid., p. 53; Heather Goodall, 'Barker, James (Jimmie) (1900–1972)', *Australian Dictionary of Biography,* vol. 13, Melbourne University Press, 1993, pp. 113–14.
47 Barker, *Two Worlds of Jimmie Barker,* pp. 56–7.
48 Massola, *Coranderrk,* pp. 55–6.
49 Barker, *Two Worlds of Jimmie Barker,* p. 69.

CHAPTER 6: THE AGE OF RACE AND NORTHERN FRONTIERS

1 P. Bratlinger, *Dark Vanishings: Discourses on the Extinction of Primitive Races, 1800–1930,* Cornell University Press, Ithaca, 2003, chap. 1; N. Stepan, *The Idea of Race in Science, Great Britain, 1800–1960,* Archon Books, Hamden, 1982, chap. 1; R. McGregor, *Imagined Destinies: Aboriginal Australians and the Doomed Race Theory, 1880–1939,* University of Melbourne Press, Melbourne, 1997, chap. 1.
2 S.J. Gould, *The Mismeasure of Man,* revised edn, Penguin, Melbourne, 1992, chap. 2.
3 Darwin, *Journal of Researches* (1839), quoted in B. Bucher, 'Darwinism, Social Darwinism and the Australian Aborigines: A re-evaluation', in R. Macleod and P.H. Rehbock (eds), *Evolutionary Theory and Natural History in the Pacific,* University of Hawaii Press, Honolulu, 1994, p. 380.
4 R.H.W. Reece, *Aborigines and Colonists: Aborigines and Colonial Society in New South Wales in the 1830s and 1840s,* Sydney University Press, Sydney, 1974, pp. 85–94.
5 Office of the High Commissioner of Human Rights, UNESCO, accessed 27 October 2008, <www.unhchr.ch/html/menu3/b/d_prejud.htm>.
6 See the comments in H. Reynolds (ed.), *Aborigines and Settlers,* Cassell, Sydney, 1972, pp. 117–20.
7 Cited in Paul Turnbull, '"Ramsay's regime": The Australian Museum and the procurement of Aboriginal bodies, c 1874–1900', *Aboriginal History,* vol. 15, part 2, p. 113.

8 L. Ryan, 'The Extinction of the Tasmanian Aborigines: Myth and reality', *Papers and Proceedings of the Tasmanian Historical Research Association,* vol. 19, no. 2, 1972, pp. 761–79.
9 Stefan Petrow, '"The Last Man": The mutilation of William Lanne in 1869 and its aftermath', *Aboriginal History,* vol. 21, 1997, pp. 90–112.
10 L. Ryan, *The Aboriginal Tasmanians,* Allen & Unwin, Sydney, 1981, p. 220.
11 L. Russell, '"Wellnigh Impossible to Describe": Dioramas, displays and representations of Australian Aborigines', *Australian Aboriginal Studies,* no. 2, 1999, pp. 35–45.
12 James Thomson to Cameron, BPA, 15 October 1885, E.M. Cameron to Captain Page, Secretary BPA, 3 February 1886, NAA B313/1 box 15.
13 H. Reynolds, *Nowhere People: How International Race Thinking Shaped Australia's Identity,* Viking, Melbourne, 2005, p. 112.
14 *Age,* 1 January 1888, cited in A. Markus (ed.), *From the Barrel of a Gun: The Oppression of the Aborigines, 1860–1900,* Victorian History Teachers' Association, Melbourne, 1974, p. 65.
15 Cited in R. Evans et al., *Exclusion, Exploitation and Extermination: Race Relations in Colonial Queensland,* Australian and New Zealand Book Co., Sydney, 1975, p. 82.
16 D. Cole, 'The Crimson Thread of Kinship: Ethnic ideas in Australia, 1870–1914', *Historical Studies,* vol. 14, no. 56, April 1971, pp. 511–25.
17 Cited in ibid., p. 351.
18 Cited in H. McQueen, *A New Britannia,* Penguin, Melbourne, 1970, p. 48.
19 Reynolds, *Nowhere People,* especially chap. 5; M. Lake and H. Reynolds, *Drawing the Global Colour Line: White Man's Countries and the Question of Racial Equality,* Melbourne University Press, Melbourne, 2008.
20 R. Broome, 'The Australian Reaction to Jack Johnson, Black Pugilist, 1907–1909', in R. Cashman and M. McKernan (eds), *Sport in History,* University of Queensland Press, Brisbane, 1979.
21 *Age,* 14 August 1869, 11 January 1888, 26 September 1896, cited in Markus (ed.), *From the Barrel of a Gun,* pp. 61, 65, 66.
22 Cited in Evans et al., *Exclusion, Exploitation and Extermination,* p. 83.
23 Cited in R. Haynes, *Seeking the Centre: The Australian Desert in Literature, Art and Film,* Cambridge University Press, Melbourne, 1988, p. 56.
24 J.C.R. Camm and J. McQuilton (eds), *Australians: A Historical Atlas,* Fairfax, Syme and Weldon, Sydney, 1987, chap. 30.
25 W. Birman, 'Wylie', *Australian Dictionary of Biography,* online edition, copyright 2006, Australian National University, <www.adb.online.anu.edu.au/biogs/A020575b.htm>.
26 A. Moorehead, 'King, John (1841–1972)', *Australian Dictionary of Biography,* online edition, copyright 2006, Australian National University, <www.adb.online.anu.edu.au/biogs/A050034b.htm>.
27 Cited in Haynes, *Seeking the Centre,* p. 49.
28 N. Loos, *Invasion and Resistance: Aboriginal–European Relations on the North Queensland Frontier 1861–1897,* Australian National University Press, Canberra, 1982, p. 23. See also G. Reid, *A Nest of Hornets: The Massacres of the Fraser Family at Hornet Banks Station, Central Queensland, 1857, and Related Events,* Oxford University Press, Melbourne, 1982, chaps 5–7, and Cullin-la-Ringo, pp. 130–6.
29 Cited in Evans et al., *Exclusion, Exploitation and Extermination,* p. 53.
30 Mary Durack, *Kings in Grass Castles,* Constable and Company, London, 1959, p. 137.
31 Cited in Loos, *Invasion and Resistance,* p. 27.
32 Cited in ibid., p. 37.
33 G. Bolton, *A Thousand Miles Away: A History of North Queensland to 1920,* Australian National University Press, Canberra, 1972, p. 38.
34 Loos, *Invasion and Resistance,* appendices pp. 193–247.

35 ibid., p. 190.
36 *Northern Territory Times*, 4 October 1884, cited in Markus, *From the Barrel of a Gun*, p. 16.
37 Cited in Tony Roberts, *Frontier Justice: A History of the Gulf Country to 1900*, University of Queensland Press, Brisbane, 2005, p. 121.
38 Cited in ibid., p. 130.
39 Cited in G. Reid, *A Picnic with the Natives: Aboriginal–European Relations in the Northern Territory to 1910*, University of Melbourne Press, Melbourne, 1990, p. 104.
40 Roberts, *Frontier Justice*, p. 130.
41 Reid, *A Picnic with the Natives*, chap. 8.
42 Roberts, *Frontier Justice*, pp. 65–6.
43 Pamela A. Smith, 'Station Camps: Legislation, labour relations and rations on pastoral leases in the Kimberley region, Western Australia', *Aboriginal History*, vol. 24, 2000, p. 79.
44 Cited in Chris Owen, '"The police appear to be a useless lot up there": Law and order in the East Kimberley 1884–1905', *Aboriginal History*, vol. 27, 2003, p. 111.
45 Durack, *Kings in Grass Castles*, p. 284.
46 Cited in Owen, 'Law and Order in the East Kimberley 1884–1905', p. 120.
47 ibid., pp. 105–30.
48 Durack, *Kings in Grass Castles*, p. 304.
49 M. Jebb, *Blood, Sweat and Welfare: A History of White Bosses and Aboriginal Pastoral Workers*, University of Western Australia Press, Perth, 2002, chap. 1.
50 A. Gill, 'Aborigines, Settlers and Police in the Kimberleys 1887–1905', *Studies in Western Australian History*, no. 1, June 1977, p. 12.
51 H. Pederson and B. Woorunmurra, *Jandamarra and the Bunuba Resistance*, Magabala Books, Broome, 1995.
52 P. Biskup, *Not Slaves, Not Citizens: The Aboriginal Problem in Western Australia 1898–1954*, University of Queensland Press, St Lucia, Queensland, 1973, pp. 21–2; A. McGrath, 'Not Afraid of Police and not "Bloody Myalls": Northern Territory cattle spearing, 1911–14', seminar paper, La Trobe University, 1980, pp. 14–15.
53 Cited in Evans et al., *Exclusion, Exploitation and Extermination*, p. 88.
54 ibid., p. 107.
55 S. Sickert, *Beyond the Lattice: Broome's Early Years*, Fremantle Arts Centre Press, Fremantle, 2003; R. Ganter, *Mixed Relations: Asian–Aboriginal Contact in North Australia*, University of Western Australia Press, Perth, 2006, chaps 3–4; P Stephenson, *The Outsiders Within: Telling Australia's Indigenous–Asian Story*, UNSW Press, Sydney, 2001.
56 J. Harris, *One Blood: 200 Years of Aboriginal Encounter with Christianity: A Story of Hope*, Albatross Books, Sydney, 1990, p. 413.
57 ibid., pp. 409–27. See also Su-Jane Hunt, 'The Gribble Affair: A study in colonial politics', in B. Reece and T. Stannage (eds), *Colonial Politics in European–Aboriginal Relations in Western Australian History*, University of Western Australia Press, Perth, 1984.
58 G. Reid, *A Picnic with the Natives*, chaps 11–12.
59 For the Queensland Act 1897 and its origins, see C.D. Rowley, *The Destruction of Aboriginal Society*, Penguin, Melbourne, 1970, pp. 178–85; C.D. Rowley, *Outcasts in White Australia*, Penguin, Melbourne, 1972, pp. 109–16.
60 E. Goffman, *Asylums: Essays on the Social Situation of Mental Patients and Other Inmates*, Penguin, Ringwood, Vic., 1975.

CHAPTER 7: WORKING WITH CATTLE

1 W.E. (Bill) Harney, *North of 23°: Ramblings in North Australia*, Australasian Publishing Co., Sydney, n.d., pp. 201–6.
2 J.W. Bleakley, 'The Aboriginals and Half-Castes of Central Australia and North Australia:

Report to Commonwealth Parliament', *Commonwealth Parliamentary Papers*, no. 21, 1929, p. 12.

3 H. Reynolds, *North of Capricorn: The Untold Story of Australia's North*, Allen & Unwin, Sydney, 2003, chaps 6 and 8; R. Ganter, *Mixed Relations: Asian–Aboriginal Contact in North Australia*, University of Western Australia Press, Perth, 2006, chaps 3–4.

4 R. McGregor, *Imagined Destinies: Aboriginal Australians and the Doomed Race Theory, 1880–1939*, Melbourne University Press, Melbourne, 1997, chap. 2.

5 L. Lamilami, *Lamilami Speaks: The Cry Went Up. The Story of the People of Goulburn Island, North Australia*, Ure Smith, Sydney, 1974, p. 203; W.E. (Bill) Harney, *Brimming Billabongs*, Rigby, Adelaide, 1947, p. 166.

6 Cited in Harney, *Brimming Billabongs*, p. 101.

7 Cited in F. Stevens, *Aborigines in the Northern Territory Cattle Industry*, Australian National University Press, Canberra, 1974, p. 164.

8 Cited in Harney, *Brimming Billabongs*, p. 99.

9 Cited in K. Willey, *Boss Drover*, Rigby, Adelaide, 1971, p. ii.

10 A. McGrath, 'Aboriginal Women Workers in the N.T., 1911–1939', *Hecate*, vol. 4, no. 2, July 1978, p. 8.

11 W.E. (Bill) Harney, *Life Among the Aborigines*, Rigby, Adelaide, 1976, p. 202.

12 A. Markus, *Governing Savages*, Allen & Unwin, Sydney, 1990, pp. 54–9.

13 J. Sullivan, *Banggaiyerri: The Story of Jack Sullivan as told to Bruce Shaw*, Australian Institute of Aboriginal Studies, Canberra, 1983, p. 85.

14 A. McGrath, '"Tamed Blacks"? Frontier paternalism and control', seminar paper, La Trobe University, 1978; A. Hamilton, 'Blacks and Whites: The relationships of change', *Arena*, no. 30, 1972, p. 43.

15 Cited in F. Stevens, *Equal Wages for Aborigines: The Background to Industrial Discrimination in the Northern Territory of Australia*, Federal Council of Aborigines and Torres Strait Islanders, Sydney, 1968, p. 47; A. McGrath, *Born in the Cattle: Aborigines in Cattle Country*, Allen & Unwin, Sydney, 1987, pp. 125–9.

16 Cited in Harney, *Brimming Billabongs*, p. 103.

17 F. Stevens, *Equal Wages for Aborigines*, pp. 14–21; F.H. Gruen, 'Aborigines and the Northern Territory Cattle Industry—An Economist's View', in I. Sharp and C. Tatz (eds), *Aborigines in the Economy: Employment, Wages and Training*, Jacaranda Press, Brisbane, 1966, pp. 197–215.

18 D. May, *Aboriginal Labour and the Cattle Industry: Queensland from White Settlement to the Present*, pp. 69–74, 106–12.

19 C.D. Rowley, *The Destruction of Aboriginal Society*, Penguin, Melbourne, 1972, pp. 255–7, 261, 273.

20 McGrath, *Born in the Cattle*, p. 139.

21 P. Biskup, *Not Slaves, Not Citizens: The Aboriginal Problem in Western Australia 1898–1954*, University of Queensland Press, Brisbane, 1973, pp. 108–10.

22 Sullivan, *Banggaiyerri*, p. 77.

23 Willey, *Boss Drover*, p. 52.

24 F. Merlan, '"Making People Quiet" in the Pastoral North: Reminiscences of Elsey Station', *Aboriginal History*, vol. 2, part 1, 1978, pp. 71–106.

25 Cited in Harney, *Brimming Billabongs*, p. 93.

26 Cited in M. Jebb, *Blood, Sweat and Welfare: A History of White Bosses and Aboriginal Pastoral Workers*, University of Western Australia Press, Perth, 2002, p. 200.

27 F. Merlan, 'Making People Quiet', pp. 70–106.

28 Harney, *Life Among the Aborigines*, p. 14.

29 For a discussion, see McGrath, *Born in the Cattle*, chap. 4.

30 Harney, *Life Among the Aborigines*, p. 14.
31 A. Hamilton, 'Aboriginal Women: The means of production' in J. Mercer (ed.), *The Other Half: Women in Australian Society*, Penguin, Melbourne, 1975, pp. 170–5.
32 McGrath, *Born in the Cattle*, pp. 89–91.
33 Bleakley, 'The Aborigines and Half-castes of Central Australia and North Australia, Report'.
34 Chettle and Ellis cited in R. MacDonald, *Between Two Worlds: The Commonwealth Government and the Removal of Aboriginal Children of Part Descent in the Northern Territory*, IAD Press, Alice Springs, 1995, pp. 30, 36; see also McGregor, *Imagined Destinies*, pp. 140–7.
35 Quoted in Stevens, *Aborigines in the Northern Cattle Industry*, p. 140.
36 C. Tatz (ed.), *Black Viewpoints: The Aboriginal Experience*, Australian and New Zealand Book Co., Sydney, 1975, p. 67.
37 G. Paton, 'Humor', in E. Cashmore (ed.), *Encyclopedia of Race and Ethnic Studies*, Routledge, London, 2004, pp. 194–7.
38 Willey, *Boss Drover*, pp. 5 and 57–8; Harney, *Brimming Billabongs*, pp. 114–18.
39 B. Shaw and S. McDonald, 'They Did it Themselves: Reminiscences of seventy years', *Aboriginal History*, vol. 2, part 2, 1978, p. 129; J. Beckett, 'George Dutton's Country: Portrait of an Aboriginal drover', *Aboriginal History*, vol. 2, part 1, 1978, p. 17.
40 Sullivan, *Banggaiyerri*, p. 90.
41 K. Palmer and C. McKenna, *Somewhere Between Black and White: The Story of an Aboriginal Australian*, Macmillan, Melbourne, 1978, chaps 4–5.
42 F.G.G. Rose, *The Wind of Change in Central Australia: The Aborigines at Angus Downs*, Akademie, Verlag, Berlin, 1965, pp. 31–3, 99; W.E.H. Stanner, *White Man Got No Dreaming, Essays 1938–1973*, Australian National University Press, Canberra, 1973, pp. 90–1; C.H. Berndt, 'Women's Changing Ceremonies in Northern Australia', *L'Homme, Cahiers D'Ethnologie, De Geographie et De Linguistique*, no. 1, 1950, pp. 58–73.
43 R.M. and C.H. Berndt, *End of an Era: Aboriginal Labour in the Northern Territory*, Australian Institute of Aboriginal Studies, Canberra, 1987.
44 Ruby de Satge, 'I've Been to Sydney Too', in H. Wharton, *Cattle Camp: Murrie Drovers and their Stories*, University of Queensland Press, Brisbane, 1994, pp. 69–70.
45 McGrath, *Born in the Cattle*, p. 148.
46 ibid., p. 175.
47 Rev. J.B. Gribble, *Dark Deeds in a Sunny Land or Blacks, Whites in North-West Australia*, (1886) reprinted University of Western Australia Press, Perth, 1987, pp. 32–7.
48 A. Holland, 'Feminism, Colonialism and Aboriginal Workers: An anti-slavery crusade', A. McGrath, K. Saunders, with Jackie Huggins, *Aboriginal Workers*, Special issue, *Labour History*, no. 69, 1995, pp. 52–64.
49 H.O. Patterson, 'On Slavery and Slave Formations', *New Left Review*, vol. 117, 1979, pp. 31–67, especially pp. 31–41.
50 P. Brock, 'Pastoral Stations and Reserves in South and Central Australia, 1850s–1950s', in McGrath et al., *Aboriginal Workers*, pp. 103–8.
51 C. Williams with W. Thorpe, *Beyond Industrial Sociology: The Work of Men and Women*, Allen & Unwin, Sydney, 1992, pp. 88–107, especially pp. 95–100.
52 Berndt, *End of an Era*, chap. 8.
53 Biskup, *Not Slaves, Not Citizens*, pp. 219–22, 235–41; M. Brown, *The Black Eureka*, Australasian Book Society, Sydney, 1976; Palmer and McKenna, *Somewhere Between Black and White*, chaps 6–9.
54 K. Wilson, 'Pindan: A preliminary comment', in A.R. Pilling and R.A. Waterman (eds), *Diprotodon to Detribalization: Studies of Change among Australian Aborigines*, Michigan State University Press, East Lansing, 1970, pp. 333–46.

55 Cited in K. Gilbert, *Living Black: Blacks Talk to Kevin Gilbert*, Penguin, Melbourne, 1977, p. 163.

56 S. Taffe, *Black and White Together: FCAATSI. The Federal Council for the Advancement of Aborigines and Torres Strait Islanders 1958–1973*, University of Queensland Press, Brisbane, 2005, pp. 145–58.

57 Stevens, *Equal Wages for Aborigines*; F.H. Gruen, 'Aborigines and the Northern Territory Cattle Industry', pp. 199–200; C.D. Rowley, *The Remote Aborigines*, Penguin, Melbourne, 1972, chaps 10–14 and 16; R. Hall, *The Real John Kerr*, Angus & Robertson, Sydney, 1978, p. 103.

58 Cited in Stevens, *Aborigines in the Northern Territory Cattle Industry*, p. 153.

59 Cited in McGrath, '"Modern Stone-Age Slavery": Images of Aboriginal labour and sexuality', *Aboriginal Workers, Labour History*, no. 69, November 1999, p. 45.

60 Cited in Rowley, *The Remote Aborigines*, p. 341.

61 P. Hinton, 'Aboriginal Employment and Industrial Relations at Weipa, North Queensland', *Oceania*, vol. 38, no. 4, June 1968, pp. 281–301. See also H. Rogers, *The Industrialists and the Aborigines: A Study of Aboriginal Employment in the Australian Mining Industry*, Angus & Robertson, Sydney, 1973; D. Cousins and J. Nieuwenhuysen, *Aboriginals and the Mining Industry*, Allen & Unwin, Sydney, 1984, pp. 49–69.

62 *Age*, 3 August 1976, 27 May 1977 and 20 June 1978; Department of Aboriginal Affairs, *Statistical Section Newsletter*, no. 5, p. 1.

63 Cited in B. Bunbury, *It's Not the Money. It's the Land: Aboriginal Stockmen and the Equal Wages Case*, Fremantle Arts Centre Press, 2002, p. 115.

64 Cited in ibid., p. 171.

65 A.P. Elkin, 'Civilized Aborigines and Native Culture', *Oceania*, vol. 6, no. 2, December 1935, p. 125.

66 Beckett, 'George Dutton's Country: Portrait of an Aboriginal Drover', pp. 13 and 17–18.

67 P. Read and Engineer Jack Japaljarri, 'The Price of Tobacco: The journey of the Warlmala to Wave Hill, 1928', *Aboriginal History*, vol. 2, pt 2, 1978, p. 148.

CHAPTER 8: MIXED MISSIONARY BLESSINGS

1 M. McKenzie, *The Road to Mowanjum*, Angus & Robertson, Sydney, 1969, p. 110.

2 Cited in K. Cole, 'A Critical Appraisal of Anglican Mission Policy and Practice in Arnhem Land, 1908–1939', in R.M. Berndt (ed.), *Aborigines and Change: Australia in the '70s*, Australian Institute of Aboriginal Studies, Canberra, 1977, p. 181.

3 Cited in M. Durack, *The Rock and the Sand*, Constable, London, 1969, p. 52.

4 E. Perez, *Kalumburu: The Benedictine Mission and the Aborigines 1908–1975*, Kalumburu Benedictine Mission, Kalumburu, 1977, pp. 54–5.

5 D. Bates, *The Passing of the Aborigines*, John Murray, London, 1940, p. 10.

6 Cole, 'A Critical Appraisal of Anglican Mission Policy and Practice in Arnhem Land, 1908–1939', p. 184.

7 E.R. Gribble, *Forty Years with the Aborigines*, Angus & Robertson, Sydney, 1930, pp. 121 and 180.

8 F.X. Gsell, *'The Bishop with 150 Wives': Fifty Years as a Missionary*, Angus & Robertson, Sydney, 1956, pp. 22, 24, 34, 152.

9 Editorial, *Australian Board of Missions Review*, 12 October 1923.

10 'Kalumburu', part of the *A Big Country* series screened on ABC-TV, Melbourne, 23 March 1977.

11 Cited in McKenzie, *The Road to Mowanjum*, p. 88.

12 D. Roughsey, *Moon and Rainbow: The Autobiography of an Aboriginal*, Rigby, Adelaide, 1977, p. 38.

13 C. Choo, 'The Role of the Catholic Missionaries at Beagle Bay in the Removal of Aboriginal Children from their Families in the Kimberley Region from the 1890s', *Aboriginal History*, vol. 21, 1997, pp. 14–29.

14 L. Lamilami, *Lamilami Speaks: The Cry Went Up. The Story of the People of the Goulburn Islands, North Australia*, Ure Smith, Sydney, 1974, p. 92.

15 Cited in R.M. and C.H. Berndt, *From Black to White in South Australia*, F.W. Cheshire, Melbourne, 1951, p. 137.

16 Cole, 'A Critical Appraisal of Anglican Mission Policy and Practice in Arnhem Land, 1908–1939', pp. 188–90, 195–6.

17 *Australian Board of Missions Review*, 12 April 1926.

18 E.R. Gribble, *A Despised Race: The Vanishing Aboriginals of Australia*, Australian Board of Missions, Sydney, 1933, p. 44; P. Biskup, *Not Slaves, Not Citizens: The Aboriginal Problem in Western Australia 1898–1954*, University of Queensland Press, Brisbane, 1973, pp. 128–9.

19 C. Halse, *A Terribly Wild Man*, Allen & Unwin, Sydney, 2002, pp. 68–9, 163–4.

20 G. Roheim, *Children of the Desert: The Western Tribes of Central Australia*, vol. 1, Harper and Row, New York, 1974, p. 75.

21 J.E. Cawte, 'Australian Ethnopsychiatry in the Field: A sampling in North Kimberley', *Medical Journal of Australia*, vol. 1, no. 13, 28 March 1964, p. 470. See also J.E. Cawte, 'Tjimi and Tjagolo: Ethnopsychiatry in the Kalumburu people of north-western Australia', *Oceania*, vol. 34, no. 3, March 1964, pp. 170–90.

22 Durack, *The Rock and the Sand*, pp. 52, 131, 236–42.

23 Biskup, *Not Slaves, Not Citizens*, pp. 133–4.

24 McKenzie, *The Road to Mowanjum*, p. 52.

25 J. Harris, *One Blood: 200 Years of Aboriginal Encounter with Christianity. A Story of Hope*, Albatross Books, Sydney, 1990, p. 812.

26 McKenzie, *Mission to Arnhem Land*, Rigby, Adelaide, 1976, pp. 39–45, 80–1.

27 ibid., p. 245, also pp. 47–51, 86–90.

28 Roughsey, *Moon and Rainbow*, p. 57.

29 Berndt, *From Black to White in South Australia*, p. 139.

30 C. Choo, *Mission Girls: Aboriginal Women on Catholic Missions in the Kimberley, Western Australia, 1900–1950*, University of Western Australia Press, Perth, 2001, p. 187.

31 Lamilami, *Lamilami Speaks*, p. 89.

32 Gsell, 'The Bishop with 150 Wives', pp. 85–99.

33 Durack, *The Rock and the Sand*, p. 32.

34 See Gungar's view quoted in W.E. (Bill) Harney, *Brimming Billabongs*, Rigby, Adelaide, 1976, p. 43.

35 C.J. Fletcher, 'The Ten Commandments at Yarrabah', *North Queensland Notes*, October 1930, pp. 1714–15, cited in H. Reynolds (ed.), *Aborigines and Settlers*, Cassell, Sydney, 1972, p. 143.

36 Cited in B. Henson, *A Straight-Out Man: F.W. Albrecht and Central Australian Aborigines*, Melbourne University Press, Melbourne, 1994, p. 139.

37 Communicated by Walter Phillips, La Trobe University History Department, who heard the remark at a Christian conference in the 1960s.

38 Durack, *The Rock and the Sand*, pp. 63–4.

39 Bates, *The Passing of the Aborigines*, p. 15.

40 Choo, *Mission Girls*, p. 12.

41 Durack, *The Rock and the Sand*, p. 52.

42 R. Berndt, 'Surviving Influence of Mission Contact on the Daly River, Northern Territory of Australia, *Neue Zietschrift fur Mission Wissenschaft*, vol. 8, no. 3, 1952, pp. 81–95.

43 Cited in Harris, *One Blood,* p. 407.

44 McKenzie, *The Road to Mowanjum,* pp. 105–21.

45 Gsell, '*The Bishop with 150 Wives*', p. 59.

46 Harris, *One Blood,* pp. 517–21.

47 Henson, *A Straight-Out Man*; see index on 'Aboriginal evangelists', 'Moses' and p. 261.

48 'Kalumburu', part of the *A Big Country* series, ABC-TV, 23 March 1977.

49 Harris, *One Blood,* pp. 788–94.

50 Cited in W.M. Hilliard, *The People in Between: The Pitjantjatjara People of Ernabella,* Rigby, Adelaide, 1976, p. 94.

51 C. Duguid, *No Dying Race,* Rigby, Adelaide, 1963, p. 81.

52 D. Trudinger, 'The Language(s) of Love: JRB Love and contesting tongues at Ernabella mission station, 1940–46', *Aboriginal History,* vol. 31, 2007, pp. 26–44.

53 Bill Edwards, '*Tjukurpa Playa*—The Good Word: Pitjantjatjara responses to Christianity', in P. Brock (ed.), *Indigenous Peoples and Religious Change,* in *Studies in Christian Mission,* vol. 31, Brill. Leiden, 2005, p. 149.

54 R. Tonkinson, *The Jigalong Mob: Aboriginal Victors of the Desert Crusade,* Cummings Publishing Co., Menlo Park, Calif., 1974, p. 121.

55 ibid., p. 149.

56 D. Trigger, 'Christianity, Domination and Resistance in Colonial Social Relations: The case of Doomadgee, northwest Queensland', in T. Swain and D. Bird Rose (eds), *Aboriginal Australians and Christian Missions: Ethnographic and Historical Studies,* Australian Association for the Study of Religions, Adelaide, 1988, pp. 213–35.

57 R. Broome, *Aboriginal Victorians: A History Since 1800,* Allen & Unwin, Sydney, 2005, pp. 271–2, 290–1.

58 M. Calley, 'Pentecostalism among the Bandjalang', in M. Reay (ed.), *Aborigines Now,* Angus & Robertson, Sydney, 1964, pp. 48–57.

59 Harris, *One Blood,* pp. 873–7.

60 ibid., pp. 882–900.

CHAPTER 9: CONTROLLED BY BOARDS AND CASTE BARRIERS

1 C.D. Rowley, *Outcasts in White Australia,* Penguin, Melbourne, 1972, p. 81.

2 A. Haebich, *For Their Own Good: Aborigines and Government in the Southwest of Western Australia, 1900–1940,* University of Western Australia Press, Perth, 1988, pp. 153–65.

3 Cited in Haebich, *For Their Own Good,* p. 198.

4 R. Van den Berg, *No Options, No Choice! My Father, Thomas Corbett, an Aboriginal Half-caste,* Magabala Books, Broome, 1994, pp. 59, 61.

5 Alice Nannup, with Lauren Marsh and Stephen Kinnane, *When the Pelican Laughed,* Fremantle Arts Centre Press, Fremantle, 1992, p. 69.

6 Nannup et al, *When the Pelican Laughed,* pp. 60–88.

7 K. Cheeson, *Jack Davis: A Life Story,* Dent, Melbourne, 1998, pp. 20–2.

8 I. West, *Pride against Prejudice: Reminiscences of a Tasmanian Aborigine,* Australian Institute of Aboriginal Studies, Canberra, 1987, p. 51.

9 C.D. Clark, 'Aborigines in the First AIF', *Army Journal,* no. 286, 1973, pp. 21–6; R. Kidd, *The Way We Civilise,* University of Queensland Press, Brisbane, 1997, p. 74; Haebich, *For Their Own Good,* p. 161; R. Broome, *Aboriginal Victorians: A History since 1800,* Allen & Unwin, Sydney, 2005, pp. 199–202.

10 S. Robinson, '"We Do Not Want One Who Is Too Old": Aboriginal child domestic servants in Queensland, 1842–1945', *Aboriginal History,* vol. 27, 2003, pp. 162–82.

11 Haebich, *For Their Own Good,* pp. 251, 286.

12 Robinson, 'We Do Not Want The One Who Is Too Old', pp. 162–82.

13 V. Haskins, '"A Better Chance?" Sexual abuse and the apprenticeship of Aboriginal girls under the NSW Aborigines Protection Board', *Aboriginal History*, vol. 28, p. 41.
14 Haskins, 'A Better Chance', p. 530.
15 Haebich, *For Their Own Good*, p. 260.
16 Nannup et al., *When the Pelican Laughed*, p. 127.
17 M. Calley, 'Race Relations on the North Coast of New South Wales', *Oceania*, vol. 27, no. 3, March 1957, pp. 190–209; L. Lippmann, *Words or Blows: Racial attitudes in Australia*, Penguin, Melbourne, 1973.
18 M. Cozzolino and F. Rutherford (eds), *Symbols of Australia*, Penguin, Melbourne, 1987, pp. 45–50.
19 Lippmann, *Words or Blows*; G. Cowlishaw, *Black, White or Brindle: Race in Rural Australia*, Cambridge University Press, Melbourne, 1988.
20 Cited in C. Tatz, *Black Viewpoints: The Aboriginal Experience*, Australian and New Zealand Book Co., Sydney, 1975, p. 49.
21 Rowley, *Outcasts in White Australia*, p. 27.
22 Rowley, *Outcasts in White Australia*, pp. 336–40. See also M. Calley, ibid., pp. 200–13; R.G. Castle and J.S. Hagan, 'Dependence and Independence: Aboriginal workers on the far coast of N.S.W. 1920–75', in A. Curthoys and A. Markus (eds), *Who Are our Enemies? Racism and the Australian Working Class*, Hale and Iremonger, Sydney, 1978, pp. 158–71.
23 S. Hodson, 'Nyungars and Work: Aboriginal experiences in the rural economy of the great southern region of Western Australia', *Aboriginal History*, vol. 17, p. 75.
24 C.D. Rowley, *A Matter of Justice*, Australian National University Press, Canberra, 1978, p. 123.
25 M. Kamien, *The Dark People of Bourke: A Study of Planned Social Change*, Australian Institute of Aboriginal Studies, Canberra, 1978, pp. 178–81.
26 R. Broome, '"No One thinks of Us": The Framlingham Aboriginal Community in the Great Depression', in P. Bastien and R. Bell (eds), *Through Depression and War: The United States and Australia*, Australian and American Fulbright Commission & Australian and New Zealand American Studies Association, 2002, pp. 62–81.
27 Cited in A. Jackmos and D. Fowells (eds), *Living Aboriginal History of Victoria: Stories in the Oral Tradition*, Cambridge University Press, Melbourne, 1991, p. 20.
28 P. Moodie, *Aboriginal Health*, Australian National University Press, Canberra, 1973, pp. 106–7 and p. 54.
29 Kamien, *The Dark People of Bourke*, p. 107.
30 Cited in Tatz, *Black Viewpoints*, p. 32.
31 Moodie, *Aboriginal Health*, pp. 193–4.
32 Kamien, *The Dark People of Bourke*, p. 108; Moodie, *Aboriginal Health*, pp. 184–7, p. 202.
33 R.T. Fitzgerald, *Poverty and Education in Australia*, AGPS, Canberra, 1976, p. 193.
34 Lippmann, *Words or Blows*, pp. 89–90.
35 Rowley, *Outcasts in White Australia*, p. 340.
36 O. Lewis, 'The Culture of Poverty', *Scientific American*, vol. 215, October 1966, pp. 19–25.
37 K. Gilbert, *Because a White Man'll Never Do It*, Angus and Robertson, Sydney, 1973, p. 153.
38 ibid., p. 156; Rowley, *Outcasts in White Australia*, pp. 135–6.
39 Lippmann, *Words or Blows*, p. 144.
40 Kamien, 'Aborigines and Alcohol: Intake, effects and social implications in a rural community in western New South Wales', *Medical Journal of Australia*, 8 March 1975, pp. 291–8. See also J. Beckett, 'Aborigines, Alcohol and Assimilation', in M. Reay (ed.), *Aborigines Now*, pp. 32–47; and House of Representatives, Standing Committee on Aboriginal Affairs, *Alcohol Problems of Aborigines*, Final Report, AGPS, Canberra, 1977.
41 M. Kamien, 'A Survey of Drug Use in a Part-Aboriginal Community', *Medical Journal of Australia*, 1 March 1975, pp. 261–4.

42 R.A. Fink, 'The Caste Barrier—An obstacle to the assimilation of part-Aborigines in north-west New South Wales', *Oceania,* vol. 28, no. 2, December 1957, p. 103. See also R.A. Fink, 'The Contemporary Situation of Change among Part-Aborigines in Western Australia', in R.M. and C.H. Berndt (eds), *Aboriginal Man in Australia,* p. 432.

43 Cited in Kamien, *The Dark People of Bourke,* p. 40.

44 West, *Pride against Prejudice,* p. 23.

45 A. Memmi, *The Colonizer and the Colonized,* Beacon Press, Boston, 1967, pp. 121–2.

46 Rowley, *Outcasts in White Australia,* p. 235, and Lippmann, *Words or Blows,* p. 143.

47 See 'Fringe Dwellers', Ministry for Territories, Canberra, 1959.

48 M. Reay, 'Native Thought in Rural New South Wales', *Oceania,* vol. 20, no. 2, December 1949, p. 90.

49 Kamien, *The Dark People of Bourke,* pp. 36–9.

50 Cited in Lippmann, *Words or Blows,* p. 189.

51 Cowlishaw, *Black, White or Brindle,* pp. 232–44.

52 J. Beckett, 'Aborigines Make Music', *Quadrant,* Spring 1958, p. 42.

53 R. Broome with A. Jackomos, *Sideshow Alley,* Allen & Unwin, Sydney, 1998, p. 183.

54 R. Broome, 'Professional Aboriginal Boxers in Eastern Australia 1930–1979', *Aboriginal History,* vol. 4, 1980, pp. 48–71.

55 P. Pepper, *You Are What You Make Yourself To Be: The Story of a Victorian Aboriginal Family 1842–1980,* Hyland House, Melbourne, 1980; see also S. Flagg, *Footprints: The Journey of Lucy and Percy Pepper,* NAA & PROV, Melbourne, 2008.

56 Richard Broome interview with Myra Grinter, Mildura, 14 October 2002; and with Sandra Stewart, Mildura, 24 August 2002.

57 Cited in Haebich, *For Their Own Good,* pp. 224–5.

58 For an outline of Bill Reid's life, see Kamien, *The Dark People of Bourke,* pp. 270–2.

CHAPTER 10: FIGHTING FOR CIVIL RIGHTS

1 A.P. Elkin, 'Australian Aboriginal and White Relations: A personal record', *Journal of the Royal Australian Historical Society,* vol. 48, part 3, July 1962, p. 230.

2 C.D. Rowley, *The Destruction of Aboriginal Society,* Penguin, Melbourne, 1970, p. 184.

3 P. Read, *A Hundred Years War: The Wiradjuri People and the State,* Australia National University Press, Canberra, 1988, p. 88.

4 J. Collman, *Fringe-Dwellers and Welfare: The Aboriginal Response to Bureaucracy,* University of Queensland Press, Brisbane, 1988, p. 90.

5 Rowley, *Outcasts in White Australia,* Australian National University Press, Canberra, 1971, p. 60. For a fuller outline of the various Aboriginal Acts, see Rowley, *The Destruction of Aboriginal Society,* Australian National University Press, Canberra, 1970.

6 H. Reynolds, *Nowhere People: How International Race Thinking Shaped Australia's Identity,* Viking, Melbourne, 2005.

7 J.W. Bleakley, 'The Aboriginals and Half-Castes of Central Australia'. Most of his recommendations are conveniently reprinted in S. Stone (ed.), *Aborigines in White Australia,* Heinemann, Melbourne, 1974, pp. 154–66.

8 F. Stevens, 'Parliamentary Attitudes to Aboriginal Affairs', in F. Stevens (ed.), *Racism: The Australian Experience,* vol. 2, p. 123.

9 R. McGregor, '"Breed out the Colour", or the Importance of Being White', *Australian Historical Studies,* no. 120, October 2002, p. 286.

10 Cited in A. Markus, *Governing Savages,* Allen & Unwin, Sydney, 1990, p. 92.

11 C. Cook to the Administrator, Northern Territory, 7 February 1933, cited in R. MacDonald, *Between Two Worlds: The Commonwealth Government and the Removal of*

Aboriginal Children of Part Descent in the Northern Territory, IAD Press, Alice Springs, 1995, p. 24.

12 H. Zogbaum, 'Herbert Basedow and the Removal of Aboriginal Children of Mixed Descent from their Families', *Australian Historical Studies*, no. 121, April 2003, p. 132.

13 A. Nannup with L. Marsh and S. Kinnane, *When the Pelican Laughed*, Fremantle Arts Centre Press, Fremantle, 1992, pp. 147–8.

14 Zogbaum, 'Herbert Basedow and the Removal of Aboriginal Children of Mixed Descent from their Families', p. 132.

15 Cited in P. Jacobs, 'Science and Veiled Assumptions: Miscegenation in W. A. 1930–1937', *Australian Aboriginal Studies*, no. 2, 1986, p. 19.

16 Cited in P. Jacobs, 'Science and Veiled Assumptions', p. 21.

17 C. Raynes, *The Last Protector: The Illegal Removal of Aboriginal Children from Their Parents in South Australia*, Wakefield Press, Adelaide, 2009.

18 McGregor, 'Breed out the Colour', p. 300.

19 Tigger Wise, 'Elkin, Adolphus Peter (1891–1979)', *Australian Dictionary of Biography*, vol. 14, Melbourne University Press, Melbourne, pp. 87–8.

20 F. Paisley, 'Federalising the Aborigines? Constitutional reform in the late 1920s', *Australian Historical Studies*, no. 111, October 1998, pp. 248–66.

21 Typescript on VAG's beginnings, April 1957, and final annual report 1971, SLV, MS 9212, Box 2; P. Matthews, '"Uplifting our Aboriginal People": The Victorian Aboriginal Group, 1930–1971', BA Hons thesis, Monash University, 1985.

22 G.C. Bolton and H.J. Gibbney, 'Bennett, Mary Montgomerie (1881–1961)', *Australian Dictionary of Biography*, vol. 7, pp. 270–1.

23 M. Lake, 'Feminism and the Gendered Politics of Antiracism, Australia 1927–1957. From maternal protectionism to leftist assimilationism', in *Australian Historical Studies*, no. 110, April 1998, pp. 91–108.

24 Helen Baillie ASIO file, NAA A6126/XMO, item 23.

25 John Cribbin, *The Killing Times*, Fontana, Sydney, 1984.

26 See T. Egan, *Justice All Their Own: The Caledon Bay and Woodah Island Killings, 1932–1933*, Melbourne University Press, Melbourne, 1996, chaps 11, 12 and pp. 203–5. Personal communication with Reverend Keith Cole, who has researched the oral history of the area.

27 Rowley, *The Destruction of Aboriginal Society*, pp. 328–9, 330.

28 J. Maynard, 'Fred Maynard and the Australian Aboriginal Progressive Association (AAPA): One god, one aim, one destiny', *Aboriginal History*, vol. 21, 1997, pp. 1–13; J. Maynard, 'Vision, Voice and Influence: The rise of the Australian Aborigines Progressive Association', *Australian Historical Studies*, vol. 34, no. 121, April, 2003, pp. 1–25; J. Maynard, '"In the Interests of Our People": The influence of Garveyism on the rise of Australian Aboriginal political activism', *Aboriginal History*, vol. 29, 2005, pp. 1–22.

29 P. Biskup, *Not Slaves, Not Citizens*, p. 160; A. Haebich, *For Their Own Good: Aborigines and Government in the Southwest of Western Australia, 1900–1940*, University of Western Australia Press, Perth, 1988, pp. 269–76.

30 Biskup, *Not Slaves, Not Citizens*, p. 163.

31 *Age*, 8 November 2008.

32 For AAL see B. Attwood and A. Markus, *Thinking Black: William Cooper and the Australian Aborigines' League*, Aboriginal Studies Press, Canberra, 2004; for the APA, see J. Horner, *Vote Ferguson for Aboriginal Freedom*, Australian & New Zealand Book Co., Sydney, 1974; H. Goodall, *Invasion to Embassy: Land in Aboriginal Politics in New South Wales, 1770–1972*, Allen & Unwin, Sydney, 1996.

33 For the Manifesto, see appendix, Horner, *Vote Ferguson for Aboriginal Freedom*.

34 ibid., pp. 56–71.

35 Cited in M. Kamien, *The Dark People of Bourke*, Australian Institute of Aboriginal Studies, Canberra, 1978, p. 273.

36 Goodall, *Invasion to Embassy*, chap. 18.

37 *Sun*, 17 January 1940.

38 R. Hall, *The Black Diggers: Aborigines and Torres Strait Islanders in the Second World War*, Allen & Unwin, Sydney, 1989; R. Hall, *Fighters from the Fringe: Aborigines and Torres Strait Islanders Recall the Second World War*, Aboriginal Studies Press, Canberra, 1995.

39 H. Goodall, 'New South Wales', in A. McGrath (ed.), *Contested Ground: Australian Aborigines under the British Crown*, Allen & Unwin, Sydney, 1995, p. 89.

40 J. Chesterman and B. Galligan, *Citizens Without Rights: Aborigines and Australian Citizenship*, Cambridge University Press, Melbourne, 1997, pp. 132–3, 166.

41 Goodall, 'New South Wales', pp. 89–90.

42 Chesterman and Galligan, *Citizens Without Rights*, p. 157.

43 Cited in M. Thorpe Clarke, *Pastor Doug: The Story of Sir Doug Nicholls, Aboriginal Leader*, Rigby, Sydney, 1965, p. 157.

44 Cited in Jacobs, 'Science and Veiled Assumptions', p. 15. See also P. Jacobs, *Mister Neville*, Fremantle Arts Centre Press, Fremantle, 1990, pp. 254–8.

45 McGregor, *Imagined Destinies: Aboriginal Australians and the Doomed Race Theory, 1880–1939*, Melbourne University Press, Melbourne, 1997, p. 223.

46 Cited in A. Haebich, 'The Formative Years: Paul Hasluck and Aboriginal issues during the 1930s', in T. Stannage, K. Saunders and R. Nile, (eds), *Paul Hasluck in Australian History: Civic Personality and Public Life*, University of Queensland Press, Brisbane, n.d., p. 100.

47 Cited in Stone (ed.), *Aborigines in White Australia*, p. 192.

48 Cited in ibid., p. 196.

49 Cited in ibid., pp. 195–7.

50 Cited in ibid., p. 196.

51 M. Lake, 'Paul Hasluck's Horror of the Two-headed Calf', in T. Rowse (ed.), *Contesting Assimiliation*, API Network, Perth, 2005, pp. 253–70.

52 W. Sanders, 'An Abiding Interest and a Constant Approach: Paul Hasluck as historian, reformer and critic of Aboriginal affairs', in Stannage et al., *Paul Hasluck in Australian History*, p. 110.

53 R. White, 'The Australian Way of Life', *Historical Studies*, vol. 18, no. 73, October 1979, pp. 528–45.

54 T. Rowse, 'The Modesty of the State: Hasluck and the anthropological critics of assimilation', in Stannage et al., *Paul Hasluck*, p. 119.

55 A. Haebich, 'Imagining Assimilation', *Australian Historical Studies*, no. 118, 2002, pp. 61–70.

56 Cited in M. Rose, *For the Record: 160 Years of Aboriginal Print Journalism*, Allen & Unwin, Sydney, 1996, p. 51.

57 Cited in R. Folds, *Crossed Purposes: The Pintupi and Australia's Indigenous Policy*, UNSW Press, Sydney, 2001, p. 22.

58 J. Wells and M.F. Christie, 'Namatjira and the Burden of Citizenship', *Australian Historical Studies*, no. 114, April 2000, pp. 110–30.

59 See R. Broome, *Aboriginal Victorians*, pp. 362–4; P. Read, *A Rape of the Soul so Profound: The Return of the Stolen Generations*, Allen & Unwin, Sydney, 1999, pp. 25–31; *Courier Mail*, 21, 22 June 1996.

60 Cited in Lake, 'Paul Hasluck's Horror of the Two-headed Calf', p. 265.

61 Cited in B. Attwood and A. Markus (eds), *The Struggle for Aboriginal Rights: A Documentary History*, Allen & Unwin, Sydney, 1999, pp. 188–9.

62 Folds, *Crossed Purposes*, pp. 29–30.
63 Rowley, *The Destruction of Aboriginal Society*, appendix 1; Department of Aboriginal Affairs, *Statistical Section Newsletter*, No. 8, July 1979, pp. 7–42, No. 9, May 1980, pp. 7–13.
64 G.F. Gale and A. Brookman (eds), *Race Relations in Australia—The Aborigines*, McGraw-Hill Book Company, Sydney, 1975, p. 72.
65 M. Lake, *Faith: Faith Bandler, Gentle Activist*, Allen & Unwin, Sydney, 2002.
66 M. Duberman, *Paul Robeson*, Bodley Head, London, 1989, p. 490.
67 Broome, *Aboriginal Victorians*, pp. 330–6, 346.
68 *Origin*, 18 September 1969.
69 Rowley, *Outcasts in White Australia*, p. 404.
70 C. Perkins, *A Bastard Like Me*, Ure Smith, Sydney, 1975, p. 80.
71 Interview on 'Broadband', ABC Radio, 20 February 1978. See also Perkins, *A Bastard Like Me*, chap. 8.
72 Cited in S. Taffe, *Black and White Together. FCAATSI: The Federal Council for the Advancement of Aborigines and Torres Strait Islanders 1958–1973*, University of Queensland Press, Brisbane, 2005, p. 114.
73 Cited in Taffe, *Black and White Together*. p. 123.
74 Cited in J. Watson, '"We Couldn't Tolerate Any More": The Palm Island strike of 1957', in A. McGrath, K. Saunders with J. Huggins (eds), *Aboriginal Workers,* special issue *Labour History*, no. 69, 1995, p. 157.
75 ibid., pp. 149–70.
76 C.D. Rowley, *The Remote Aborigines*, Penguin, Melbourne, 1982, p. 98.
77 C. Tatz, 'Queensland's Aborigines: Natural justice and the rule of law', *Australian Quarterly*, vol. 35, no. 3, September 1963, pp. 33–49.
78 C. Tatz, 'Aborigines: Equality or inequality', *Australian Quarterly*, vol. 38, no. 1, March 1966, pp. 73–90.
79 W. Rosser, *This is Palm Island*, Australian Institute of Aboriginal Studies, Canberra, 1978.
80 See *Age*, 8 November 1977; 31 May 1978; 14 July 1979; *Melbourne Times*, 3 December 1980.
81 W. McNally, *The Angry Australians*, Scope Publishing, Melbourne, 1974, p. 65.
82 E. Eggleston, *Fear, Favour or Affection: Aborigines and the Criminal Law in Victoria, South Australia and Western Australia*, Australian National University Press, Canberra, 1976, p. 326.
83 C. Tatz (ed.), *Black Viewpoints: The Aboriginal Experience*, Australian and New Zealand Book Co., Sydney, 1975, p. 36.
84 Eggleston, *Fear, Favour or Affection*, pp. 13 and 172; W. McNally, *Goodbye Dreamtime*, Nelson, Melbourne, 1973, pp. 146–7; Department of Aboriginal Affairs, *Statistical Section Newsletter*, No. 7, April 1979, p. 12; *Age*, 10 March 1981.

CHAPTER 11: STRUGGLING FOR INDIGENOUS RIGHTS

 1 Yirrkala men to Gordon Bryant on 23 July 1963, cited in B. Attwood and A. Markus (eds), *The Struggle for Aboriginal Rights: A Documentary History*, Allen & Unwin, Sydney, 1999, p. 199.
 2 G.F. Gale and A. Brookman (eds), *Race Relations in Australia—The Aborigines*, McGraw-Hill Book Company, Sydney, 1975, p. 83.
 3 B. Attwood and A. Markus (eds), *The Struggle for Aboriginal Rights*, Allen & Unwin, Sydney, 1999, pp. 202–3.
 4 Cited in C.D. Rowley, *A Matter of Justice*, Australian National University Press, Canberra, 1978, p. 58.

5 S. Taffe, *Black and White Together. FCAATSI: The Federal Council for the Advancement of Aborigines and Torres Strait Islanders 1958–1973*, University of Queensland Press, Brisbane, 2005, p. 208.

6 H. Morphy, '"Now You Understand": An analysis of the way Yolngu have used sacred knowledge to retain their autonomy', in N. Peterson and M. Langton (eds), *Aborigines, Land and Land Rights*, Australian Institute of Aboriginal Studies, Canberra, 1983, pp. 110–33.

7 Attwood and Markus, *The Struggle for Aboriginal Rights*, pp. 252–3.

8 ibid., p 255.

9 Cited in K. Gilbert, *Because a White Man'll Never Do It*, Angus & Robertson, Sydney, 1973, p. 49.

10 Attwood and Markus, *The Struggle for Aboriginal Rights*, p. 236.

11 ibid., pp. 257–8.

12 Cited in C. Tatz (ed.), *Black Viewpoints: The Aboriginal Experience*, Australia and New Zealand Book Co., Sydney 1975, p. 49.

13 Cited in J. Andrews et al., 'Aboriginaland', *Australian New Left Review*, no. 60, July 1977, p. 17.

14 Gale and Brookman, *Race Relations in Australia—The Aborigines*, pp. 100–2.

15 Department of Aboriginal Affairs, *Statistical Section Newsletter*, No. 7, April 1979, p. 16. Figures are to the nearest million and do not include salaries and administrative costs.

16 C. Perkins, *A Bastard Like Me*, Ure Smith, Sydney, 1975, pp. 197.

17 C. Walker, *Buried Country: The Story of Aboriginal Country Music*, Pluto Press, Sydney, 2000, pp. 152–3.

18 T. Rowse, *Obliged to be Difficult: Nuggett Coombs' Legacy in Indigenous Affairs*, Cambridge University Press, Melbourne, 2000; C. Tatz, 'Aborigines: Political options and strategies', in R.M. Berndt (ed.), *Aborigines and Change: Australia in the '70s*, Australian Institute of Aboriginal Studies, 1977, pp. 384–401. Thanks to Bill Brown, my honours student at La Trobe University in 2009, for insights on the NACC.

19 A.E. Woodward, *Land Rights Commission. First and Second Report*, AGPS, Canberra, 1973, 1974.

20 R.W. Fox et al., *Ranger Uranium Environmental Inquiry Second Report*, AGPS, Canberra, 1977, p. 47.

21 ibid., p. 233.

22 ibid.

23 *Age*, 26 August 1977.

24 *Age*, 7 November 1979.

25 See *Age*, February–March, August–November 1978.

26 *Age*, 27 September 1978.

27 *Land Claims by Alyawarra and Kaititja. Report by the Aboriginal Land Commissioner, Mr Justice Toohey, to the Minister for Aboriginal Affairs*, AGPS, Canberra, 1979, p. 23.

28 ibid., p. 22.

29 *Age*, 26 September 1985.

30 *Age*, 2 and 10 October 1978.

31 *Age*, 2 March, 31 March, 2 April, 12 May and 8 October 1982.

32 The statistics in this paragraph are from S. Harris, *'It's Coming Yet': An Aboriginal Treaty within Australia between Australians*, for the Treaty Committee, Canberra, 1979, pp. 49–50.

33 *Age*, 3 December 1981.

34 *Age*, 22 November 1993.

35 *Age*, 12 August 1984. See also C. Tatz, *Aborigines and Uranium and other Essays*, Heinemann Educational, Melbourne, 1982, chaps 5–6.
36 *Age*, 4 August 1990.
37 *Age*, 24 November 1981, 18 May 1982, 31 January 1983.
38 *Age*, 3 June 1982.
39 *Age*, 18 April 1983.
40 *Age*, 14 May 1992.
41 *Age*, 25 March 1983.
42 *Age*, 16 and 27 April 1983.
43 *Age*, 9 December 1983.
44 *Age*, 29 May 1982.
45 *Age*, 3 May 1984.
46 *Age*, 9 May 1984.
47 *Age*, 21, 10 and 30 July 1984.
48 *Age*, 4 October 1984.
49 *Age*, 15 October 1984.
50 *Courier Mail*, 13 October 1987.
51 M. Groot, 'Public Opinion', in W. Vamplew (ed.), *Australians: Historical Statistics*, Fairfax, Syme and Weldon, Sydney, 1987, p. 440.
52 *Age*, 28 September 1984.
53 *Age*, 19 and 20 October 1984.
54 *Age*, 22 November 1984.
55 *Age*, 28 October 1985.
56 *Age*, 4, 5 and 21 November 1985.
57 *Age*, 4 March 1986.
58 *Age*, 16 May 1986, 3 December 1988.
59 R. McGregor, 'Another Nation: Aboriginal activism in the late 1960s and early 1970s', *Australian Historical Studies*, vol. 40, issue 2, September 2009, forthcoming.
60 *Identity*, vol. 1, no. 7, July 1973, pp. 28–9; vol. 2, no. 1, July 1974, pp. 39; vol. 3, no. 11, November 1979.
61 *Identity*, vol. 4, no. 2, winter 1981, pp. 21–36.
62 D. Sanders, 'The Formation of the World Council of Indigenous Peoples', 1980, <www.halycon.com/pub/FWDP/International/wcipubfi.txt>.
63 Rowse, *Obliged to be Difficult*, chap. 10.
64 N. Wallace, 'Pitjantjatjara Decentralisation in North-West South Australia'; W.J. Gray, 'Decentralisation Trends in Arnhem Land', both in R.M. Berndt (ed.), *Aborigines and Change: Australia in the '70s*, pp. 124–35 and pp. 114–23.
65 S. Turnbull, *Economic Development of Aboriginal Communities in the Northern Territory. Second Report: Self-sufficiency (with Land Rights)*, Commonwealth Government Printer, Canberra, 1979, p. 37.
66 Cited in Gilbert, *Because A White Man'll Never Do It*, p. 188.
67 Quoted in P. Nathan, *A Home Away From Home: A Study of the Aboriginal Health Service in Fitzroy*, Victoria, Preston Institute of Technology, Bundoora, 1980, p. 114.
68 Editorial, *Age*, 1 September 1980; Nathan, *A Home Away from Home*.
69 M. Kamien, *The Dark People of Bourke*, Australian Institute of Aboriginal Studies, Canberra, 1978, p. 76.
70 See, for instance, J.H. Downing, 'Consultation and Self-determination in the Social Development of Aborigines', in R.M. Berndt (ed.), *A Question of Choice: An Australian Aboriginal Dilemma*, University of Western Australia Press, Perth, 1971, pp. 61–90.

71 C. Tatz, *Race Politics in Australia: Aborigines, Politics and Law*, University of New England Publishing Unit, Armidale, 1979, pp. 66–81.
72 G. Foley, 'Blacks on Film in the Seventies', *Identity*, vol. 11, no. 3, November–December 1979, pp. 8–10.
73 Walker, *Buried Country: The Story of Aboriginal Country Music*, p. 13.
74 Cited in ibid., p. 224.
75 *Aboriginal and Islander Identity*, vol. 3, no. 2, April 1977, p. 20.
76 *Age*, 21 April 1980.
77 *Identity*, January 1972.

CHAPTER 12: HOPING FOR EQUALITY

1 Cited in C. O'Faircheallaigh, 'The Economic Impact on Aboriginal Communities of the Ranger Project: 1979–1985', *Australian Aboriginal Studies*, 1986, no. 2, p. 3.
2 *Age*, 4 May 1982.
3 David Cousins and John Nieuwenhuysen, *Aboriginals and the Mining Industry*, George Allen & Unwin, Sydney, 1984, p. 168.
4 *Age*, 26 March 1982.
5 *Age*, 20 April 1983.
6 *Age*, 3 June 1988.
7 *Age*, 6 December 1984.
8 *Age*, 21 March and 8 April 1989.
9 J. Altman and N. Peterson, 'A Case for Retaining Aboriginal Mining Veto and Royalty Rights in the Northern Territory', *Australian Aboriginal Studies*, 1984, no. 2, p. 50.
10 C. O'Faircheallaigh, 'Mining as a Source of Employment in the Northern Territory', in D. Wade-Marshall and P. Loveday (eds), *Employment and Unemployment*, ANU, Darwin, 1985, p. 55.
11 O'Faircheallaigh, 'The Economic Impact on Aboriginal Communities of the Ranger Project: 1979–1985', pp. 2–14.
12 *Age*, 29 October 1985 and 29 October 1986.
13 C. O'Faircheallaigh, 'Uranium Royalties and Aboriginal Economic Development', in D. Wade-Marshall and P. Loveday (eds), *Contemporary Issues in Development*, ANU, Darwin, 1988, pp. 155–82.
14 *Age*, 19 June 1985.
15 Cousins and Nieuwenhuysen, *Aboriginals and the Mining Industry*, pp. 167, 159.
16 E. Young, 'Aboriginal Economic Enterprises: Problems and prospects', in D. Wade-Marshall and P. Loveday (eds), *Contemporary Issues in Development*, ANU, Darwin, 1988, pp. 182–9.
17 E. Young, 'Aboriginal Economic Enterprises: Problems and profits', pp. 189–200; L. Ellana, P. Loveday, O. Stanley and E. Young with the assistance of I. White (eds), *Economic Enterprises in Aboriginal Communities in the Northern Territory*, ANU, Darwin, 1988, p. 261. See chaps 7, 9 and 10.
18 O. Stanley, 'Economic Development Problems in Remote Aboriginal Communities', in P. Loveday and D. Wade-Marshall (eds), *Economy and People in the North*, ANU, Darwin, 1985, pp. 111–14.
19 ibid., p. 116.
20 House of Representatives Standing Committee on Aboriginal Affairs, *Return to Country: The Aboriginal Homelands Movement in Australia*, AGPS, Canberra, 1987, p. 30.
21 J. Altman, *Hunter-Gatherer Today: An Aboriginal Economy in North Australia*, AIAS, Canberra, 1987; *Return to Country*, pp. 132–4; L. Head and R. Fullagar, 'We All "As One

Land": Pastoral excursions and Aboriginal resource use', *Australian Aboriginal Studies*, 1991, no. 1, pp. 39–52.

22 L. Sackett, 'Welfare Colonialism: Developing Divisions at Wiluna', in R. Tonkins and M. Howard (eds), *'Going it Alone': Prospects for Aboriginal Autonomy*, AIAS, Canberra, 1990, pp. 201–18.

23 G. Bernardi, 'The CDEP Scheme: A case of welfare colonialism', *Australian Aboriginal Studies*, 1997, no. 2, pp. 36–46.

24 R. Moroney, 'The Community Development Employment Projects (CDEP) Scheme', in J. Altman (ed.), *Aboriginal Employment Equity by the Year 2000*, Academy of Social Science in Australia, Canberra, 1991, pp. 101–5.

25 Discussion with the manager, Mark Edmonds, 18 October 2002.

26 M.L. Treadgold, 'Intercensal Change in Aboriginal Incomes, 1976–1986', *Australian Labour Bulletin*, vol. 14, no. 4, September 1988, pp. 592–609.

27 F. Jones, 'Economic Status of Aboriginal and Other Australians: A comparison', in Altman (ed.), *Aboriginal Employment Equity*, p. 28.

28 J. Altman and W. Sanders, *From Exclusion to Dependence: Aborigines and the Welfare State in Australia*, Centre of Aboriginal Economic Policy Research, ANU, Canberra, 1991.

29 R.G. Gregory, '"The American Dilemma" Down Under: A comparison of the economic status of US Indian and Blacks and Aboriginal Australians', in Altman (ed.), *Aboriginal Employment Equity*, pp. 141–5.

30 R.T. Ross, 'Employment Prospects for Aborigines in New South Wales', in Altman (ed.), *Aboriginal Employment Equity*, p. 121.

31 P.W. Miller, 'Aboriginal and non-Aboriginal Youth Unemployment', in Altman (ed.), *Aboriginal Employment Equity*, p. 81.

32 W.S. Arthur, 'The Prospects for Employment Equity in Remote Areas: The Torres Strait Case', in Altman (ed.), *Aboriginal Employment Equity*, pp. 107–19. D. Cousins, 'Aboriginal Employment in the Mining Industry', in Loveday and Wade-Marshall, *Economy and People in the North*, pp. 178–93.

33 A. Gray, *Progress without Grant: Employment in Some Aboriginal Communities*, ANU, Department of Demography, 1987.

34 C. Manuel, 'Equal Employment Opportunities in Darwin? Aborigines in the workforce', in Wade-Marshall and Loveday (eds), *Employment and Unemployment*, pp. 97–115.

35 Jones, 'Economic Status of Aboriginal and Other Australians', pp. 32–3.

36 J. Altman, 'Aboriginal Employment in the Informal Sector: The outstation case', in Wade-Marshall and Loveday (eds), *Employment and Unemployment*, pp. 163–73; E. Young, 'Aboriginal Employment—To What Purpose?', in Wade-Marshall and Loveday (eds), *Employment and Unemployment*, pp. 23–33.

37 P. Loveday, 'Aboriginal Employment in Katherine', in Wade-Marshall and Loveday (eds), *Employment and Unemployment*, p. 134.

38 *Age*, 1 February and 26 September 1990; A. Gray and H. Tesfaghiorghis, *Social Indicators of the Aboriginal Population of Australia*, Centre for Aboriginal Economic Policy Research, Canberra, 1991, pp. 12–14.

39 *Age*, 26 September 1990.

40 *Age*, 4 May 1993.

41 *Age*, 6 May 1989.

42 *Age*, 26 September and 18 December 1990.

43 *Age*, 21 January 1994.

44 *Age*, 22 November 1993.

45 Report on Morbidity and Mortality, *Age*, 20 August 1994; P. Torzillo et al., 'Invasive Pneumococcal Disease in Central Australia', *Medical Journal of Australia*, vol. 162, 1995,

pp. 182–6; B. Bartlett and D. Legge, *Beyond the Maze: Proposals for the More Effective Administration of Aboriginal Health Programs*, Australian National University, Canberra, 1994.

46 *Age*, 28 September 1990.

47 Human Rights and Equal Opportunity Commission, *Toomelah Report: Report on the Problems and Needs of Aborigines Living on the NSW–Queensland Border*, AGPS, Sydney, 1988.

48 *Age*, 12 January 1987.

49 *Australian*, 13–14 October 1990.

50 C. Choo, *Aboriginal Child Poverty*, Brotherhood of St Lawrence, Melbourne, 1990, p. 42.

51 *Age*, 6 August 1993.

52 P. Wilson, *Black Death, White Hands*, Allen & Unwin, Sydney 1982, p. 33. See also chaps 1 and 3.

53 *Age*, 29 April 1993.

54 *Sydney Morning Herald*, 14 November 1987.

55 Human Rights and Equal Opportunity Commission, *Racist Violence: Report on the National Inquiry into Racist Violence in Australia*, AGPS, Canberra, 1991, p. 209.

56 ibid., p. 210.

57 ibid., pp. 90–104; see also G. Lyons, 'Aboriginal Perceptions of Courts and Police: A Victorian study', *Australian Aboriginal Studies*, 1983, no. 2, pp. 45–61; K. Hazelhurst, 'Aboriginal and Police Relations', in P. Moir and H. Eijkman, *Policing Australia: Old Issues and New Perspectives*, Macmillan, Melbourne, 1992, pp. 236–65.

58 *Age*, 9 February 1990.

59 *Racist Violence*, pp. 95–6.

60 Chris Cunneen, 'Judicial Racism', *Aboriginal Law Bulletin*, vol. 2, no. 58, October, 1992, pp. 9–11.

61 *Racist Violence*, pp. 91–2.

62 *Age*, 26 May 1981.

63 *Age*, 6 and 7 March 1992.

64 *Age*, 10 August 1993.

65 *Canberra Times*, 5 January 1994.

66 *Age*, 26 April 1993.

67 *Age*, 14 July 1993 and 17 May 1994. AFL Code rule 30 to combat racial and religious vilification.

68 *Age*, 8 October 1983; *National Times*, 16–22 November 1984.

69 *Age*, 12 and 13 August 1987.

70 *Royal Commission into Aboriginal Deaths in Custody (RCIADIC) Interim Report*, AGPS, Canberra, 1988.

71 Ken Baker (ed.), *A Treaty with the Aborigines*, Institute of Public Affairs, 1988, p. 1.

72 *Age*, 26 August and 3, 4, 7, 18, 15, 22 September 1987.

73 *Age*, 6 October 1987.

74 *Age*, 17 December 1987.

75 *Age*, 24 August 1988.

76 *Age*, 27 and 28 January 1988.

77 *Age*, 14, 19, 22 and 25 January 1988.

78 *Age*, 23 February 1988.

79 *Age*, 24 February 1988.

80 *Age*, 16 June 1988.

81 Kevin Gilbert, *Aboriginal Sovereignty, Justice, the Law and Land*, 3rd edn, Burrambinga Books, Canberra, 1993.

82 Baker, *A Treaty With the Aborigines?*, passim.

83 *Age*, 4 July 1988.

84 *Age*, 16 August 1989. For the controversy, see 19, 27 October and 5 November 1988, 16 August 1989.

85 Peter Read, *The Stolen Generations: The Removal of Aboriginal Children in New South Wales 1883 to 1969*, NSW Ministry of Aboriginal Affairs, Sydney, 1983, pp. 8–9.

86 R. Broome and C. Manning, *A Man of All Tribes: The Life of Alick Jackomos*, Allen & Unwin, Sydney, 2006, pp. 241–2.

87 *Age*, 5, 10 September and 11, 12 December 1989, 25 January 1990.

88 *Australian*, 29 June 1993.

89 Analysis of *RCIADIC*, vol. 5, pp. 547–600.

90 ibid., vol. 1, p. 3.

91 *RCIADIC*, vol. 1, pp. 1–31.

92 'Too Much Sorry Business', *RCIADIC*, vol. 5, pp. 275–512.

93 ibid., vol. 1, pp. 223.

94 ibid., vol. 1, pp. 38–55.

95 E. Johnson, *National Report. Overview and Recommendations, Royal Commission into Aboriginal Deaths in Custody*, AGPS, Canberra, 1991, pp. 7 and 22.

96 *Age*, 10, 11 May 1991; Ron Brunton, *Black Suffering, White Guilt? Aboriginal Disadvantage and the Royal Commission into Deaths in Custody*, Institute of Public Affairs, Perth, 1993.

97 *Justice under Scrutiny*, AGPS, Canberra, 1994.

98 *Age*, 25 and 26 November 1996; HREOC, *Indigenous Deaths in Custody 1989 to 1996*, Canberra, AGPS, 1996, pp. xxii–xxxi.

99 *Age*, 19 April 2001; for Clark's address, see *Age*, 18 April 2001.

100 *Age*, 13 and 14 March 1992.

101 *Age*, 9 May 1992. For her son's death, see *Age*, 22 July, 1987 and James Muirhead, *Report of the Inquiry into the Death of Kingsley Richard Dixon*, AGPS, Canberra, 1989. For her belief that he was murdered and did not commit suicide, see *Age*, 10 May 1991.

102 *Age*, 21 October 1983, 28 January and 14 September 1984, 27 June 1988, 16 June 1989.

103 *Age*, 26 June 1990, 18 January 1992.

104 *Age*, 26 July 1993.

105 *Age Good Weekend*, 20 January 1996.

106 *Age*, 1 November 1993.

107 *Age*, 23 August 1986.

108 Noel Butlin, *Economics and the Dreamtime: A Hypothetical History*, Cambridge University Press, Melbourne, 1993, pp. 133–9.

109 *Age*, 7 August 1990.

110 D. Mowljarlai and C. Peck, 'Ngarinyin Cultural Continuity: A project to teach the young people the culture, including the re-painting of Wandjina rock art sites', *Australian Aboriginal Studies*, 1987, no. 2, p. 72.

CHAPTER 13: UNDER SIEGE

1 *Age*, 11 February 1992.

2 'Mabo v Queensland', *The Australian Law Journal Reports*, vol. 66, January 1992– December 1992, p. 429.

3 *Aboriginal Law Bulletin*, vol. 3, no. 61, April, 1993, p. 5.

4 *Age*, 13 October 1992.

5 *Age*, 7 July 1993.

6 *Age*, 7 July and 1 November 1993.

7 *Age*, 17 June and 15 September 1993.

8 *Age*, 11 July 1993.

9 *Age*, 28 July 1993.

10 *Age*, 2 July 1993.

11 *Age*, 9, 11 and 19 November and 1 December 1993.

12 *Age*, 22 June 1993.

13 *Age*, 2 April and 4 August 1993.

14 *Age*, 4 June 1993.

15 *Age*, 10 June 1993.

16 *Age*, 6 August 1993.

17 *Age*, 21 August 1993.

18 *Age*, 19 October 1993; 14 February 1994; K. Wimp, 'Mabo: The Inside Story', *Arena*, no. 9, February/March, 1994, pp. 16–20.

19 *Age*, 19 October 1993.

20 *Age*, 22 November and 3, 4 December 1993.

21 *Age*, 8 December 1993.

22 *Sydney Morning Herald*, 22 December 1993.

23 *Age*, 17 February, 7 September and 26 December 1994.

24 *Age*, 3 and 4 March 1995.

25 *Age*, 17 March 1995.

26 *Courier Mail*, 22 April 1997.

27 *Courier Mail*, 6 October 1995.

28 *Age*, 9 and 19 February 1996.

29 *Courier Mail*, 21 and 22 June 1996.

30 Major references on the affair include *Age* 22 and 23 May 1995, *Courier Mail*, 23 May, 7 and 8 June, 26 August, 8 and 23 December 1995, 21 May 1997. See C. James 'The Bridge over Troubled Waters' for a good analysis to May 1995, *Courier Mail*, 27 May 1995, 7 and 18 September 1996.

31 C. Forbes, 'Coronation Hill', *Age*, 11 November 1989, *Age*, 20 June 1991.

32 D. Bell, *Ngarrindjeri Wurruwarrin: A World That Is, Was, and Will Be*, Spinifex Press, Melbourne, 1998, especially, pp. 1–39. See also S. Hemming, 'Hindmarsh Island (Kumarangk): Challenging Australian mythologies' in S. Kleinert and M. Neale (eds), *The Oxford Companion to Aboriginal Art and Culture*, Oxford University Press, Melbourne, 2000, pp. 441–4.

33 *Age*, 6 June 1995.

34 <http://www.cityofsydney.nsw.gov.au/Barani/news/KeatingsRedfernAddressanunforgettablespeech.htm>.

35 *Courier Mail*, 2 January 1996.

36 *Age*, 7 March 1996. For Howard's role in the rise of Hanson and New Right politics, see A. Markus, *Race: John Howard and the Remaking of Australia*, Allen & Unwin, Sydney, 2001.

37 *Sunday Herald*, 13 October 1996 and *Age*, 15 November 1996 for an analysis of the speech by Laura Tingle. See also J. Brett, 'John Howard, Pauline Hanson and the Politics of Envy', in G. Gray and C. Winter (eds), *The Resurgence of Racism: Howard, Hanson and the Race Debate*, Monash Publications in History, 24, Melbourne, 1997, pp. 7–28.

38 *Age*, 23 September 1996.

39 *Age*, 7 May 1997.

40 *Age*, 30 April 1994.

41 *Age*, 2 April 1996. See also *Age*, 6–7 April 1996.

42 *Courier Mail*, 8 April 1996.

43 *Age*, 4 July 1996.

44 *Courier Mail*, 15 October, 12 November 1996.
45 *Age*, 15 April 1998.
46 *Courier Mail*, 11 and 21 May and R. Farley, 'Workable Native Title Deal', 17 May 1996.
47 D. Solomon, 'Court Prolongs Land-Title Uncertainty', *Courier Mail*, 24 December 1996.
48 *Courier Mail*, 18 January 1997.
49 *Courier Mail*, 3 March 1997.
50 *Age*, 29 April 1997. See also L. Tingle, 'Law of the Land', *Age*, 25 March 1997.
51 *Sunday Mail*, 25 May 1997.
52 *Age*, 4 November 1997.
53 *Age*, 8 November 1997.
54 *Age*, 22 November 1997.
55 *Age*, 13 November 1997.
56 *Age*, 22 November 1997.
57 *Age*, 9 December 1997.
58 *Age*, 31 March 1998.
59 *Age*, 1 April 1998.
60 For the speech and the reaction, see *Age*, 4 June 1998.
61 *Age*, 3 July 1998.
62 *ATSIC, Annual Report*, 1999–2000, pp. 124–5.
63 *Age*, 7 March 1998.
64 *Age*, 17 October, 29 November 2000.
65 For Dunghuti, see *Courier Mail*, 10 October 1996, *Age*, 8 April 1997. For Miriuwung Gajerrong decision, see *Age*, 25 November and 13 December 1998.
66 *Green Left Weekly*, 21 August 2002, <www.greenleft.org.au/2002/505/27649>.
67 *Age*, 15 June 2001.
68 *Age*, 31 July 2008.
69 *ATSIC, Annual Report*, 1999–2000, p. 113.
70 *Indigenous Land Corporation, Annual Report*, 1999–2000, pp. 19–47.
71 *Age*, 19 December 1998.
72 *Age*, 13 December 2002.
73 *Age*, 4 November 2002, 21 November 2003.
74 P. Wolfe, 'Nation and Miscegenation: Discursive continuity in the post-Mabo era', *Social Analysis*, no. 36, October 1994, pp. 93–152.
75 *Courier Mail*, 1 June 2002.
76 National Report: Native Title, June 2008. For more on native title, see C. Choo and S. Hollbach (eds), *History and Native Title, Studies in Western Australian History*, vol. 23, 2003.
77 *Australia Council, Annual Report*, 1996–97, pp. 20–2 and 1999–2000, pp. 96–8.
78 Record sale prices, *Age*, 19 June 1995, 2 July 1997 and 10 July 2001. For annual sales estimates, *Age*, 26 September 1999.
79 *Age*, 25 July 2007.
80 See A. Attwood, 'Australian Tragedy: Our Aboriginal icons', in *Age*, 17 May 1997; *Age*, 2 July 1997.
81 R. Lancashire, 'A Whole Lot of Emily', *Age*, August 1998. For an outline of the Central Australian Indigenous art movement, see Kleinert and Neale (eds), *Oxford Companion to Aboriginal Art and Culture*, pp. 197–225.
82 *Age*, 23 September 1998. See also H. Morphy, '"Now You Understand": An analysis of the way Yolngu have used sacred knowledge to retain their autonomy', in N. Peterson and M. Langton (eds), *Aborigines, Land and Land Rights*, Australian Institute of Aboriginal Studies, Canberra, 1983, pp. 110–33.

83 On fakes, *Age*, 28 May 1998, 22 November 1999. On the NIAAA, *Age*, 17 November 1999.

84 *Age,* 4 October 2008.

85 *Age*, day unrecorded, September 1997. See also 8 March 1997, 26 May 2000.

86 House of Representatives Standing Committee on Aboriginal and Torres Strait Islander Affairs, *Torres Strait Islanders, A New Deal*, AGPS, Canberra, 1997, pp. xv–xxxi.

87 Press release, 13 September 2000 and *Torres Strait Regional Authority, Annual Report,* 1999–2000, p. 4.

88 *Age*, 7 October 1996.

89 HREOC, *Bringing Them Home: Report of the National Inquiry into the Separation of Aboriginal and Torres Strait Islander Children from their Families*, Sterling Press, 1997, chap. 13.

90 ibid., p. 653.

91 *Age*, 22 May 1997.

92 *Sydney Morning Herald*, 23 April 1997; *Courier Mail*, 24 April 1997; *Age*, 29 April 1997.

93 *Age*, 17 December 1997.

94 *Age*, 1 August 1997.

95 *Age*, 12 August 2000.

96 See, for instance, P. Howson, 'Rescued from the Rabbit Burrow', *Quadrant,* June 1999, pp. 10–14, and other articles in 1999 and 2000.

97 R. Manne, *In Denial: The Stolen Generations and the Right*, in *Australian Quarterly Essay,* no. 1, 2001, Schwartz Publishing, Melbourne, 2001. For the conservative response to *In Denial*, see P. Howson and R. Brunton, *Age*, 3 and 4 April 2001 respectively, and *The Australian Quarterly Essay*, no. 2, 2001.

98 I used this term 'benign genocide' in the first edition in 1982, p. 165.

99 *Age*, 3 April 2000.

100 *Age*, 5 April 2000.

101 Anna Haebich, *Broken Circles: Fragmenting Indigenous Families, 1800–2000*, Fremantle Arts Centre Press, Fremantle, 2000, p. 130.

102 P. Howson, 'There is No Stolen Generation. There is Separatism', *Age*, 24 August 2000.

103 Robert Manne, 'A Colorblind Judgement', *Age*, 14 August 2000 and Malcolm Fraser, *Age*, 25 August 2000.

104 John McDonnell, 'Darwin, Rhetta Dixon and the Buffaloes', *Quadrant*, December 2000, p. 36.

105 *Courier Mail*, 29 October and 2 November 1996.

106 *Age*, 24 and 29 May 1999.

107 *Herald Sun*, 23 February 2001.

108 Press release, 1 March 2001. See also *Age*, 24 February 2001.

109 *Age*, 24 February 2001. See also comment by M. Flanagan and R. Manne, *Age*, 1 and 5 March 2001 respectively.

110 *Age*, 2 August 2007.

111 *Age*, 27 May 1997.

112 *Age*, 8 November 2000.

113 *Age*, 30 June 2003.

114 G. Partington has put this view in his *Hasluck versus Coombs: White Politics and Australia's Aborigines*, Quakers Hill Press, Sydney, 1996.

115 Howson, 'Reality and Fantasy: The abject failure of Aboriginal policy', *Quadrant*, April 2000, p. 24.

116 G. Blainey, 'Drawing up a Balance Sheet of Our History', *Quadrant*, July–August, 1993, pp. 10–15. On the use of the term, see M. McKenna, 'Black-armband History', in

G. Davison et al., *The Oxford Companion to Australian History*, Oxford University Press, 1998, pp. 72–3.

117 See Keith Windschuttle's three articles in *Quadrant*, September, October, December 2000, and replies by Henry Reynolds, *Age*, 28 September 2000; Andrew Markus, *Age*, 1 October 2000; and Lyndall Ryan, 'Postcolonialism and the Historian: The Aboriginal History Wars', in *Australian Historical Association Bulletin*, no. 92, June 2001, pp. 31–37; Manne, *In Denial*, pp. 93–105; Raymond Evans and Bill Thorpe, 'Indigenocide and the Massacre of Aboriginal History', *Overland*, no. 163, Winter 2001, pp. 21–39.

118 *Age*, 21 January 1998.

119 *Age*, 4 June 1999.

120 *Age*, 23 and 24 March, 24 June, 3 July and 12 August 1999.

121 *Age*, 4 and 8 March, and for the allegations, 11 April 2000.

122 *Age*, 11 May 2000.

123 *Age*, 22 May 2000.

124 M. Dodson, 'Our Generation, Mr Howard', *Age*, 30 May 2000.

125 G. Clark and J. Howard, *Age*, 29 and 30 May 2000.

126 *Age*, 26–28 October 2000.

127 *Age*, 8 November 2000.

128 *Age*, 9 November and 14 December 2000.

CHAPTER 14: CRISIS, INTERVENTION AND APOLOGY

1 Age, 15 August 2002.

2 Age, 12 July 2008.

3 *Age*, 8 February 2009.

4 *Age*, 27 March 1999.

5 *Age*, 14 January 1992, 27 March 1999.

6 *Age*, 19 May 1995.

7 G. Banks, *Overcoming Indigenous Disadvantage in Australia*, pp. 1–32, <www.pc.gov.au/speeches/cs20070629>.

8 *Courier Mail*, 18 and 26 August 1995.

9 Indigenous Governance Awards, <www.reconciliation.org.au/igawards/>.

10 Information from *The Rumbarumbles*, no. 7, 1 August 2007; ASHE Course Information, 2007.

11 Information from author's visit and from community adviser Rob Bamkin, October 2008.

12 See J. Altman and L. Taylor, *The Economic Viability of Aboriginal Outstations and Homelands*, AGPS, Canberra, 1987.

13 *Courier Mail*, 21 June 1996, 18 May 1997.

14 J. Altman, 'Development Options on Aboriginal Land: Sustainable indigenous hybrid economies in the twenty-first century', in L. Taylor, G.K. Ward, G. Henderson, R. Davis and L.A. Wallis (eds), *The Power of Knowledge: The Resonance of Tradition*, Aboriginal Studies Press, Canberra, 2005, pp. 35–48.

15 A.B. Pittock, 'Climate Change: Desert Challenge and Opportunity', 2009 unpublished paper lent by the author and available on the Desert Knowledge CRC website <www. desertknowledgecrc.com.au>.

16 Paul Memmot, 'Queensland Aboriginal Cultures and the Deaths in Custody Victims', in L.F. Wyvill, *Regional Report of Inquiry in Queensland*, RCIADIC, 1991, appendix 2, p. 276.

17 ibid., p. 222.

18 D. McKnight, 'Fighting in an Australian Aboriginal Supercamp', in D. Riches (ed.), *The Anthropology of Violence*, Basil Blackwell, Oxford, 1986, pp. 136–63.

19 *Courier Mail*, 26 September 1995.

20 Wilson and Barber quoted in J. Van Tiggelen, 'The Island Life', *Age*, 9 July 1994.

21 *Courier Mail*, 7 December 1996.

22 *Courier Mail*, 7 December 1996. See also *Australian*, 23–24 July 1994, *Courier Mail*, 31 May 1996.

23 Australian Bureau of Statistics, *The Health and Welfare of Australia's Aboriginal and Torres Strait Islander People*, AGPS, Canberra, 1997, pp. 28–35.

24 D. McKnight, *From Hunting to Drinking: The Devastating Effects of Alcohol on an Australian Aboriginal Community*, Routledge, London and New York, 2002, p. 115; see also chaps 8–9.

25 *Courier Mail*, 23 December 1995.

26 ibid., p. 216.

27 *Courier Mail*, 12 July 1995.

28 *Age*, 4 December 1995.

29 *Age*, 18 March 1996.

30 *Age*, 26 August 1996.

31 *Age*, 18 December 1997.

32 M. Brady, *Heavy Metal: The Social Meaning of Petrol Sniffing in Australia*, Aboriginal Studies Press, Canberra, 1992, chap. 7 on its incidence and chaps 3–4 on effects.

33 ibid., p. 190.

34 ibid., p. 193.

35 B. Lagan, 'Desert Visions Turn Deadly', *Age*, 22 August 2000.

36 A. Bolger, *Aboriginal Women and Violence*, Australian National University North Australian Research Unit, Darwin, 1991, p. 98.

37 ibid., pp. 11–12.

38 Australian Bureau of Statistics, *The Health and Welfare of Australia's Aboriginal and Torres Strait Islander Peoples 1999*, ABS, Canberra, 1999, pp. 45–60, 128–33, 11–24.

39 Mrs Jonny cited in B. Robertson, *Aboriginal and Torres Strait Islander Women's Task Force on Violence Report*, October 1999, p. 8.

40 *Courier Mail*, 6 November 1998. See also *Courier Mail*, 30 October, 2–6 November 1998.

41 Robertson, *Aboriginal and Torres Strait Islander Women's Task Force on Violence Report*, p. 4.

42 *Age*, 9 May 2001.

43 *Age*, 20 September 2000.

44 *Age*, 14 June 2001.

45 *Age* editorial, 16 June 2001.

46 Evelyn Scott and Sam Backo, *Courier Mail*, 20, 21 June 2001.

47 *Age*, 5 December 2003, 28 August 2004.

48 *Age*, 10 December 2003.

49 *Age*, 2 February 2007.

50 For the Koch articles, see *Courier Mail*, 30 June 2001. For the inquiry and Pearson's views, see *Courier Mail*, 14 July 2001.

51 *Four Corners*, ABC Television, 3 September 2001.

52 *Age*, 24 June 2001 and *Four Corners*, ABC Television, 3 September 2001.

53 *Age*, 28 December 2000 and for ATSIC's view, see *Age*, 14 March 2001.

54 *Age*, 18–19 April 2003.

55 *Age*, 1 April 2004.

56 *Age*, 24 November 2004.

57 *Age*, 22 April 2005.

58 *Age*, 15 and 29 December 2004.

59 *Australian*, 2, 7 and 25 April 2005, 28 May 2005.

60 *Age*, 10 April 2005.
61 Age, 11 April 2005.
62 *Age*, 25 July 2005.
63 *Age*, 5 August 2005.
64 *Age*, 26 October 2005.
65 *Age*, 23 and 24 July 2003.
66 *Age*, 6 August 2003.
67 *Age*, 22 July 2003.
68 *Age*, 24 June 2006.
69 *Age*, 27 June 2006.
70 *Age*, 21 September 2006.
71 R. Wild and P. Anderson, *'Little Children are Sacred': Board of Inquiry into the Protection of Aboriginal Children from Sexual Abuse*, Northern Territory, p. 57, <www.nt.gov.au/dcm/inquirysaac/pdf/bipacsa_final_report.pdf>.
72 This is revealed by Russell Skelton, *Age*, 21 June 2007.
73 *Age*, 20 June 2007.
74 *Age*, 22 June 2007; Northern Territory Emergency Response Fact Sheets, 24 August no. 1–24, Australian Government.
75 *Age*, 22–25 June 2007.
76 *Age*, 26 June 2007.
77 *Age*, 27 June 2007.
78 ibid.
79 *Age*, 26 June 2007.
80 *Age*, 30 June 2007.
81 *Age*, 24 July 2007.
82 *Age*, 10 July 2007.
83 *Age*, 7–18 August 2007.
84 *Age*, 21 August 2007.
85 *Age*, 12 October 2007.
86 *Age*, 25 October 2007.
87 *Age*, 21 June 2008.
88 *Australian*, 5 June 2008.
89 *Australian*, 15 October 2008.
90 <www.nterreview.gov.au/docs/report_nter_review/ch3.htm>.
91 *Age*, 24 and 29 October 2008.
92 *Age*, 25 November 2008.
93 PAPA media release, 3 February 2009.
94 *Age*, 5 April 2009.
95 Productivity Commission, 'Overcoming Indigenous Disadvantage: Key Indicators 2009', section 4.10, <www.pc.gov.au/reports/indigenous/keyindcators2009>.
96 *Age*, 27 March 2009.
97 *Age*, 10–11 April 2009.
98 *Age*, 26 August 2009.
99 *Age*, 27 November 2007.
100 *Age*, 13 February 2008.
101 *Australian*, 24 July 2008.
102 <http://en.wikipedia.org/wiki/List_of_Australian_of_the_Year_Award_recipients>.

SELECT BIBLIOGRAPHY

To extend your reading in Aboriginal history, you should consult the select bibliography below and the following journals: *Aboriginal History* (1977+), *Australian Aboriginal Studies* (1983+), *Mankind* (1931) and *Oceania* (1930+). There are many articles in *Australian Historical Studies* and the *Journal of Australian Studies* since about 1990 and *History Australia* since 2003. Useful reference works include: D. Horton (ed.), *The Encyclopaedia of Aboriginal Australia*, 2 vols, Aboriginal Studies Press, Canberra, 1994; S. Kleinert and M. Neale (eds), *The Oxford Companion to Aboriginal Art and Culture*, Oxford University Press, Melbourne, 2000; W. Arthur and F. Morphy (eds), *Macquarie Atlas of Indigenous Australia*, Macquarie Library, Sydney, 2005. The following major printed books will also be very useful.

WORKS BY NON-INDIGENOUS AUTHORS
Attwood, B., *Rights for Aborigines*, Allen & Unwin, Sydney, 2003.
Attwood, B. and Foster, S.G., *Frontier Conflict: The Australian Experience*, National Museum of Australia, Canberra, 2003.
Attwood, B. and Markus, A. (eds), *The Struggle for Aboriginal Rights: A Documentary History*, Allen & Unwin, Sydney, 1999.
Barwick, D., and L.E. and R.E. Barwick (eds), *Rebellion at Coranderrk*, Aboriginal Studies Press, Canberra, 1998.
Beckett, J., *Torres Strait Islanders: Custom and Colonialism*, Cambridge University Press, Cambridge, 1987.
——(ed.), *Past and Present: The Construction of Aboriginality*, Aboriginal Studies Press, Canberra, 1988.
Bennett, S., *Aborigines and Political Power*, Allen & Unwin, Sydney, 1989.
Berndt, R.M. and C.H. (eds), *The World of the First Australians*, 2nd edn, Ure Smith, Sydney, 1974.
Biskup, P., *Not Slaves, Not Citizens: The Aboriginal Problem in Western Australia 1898–1954*, University of Queensland Press, Brisbane, 1973.
Brook, J. and Kohen, J., *The Parramatta Native Institution and the Black Town*, University of New South Wales Press, Sydney, 1991.
Broome, R., *Aboriginal Victorians: A History since 1800*, Allen & Unwin, Sydney, 2005.

Butlin, N., *Our Original Aggression: Aboriginal Populations of Southeastern Australia 1788–1850*, Allen & Unwin, Sydney, 1983.

Campbell, J., *Invisible Invaders: Smallpox and Other Diseases in Aboriginal Australia 1780–1880*, Melbourne University Press, Melbourne, 2002.

Cato, N., *Mister Maloga: Daniel Matthews and his Mission, Murray River, 1864–1902*, University of Queensland Press, Brisbane, 1976.

Chesterman, J., *Civil Rights: How Indigenous Australians Won Formal Equality*, University of Queensland Press, Brisbane, 2005.

Chesterman, J. and Galligan, B. (eds), *Citizens Without Rights*, Cambridge University Press, Melbourne, 1997.

Christie, M.F., *Aborigines in Colonial Victoria 1835–86*, Sydney University Press, Sydney, 1979.

Collman, J., *Fringe-Dwellers and Welfare: The Aboriginal Response to Bureaucracy*, University of Queensland Press, Brisbane, 1988.

Cowlishaw, G., *Black, White and Brindle: Race in Rural Australia*, Cambridge University Press, Cambridge, 1988.

Critchett, J., *'A Distant Field of Murder': Western District Frontiers 1834–1848*, Melbourne University Press, Melbourne, 1990.

Dutton, G., *White on Black: The Australian Aborigine Portrayed in Art*, Macmillan, Melbourne, 1974.

Eggleston, E., *Fear, Favour or Affection: Aborigines and the Criminal Law in Victoria, South Australia and Western Australia*, Australian National University Press, Canberra, 1976.

Evans, R., Saunders, K. and Cronin, K., *Exclusion, Exploitation and Extermination: Race Relations in Colonial Queensland*, Australian and New Zealand Book Co., Sydney, 1975.

Fels, M., *Good Men and True: The Aboriginal Police of the Port Phillip District 1837–1853*, Melbourne University Press, Melbourne, 1988.

Gale, F. (ed.), *Woman's Role in Aboriginal Society*, 2nd edn, Australian Institute of Aboriginal Studies, Canberra, 1974.

Ganter, R., *Mixed Relations: Asian–Aboriginal contact in North Australia*, University of Western Australia Press, Perth, 2006.

Goodall, H., *Invasion to Embassy: Land in Aboriginal Politics in New South Wales 1770–1972*, Allen & Unwin and Black Books Inc., Sydney, 1996.

Haebich, A., *For Their Own Good: Aborigines and Government in the Southwest of Western Australia, 1900–1940*, University of Western Australia Press, Perth, 1988.

——*Broken Circles: Fragmenting Indigenous Families, 1800–2000*, Fremantle Arts Centre, Fremantle, 2000.

Hall, R., *The Black Diggers: Aborigines and Torres Strait Islanders in the Second World War*, Allen & Unwin, Sydney, 1989.

Harris, J., *One Blood: 200 Years of Aboriginal Encounter with Christianity; A Story of Hope*, Albatross, Claremont, 1990.

Horner, J., *Vote Ferguson for Aboriginal Freedom*, Australian and New Zealand Book Co., Sydney, 1974.

Jebb, M., *Blood, Sweat and Welfare: A History of White Bosses and Aboriginal Pastoral Workers*, University of Western Australia Press, Perth, 2002.

Jenkin, G., *Conquest of the Ngarrindjeri*, Rigby, Adelaide, 1979.

Keen, I. (ed.), *Being Black: Aboriginal Cultures in 'Settled' Australia*, Aboriginal Studies Press, Canberra, 1988.

Kidd, R., *The Way We Civilise: Aboriginal Affairs, the Untold Story*, University of Queensland Press, Brisbane, 1997.

Loos, N. *Invasion and Resistance: Aboriginal–European Relations on the North Queensland Frontier 1861–1897*, Australian National University Press, Canberra, 1982.

Markus, A., *From the Barrel of a Gun: The Oppression of the Aborigines, 1860–1900*, Victorian History Teachers' Association, Melbourne, 1974.

——*Governing Savages*, Allen & Unwin, Sydney, 1990.

——*Australian Race Relations*, Allen & Unwin, Sydney, 1994.

May, D., *Aboriginal Labour and the Cattle Industry*, Cambridge University Press, Melbourne, 1994.

McGrath, A., *'Born in the Cattle': Aborigines in Cattle Country*, Allen & Unwin, Sydney, 1987.

——*Contested Ground: Aboriginal Australians under the British Crown*, Allen & Unwin, Sydney, 1995.

McGregor, R., *Imagined Destinies: Aboriginal Australians and the Doomed Race Theory 1880–1939*, Melbourne University Press, Melbourne, 1997.

Mulvaney, D.J. and White, J.P. (eds), *Australians to 1788*, Fairfax, Syme and Weldon, Sydney, 1987.

Plomley, B. (ed.), *Weep in Silence: A History of the Flinders Island Aboriginal Settlement*, Blubber Head Press, Hobart, 1987.

Read, P., *A Hundred Years War: The Wiradjuri People and the State*, Australian National University Press, Canberra, 1988.

——*A Rape of the Soul so Profound: The Return of the Stolen Generations*, Allen & Unwin, Sydney, 1999.

Reece, R.H.W., *Aborigines and Colonists: Aborigines and Colonial Society in New South Wales in the 1830s and 1840s*, Sydney University Press, Sydney, 1974.

Reid, G., *A Picnic with the Natives: Aboriginal–European Relations in the Northern Territory to 1910*, Melbourne University Press, Melbourne, 1990.

Reynolds, H. (ed.), *Aborigines and Settlers: The Australian Experience 1788–1939*, Cassell Australia, North Melbourne, 1972.

Reynolds, H., *The Other Side of the Frontier: An Interpretation of the Aboriginal Response to the Invasion and Settlement of Australia*, James Cook University, Townsville, 1981.

——*Frontier: Aborigines, Settlers and Land*, Allen & Unwin, Sydney, 1987.

——*The Law of the Land*, Penguin, Melbourne, 1987.

——*With the White People*, Penguin, Melbourne, 1990.

——*Fate of a Free People*, Penguin, Melbourne, 1995.

——*Aboriginal Sovereignty*, Allen & Unwin, Sydney, 1996.

——*The Question of Genocide in Australia's History: An Indelible Stain*, Viking, Melbourne, 2001.

——*Nowhere People: How International Race Thinking Shaped Australia's Identity*, Viking, Melbourne, 2005.

Rowley, C.D., *The Destruction of Aboriginal Society*, Penguin, Melbourne, 1972.

——*Outcasts in White Australia*, Penguin, Melbourne, 1972.

——*The Remote Aborigines*, Penguin, Melbourne, 1972.

Rowse, T., *White Flour, White Power: From Rations to Citizenship in Central Australia*, Cambridge University Press, Melbourne, 1998.

——(ed.), *Contesting Assimilation*, API Network, Perth, 2005.

Ryan, L., *Aboriginal Tasmanians*, Allen & Unwin, Sydney, 2nd edn, 1996.

Sharp, N., *Stars of Tagai: The Torres Strait Islanders*, Aboriginal Studies Press, Canberra, 1993.

Stanner, W.E.H., *After the Dreaming: Black and White Australians—An Anthropologist's Views*, (Boyer lectures 1968), Australian Broadcasting Commission, Sydney, 1969.

——*White Man Got No Dreaming: Essays 1938–1973*, Australian National University Press, Canberra, 1979.

Stevens, F.S., *Aborigines in the Northern Territory Cattle Industry*, Australian National University Press, Canberra, 1974.

——(ed.), *Racism: The Australian Experience. A Study of Race Prejudice in Australia*, 3 vols, Australian and New Zealand Book Co., Sydney, 1974.

Stone, S. (ed.), *Aborigines in White Australia: A Documentary History of the Attitudes Affecting Official Policy and the Australian Aborigine 1697–1973*, Heinemann, Melbourne, 1974.

Swain, T. and Bird Rose, D. (eds), *Aboriginal Australians and Christian Missions: Ethnographic and Historical Studies*, Australian Association for the Study of Religions, Adelaide, 1988.

Taffe, S., *Black and White Together. FCAATSI: The Federal Council for the Advancement of Aborigines and Torres Strait Islanders 1958–1973*, University of Queensland Press, Brisbane, 2005.

Walker, C., *Buried Country: The Story of Aboriginal Country Music*, Pluto Press, Sydney, 2000.

Woolmington, J. (ed.), *Aborigines in Colonial Society: 1788–1850*, Cassell Australia, Melbourne, 1973.

WORKS BY INDIGENOUS AUTHORS AND 'AS TOLD TO' LIFE STORIES

Barker, J., *The Two Worlds of Jimmie Barker: The Life of an Australian Aboriginal 1900–1972, as told to Janet Matthews*, Australian Institute of Aboriginal Studies, Canberra, 1977.

Bohemia, J. and McGregor, W., *Nyibayarri: Kimberley Tracker*, Aboriginal Studies Press, Canberra, 1995.

Cheeson, K., *Jack Davis: A Life-story*, Dent, Melbourne, 1988.

Cohen, W., *To My Delight: The Autobiography of Bill Cohen, a Grandson of the Gumbangarri*, Aboriginal Studies Press, Canberra, 1987.

Crawford, E., *Over My Tracks: A Remarkable Life*, Penguin, Melbourne, 1993.

Edwards, C. and Read, P., *The Lost Children*, Doubleday, Sydney, 1989.

Gaffney, E., *Somebody Now: The Autobiography of Ellie Gaffney, a Woman of Torres Strait*, Aboriginal Studies Press, Canberra, 1989.

Gilbert, K., *Because a White Man'll Never Do It*, Angus & Robertson, Sydney, 1973.

——(ed.), *Living Black: Blacks Talk to Kevin Gilbert*, Allen Lane, Penguin, Melbourne, 1977.

Harney, Y.B., told by J. Wositzky, *Born Under the Paperbark Tree: A Man's Life*, ABC Books, Sydney, 2001.

Huggins, R. and Huggins, J., *Auntie Rita*, Aboriginal Studies Press, Canberra, 1994.

Kennedy, M., *Born a Half-caste*, Aboriginal Studies Press, Canberra, revised edn, 1990.

Lamilami, L., *Lamilami Speaks: The Cry Went Up. The Story of the People of Goulburn Islands, North Australia*, Ure Smith, Sydney, 1974.

Langford, R., *Don't Take Your Love to Town*, Penguin, Melbourne, 1988.

Lester, Y., *The Autobiography of Yami Lester*, I.A.D. Publishers, Canberra, 1993.

McAdam, C., *Boundary Lines: A Family's Story of Winning against the Odds*, McPhee Gribble, Melbourne, 1995.

McGinness, J., *Joe McGinness: Son of Alyandabu*, University of Queensland Press, Brisbane, 1991.

Morgan, E., *The Calling of the Spirits*, Aboriginal Studies Press, Canberra, 1995.

Morgan, S., *My Place*, Fremantle Arts Centre Press, Fremantle, 1987.

——*Wanamurraganya: The story of Jack McPhee*, Fremantle Arts Centre Press, Fremantle, 1989.

Nannup, A. with L. Marsh and S. Kinnane, *When the Pelican Laughed*, Fremantle Arts Centre Press, Fremantle, 1992.

Napanangka, T.F. et al., *Yarrtji: Six Women's Stories from the Great Sandy Desert*, Aboriginal Studies Press, Canberra, 1997.

Palmer, K. and McKenna, C., *Somewhere Between Black and White: The Story of an Aboriginal Australian*, Macmillan, Melbourne, 1978.

Pascoe, B. (ed.), *Wathaurong: Too Bloody Strong. Stories and Life Journeys of People from Wathaurong*, Pascoe Publishing, Apollo Bay, 1997.

Pepper, P., *You Are What You Make Yourself to Be: Story of a Victorian Aboriginal Family 1842–1980*, Hyland House, Melbourne, 1980.

Perkins, C., *A Bastard Like Me*, Ure Smith, Sydney, 1975.

Read, P. (ed.), *Down There with Me on the Cowra Mission*, Pergamon Press, Sydney, 1984.

Rosser, W., *This is Palm Island*, Australian Institute of Aboriginal Studies, Canberra, 1978.

——*Dreamtime Nightmares: Biographies of Aborigines under the Queensland Aborigines Act*, Australian Institute of Aboriginal Studies, Canberra, 1985.

——*Return to Palm Island*, Aboriginal Studies Press, Canberra, 1995.

Roughsey, R. (Goobalathaldin), *Moon and Rainbow: The Autobiography of an Aboriginal*, Rigby, Adelaide, 1971.

Saunders, K., *Learning the Ropes*, Aboriginal Studies Press, Canberra, 1992.

——*Myall Road*, Aboriginal Studies Press, Canberra, 1998.

Shaw, B., *Countrymen. The Life Histories of Four Aboriginal Men as Told to Bruce Shaw*, Australian Institute of Aboriginal Studies, Canberra, 1986.

Simon, E., *Through My Eyes*, Collins Dove, Melbourne, 1987.

Smith, S., *Mum Shirl: An Autobiography with the Assistance of Bobbi Sykes*, Heinemann Educational, Melbourne, 1981.

Somerville, M. et al., *The Sun Dancin': People and Place in Coonabarabran*, Aboriginal Studies Press, Canberra, 1992.

Tatz, C. (ed.), *Black Viewpoints: The Aboriginal Experience*, Australian and New Zealand Book Co., Sydney, 1975.

Thaiday, W., *Under the Act*, Townsville, North Queensland Publishing Co., 1981.

Thomson, J., *Reaching Back: Queensland Aboriginal People Recall Early Days of Yarrabah Mission*, Aboriginal Studies Press, Canberra, 1989.

Tucker, M., *If Everyone Cared*, Ure Smith, Sydney, 1977.

Van den Berg, R., *No Option, No Choice: My Father, Thomas Corbett, an Aboriginal Half-caste*, Magabala Books, Broome, 1994.

Walker, D., *Me and You: The Life Story of Della Walker as told to Tina Coutts*, Aboriginal Studies Press, Canberra, 1989.

Ward, G. *Wandering Girl*, Magabala Books, Broome, 1987.

West, I., *Pride against Prejudice: Reminiscences of a Tasmanian Aborigine*, Australian Institute of Aboriginal Studies, Canberra, 1987.

Wharton, H. (ed.), *Cattle Camp: Murrie Drovers and their Stories*, University of Queensland Press, Brisbane, 1994.

INDEX

Page numbers followed by *ill* indicate an illustration.

and northern cattle industry, 134–137
sexual abuse of, 134, 177–178, 333, 338,
   340
victims of violence, 79, 332–333, 338
Wonga, Simon, 82–85
work
   Aboriginal attitudes to, 60–61, 70, 263
   unemployment in 1980s, 261–262
World Council of Indigenous Peoples,
   245–246
World War I, 175–176
World War II
   Aboriginal enlistments, 207–208
   civil rights gains, 207–210
   impact on northern pastoral industry, 141

Wybaleena, 72–74

Yagan, 44
Yarraba mission, 161, 164
yaws, 8, 65, 151
Yemmerrawannie, 33
Yirrkala mission, 147, 227
Yolgnu people
   Gove case, 227, 229
   land rights petitions, 227, 229
Yorta Yorta case, 304–305
Yuendumu community, 258–259
Yunupingu, Galarrwuy, 236–237, 272, 273ill,
   279, 349–350
Yunupingu, Mandawuy, 268, 279